Jihad and Just War in the War on Terror

ALIA BRAHIMI

OXFORD
UNIVERSITY PRESS

OXFORD

UNIVERSITY PRESS

Great Clarendon Street, Oxford OX2 6DP

Oxford University Press is a department of the University of Oxford.
It furthers the University's objective of excellence in research, scholarship,
and education by publishing worldwide in

Oxford New York

Auckland Cape Town Dar es Salaam Hong Kong Karachi
Kuala Lumpur Madrid Melbourne Mexico City Nairobi
New Delhi Shanghai Taipei Toronto

With offices in

Argentina Austria Brazil Chile Czech Republic France Greece
Guatemala Hungary Italy Japan Poland Portugal Singapore
South Korea Switzerland Thailand Turkey Ukraine Vietnam

Oxford is a registered trade mark of Oxford University Press
in the UK and in certain other countries

Published in the United States
by Oxford University Press Inc., New York

British Library Cataloguing in Publication Data

Data available

Library of Congress Cataloging in Publication Data

Library of Congress Control Number: 2010933140

Typeset by SPI Publisher Services, Pondicherry, India
Printed in Great Britain
on acid-free paper by
MPG Biddles

ISBN 978–0–19–956296–1

1 3 5 7 9 10 8 6 4 2

For my parents, Farouk and Kathy Brahimi

Acknowledgements

I am inevitably and irredeemably indebted to James Piscatori, for supervising my work as a doctoral student, where this research began, and for the example he has set with his dedication, graciousness, and consistent good humour. The opportunity to work with him was an honour; the years spent under his tutelage, a true privilege.

Thank you, too, to the Department of Politics and International Relations at the University of Oxford for its help through the various stages of this process and, in particular, to the Changing Character of War programme. Funding from the Leverhulme Trust made possible the wonderful years I spent as a research associate at the programme, and Hew Strachan's support made a profound difference to my work and to my confidence. That this book has seen the light of day is in no small part due to supplies of morale from Avi Shlaim, Gil-Li Vardi, and Sibylle Scheipers. Adam Roberts was ever a reliable source of wisdom, and a steadfast friend. To Henry Shue I owe an enormous debt for ploughing through everything from hastily scribbled streams of half-formed thoughts to draft upon draft of overlong chapters, and for always cushioning any blows. George Joffe also went beyond the call of duty as my thesis examiner.

My sisters—Leila and Samia Brahimi—have shown such love and encouragement that I was able to forget the long distance; and, from far-flung corners of the globe, dear friends have been as devoted as ever. At Oxford, in the friendships of a lifetime, I discovered a home away from home. Thank you Erica Moret. For moving grand ambitions into the realm of possibility, I must express my abiding gratitude to Hamad K. And thank you Hasan Hameed, for everything.

Contents

A note on transliteration

Given the variation in Arabic–English transliteration schemes, I have chosen to follow commonly used media spellings, owing to their prevalence. For example, 'Osama' is employed rather than 'Usama', and 'Sheikh' rather than 'Shaykh'.

Introduction

The *jihadi* inhabits a moral universe, the boundaries of which are constantly contested. In eighteenth-century Malabar, as Muslims launched suicidal attacks against their European colonizers, one East India Company report noted that 'the more prudent part of the Moors deny that such evil practices are conformable to their religion'.[1] When, in 1983, Hizballah in Lebanon imitated the methods of the Syrian Nationalist Party—a secular organization comprised of a large number of Arab Christians—by launching its first suicide bombing against American and French troops in Beirut, the attacker was criticized by virtually every Shia authority in the land.[2] As the Groupe Islamique Armé plumbed new depths of savagery in Algeria in the late 1990s, it was condemned by the firebrand Palestinian cleric Abu Qatada, the Egyptian terrorist group Gama'at Islamiyya, and Osama bin Laden. In turn, when it became clear, by late 2007, that al-Qaeda's *jihad* was primarily and senselessly directed against innocents, bin Laden himself was denounced by a series of radical Muslims.

However, just as al-Qaeda's *jihad* has been criticized, so it has been painstakingly legitimized. The US-led 'war on terror' was initiated in September 2001 after al-Qaeda, an international terrorist network, successfully executed a devastating attack upon American soil which massacred some 3000 civilians. Significant for international relations scholars are the manifold issues raised by such a non-state actor's subversion of international order through unconventional warfare. Compelling theoretical and practical questions are provoked by this elusive network of covert operatives targeting the superpower, as well as by the means and strategies that America and its allies have devised to counter it. Equally interesting, however, is the fact that both 'sides' of the 'war on terror'—that is, George W. Bush's administration and al-Qaeda—have taken great pains to justify their actions in moral terms.

For the Americans, the self-proclaimed 'defenders of civilisation',[3] the 'just war' tradition provides a repository of concepts and conditions to appeal to when making the moral case for war. Just war theory emerged out of the ruminations of Christianity, but it is now available in a more secularized form as moral philosophers have engaged with its central ideas, and international law has codified some of its key tenets. Islam too has a long history of discussion about the morally legitimate use of military force. Osama bin Laden, who sets himself up as an Islamic authority, has sought to portray his *jihad* as an individual duty conferred by Islam and incumbent upon all Muslims. The Bush administration and al-Qaeda have each deliberately invoked their respective just war traditions. But especially significant is the controversy that such invocations have excited. Within each tradition, the arguments put forward for the resort to war and for the way in which war is fought have been feverishly contested.

President Bush, for example, said of the US-led invasion of Iraq that 'by our actions in this war we serve a great and just cause'.[4] The prominent political theorist, Michael Walzer, however, concluded that an Iraq invasion was 'unjust'.[5] Furthermore, the 'near-unanimous view of international lawyers' was that an invasion of Iraq would be illegal,[6] and the World Council of Churches urged that it would be 'immoral and unwise'.[7] Indeed, 'most of the religious response to the unfolding of the Bush Iraq policy use[d] elements of the just war theory in making its case against the war'.[8]

Similarly, Osama bin Laden confidently employed Quranic verses in support of his commands to 'kill the Americans and their allies—civilians and military'.[9] Decrying the attacks of 11 September, however, another radical (Sunni) contemporary of bin Laden, Sheikh Yusuf al Qaradawi, quoted different verses from the Quran[10] and argued that 'Islam ... considers the attack against innocent human beings a grave sin'. The influential Egyptian cleric concluded by stating: 'I categorically go against a committed Muslim's embarking upon such attacks. Islam never allows a Muslim to kill the innocent and the helpless'.[11] This reassertion of the principle of non-combatant immunity in Islam was echoed throughout the Muslim world by such diverse figures as the Grand Mufti of Saudi Arabia, Sheikh Abd-al Aziz al-Sheikh[12]; the spiritual leader of Iran, Ayatollah Ali Khamenei[13]; and the opposition Islamist group in Egypt, the Muslim Brotherhood.[14]

Thus, the normative clashes within the Western and Islamic worlds appear as relevant as any supposed clash between them. This book seeks to engage critically with the moral traditions—namely, 'just war' and *jihad*—to which the protagonists in the 'war on terror' appeal. This involves applying the various just war ideas and theoretical concepts of both traditions to the arguments which draw upon those traditions. The central argument is that, in important ways, the normative justifications advanced on both 'sides' of the war on terror are not directly consistent with the moral traditions they invoke. This will be suggested with reference to historical expositions of Western and Islamic just war doctrine as well as the views of Bush and bin Laden's contemporaries. In considering this contemporary criticism of bin

Laden, we must question Rohan Gunaratna's assertion that those Islamists who denounced the 11 September assault only did so because they disputed the wisdom of its timing or because they sought to avoid retaliation from the United States and its allies.[15] We shall see that moral and theological reasoning featured prominently in condemnations of al-Qaeda.

The 11 September attacks ('9/11') and America's pursuant 'war on terror' heaped a series of legally contentious and morally urgent questions upon the international community. The Anglo-American decision to press ahead with an invasion of Iraq, without a prior attack by Iraq and against the will of the United Nations, induced a worldwide debate on the difference between aggression and self-defence. The Bush administration's detention of suspected terrorists at Guantanamo Bay, wherein the Geneva Conventions' guidelines on treating prisoners of war were not applied, raised issues about the limits to safeguarding national security. Osama bin Laden's powerful and highly sophisticated arguments have confronted the Islamic world with the dilemma of whether the defence of Muslims can ever justify the deliberate murder of civilians. Similarly, Islamic jurists have been forced to grapple with, and exchange *fatwas* over, the question of whether suicide bombing can be countenanced as part of a lawful *jihad*. War is an important component of international relations, and the answers to such questions bear upon the two principal issues about war: what type of conduct is acceptable in war and when it is legitimate to use force in the first place.

Both the Bush administration and al-Qaeda have defined this conflict as representative of a new kind of war. Justifying the type of terrorist acts that al-Qaeda perpetrates, bin Laden reflected that 'in today's wars, there are no morals, and it is clear that mankind has descended to the lowest degrees of decadence and oppression'.[16] Similarly, Cofer Black of the CIA informed the Joint House and Senate Select Intelligence Committee: 'all you need to know is that there was a before 9/11 and an after 9/11. After 9/11 the gloves came off'.[17] Such admissions put pressure on the received ideas about justice and warfare embodied in the Western and Islamic just war traditions. At the same time, however, such traditions are not stagnant and their injunctions are not immutable. Bush and bin Laden both depict their actions as manifestations of justice and, in so doing, they both endeavour to make contributions to their just war traditions. In short, their arguments could have a lasting impact upon the constantly evolving just war traditions of Islam and the West. As Kanan Makiya and Hassan Mneimneh advised with regard to the 'spiritual manual' found in the luggage of one 9/11 hijacker, 'we should ask whether the ideas in the document will become part of the tradition that they misrepresent'.[18]

This book endeavours to provide a clarification of the arguments put forward with reference to the use of force in the 'war on terror', and to argue that, in the end, the positions of both the Bush administration and al-Qaeda present challenges to accepted ideas about justice in war. In so doing, this book also offers up one possible way of understanding the 'war on terror'. Referring to the rift between Europe and the United States during the run-up to the US-led invasion of Iraq, one Indian columnist observed that 'the western world is dangerously at odds with itself today'.[19] The same could be said of the Muslim world, with regard to al-Qaeda's deeply controversial attacks. Indeed, the gravest challenge that such contentious policies pose is to their own traditions—their own 'civilizations', so to speak. In a very real sense, then, the pertinent struggle is that between each tradition and modern attempts to reinterpret them. Though the 'war on terror' has been repeatedly framed in terms of a 'clash of civilizations', the proposition here is that the significant clash is occurring intra-civilizationally: within each tradition, a set of actors (e.g. the Bush administration, al-Qaeda) have brazenly confronted received ideas about the morally appropriate use of violence. Thus, it is as a result of the reinterpretation of tradition *within* each civilization that the 'war on terror' took place.

This book also holds some implications for the way in which al-Qaeda's *jihad* ought to be understood. While Western scholarship tends to assume that Bush made a moral case for war (beyond fighting Muslims) and that just war is not holy war, with regard to Islam, confusions abound. Bin Laden is all too often depicted as an apocalyptic fanatic who believes himself to be divinely ordained to commit catastrophic terrorism. Certainly, the suggestion that bin Laden and his cohorts are capable of moral argument undermines the dramatization of the 'war on terror' as a binary struggle between civilization and barbarism. However, the recurring focus on 'nihilism' and 'evil' works to obscure the refined Islamic reasoning underpinning bin Laden's case for war, which, in turn, undervalues the potential mass appeal of his self-defined 'liberation' movement among disenfranchised Muslims. Indeed, whatever his ultimate ambitions, bin Laden sets out a series of nuanced arguments for a just and limited war against America and its allies. This book seeks to engage with the content of what bin Laden has been saying to Muslims, and to the world.

The *jihad* concept, too, is commonly conflated with aggressive and boundless warfare in the name of Allah's sovereignty. However, just as Western just war is distinguished from pacifism on one end of the spectrum and holy war on the other, Islamic *jihad* is understood, in this volume, as justified warfare within limits. Far from denoting indiscriminate slaughter to enforce religious conversion, we shall see that *jihad* embodies a strict ethical code on the permissible and the impermissible in war, in terms of both justification and conduct. No doubt, to the minds of some people this definition of the *jihad* tradition smacks of apologia. But perhaps the strongest testament to its applicability is contained in the words and arguments of al-Qaeda's leaders themselves. Bin Laden and his sort represent the hard case for the proposition that *jihad* is the Islamic counterpart to just war (as opposed to holy war). Yet, at every turn, these supposed archetypes of 'jihadi' fanaticism accompany their death-dealing with arguments about self-defence, last resort, necessity, collateral damage, pure intention, and accidental manslaughter.

As this research engages analytically with the just war arguments put forward on both sides of the 'war on terror', it is underpinned by two theoretical assumptions.

I.1. CONCEPTUAL ASSUMPTIONS

I.1.1. Tradition as perpetual evolution

Contest is fundamental to the notion of tradition. Though they embody durable practices, traditions are neither stagnant nor uniform doctrines. Paul van Tongeren has described tradition as an ongoing process in which the participants actively shape that in which they participate. Far from an imposed form, tradition is 'an ongoing discussion (or struggle) between various attempts at grasping meaning, between different interpretations of meaning'. Meaning cannot be fixed or established, as it only exists in the discussion between interpretations—in tradition.[20]

Of course, necessary to any such interpretive disagreements is a sufficient degree of agreement. The starting point of any discussion must be some basic shared concepts and beliefs, as well as a shared language. However, the existence of common characteristics does not guard against widely diverging positions and conclusions. As Alasdair MacIntyre asserted, most important conflicts take place within social orders as well as between them.[21]

This is a point repeatedly made by the group of scholars focusing on the resurgent importance of religion in international relations. Cecilia Lynch, for example, suggests that religions are often treated as essentialist, which ignores the lively debates within religious thought itself.[22] Scott Thomas singles out the 'clash of civilizations' theory as overlooking 'on-going debates within the Islamic world over the possibility of an "Islamic" form of civil society and its compatibility with democracy'.[23] Thomas also makes the point that 'the great world religions may have fixed texts but they do not have fixed beliefs, only fixed interpretations of those beliefs'.[24] Religious interpretations, he observes, cannot be separated from politics (indeed, more than two decades ago James Piscatori was troubled by the widespread assumption that religion determines politics, rather than the other way around[25]). Because interpretations are rooted in historical circumstance, the arguments made within various traditions must be considered historically.

In fact, with reference to the Islamic tradition, such an approach can guard against one of Lawrence Rosen's characteristics of Orientalism. He notes that 'no self-respecting contemporary Orientalist comments on a text or word without showing its "original" meaning, commonly implying that, whatever accretions may have attached themselves over the centuries, the word's true meaning is its first meaning'. This assumption, described by Rosen as 'etymology is destiny', strips language of its living and psychological contexts, it blocks the possibility for interdisciplinary insight, and it can perpetuate the notion that the scholar knows better than the speaker the true meaning of his or her expression.[26] But, as with any other tradition, both language and ideas in Islam are alive and contested, and they have evolved significantly since 'first meanings' were attributed. As John Kelsay makes clear in *Arguing the Just War in Islam,* Islam is a *living* tradition.[27]

Tradition, then, ought not to be reified. Edward Shils observes that traditions can change while they are in the 'possession of their recipients', because 'the desire to create something truer and better or more convenient is alive in those who acquire and possess them'.[28] Owing to the nature of tradition, participants such as Bush and bin Laden may also contribute to the interpretive direction of their just war traditions. Terry Nardin emphasizes that an ethical tradition is not a theoretical system of general principles—it involves the interpretation and application of principles in certain circumstances by certain people. Moreover, his conclusion suggests the significance of an academic inquiry into the content of traditions: 'ethical traditions shape the particular controversies over right and wrong that have always been a central feature of international relations'.[29]

I.1.2. Ideas in international relations

The starting point of this study is that each state is, in Michael Barnett's words, embedded in an 'increasingly dense normative web', which acts to constrain its use of force. At the same time, however, the centrality of power in international relations is not denied. On the contrary, as Robert Jackson has observed, 'to study justice is not to ignore power but rather to give it pride of place by focusing on the fundamental normative issues it provokes, which are part and parcel of reality and not separate from it'.[30] The issue is that power properly construed is not solely comprised of the material factors privileged by neorealist theories of international relations (weapons capability, economy, or geography). The pursuit of legitimacy—a social concept—permeates the just war invocations looked at in this thesis. Nicholas Wheeler notes that 'although the strongest are in a position to substitute brute power for legitimacy, what's surprising is how rarely this happens'.[31] International actors routinely offer up normative arguments in search of moral and legal power, of legitimacy, authenticity even. In addition, as expertly demonstrated by bin Laden's ability to recruit *jihadis* worldwide, such arguments can be a source of power that rivals the most asymmetric distribution of capabilities.[32]

In the context of the 'war on terror' in the twenty-first century, the task of justifying violence becomes especially urgent. As head of a democratic state, with the executive branch of government beholden to the Congress, the American President and his administration have the constitutional duty to convince representatives of the people that a war ought to be fought. It is incumbent upon al-Qaeda, too, as a non-state actor which possesses the capacity to exert power on the world stage in proportion to the numbers which swell its ranks, to persuade its foot soldiers that fighting is warranted. With reference to the Bush administration and al-Qaeda, then, there is a direct relationship between the arguments made for war and the physical manifestation of hostilities. But this is not merely about instrumentality— that is to say, the language employed is not only significant for its usefulness to the bellwethers of war. A striking feature of this dialogue is that it is frequently framed in a moral vocabulary and it often involves a recognition of the importance of limits in warfare.

Moreover, such language grasps towards standards and intersubjectively held beliefs that are necessarily independent of the discourses which instrumentalize them. As Hedley Bull argued, 'ideologies provide justifications that reach out from the group itself and provide an explanation and rationale *to others*, not simply to oneself . . . they are tainted with special interests and motivated by them, but they stretch out towards something else'.[33] Indeed, to the common materialist argument that moral language and ideational justifications function as 'window dressing' to mask the interminable quest for power, Christian Reus-Smit observed that such tactics only work because norms and ideas *already* have moral force in a given social context. Further, it is only a viable strategy if the behaviour proposed is to some extent consistent with the proclaimed principles.[34] On this latter notion, the insights of Quentin Skinner are invaluable:

The aim is to argue that a favourable evaluative-descriptive term is being applied in the ordinary way, while trying at the same time to drop some of the criteria for applying it, thereby extending the range of the actions which it can properly be used to describe and commend. This will fail if too many of the criteria are dropped, for in this case the fact that the term has undergone a 'change of meaning' will become too obvious. But it will also fail if not enough are dropped, for in this case the capacity of the term to cover and thus to legitimate new forms of social action will not have been extended after all.[35]

Thus, the problem is not simply the instrumental one of tailoring an account of one's principles in order to fit a proposed project; it must in part be the problem of tailoring projects in order to make them answer to the pre-existing language of moral principles.[36]

It is worth noting that, while this book will consider the moral cases made for war by members of the Bush administration and al-Qaeda, it is deliberately indifferent to the question of whether such moral claims were internalized. The purpose herein is not to show that Bush and bin Laden personally believed in the rightness of the just war arguments they made. The possibility that they could be lying or dissembling does not bear on the content of their statements. The point is that both were impelled or constrained by expectations about just wars and so put forward arguments. Neta Crawford's assertion that 'lies indicate the bounds of the acceptable'[37] is supported by Walzer's notion that 'wherever we find hypocrisy, we also find moral knowledge'.[38]

Integral to international politics are arguments which self-consciously link what is being done to what ought to be done. The use of force is routinely accompanied by a normative transcript that conveys ideas about what is right and wrong in warfare. In examining such discourse, this book proceeds from the assumption that insight of some value can be gained from a focus on the articulated normative dimensions of war. We will see that, even in high-stakes situations of war and killing, the linguistic landscape is replete with references to ideas—and ideals. Indeed, especially at such critical junctures do normative constructions of 'right' and 'wrong' come to the fore and intermingle intelligibly with the projection of material power.

I.2. OVERVIEW

This book explores the just war claims set forward by the Bush administration and al-Qaeda, discussed in relation to authoritative theories of just war and the counterclaims of Bush and bin Laden's contemporaries. It is comprised of two parts: one deals with just war theory and the Bush administration's strategies, while the second describes the Islamic tradition and al-Qaeda's justifications for *jihad* against America. Within each part, claims about the justice of resorting to war (*jus ad bellum*) and the justice of the way in which war is fought (*jus in bello*) are evaluated.

Part I applies Western just war theory to the Bush administration's arguments for the 'war on terror' and it is made up of three chapters. Chapter 1 begins with an overview of the just war tradition and then focuses on issues concerning the *jus ad bellum*. The US-led invasion of Iraq in March 2003 is singled out as a case study because its controversy, on many levels, provoked much discussion about just war. Of course, the military intervention in Afghanistan raised fascinating issues of its own, but the divisiveness of the Iraq war made it the slightly more interesting focus. The chapter considers the invasion in light of seven just war criteria: it sets out the Bush administration's case for war and shows how, on each count, its argumentation was resisted by dissidents using the language and conceptual contours of the just war tradition.

Chapter 2 then engages with one issue of the *jus ad bellum* and the Iraq war extensively: the doctrine of pre-emption. Pre-emption is focused upon comprehensively because it was both the cornerstone of the Bush administration's case for just cause and the most dramatic bone of contention between proponents of the war and its critics. The chapter will suggest that while 'pre-emptive' war was widely cast as legitimate by contemporary churchmen, philosophers, and international lawyers, the Bush administration's seemingly 'preventive' war was approached with considerably more moral scepticism.

Chapter 3 takes up issues of justice in war by applying the principles of 'proportionality' and 'discrimination' to the invasion of Iraq. The analysis then turns to one highly charged issue of the *jus in bello* as it focuses on the Bush administration's justifications for the treatment of 'non-lawful combatants' at Guantanamo Bay. The chapter contends that using the logic of 'supreme emergency', alleged terrorists are stripped of Geneva Convention protections because the defensive just cause is presented as unusually urgent and the stakes are said to be civilizational. First-order principles such as the prohibition against torture are qualified by the emergency of the *jus ad bellum*, thus rendering purportedly absolute human rights contingent upon the state of the world. This strategy, presented by one administration lawyer as a 'choice of evils',[39] was critiqued by other lawyers, governments, and human rights groups worldwide, as well as by members of the Bush administration's own Department of State.

Part II of the book is also made up of three chapters. It centres on Islamic just war theory and al-Qaeda's attacks against America on 11 September. Its structure mirrors that of Part I, in that Chapters 4 and 5 deal with *jus ad bellum* criteria, while Chapter 6 engages with the *jus in bello* of the *jihad* tradition. Chapter 4 offers an overview of the development through the centuries of an Islamic body of thought concerned with the use of force and

its limits, before narrowing the focus to the critical issue of just cause. Osama
bin Laden and his deputy, Ayman al-Zawahiri, consistently maintain that
aggression is both wrong and illegal, and that in using violence al-Qaeda is
merely repelling America's attacks. However, since the United States had
launched no invasion of bin Laden's country before 11 September, be it
Saudi Arabia, Sudan, or Afghanistan, it was incumbent upon him to attempt
to redefine the concept of 'aggression', an attempt which was shunned by the
series of Muslim leaders who described al-Qaeda as the belligerent party on
9/11. Chapter 5 continues the discussion of the Islamic *jus ad bellum* by
looking at bin Laden's claims in three other areas. Despite the numerous,
and often nuanced, arguments put forward by al-Qaeda's leaders, the *jihad*
tradition provides grounds for doubting some of their crucial assertions.

Islamic *jus in bello* guidelines are the subject of Chapter 6. The 'spiritual
manual' found in the luggage of one of the 9/11 hijackers cited the *hadith* in
which Ali, the fourth caliph, moves to slay a man in battle, but the man spits
in his face and then Ali lets him go. When the befuddled man wonders why,
Ali affirms that Muslims are instructed never to kill in anger; the man is so
impressed that he converts to Islam on the spot. Al-Qaeda's actions are
assessed generally in light of similar Islamic norms about fighting within
stringent limits, and the chapter then considers the divisive issue of suicide
bombing and 'martyrdom' in Islam. Indeed, in the aftermath of the 9/11
attacks, a newspaper editorial addressed a series of questions to the clerical
establishment, one of which wondered: 'are those who committed that act
really martyrs according to Islamic *sharia* ruling?'[40] Hence, the chapter will
provide an overview of the Islamic debate thrown up by the means favoured
by al-Qaeda on 9/11. It will then examine the group's defence of its civilian
targets. Even the famous thirteenth-century jurist ibn Taymiyyah, whose
authority is drawn upon by al-Qaeda, prohibits the killing of 'those who are
not belligerent and do not participate in war, such as women, children,
hermits, old men, the blind, the chronically ill and the like'.[41] As a result,
bin Laden devises an uncomfortable, and often inconsistent, case which
deems the protection of civilian immunity null and void for American
citizens, a position which is hotly contested by historical and contemporary
voices from within the Islamic tradition.

I.3. CAUTIONARY POINTS

In the discussion of *jihad*, the author employs categories associated with,
and adopts the terminology of, Western just war theory ('just cause', 'right

authority', 'proportionality', and 'non-combatant immunity etc.'). This book does not intend to deny the distinctiveness of the historical development and epistemologies of the Western and Islamic just war traditions (well taken is Olivier Roy's point about the mistake of investigating Islamic culture with the concepts of Western culture),[42] but it resorts to the explicit language of one tradition in search of organizational symmetry, and in order to make possible points of comparison. This decision, however, is not entirely expediential: it is driven by the more positive claim that the questions posed by issues of justice in war are, in a sense, universal.

The influence of Islam upon European international law has been noted by a range of commentators, including Ernest Nys,[43] Mohammed Hamidullah,[44] and Sayyed Qutb, with the latter contending that, up until the eighteenth century, 'Europe had no concept of international law except for what it learnt through its dealings with the Muslim world'.[45] Of course, there were extensive cultural contacts between the two traditions, not least during the crusades and in Islamic Spain, and the chain of intellectual debt was in no way unidirectional. The Islamic philosophers Ibn Sina and Ibn Rushd, for example, borrowed heavily from the Greeks in arguing that rationalism could parallel belief in achieving revelation (which, in turn, influenced the writings of Thomas Aquinas).[46] In the nineteenth century, Cheragh Ali cited the American Lawyer Francis Lieber on the legitimacy of trying rebel leaders under certain conditions.[47]

However, the point here is not to make any authoritative claims about the causal influence of one tradition upon the evolution of the other. Instead, this book will follow James Turner Johnson in his observation that 'both the traditions of the Islamic world and those of western culture share concerns that can be classified within the categories of the just war tradition: just cause, right authority, right intention, and so forth'.[48] John Kelsay, Johnson's co-editor of another comparative volume, argues that:

It is difficult to deny the persistence of certain concerns across the boundaries of particular cultures: that violence not be gratuitous; that wars be justified; and that conflicts be governed by a concern to distinguish the innocent from the guilty. These, I submit, are human concerns, tied to the necessities of ordering social life.[49]

The interpretations of just war concepts at particular times are undeniably informed by history—just as Francisco di Vitoria's expositions were profoundly affected by the Spanish encounter with the Indians of the Americas, the medieval Islamic jurists' understanding of just cause was intimately bound up with the existence of an expansionary Islamic empire. The concepts themselves, however, seem to stand apart from experience. Thus, the just war ideas discussed in the *jihad* section will be formulated in vocabulary borrowed from the Western tradition, but the author follows Johnson and Kelsay in their assertion that the moral concerns addressed inhere in both traditions.

When making judgements about tradition, two related worries present themselves. Firstly, as Andrew Vincent put it, there can be no absolute Archimedean onlookers on the ideological scene. In describing the Western and Islamic just war traditions, it is not possible for two fixed traditions to be observed from the standpoint of omniscient observer—as we have seen, one of the central assumptions of this book is that traditions are multivocal and in constant development. Though the built-in methodological problem of this research lies in the danger of typifying each tradition, every effort can be made to avoid essentializing both. After considering a variety of positions, it will remain possible to discuss leading or dominant schools of thought, and the existence of broad consensus serves as a useful benchmark when engaging with living traditions. As Vincent also acknowledges, some distance can be attained in the very fact of theorizing self-consciously.[50]

Secondly, the author is aware of the endless controversy that comes along with judgements about who are the appropriate spokesmen for traditions. This problem has been particularly acute for Islamic legal scholarship as *ulema* (scholars) fiercely debate which *ijma* (consensus) is to be counted and which individuals can lawfully exercise *ijtihad* (interpretive judgement)— raising concomitant questions about whether the exercise of *ijtihad* is still even a possibility.[51] Piscatori's inescapable conclusion regarding Islam— 'that it is nearly impossible to say with authority at any moment what Islam is and what it is not'[52]—holds true for almost any tradition of thought, yet even in multivocal contestation common themes can be suggested and claims about broad agreement can be set forth with caution. In proposing any such consensus, an assortment of voices are consulted as the book draws upon the expressed views of theologians, politicians, lawyers, religious figures, and public intellectuals.

For Western just war, these extend from St Augustine of Hippo in the fourth century ('the only Catholic Saint the Protestant tradition has consistently recognised as an authoritative source of wisdom'[53]), through the theological writings of Thomas Aquinas and Francisco di Vitoria, up to twentieth-century ethicists like Paul Ramsey, Ralph Potter, and William O'Brien, 'an authority on just war doctrine'.[54] Modern-day sources are also appealed to, ranging from Catholic newspapers, to UN resolutions, to prominent just war commentators like Michael Walzer, whose 1977 treatise is considered by many to be 'unambiguously the most influential academic reconsideration of the tradition in recent times'.[55] This book's Islamic section invokes classical writers like Mohammad ibn al-Hasan al-Shaybani, as well as medieval jurists such as Taqi al-Din ibn Taymiyyah (Sunni) and Nasr al-Din

Tusi (Shia). The nineteenth-century reformist movement is also considered, as are twentieth-century Islamists like Sayyed Qutb and influential contemporary figures like Grand Ayatollah Mohammad Hussein Fadlallah, the spiritual leader of the Shia in Lebanon, and Sheikh Yusuf al-Qaradawi, a hugely popular professor of *sharia* who hosts an opinion programme on an Arabic television station with a daily viewership of 50 million[56] (according to Azzam Tamimi, 'when you're talking about Sheikh Qaradawi, you're talking about an audience of hundreds of millions of Muslims across the world, someone who actually creates public opinion').[57] Ibn Taymiyyah, especially, is repeatedly referenced, not only on account of his status as a renowned medieval jurist, but because, in the lectures given by Osama bin Laden and Ayman al-Zawahiri to recruits in Afghanistan, 'one of the main textual sources used was the work of [this] twelfth-century [*sic*] Muslim scholar'.[58] The descriptive method adopted by this book endeavours to substantiate particular ideas by referring to thinkers across the centuries as well as religious sects. The suggestion is never that any one figure is representative of the just war tradition or the *jihad* tradition—or even of Islam or Christianity—but rather that there is an arguable consensus around the ideas in question.

With regard to another point of terminology, 'the United States' and 'the Americans' are often employed as convenient shorthand for the administration of George W. Bush. It is, of course, recognized that there were idiosyncratic differences between the beliefs, opinions, and actions of various American parties as well as individual members of Bush's government. Al-Qaeda is a more dispersed network lacking in conventional hierarchy and, as a movement, it has gained differentiation over time. However, by convention it will be possible to privilege a set of actors that centre on al-Qaeda's ideological spearhead, Osama bin Laden. Personally, bin Laden has championed al-Qaeda's broad objectives and my research will focus on statements made by him and two of his close lieutenants, Ayman al-Zawahiri and Suleiman Abu Ghaith.

The book's period of study extends from the early 1990s, when al-Qaeda was formed and its ideology formulated, up to the end of the first presidential term of George W. Bush (December 2004). The main focus will be the critical period between the months preceding the September 2001 attacks and the months following the Iraq invasion in March 2003, in which the reasons behind al-Qaeda's declaration of war and America's pursuant 'war on terror' were publicly stated, challenged, and restated. While a lot, of course, has happened since, the pathway to war, with the justifications which stretch alongside it, only plays out once. Though attempts no doubt can be made, neither event nor utterance can undo it.

Part I

Just War and the Bush Administration

1

Jus ad Bellum, Iraq, and the War on Terror

Two months prior to the US invasion of Iraq, President Bush used his State of the Union address to proclaim: 'If war is forced upon us, we will fight in a just cause and by just means, sparing in every way we can the innocent'.[1] In this single sentence, the Commander-in-Chief of the world's sole superpower invoked four of the just war tradition's central concepts (last resort, just cause, proportionality, and discrimination), making reference to both *jus ad bellum* and *jus in bello*. With a sentence of his own, a vocal opponent of the President's proposed actions, Senator Ted Kennedy, urged that 'the administration has not made a convincing case that we face such an imminent threat to our national security that a unilateral, pre-emptive American strike and an immediate war are necessary'.[2] In drawing attention to a further set of just war concepts, and deliberately contesting the Bush administration's interpretation of just war criteria, Senator Kennedy employed the same moral tradition to register his critique of the proposed policy.

While the foregoing might illustrate the controversy that comes with applying just war ideas, it also emphasizes both the relevance and the vitality of the just war tradition. Just war discourse abounds, permeating the language of international politics and framing academic debate. This chapter begins the discussion of the just war tradition by examining the *jus ad bellum* involved in the Iraq war. Section 1.1 will provide a brief overview of the just war tradition as a school of thought. Section 1.2 will consider each of the *jus ad bellum's* seven modern criteria in light of the Iraq war. The doctrine of pre-emption will be explored more fully in Chapter 2.

1.1. THE JUST WAR TRADITION

According to the just war tradition's foremost contemporary historian, 'the name *just war* stands for a broadly and consensually shaped moral tradition in western culture on the problems of justifying and restraining the violence of war'.[3] Such a moral tradition[4] owes its substance to a vast number of varied yet related sources, including international law, military rules of engagement, and applied ethics, but it is deeply rooted in Christian (and especially Catholic) moral thought. The original just war question asks, as Aquinas puts it, whether war is always a sin,[5] and the just war tradition has sought to examine the conditions under which it is morally permissible to kill the neighbour for whom Christ died.

The theological impetus for the just war is significant not only because 'Catholic formulations of just war issues persist regardless of the religious or philosophical affiliations or positions of the leading modern scholars dealing with the normative problem of war, most of whom are not Catholic',[6] but also on account of the historical development of the tradition itself. Saint Augustine, as one of the first thinkers to justify Christian participation in wars systematically, was influenced heavily by the Constantinian reform of the fourth century, which, by making Catholicism the state religion of the Roman Empire, dramatically ended the ostracism of the (previously illegal) Christian community. As such, empire and Church found themselves in a position of mutual support—indeed, the Emperor attributed his triumphs in battle to the fact he had turned to Christ, and 'in the victories of Constantine, [Bishop] Eusebius saw God intervening to destroy the power of Satan'.[7] This intermingling of policy and religion, represented starkly by the inscription of the cross on the shields of Roman soldiers, required a nuanced answer to the original just war question which, in turn, provided a rough beginning for the just war tradition.

Central to the conciliation of Christian love with the use of violence is the proposition that Christ never explicitly banned war or instructed soldiers to lay down their arms. Hugo Grotius draws attention to the fact that John the Baptist 'did not bid the [soldiers] withdraw from military service, as he must have done, if such was the will of God'.[8] Luther acknowledges that Christ did not himself bear the sword, but also points out that 'he did not take a wife or become a cobbler or a tailor' and in pursuing his own vocation he did not thereby reject all others.[9] In this vein, Jesus' crucial rebuke of Simon Peter for using his sword to cut off the ear of a guard was taken as the repudiation of a single act of unjustified violence rather than a rejection of all violence per se. In fact, the bearing of arms in certain circumstances has been taken to be a deeply Christian act of mercy, 'interior to the ethics of Christian love'[10]—but, as such, both the recourse to war and the use of arms in battle are subject to strict, love-inspired limitations.

The just war tradition, however, has never been the exclusive province of theology. In addition to religious treatises and commentaries thereupon, the tradition encompasses moral philosophy, international law, and military rules of engagement. In concert, these various sources act as 'a repository of the way in which Western culture has come to think of the values which political life exists to support, protect, and foster; the role of military force in service of those values; and the limits on the use of such force'.[11] In examining the relation of morality to politics, the sacred and secular strands of the just war have historically reinforced each other. With his detailed chronicles of the development of the tradition, Johnson makes repeated reference to this phenomenon. During the medieval period, for example, four separate streams of thought combined to form the classical just war doctrine: The (*a*) canon law tradition and (*b*) theological tradition derived from the Church, while (*c*) Roman law and theory and (*d*) the chivalric code of conduct for the knightly classes were independent of ecclesiastical reasoning. Even in drawing upon the Bible, the two religious streams were subjected 'to interpretations importantly determined by the cultural context of medieval Christendom'.[12] Ramsey also reminds us that Augustine and other great Christian thinkers were notably influenced by 'the notions of justice lying around in the Graeco-Roman world'.[13]

It is this eclectic nature of the just war's evolution that renders it a 'tradition' rather than 'doctrine', most obviously because it contains a number of individual doctrines drawn from diverse sources spanning twenty centuries.[14] Another relevant feature of just war's status as tradition is its function as a framework structuring debate rather than a series of immutable prescriptions. For Jean Bethke Elshtain, this is a non-utopian, 'ethically shaped framework' which places 'the political within a set of moral concerns and considerations'.[15] Despite the realist attempt to categorize just war theory as part of idealism, it continues to resonate as 'a mode of discourse and a language of justification'. For, indeed, it is just war *concepts* and the accompanying contest over their interpretation and application that are the mainstay of the tradition, and furnish it with meaning. Johnson illustrates this authoritatively:

> Such terms as just cause, right authority, right intention, last resort, an end of peace, proportionality of good to evil, and non-combatant immunity thus operate, in the just war tradition, as focal points about which thought and argument revolve. But . . . these terms are more than mere empty focal points; they have a content, more or less well specified and agreed upon at different moments in history but persistent nonetheless, that normatively defines the boundaries to initiating and waging war for the heirs of that tradition.[16]

While such precepts delineate normative boundaries, specific documents and international agreements, such as General Orders 100[17] and the Geneva Conventions, serve as normative benchmarks for guiding the conduct of modern war. In reflecting the heritage of the just war tradition, these developments at once become part of that tradition and proceed to shape its evolution.

The just war tradition is, by definition, dynamic, and it is contributed to by divergence as well as convergence. Such divergence flows naturally from just war as 'a set of essentially contested concepts around which political life is focused'. Elshtain suggests that contests over the range of applicability of just war concepts serve to generate and focus political debate.[18] This sort of critical dialogue is made possible by Michael Walzer's observation that 'our sharpest disagreements are structured and organised by our underlying agreements, by the meanings we share'.[19] The just war tradition expresses certain principles and embodies particular precedents, but the moral insight it reflects is not static. William O'Brien insists that it is 'a practical body of moral guidelines applicable to real life, not a museum piece to be preserved for its own sake'.[20] In so doing, he asserts that fidelity to the great writers of the tradition is not as important for just war guidelines as the requirements of the conflict-ridden world. The significance of studying this body of thought emanates from the fact that it bears an immediate and symbiotic connection with history and, more specifically, wars.

The theoretical content of just war can function in a number of ways. It has already been suggested that the tradition can play a role in the public justification of war and also act as a moral vehicle for registering opposition to it. In addition, it can serve as a useful device for assessing the moral quality of specific actions and judging the legitimacy of individual cases. For example, theorists have systematically and comprehensively applied just war principles to conflicts like the Second World War,[21] Vietnam,[22] and, more recently, the 'war on terror'.[23] The just war tradition can also impact upon the individual conscience grappling with the issues of war. In a 2003 feature film, former Defense Secretary Robert S. McNamara reflected upon the Second World War, reasoning that 'killing 50–90% of the people in 67 Japanese cities and then bombing them with two nuclear bombs is not proportional, in the minds of some people, to the objectives we were trying to achieve'.[24] Just war ideas can influence individuals prior to the fact of war as well. A British reservist, refusing 'point-blank' to serve in Iraq in January 2005, wrote of the 'futility, immorality and illegality of the war', directly appealed to the just war idea of last resort,[25] and concluded that 'you should only obey orders that are morally right'.[26] Moreover, just war teaching can serve to regulate the conduct of warfare, as with US Air Force pamphlet *AFP 110-31*, Germany's *Humanitarian Law in Armed Conflicts: Manual*, and copious other military handbooks and rules of engagement.[27] Certain international institutions (the International Committee of the Red Cross) and agreements (the Hague and Geneva Conventions) represent a significant degree of consensus upon the humanitarian precepts that have evolved out of just war wisdom.

Integral to the just war spirit is the idea that it is violence rather than non-violence that tows the burden of moral proof. But here the just war tradition parts company with pacifism, because this 'strong presumption against war'[28] is tempered by the legitimacy of those circumstances in which force is morally justified. While pacifists can criticize just war thinkers for adding elements of moral sanity to violence (thus making war appear more palatable as an instrument of state policy), just war theorists have condemned pacifists for their lack of hold on reality. Paul Ramsey was scathing in his dismissal of the Church's 'race for peace', dubbing it 'a kind of sack race in some macabre carnival mood on a picnic ground some distance from the real decisions that are shaping man's political destiny at this very hour'.[29] The just war tradition, far from being a homogeneous sequence of commandments, can nevertheless claim a broad agreement on two sets of concepts that must be brought to bear on the decision to resort to war and the manner in which war is waged.

1.2. JUS AD BELLUM

The distinction between *jus ad bellum* and *jus in bello* was first established by Vitoria in the sixteenth century; although they had emphasized the duty to wage war with kindness and for the sake of peace, Vitoria's Catholic predecessors (Augustine, Gratian, and Aquinas) had only implied just conduct in war. Vitoria's discussions on what it is permissible to do in warfare were grounded in natural law which, although derived from divine law, paved the way for Grotius' secularization of just war theory. For both Vitoria and Grotius, *jus in bello* rules were absolutely binding and applicable in every war against every sort of enemy: 'it follows that even in wars against the Turks we may not kill children . . . nor women'.[30] However, with the advance of *jus in bello*, the justice of the resort to war was increasingly marginalized. By the eighteenth century, the ethic of *raison d'état* had strongly taken hold in the European state system, whereby sovereigns were deemed to hold the discretionary right to wage war as an instrument of national policy. In adding credibility to the Clausewitzian dictum that war is the continuation of politics by other means, the right of war was presumed to belong to states in pursuit of their national interest. This manifested itself in an emphasis on the formal declaration of war and the rights and obligations of belligerents, rendering the deeper questions of *jus ad bellum* irrelevant. Issues about the justice of resorting to war were not adequately raised and explored until the culmination of balance-of-power politics with the First World War.

The *jus ad bellum* received renewed attention in the ensuant Covenant of the League of Nations, which was essentially an attempt to extirpate war from international relations. The 1928 Kellogg–Briand Pact reinforced this trend when its signatories agreed to outlaw war and renounce it as an instrument of policy, although the treaty was commonly interpreted as permitting defensive war. The United Nations Charter of 1945 also abrogated the right of states to wage offensive war by banning the first use of force, but the 'inherent right' of self-defence remains in effect. These developments and their implications will be considered further in Chapter 2—the purpose here is to note that after a 300-year lull the bloody course of the twentieth century has revived debate about the morality of resorting to war in the first place.

The just war tradition requires that the following seven criteria be satisfied for the recourse to force to be justified: just cause, right authority, right intention, the goal of peace, overall proportionality of good over evil, last resort, and reasonable hope of success. Modern just war theory treats these as the authoritative requirements at which the tradition has arrived; that these are indeed the relevant criteria is fairly uncontroversial. The contest arises over issues surrounding interpretations of the criteria, their scope, and their proper content. It is worth noting that some vagaries do exist—for example, right intention and goal of peace are often collapsed into one (as the latter is a positive indicator of the former) and international law is in fact silent on issues such as right intent and the probability of success. When drawing upon the larger just war tradition, however, it is fair to say that these seven moral concepts comprise the received wisdom on *jus ad bellum*. Hence, the following seven sections will examine each criterion with reference to the Bush administration's invasion of Iraq in the context of its 'war on terror'.

Just cause, right authority, and right intention are considered first because they are logically prior to the other four. This is true 'both historically and in terms of the inner logic of the just war idea'.[31] Johnson argues that these three concepts are *deontological* criteria of a qualitatively different character to the *prudential* nature of the remaining four. The prudential tests were derived historically from Roman practice by Augustine, and they serve to counsel political prudence rather than moral obligation. Though secondary to the deontological requirements, the prudential criteria remain significant to the *jus ad bellum* and any decision to resort to war must come to terms with them. The idea is to guard against situations where the lack of proportionality[32] or a reasonable hope of success[33] might cancel the moral justification for the use of force which has a just cause, is sanctioned by the right authority, and is employed with the right intention. Such (extreme) cases involve a decision to use force that is unwise or imprudent but, given the ultimate priority of the deontological tests, this does not necessarily render the use of force unjust.

While Johnson's distinction is reasonable, it is worth noting two potential difficulties. In the first place, the use of the term 'prudential' implies (inadvertently, I think) that the judgements made concern only one's *own* welfare. However, evaluations of proportionality, for example, are supposed to include the interests of both sides as well as any relevant third parties—that is, proportionality is not meant to be purely self-regarding. 'Prudential' might be more effectively substituted with terms like 'teleological',[34] 'pragmatic', 'expediential', or 'consequentialist', although some or all of these might be seen as denying the intrinsic moral weight of the criteria. This is related to the second difficulty. Where Johnson allows for just wars in which one or some of the 'prudential' criteria are not satisfied, other theorists would insist that each of the seven conditions is individually necessary. Lord Guthrie, for example, believes that all *jus ad bellum* tests must be satisfied: 'five out of six is not a pass mark'.[35] Further, as illustrated by Thomas Hurka, considerations of proportionality can be strong enough to cancel the just cause: 'the Soviet Union's invasion of Czechoslovakia in 1968 gave NATO a just cause for war, but most people think a military defence of that country would have been horribly wrong because it risked starting a global nuclear war'.[36] In an important sense, then, the requirement of proportionality does appear to confer a moral obligation, beyond the counselling of political prudence. In the round, however, it seems that Johnson principally intends, as Suaraz did, to uphold the right of self-defence in the face of a much stronger invader, as was the situation of the Poles, Dutch, and Belgians in the Second World War. It is to the issues of just cause and self-defence that the discussion now turns.

1.2.1. Just cause

'Goddamn, what the fuck are they talking about?'[37] Such was the reaction of General Tommy Franks, the Commander-in-Chief of United States Central Command, to the Bush administration's request for a detailed war plan for Iraq. Indeed, the announcement of Iraq as a choice of target in the 'war on terror' was met with dubiousness and incredulity worldwide. To the mind of Democratic Senator Bob Graham, 'it was the equivalent of the Allies declaring war on Mussolini's Italy and ignoring Hitler's Germany'.[38] But for the Bush administration, the Iraq war was a fundamental juncture in the 'war on terror'. This section will explore the American just cause generally before examining three individual elements of the argument: weapons of mass destruction (WMD), the al-Qaeda connection, and the nature of the Iraqi regime.

Augustine originally spelled out the crucial feature of the just cause when he stressed that 'it is the wrongdoing of the opposing side that lays on the wise man the duty of waging wars'.[39] Thus, *'justa bella ulciscuntur injuries'* (just wars avenge injuries). Aquinas too emphasized that 'those who are attacked, should be attacked because they deserve it on account of some fault'.[40] The notion that war ought only to be waged in order to right a wrong was carried over by the Spanish neo-scholastics. Suarez asserted that the only sufficient cause was 'a grave injustice that cannot be avenged or repaired in any other way',[41] and Vitoria opined that 'the sole and only just cause for waging war is when harm has been inflicted'.[42] A transgression by the enemy was the substratum of the just cause conceived in its Catholic form.

This idea gave rise to a classical expression of the just cause which involved one or more of three conditions: defence against an armed attack, recovery of something wrongly taken, or the punishment of evildoers.[43] This last condition worried the neo-scholastics and, in their efforts to counter holy war thinking and stamp out the crusade, they maintained that 'a war was just only if waged to correct some perfectly definite wrong'.[44] The idea was to insist upon a conception of just cause objective and precise enough to be adjudicated in a law court. With the post-First World War revival of interest in *jus ad bellum*, international law codified this current by outlawing all aggressive war such that 'in the conditions of the second half of the twentieth century, to resort to war against another state except in self-defence or under the provisions of the UN Charter is a crime, in both the moral and legal senses of the word'.[45] Thus, the particular evil of aggression underpins the modern notion of just cause. In fact, 'punishment of evil' and 'recovery of something wrongly taken' are now subsumed under the predominating condition of self-defence. Iraq's invasion of Kuwait in 1990 was a paradigmatic example of this: Kuwait had to be defended against armed attack, its wrongly seized territory had to be recovered, and Iraq's aggression had to be punished.[46]

The analysis of just cause as confined to self-defence against armed attack—embodied in Articles 2 and 51 of the UN Charter—is the most restrictive in the history of the just war tradition (though not identical with the just war tradition, international law is 'recognizably a continuation of the just war tradition').[47] It is also the mainstay of the modern state system, which assigns rights such as political sovereignty and territorial integrity to states. But state sovereignty is not merely a legal condition; it is regarded by 'communitarian' political theorists as a moral condition. Michael Walzer, for example, draws upon social contract theory to argue that 'rights in the world have value only if they have dimension'. For Walzer, state boundary lines establish habitable worlds in which conceptions of the good are realized, rights are conferred, and men and women are provided with safety. Aggression, therefore, 'in all its forms challenges rights that are worth dying for'. It interrupts the 'peace with rights' condition and forces people to risk their lives for the sake of their rights. Aggression is 'morally and physically coercive', and that is why it is a crime.[48] Walzer articulates an eloquent and succinct 'theory of aggression', summed up in six propositions,[49] which serves as a neat summary of the case against aggression from the perspective of moral philosophy.

Thus, in the words of Pope Pius XII, aggression by one state against another has come to be regarded both morally and legally as 'a sin, an offence, an outrage'. The claim of self-defence is therefore pivotal to contemporary presentations of just cause. Given the fact of the attacks on US soil on September 11 and the belief that they could be 'a prelude to far greater horrors',[50] the Bush administration's war on terror is presented as a case of self-defence. September 11 was described by Bush as the Pearl Harbour of the twenty-first century. For, indeed, 'with those attacks the terrorists and their supporters declared war on the US, and war is what they got'.[51] The invasion of Iraq was depicted as part of this defensive war on terror—as an 'essential step',[52] the administration insisted that Iraq had to be understood in 'the context of the war on terror'.[53] But, considering that Saddam Hussein had not himself attacked or declared war on the United States, the Bush administration justified the Iraq war by appealing to the just war doctrine of pre-emption. This sizeable, controversial issue will be engaged more extensively in Chapter 2. For now, it is noted that the notion of self-defence as the only justification for war was given credence by the Bush administration. At the same time, however, the accepted idea of 'self-defence' was reconceptualized. An appeal to pre-emption challenges the simple aggressor–defender distinction that concentrates on the *first* use of force as the defining characteristic of the unjust side. In drawing upon the broader just war tradition, the Bush administration contested the legal tendency to view the initiator of hostilities as the wrongdoer.

As part of its just cause, the war on terror qualified 'aggression' in a second way. Terrorism was dubbed 'the great evil of our time'.[54] According to Douglas Feith, 'the international murder of civilians, including children, forces us to speak in moral terms about basic ideas—about good and evil. President Bush states the case starkly: terrorism is evil'.[55] In this way, the third classical condition of 'punishment of evil' was revived and emphasized. Aquinas justified such punishment by quoting Romans 13:4: '[the soldier] beareth not the sword in vain, for he is God's minister, an avenger to execute wrath upon him that doth evil'.[56] By postulating the existence of an 'axis of evil' and deeming that 'evil is real and it must be opposed',[57] Bush's stark, biblical terminology evoked a moral battle between the forces of darkness and light. In fact, a graphic choice was presented between 'a world at peace and a world of chaos'.[58] 'Freedom and fear' were said to be 'at war',[59] and military action was justified because 'the measured use of force is all that protects us from a chaotic world ruled by force'.[60] The president affirmed that the two visions which clashed in Afghanistan—'one of tyranny and murder, the other of liberty and life'[61]—then met in Iraq and contended for the future of that country. For, like 'the terrorists', the Baathist regime was evil. Upon describing Saddam's torture chambers, Bush reasoned that 'if this is not evil, then evil has no meaning'.[62]

This impulse clearly runs counter to the neo-scholastic attempt to avoid defining evil in ideological terms, but it can be construed as a part of the broader just war tradition which understands just cause as the protection and preservation of value. Because the United States led an attack against Iraq without a prior attack from Iraq, the US invasion of Iraq violated the modern prohibition against the first use of force and the secular conception of 'value' as state sovereignty. Yet even if the appeal to self-defence by pre-emption is rejected, the invasion could be viewed as consistent with the just war tradition's vision of war as an instrument of God's justice. Bush's statements share with Reinhold Niebuhr the belief that justice is related to divine love, and that military action can indeed serve the will of God. This agenda has been marginalized in more recent times as the crusade was considered to be wholly distinct from the just war. The question of 'evil' will be taken up again in Chapter 3. But the ideological agenda of the war on terror need not be defined in religious terms—put in a secular way, 'our enemies are engaged in a war on freedom'[63] and it is up to the United States to 'fight freedom's fight'.[64]

The just cause of the war on terror was thus double-pronged: it involved safeguarding national security as well as a value-laden contest between ways of life. It was both 'the security challenge and the moral mission of our time'.[65] Indeed, 'we fight not to impose our will but to defend ourselves and extend the blessings of freedom'.[66] This 'defend and extend' justification was manifested in the Iraq war with reference to three phenomena. The three interrelated branches of the Bush administration's just cause in Iraq were (*a*) WMD, (*b*) the al-Qaeda connection, and (*c*) the nature of the Iraqi regime. Each factor will be examined below in the light of both the strategic and the ideological objectives of the war on terror.

1.2.1.1. *Weapons of mass destruction*

Douglas Feith's confidence in 2004 that 'no one can properly assert that the failure, so far, to find Iraqi WMD stockpiles undermines the reasons for war'[67] seems misplaced given that the principal stated reason for war was to 'disarm Iraq'. Indeed, the WMD issue was pivotal to the justification for the war along the conventional lines of self-defence. The existence of WMD meant that the administration could speak of great threat and employ concepts such as 'common defence' and 'disarmament', and the war's objective could be painted in terms of 'the end of terrible threats to the civilised world'.[68] Indeed, the president declared that 'by our actions we serve a great and just cause: we will remove weapons of mass destruction from the hands of mass murderers'.[69]

The WMD issue also allowed for the use of imagery that implicitly connected the Iraqi threat with the events of September 11,[70] which will be explored in the next section. The proposition that Saddam Hussein could arm al-Qaeda was certainly crucial to the impression that Iraq fell under the ambit of the war on terror. The alleged Iraqi arsenal was made a legitimate target by the 'National Strategy to Combat Weapons of Mass Destruction', because linkages between terrorist groups and state sponsors of terror warranted 'priority attention'.[71] Iraq was a cornerstone of the strategic objectives of the war on terror because 'the terrorist threat to America and to the world will be diminished the moment that Saddam Hussein is disarmed'.[72] Such arguments, however, rested entirely upon the assumption that Iraq did possess WMD.

This 'fact' was established by a sophisticated case that rendered the Iraqi stockpile both knowable and unknowable simultaneously. Detailed catalogues of deadly materials were put forward, including 25,000 litres of anthrax; 500 tons of sarin, mustard, and VX nerve agents; 38,000 litres of botolinum toxin; between 100 and 500 tons of chemical weapons agent; dozens of Scud-variant ballistic missiles; and five different methods of enriching uranium for a nuclear bomb. This threat was buttressed by references to mobile production facilities, dual-use infrastructure, F1 Mirage jets with modified aerial fuel tanks, and unmanned aerial vehicles for dispensing chemical and biological agents. As well as cataclysmic images of mushroom clouds, respiratory failure, circulatory failure, plague, typhus, tetanus, cholera, camelpox, hemorrhagic fever, and smallpox were alluded to.[73] That Iraq was actively developing such dangerous, mendacious programmes was said to be beyond doubt: 'there is no doubt that Saddam Hussein now has weapons of mass destruction' (Cheney, 27 August 2002); 'intelligence . . . leaves no doubt that the Iraqi regime continues to possess and conceal some of the most lethal weapons ever devised' (Bush, 17 March 2003); 'people will continue to debate this issue but there is no doubt in my mind' (Powell, 5 February 2003).

The certainty that Saddam Hussein was in possession of prohibited WMD was coupled with a subtle case for the inherent mysteriousness of the stockpile. The Baathist regime was alleged to be 'moving'[74] its arsenal, 'tunnel [ing] underground',[75] and generally 'housecleaning'[76] in order to evade inspectors. The secretive, impenetrable nature of the regime was also offered up as a reason for the intangibility of the illicit weapons programme—speaking after the war, Bush reasoned that 'there is no such thing necessarily in a dictatorial regime of ironclad, absolutely solid evidence'.[77] It was therefore argued that 'the first time we can be completely certain he has nuclear weapons is when, God forbid, he uses one' (Bush, 12 September 2002). This tacit admission that complete certainty had not yet been attained jars with the 'no doubt' claims that hurried the path to war. But this seeming contradiction worked well in both heightening the perception of danger and lessening the burden of proof. What was known about Iraq was said to be the mere tip of a submerged iceberg and to await full knowledge of the rest of the stockpile was presented as suicidal. Similarly, the Americans could go to war without a 'smoking gun' of evidence because, almost by definition, a smoking gun in Iraq was impossible to find.

As it transpired, evidence of WMD was not uncovered in Iraq. Rice had claimed that 'the intelligence against Saddam and his weapons of mass destruction is a broad and deep case from multiple sources over 12 years from many, many different intelligence agencies, from the UN itself'.[78] Such intelligence was, apparently, incorrect—what's more, there were doubts about the viability of the intelligence before the war commenced. This led to a series of scandals[79] and panels[80], after the fact, surrounding the question of whether the intelligence was 'sexed-up'. Indeed, the case for war based on Saddam's possession of WMD was problematic. Bush had claimed in his 2003 State of the Union address that Iraq was trying to purchase uranium from Africa,[81] but Stephen Hadley later admitted that he had been warned twice by the CIA that the agency would not stand by that information and that it should be removed from the speech.[82] Much a-do was made of Iraq's attempts to 'buy high-strength aluminium tubes used to enrich uranium',[83] but the International Atomic Energy Agency (IAEA) team had concluded that 'Iraq's efforts to import aluminium tubes were not likely to be related to the manufacture of gas centrifuges'.[84] The British had suggested that Iraq could launch a chemical or biological attack in as little as forty-five minutes,[85] but it was widely known that the director of the CIA, George Tenet, privately spoke of the 'they-can-attack-in-45-minutes shit'.[86] Bush had alleged to his cabinet that the time frame for Iraq to develop a nuclear weapon would be six months,[87] but the IAEA inspection report, published twelve days before the invasion of Iraq, concluded that 'we have to date found no evidence or plausible indication of the revival of a nuclear weapons programme in Iraq'.[88]

At best, this situation was embarrassing for the administration. There is some irony to Rice's *New York Times* article, entitled 'Why We Know Iraq is Lying', and Powell's statement that 'most brazenly of all the Iraqi declaration[89] denies the existence of any prohibited weapons programs at all'.[90] At worst, contra Feith, the lack of WMD in Iraq totally subverted the principal reason for war. The just cause was portrayed as ridding Iraq of lethal weapons; there were no weapons to be rid of. The existence of WMD was, moreover, crucial to the case for pre-emptive war, which will be set out fully in Chapter 2.

1.2.1.2. *The al-Qaeda connection*

The issue of WMD was also integral to the Bush administration's attempts to link Iraq with the terrorist group that perpetrated the attacks of September 11. The Bush administration's salient argument for the invasion of Iraq proceeded as follows:

Figure 1.1   Bush administration argument for the invasion of Iraq.

1. A great threat to the United States is WMD in the hands of al-Qaeda.[91]
2. Saddam Hussein supports and harbours al-Qaeda.[92]
3. Saddam Hussein has WMD.[93]

4. Saddam Hussein is a great threat to the United States.[94]

Citing the September 11 Commission's conclusion that the US government had failed to imagine the horror of that day, Bush argued that 'after September 11th we cannot fail to imagine that a brutal tyrant' might 'share this deadly capability with terrorists'.[95] But, in order to establish that his case for war was based on more than mere imaginings, the evidentiary propositions inhering in (2) and (3) were pivotal to the validity of the argument. The viability of (3) was examined in the previous subsection; (2) will be considered here.

The first element of Iraq's connection with al-Qaeda, indicated in (2) above, was the idea that Iraq was a material 'ally of al-Qaeda'.[96] It was repeatedly charged that there exists a 'sinister nexus between Iraq and the al-Qaeda terrorist network',[97] that Saddam had 'an established relationship with al-Qaeda',[98] and that 'the passing of Saddam Hussein will deprive terrorist networks of a wealthy patron that pays for terrorist training'.[99] Dick Cheney was particularly vocal on this issue, insisting:

We learned more and more that there was a relationship between Iraq and al-Qaeda that stretched back through most of the decade of the '90s, that it involved training, for example, on BW and CW, that al-Qaeda sent personnel to Baghdad to get trained on the systems that are involved. The Iraqis providing [*sic*] bomb-making expertise and advice to the al-Qaeda organization.[100]

The vice-president also spearheaded a discredited accusation that Moham-mad Ata, one of the 9/11 hijackers, had met with an Iraqi intelligence agent in Prague.[101] Indeed, the 9/11–Iraq connection is said to have been Cheney's *idée fixe*, described by some of his colleagues as a 'fever' bordering on obsession.[102]

In terms of the events of 9/11, 'neither the CIA nor the congressional joint inquiry that investigated the assault on the World Trade Centre and the Pentagon found any evidence linking Iraq to the hijackers or the attacks'.[103] More generally, former counterterrorism specialist Dick Clarke pronounced in 2004 that 'there's absolutely no evidence that Iraq was supporting al-Qaeda, ever'.[104] That there was 'scant evidence to tie Saddam to terrorist organizations, and even less to the September 11 attacks'[105] was a point repeatedly made by experts before the war. Colin Powell's speech to the United Nations in February 2003 involved a conspicuously thin case with regard to the al-Qaeda connection and, even if entirely reliable, very little of Powell's evidence implicated the Iraqi regime directly. What is more, Powell's case centred almost entirely on Abu Musab al-Zarqawi, who was the leader of Tawhid wa Jihad at the time. In fact, the slides that illustrated the connection were entitled 'Al-Zarqawi's Iraq-Linked Terrorist Network', but it was believed by some experts that Zarqawi's group was autonomous of, even a possible rival to, al-Qaeda.[106] In any case, though Powell told the United Nations that Zarqawi travelled to Baghdad in May 2002, whereupon 'nearly two dozen extremists converged on Baghdad and established a base of operations there',[107] Zarqawi was in fact staying in Syria at the time where, it is said, his phone was being tapped by a Western intelligence service.[108] Although theories continued to postulate a direct, material link between Saddam Hussein and al-Qaeda,[109] Rumsfeld's confidence about the 'bullet-proof'[110] intelligence was undermined by other conclusions that the evidence about the ties was 'sketchy'[111] and 'not compelling'.[112]

A second feature of the Bush administration's link between Iraq and al-Qaeda was an implied ideological affinity. According to Bush, there is such a thing as an 'ideology of terror',[113] and it was suggested that the Baath party and the al-Qaeda network shared it: 'our principles and security are challenged today by outlaw groups and regimes that accept no law of morality and have no limit on their violent ambitions'.[114] As a result, rogue regimes and their terrorist 'allies' constituted an 'axis of evil', a term that demarcates the enemy ideologically. However, while Baathism's ideological aims are secular, socialist, and pan-Arab, al-Qaeda's objectives are religious, funda-mentalist, and pan-Islamic, involving a global Muslim insurgency distinct from states. In fact, al-Qaeda encouraged the 'ousting of the apostate rulers of the Arabian peninsula',[115] one of whom was Saddam Hussein. For sure,

Osama bin Laden stated in 1996 that 'we, as Muslims, do not like the Iraqi regime',[116] he described the Baath party as 'infidel',[117] and he considered Saddam to be 'a thief and an apostate'.[118] Al-Qaeda's spokesman, Suleiman Abu Ghaith, too, made his name through sermons vigorously denouncing Saddam Hussein for his invasion of Kuwait. Moreover, excessive religiosity was seen as a threat to Iraqi national unity, and Saddam was well known for his brutal crackdowns on clerics and their families. Karsh and Rautsi point out that bin Laden's hatred of the United States was 'far more ideological, if no less intense, than that of the Iraqi tyrant. . . . For Saddam, it was a strictly personal matter'.[119] The ideological overlap that would entail an alliance between the Iraqi regime and al-Qaeda was virtually non-existent.

The implication that Saddam and his cronies were themselves 'terrorists' is the third element of the Iraq–al-Qaeda connection. The administration often referred to 'the terror regime in Iraq'.[120] Whether deliberate or not, this evoked a tacit affiliation between the way in which a dictator 'terrorizes' his own population and the very different phenomenon of international terrorism. Rumsfeld exemplified this well when he spoke of 'the tyranny of terrorism'.[121] Wolfowitz too took to describing Iraq's alleged WMD stockpile as 'weapons of mass terror' and 'an arsenal of terror'.[122] Speaking about Iraq, Bush stated quite plainly that 'we're in a war against these terrorists'.[123] However, Iraq's status as an outlaw regime, its flouting of international law, and its authoritarian rule is surely distinct from terrorism as it is conventionally understood. Nevertheless, there was an implicit attempt by the administration to elide the two concepts.[124] Indeed, Bush was remarkably candid about this when he explained to the Australian Prime Minister, John Howard, that 'every speech I give I remind them of the atrocities of the [Iraqi] regime just to make the point that they acted like terrorists'.[125]

Interestingly, a *Washington Post* poll conducted five months after the Iraq invasion found that 69 per cent of the American people believed Saddam Hussein was personally involved in the September 11 attacks, while 82 per cent thought he had assisted bin Laden and the al-Qaeda network.[126] Whether such beliefs were independent of the Bush administration's attempts to prove a connection or whether they were a consequence of the Bush administration's efforts, there are grounds on which each of the three elements of proposition (2) can be questioned. However, the Bush administration's just cause necessitated the claim that Saddam Hussein supported and harboured al-Qaeda. In the first place, (2) was integral to the justification of the war as pre-emptive self-defence: the United States claimed to be defending against the contingency that Iraq would arm al-Qaeda with WMD. Such a prospect would be impossible if Iraq and al-Qaeda were unconnected. Furthermore, if Saddam Hussein was indeed linked with the perpetrators of September 11, the

Bush administration's just cause could involve retaliation, which is permitted by the just war tradition (the pursuit and punishment of an aggressor falls under self-defence). So, like al-Qaeda, on top of being evil, Saddam Hussein had also *done* evil to the American people. In this way, the United States could 'punish the evildoers' who had helped commit the modern 'evil' of aggression against the United States on September 11.

1.2.1.3. *The nature of the Iraqi regime*

Saddam Hussein's dictatorial regime and sometime appalling human rights record were also brought into play for the case against him. Thus, the administration highlighted his 'evil', dubbing him 'a student of Stalin',[127] and invoking United Nations Commission on Human Rights reports of his grave abuses. As a result, Iraq as a target was consistent with the ideological objectives of the war on terror, which involved extending freedom's 'blessings'. In fact, the brutal nature of the Iraqi regime was key to the ideological objectives of the US invasion, which could take on a hue that was over and above power politics and national interest—'America's cause is right and just: liberty for an oppressed people and security for the American people'.[128] To Powell's mind, Saddam Hussein had shown contempt for the United Nations and contempt for the truth, but 'most damning of all' was 'his utter contempt for human life'.[129]

Perhaps the most well-demarcated trend in the just war tradition, which takes its cue from the fact of vicious regimes and human rights abuses, is that of 'humanitarian intervention'. In the sixteenth century, Grotius argued that the rights of a sovereign were limited by principles of humanity and, accordingly, others could justifiably take up arms against a tyrant practising atrocities 'as no one is warranted in inflicting'.[130] This sentiment has been strengthened over time and spawned the 'solidarist' school of thought in international relations. As well as an ever-growing body of moral,[131] legal,[132] and political theory[133] on the subject, the end of the Cold War and revitalization of the Security Council has brought a series of interventions justified (to varying degrees) on humanitarian grounds, including Somalia, Kosovo, Haiti, East Timor, Liberia, and Congo. Humanitarian intervention is taken to be 'coercive interference in the internal affairs of a state, involving the use of armed force, with the purposes of addressing massive human rights violations or preventing widespread human suffering'.[134] Although there has been a move towards the doctrine in both theory and state practice, because of its implications for sovereignty the acceptable instance of humanitarian intervention is also the strictly limited one.

Given emerging concerns, the Iraq war can be seen as a problematic case of humanitarian intervention in (at least) three major ways. Firstly, the means used in the Iraq war were inconsistent with an end of humanitarian intervention. The character of the US conduct—a 'shock and awe' bombing campaign followed by 150,000 ground troops and the use of cluster munitions in populated areas—was clearly not designed with the objective of ending human rights abuses. The disbanding of the Iraqi police forces and the failure to prepare adequately for the rampant violence and disorder of post-Saddam Iraq further underlines the discrepancy between the coalition's actual intervention and any possible pretext of humanitarian intervention. Secondly, there is no evidence of the triggering mechanism for a humanitarian intervention in Iraq—namely, 'crimes that shock humanity'. According to Human Rights Watch, 'the Iraq war was not mainly about saving the Iraqi people from mass slaughter' because 'no such slaughter was then ongoing or imminent'.[135] Thirdly, humanitarian motives were clearly not dominant,[136] as it is reasonable to suggest that the war would not have occurred in the absence of the issues of WMD and the al-Qaeda connection. In Powell's February presentation to the United Nations, even his slides relating to human rights violations were labelled, 'Iraq: Failing to Disarm'.

Perhaps the most compelling illustration of the fact that the Iraq war was not a viable case of humanitarian intervention is provided by comparison with the humanitarian action taken after the Gulf War in 1991, however imperfect a mission it was. Operation Provide Comfort came in response to Saddam's brutal counteroffensive to the Shia revolt, during which helicopters were used to dispense napalm and a million terrified refugees fled to the mountains of Iran and Turkey. Up to a thousand people were dying each day—'no fly zones' were thus designed to ensure the delivery of humanitarian aid and protect the besieged civilians. As well as having a UN Chapter VII mandate, this intervention was a response to a genuine humanitarian emergency and the means it adopted displayed an explicit connection with the humanitarian ends of the mission.

While the administration never appealed to the doctrine of humanitarian intervention, a sustained effort was made to justify the invasion of Iraq with reference to the well-being of Iraqis. In the absence of ongoing or imminent mass slaughter, this centred on Saddam's 'police state' and the climate of political repression in Iraq, which were part of the broader 'freedom deficit' in the Middle East. Consequently, 'liberty for the Iraqi people is a great moral cause and a great strategic goal'.[137] However, 'liberty' as both the moral cause and the strategic goal of the Iraq invasion can be viewed with some moral scepticism.

The war on terror comprises the ultimate strategic-cum-ideological foreign policy objective: 'a balance of power that favours freedom'.[138] In citing values, the war on terror is not anomalous. This chapter has already touched upon the larger conception of the just war as the preservation and protection of value—for Augustine and, more recently, Ramsey, fundamental to the just war was the protection of innocents. Such a moral goal is said to be universalizable. For the Bush administration, and 'neoconservatives' more generally, the 'cause of liberty' was depicted as an equally fundamental moral goal: 'we serve the cause of liberty, and that is always and everywhere a cause worth serving'.[139] Buttressing this claim was Wolfowitz's stated belief that 'the values we call Western are indeed universal'.[140] Interestingly, figures such as Mahathir Mohammed would argue that 'Western values [are] merely Western, while Islamic values [are] universal'.[141] In any case, the ideals of 'liberty' and 'freedom' as realized by liberal-democratic political systems are not as clearly basic as the protection of innocent life and other core just war values, which have prompted and shaped the norm of humanitarian intervention. The 'freedom' to which Bush so often appealed can conceivably be realized in a number of varying ways. Bin Laden himself offered such an argument, declaring that al-Qaeda fights 'because we are free men who cannot acquiesce in injustice'.[142] In short, the legitimacy of Bush's value-laden agenda was merely assumed—he did not offer a full account of why 'freedom' in the form of *democratization* might be as obvious a just cause for war as protecting the inalienable right to life threatened by such occurrences as aggressive war or genocide.

In terms of strategic interests, there was certainly an element of long-term self-defence in the Bush administration's hopes to export democracy to the Middle East: 'the transformation of the Middle East is the *only guarantee* that it will no longer produce ideologies of hatred that lead men to fly airplanes into buildings in New York or Washington'.[143] America's chosen means to redress the freedom deficit in Iraq—namely, invasion—was arguably illegal, as it violated state sovereignty. The Bush administration therefore appealed to pre-emptive self-defence by invoking WMD and the al-Qaeda connection. But, changing Iraq's regime can also be seen as part of the self-defence package. The strategic objective aimed to preclude the possibility of current and future enemies by 'transforming' a whole region. However, there are reasons for thinking that there ought to be limits to securing national security goals. The very essence of a modern just war is to have objectives that are limited to dealing with the danger posed and neutralizing concrete threats. This tenet did not fit easily with the stated objective of political 'transformation' in the Middle East, and the moral, if not legal, legitimacy of such a broad objective was never systematically defended by members of the US administration.

This section has examined the Bush administration's presentation of just cause, which was broken down into the three factors of WMD, the al-Qaeda connection, and the nature of the Iraqi regime. The allegations that Saddam Hussein was developing WMD and that he was linked to al-Qaeda were both necessary features of the just cause. Neither was, by itself, sufficient. The just cause for an invasion of Iraq as part of the war on terror relied on a combination of the two charges.[144] The third element of the just case, the brutal excesses of the Baathist regime, was neither sufficient for an invasion (very many other states were implicated in serious human rights abuses at the time of invasion) nor necessary (the grave allegation that Saddam was planning to arm al-Qaeda with prohibited WMD was adequate). Indeed, regime change was originally treated as epiphenomenal by the British—an unintended but positive outcome of disarming Iraq.[145] Nonetheless, in the absence of proof of WMD and/or a connection between Saddam Hussein and al-Qaeda, this third feature of the just cause was increasingly pointed to as the dominant justification for the US-led invasion.[146]

1.2.2. Right authority

Whereas, today, just cause is the dominant category, the proviso that legitimate uses of force be sanctioned by right authority was once the most pressing just war criterion. This was because, for medievalists, right authority was regarded as vital to protecting the peace and limiting the occurrence of violence, as its purpose was to circumscribe the right of lawless brigands and thugs to resort to force. Augustine duly restricted the right to wage war to the divinely sanctioned sovereign: 'for the natural order which seeks the peace of mankind, ordains that the monarch should have the power of undertaking war if he thinks it advisable'. Aquinas, quoting Augustine, further developed the concept of right authority such that its basis became secular. A private citizen had no need to declare war because he could 'seek for redress of his rights from the tribunal of his superior'; what's more, it was the sovereign's responsibility to 'watch over the common weal of the city' and to protect it from both internal disturbances and external attack.[147] In this way, bands of strongmen as well as churchmen had no business making war.

The stipulation that only rulers of recognized sovereign political entities had the authority to wage war evolved into a formalistic *competence de guerre*, the doctrine that a prince could initiate war based on his own authority and his own assessment of whether a just cause exists. This state of affairs predominated in Grotius' work and was well realized by the sovereign wars of the eighteenth century, the effects of which lasted up until the First World War. The League of Nations, however, moved drastically to divert war-making authority from sovereigns to international institutions of collective security.

These efforts were buttressed by Catholic pronouncements such as the Conventus of Fribourg of 1931, which argued that a war declared without recourse to the League of Nations' arbitration mechanism could not be a lawful social process. After the Second World War, the United Nations succeeded the League of Nations as the pre-eminent international body with the legitimacy to wage war. By positive international law, the authority for the offensive use of force is located in the United Nations Security Council.

At the dawn of the twenty-first century, the question of right authority tends to revolve around issues of unilateralism versus multilateralism, brought to a dramatic head with the US-led invasion of Iraq. A significant aspect of the furore surrounding the war was whether the United States and Britain possessed the authority to declare it—indeed, the legal debate centred on the necessity (or not) of a second UN resolution.[148] The Bush administration's approach to the question of right authority took on two mantles.

In the first place, the administration staunchly reserved for itself the unilateral right to be 'in charge' of its own defence.[149] Cheney's vigorous assertions that 'the United States will never seek a permission slip to defend the security of our country'[150] were echoed by the President's insistence that 'America must never outsource its national security decisions to leaders of other countries'.[151] Indeed, the internationalism[152] of Senator John Kerry, Bush's challenger in the 2004 presidential elections, was lambasted as unpatriotic and derided as 'soft-on-defence liberal[ism]'.[153] Even in seeking a second resolution from the United Nations, Bush informed its delegates that 'by heritage and by choice, the United States of America will make [a] stand. Delegates to the United Nations, you have the right to make that stand as well'.[154] Implicit in this statement, and others,[155] was the idea that the Americans were going to take action anyway; the approach to the United Nations was merely an invitation to jump on a bandwagon that had already hit the road. The Bush administration's threats of unilateral action in the absence of proper UN approbation allowed it to project an image of unbridled strength in the war on terror, but it also vested the US Congress with *competence de guerre*, UN approval being an added bonus.[156] When Lord Butler asked Rice whether the war was legal, she instantly responded: 'Of course, Congress approved it'.[157]

Simultaneously, however, the American administration made a direct appeal to the United Nations' authority in framing the argument for war. Pivotal to both the legal and moral case against Iraq was that it had 'been found guilty of material breach of its obligations stretching back over 16 previous resolutions and 12 years'.[158] In fact, the case for war was laden with references to UN determinations, inspectors, sanctions, and resolutions, and one of the triggering justifications for war was the following: 'The United Nations Security

Council has not lived up to its responsibilities, so we will rise to ours'.[159] Bush had spoken repeatedly of the Iraq issue as a 'difficult and defining moment' for the UN,[160] a chance for the Security Council to 'rise to the moment',[161] and he later portrayed the action in Iraq as preventing 'the UN from solemnly choosing its own irrelevance and inviting the fate of the League of Nations'.[162] In order to square the circle of US unilateralism grounded in the legal licence of UN resolutions, the Bush administration depicted its invasion of Iraq as upholding, rather than contravening, UN authority: 'We believe in the Security Council—so much that we want its words to have meaning'.[163] In addition, the international nature of the 'coalition of the willing' was emphasized: 'Every major race, religion and ethnic group in the world is represented. The coalition includes nations from every continent on the globe'.[164]

After September 11, the 'National Security Strategy' proposed a 'distinctly American internationalism'—certainly, the US position with regard to Iraq was distinctive. In declaring itself the champion of the UN's will (as represented by a series of resolutions), the United States could proceed on its own accord without a Security Council mandate and yet maintain that its action was consistent with the right authority of the United Nations. The question of proper authority became a key point of controversy over the Iraq war: Although the British Attorney General advised that authority to use force existed from 'the combined effect' of three Security Council resolutions (678, 687, and 1441),[165] other eminent academic lawyers argued that 'there is no justification under international law for the use of military force against Iraq...neither Security Council resolution 1441 nor any prior resolution authorises the proposed use of force in the present circumstances'.[166] Key figures in the run-up to war such as Jacques Chirac,[167] Hans Blix,[168] and Kofi Annan[169] declared the US action 'illegal', and there was even speculation that Bush and Blair could one day face criminal charges.[170] For the most part, churches worldwide also insisted upon UN authority, with New Zealand's church leaders jointly stressing that to 'by-pass the appropriate international authority which does exist, the United Nations Security Council, is immoral'.[171] The legality of the war was disputed at the time hostilities commenced and will remain contentious. Regardless, Bush's attempt to have his cake and eat it represents the modern and widely shared importance attached to UN authority for the legitimacy of waging war.

1.2.3. Right intention

We come to Iraq with respect for its citizens, for their great civilisation and for the religious faiths they practice. We have no ambition in Iraq except to remove a threat and restore that country to its own people.[172]

For Aquinas, 'it may happen that the war is declared by the legitimate authority, and for a just cause, and yet be rendered unlawful through a wicked intention'.[173] Such malicious intent was defined by Augustine as 'the passion for inflicting harm, the cruelty in taking vengeance, an unpacific and relentless spirit, the fever of rebellion, the lust for domination, and such like things'.[174] Aquinas summarizes right intention as involving 'the advancement of good, or the avoidance of evil',[175] which draws attention to its dynamic link with *jus in bello*. In fact, as James Turner Johnson has argued, 'this is as close as Thomas [Aquinas] came to the stipulation of a *jus in bello*. For him, right conduct in war would follow from the virtuousness of its purpose and of those who fought in accordance with that purpose'.[176] Grady Scott Davis, too, points out that failure to respect the principle of proportionality *in bello*, for example, registers indifference to the principle of discrimination, which calls into question your (*ad bellum*) intent.[177] In important ways, then, right intention serves as a lynchpin between the two spheres of justice.

A rightful intention would impact the *jus in bello* by ensuring that the war is fought in accordance with the overarching desire to advance good. While 'wrong' intentions cannot be bleached out of the complex texture of human and political motivation, the idea is that whatever bad feelings are harboured towards the enemy, these must not be translated into behaviour.[178] The duty this criterion placed on individuals was reflected in a practice that carried well into the Middle Ages, whereby the Church required that soldiers do penance after battle on the chance that they had carried sinful motivations in their hearts.[179] Individual manifestations of 'wrong intention' are perhaps easier to capture in the modern era because of advances in media technology—it was with graphic photographic evidence that the abuse at the Abu Ghraib prison first came to the attention of the global press, and it was a Channel Four camera crew that captured the message discovered by one Fallujah family scrawled in lipstick on the bedroom mirror: 'Fuck Iraq and every Iraqi in it'.[180] In Chapter 3, we shall see how the notion of 'intention' is important to the *jus in bello* in a second way, as it resurfaces in the context of targeting, proportionality, and the doctrine of double effect.

In terms of the *jus ad bellum*, right intention deals with a state's motivation for resorting to war. In a just war, the state is circumscribed from prosecuting a war that is rooted in malice or hatred. Douglas Lackey notes that Augustine would surely condemn as sinful the US campaign of extermination against Japanese cities, the dropping of two atomic bombs, and the four-year internment of 180,000 innocent Japanese Americans during the Second World War, because it was based on a racial hatred of the Japanese.[181] In fact, Osama bin Laden has made the argument that the United States has waged a war to 'annihilate Islam'.[182] Accordingly, in making the case for the war on terror, members of the Bush administration went to some length to emphasize that US action in no way represented an assault on Islam or Arabs. The National Security Strategy deliberately invoked and rejected Samuel Huntington's thesis by affirming that 'the war on terrorism is not a clash of civilisations',[183] and various members of the Bush administration publicly outlined their admiration for Arab culture and Islam as 'a great faith that inspires people to lead lives based on honesty, justice and compassion'.[184] Of course, the administration's efforts to this end were compromised somewhat by allegations of deliberately mocking Islamic practices at Guantanamo Bay, ranging from forced nudity,[185] to flushing the Koran down the toilet,[186] to smearing detainees with the menstrual blood of prostitutes during interrogation,[187] to the words 'Fuck Islam' scrawled above the latrines.[188]

But does the presence of hatred vitiate the right to wage war, even if there is a just cause? This is subject to debate. James Childress argues that if all the other conditions of a just war are met, the presence of vicious motives does not, in fact, obliterate the *jus ad bellum*. Yet Grady Scott Davis maintains that a war carried out in hate cannot be just. Venturing an analysis of the moral psychology of the person who hates, Davis argues that the hater hates in the absence of a just cause—he wants to inflict injury, whether or not this is due, 'and this desire is contrary to justice'.[189] This position is in line with his view that the *jus ad bellum* criteria are, as conditions for justice, individually necessary and only conjointly sufficient to secure a just war: 'They are like dominoes; when one falls they all go down'.[190]

The right intentions of a state should centre on goals like protecting or restoring national or human rights and upholding territorial integrity, which rules out 'taking another state's territory, violating the rights of individuals or nations, and deliberately depriving a nation of peace and stability'.[191] With reference to Iraq, time and time again it was emphasized that the United States did not seek to conquer, for America is 'not an imperial power.... We're a liberating power',[192] a fact to which Japan and Germany were said to attest. Hence, in bearing witness to 'the liberation of Iraq' with his first visit, Rumsfeld took the opportunity on national radio to 'be clear: Iraq belongs to you. We do not want to run it'.[193] Indeed, the President promised from the outset that the United States had no intention of determining the precise form of a new Iraqi government,[194] and Rumsfeld pointed to the *loya jirga* system taking root in Afghanistan as evidence that the United States would not 'impose an American-style template on Iraq'.[195] In confirming this intention, Douglas Feith noted that certain proposals were dropped when they proved unpopular with the Iraqis, and the Transitional Administrative Law was debated and approved by the representative government of Iraq, rather than decreed by the Americans.[196]

Mainly due to doubts over the existence of Saddam's allegedly sophisticated weapons programme, a wealth of illegitimate intentions were attributed to the Bush administration's actions in Iraq, including the neocolonial desire to hijack its vast oil reserves,[197] profit from lucrative reconstruction contracts,[198] and create a puppet-state friendly to Israel.[199] These are all accusations the administration would, and did, vociferously deny.[200] However, it is worth considering the value of an intention to which the Bush administration freely admitted—namely, that the Iraq war was a crucial step in the global war on terror. According to the vice-president, 'terrorists have gathered in that country and there they will be defeated. We are fighting this evil in Iraq so we do not have to fight it on the streets of our own cities'.[201] Putting aside the question of whether 'the terrorists' were in fact confined to Saddam's henchmen and foreign fighters, it is worth considering whether 'taking the fight' to another nation is an obviously legitimate intention.

Prior to the US invasion, Iraq did not suffer from the sort of terrorist carnage brought by, for example, suicide bombing, and if the targeting of innocent civilians is in fact 'the great evil of our time',[202] there is room for discussion about whether the United States was morally justified in exposing Iraqi civilians to random acts of mass murder in order to protect US civilians. Of course, it might be argued that the Americans could not foresee the breakdown in order, the influx of foreign fighters, and the proliferation of car bombings and kidnappings, but there was an element of bravado in the Bush administration's attitude to the propagation of terrorism in Iraq:

The President: This collection of killers is trying to shake the will of the United States. They do not understand us. America will never be intimidated by thugs and assassins.
Audience: USA! USA! USA!
The President: We are aggressively striking the terrorists in Iraq. We are on the offensive. We will defeat them there so we do not have to face them in our own cities.[203]

The Bush administration would, no doubt, counter this criticism by referring back to the ultimate intention of the war on terror, which was, effectively, to usher in an era of world peace.

1.2.4. Goal of peace

The goal of peace serves to reinforce right intention, and in so doing makes explicit both the legitimate ends of the just war and its spirit. Just as Augustine counselled Count Boniface, 'peace ought to be what you want . . . war is waged in order to obtain peace',[204] Michael Howard asserts that 'war is instrumental and not elemental: its only legitimate object is a better peace'.[205] The UN Charter, too, is replete with references to its mandate of 'maintaining or restoring peace and security'. The goal of peace, while being the only virtuous objective of a just war, has two related effects. Firstly, in 'cherish[ing] the spirit of a peacemaker',[206] the soldier will fight in the merciful manner that befits the peacemaker and his pursuit of the just cause will be limited. Secondly, and as a result, it will be much easier to sustain the peace after hostilities have ceased if the belligerent has sought peace all along and behaved accordingly.

The discourse surrounding the Bush administration's war on terror attests to the desirability of the image of the seeker of peace. In the war on terror generally, it was declared that 'this great country will lead the world to safety, security, peace and freedom'.[207] In Iraq specifically, 'our goal is peace—for our nation, for our friends and allies, and for the people of the Middle East'.[208] The 'cause of peace'[209] was buttressed by references to the coalition's efforts to bring water to the thirsty, clear landmines, and ship food and medicine.[210] What's more, the creation of a democracy in the long-run would, presumably, count as further evidence in this regard as democracies tend to be more peaceful states and famously 'do not fight each other'.

Howard's reference to a 'better peace' serves to remind that peace is a complex concept: it is not necessarily the mere absence of war. Aquinas touches upon this when he declares that 'those who wage war justly aim at peace, and so they are not opposed to peace, except to the evil peace'.[211] As a cluster concept, peace is therefore dependent upon other values; had the European powers surrendered to Germany in 1939 Hitler's expansionism may have been sated, but 'peace' under Nazi rule conflicts with other fundamental values such as personal liberty and equality. Although the Americans ostensibly breached the peace by commencing a war in Iraq, it behove the United States to appeal to peace as a complex concept in order to support its appearance as the peace seeker. Bush contended that 'a future lived at the mercy of terrible threats is no peace at all'[212] and it was suggested that appeasing Saddam created a state of affairs akin to Aquinas' 'evil peace': 'allowing a dangerous dictator to defy the world and harbour weapons of mass murder and terror is no peace at all. It is pretence'.[213]

The Bush administration therefore suggested that peace defined as lack of war is empty (indeed, dangerous) and proceeded to construe its own actions as instantiations of the 'cause of peace'. As a result, 'the threat to peace does not come from those who seek to enforce the just demands of the civilised world; the threat to peace comes from those who flout those demands'.[214] However, diverse critics of the war denied this characterization and pointed to Bush as a 'stupid, wicked warmonger' (Iranian newspaper editorial)[215] and 'the biggest threat to world peace' (Nelson Mandela).[216] European leaders, too, suggested that a 'war would harm peace and stability in the region'.[217] The efforts by international law to link 'peace' with the upholding of the territorial status quo are designed to circumvent the conceptual conflicts involved in subjective definitions of the 'better peace'. Sovereignty is supposed to apply to all states as a measure of equality which guards against one state's categorization of war as the 'cause of peace'. Of great importance to the US's defence here was the claim that it was forced to subvert the status quo because its war was pre-emptive of a genuine threat, which will be dealt with in Chapter 2. But the Iraq war vividly demonstrates that the just war criterion at hand is comprised of a concept that is inherently, perhaps endlessly, contestable once we abandon the straightforward equation of aggression with the first use of force against a sovereign nation. Formulations of what 'the cause of peace' would amount to in reality are highly dependent on prior understandings of what the appropriate referent objects are (individuals or states), the limits of sovereignty (whether it is an absolute right or conditional on some other state of affairs), and what values such a peace is designed to foster. While the Americans viewed their 'cause of peace' as suitably valuable to undermine Iraq's sovereignty, others, reasoning with different assumptions about world order with different conceptions of value, perceived the Iraq invasion as 'a crime against peace' (Archbishops Jean-Louis Tauran and Renato Martino).[218]

1.2.5. Proportionality

According to A. J. Coates, in its simplest form the criterion of proportionality is meant to raise the question: Is this just cause *worth* a war?[219] The principle of proportionality counsels that the overall destruction expected in war must be outweighed by the good to be achieved. As Ramsey puts it, 'it can never be right to resort to war, no matter how just the cause, unless . . . one has reason to believe that in the end more good will be done than undone or a greater measure of evil prevented'.[220] This idea was invoked by the group of bishops in 1870 who addressed a *Postulata* to Pope Pius XI and the First Vatican Council, decrying the 'hideous massacres' committed by growing national military establishments as completely out of all proportion to the good that would be expected of them. The notion that no modern war can be proportional has gained considerable momentum since and, coupled with the development of extremely destructive weaponry, 'modern-war-pacifism'[221] has taken root.

Such pacifism certainly benefits from a moral neatness not available to the just war position, as the exercise in moral judgement entailed by the principle of proportionality is arduous and the balancing act leaves much to discretion.

Indeed, Aristotle's observation that moral reasoning never amounts to the certainty of mathematics applies aptly to the just war's principle of proportionality. Moreover, even if there were a systematic way of weighing moral values, the problem of prediction persists—for example, if the coalition had prior knowledge of the scale of the insurgency in Iraq, would the war have been prosecuted nonetheless?

It seems fair to dub proportionality 'perhaps the most contentious of all just war criteria'.[222] Central to the 'calculus' of overall good versus evil are prior conceptions about good and evil. Even an appeal to one of the most fundamental values of the just war tradition—the protection of innocents—is fraught with controversy. In 2004, *The Lancet* medical journal published a (disputed) report that suggested that more innocent lives met violent ends as a result of the Iraq invasion than if the situation under Saddam Hussein had continued. In comparing mortality in the seventeen to eighteen months after the invasion with that fourteen to sixteen months prior to the invasion, the survey found not only that 'about 100,000 excess deaths, or more have happened since the 2003 invasion of Iraq' but also 'most individuals reportedly killed by coalition forces were women and children'.[223] As a result, in terms of the tangible 'evil' of civilian deaths (based on these findings), greater 'evil' resulted from the invasion than would have resulted had the invasion not occurred. However, when weighed against other less tangible values—such as the end of a brutal dictatorship and the opening up of the political system—it seems plausible that the deaths of a large number of innocents could be deemed by some as an acceptable level of 'evil'.

Proportionality is a criterion requiring the moral and political judgement of leaders before the commencement of a war and, as such, evidence of the calculation is nearly impossible. The Bush administration obviously decided that more good would be done with a war than undone, and so it led an invasion of Iraq. Others, however, used the idea of proportionality to resist the path towards war. As one of his three major conditions for a just war, the president of America's largest evangelical seminary, Dr Richard Mouw, questioned whether 'a military strike would do more good than harm' (his other two criteria being last resort and right authority).[224] Likewise, the German premier, Gerhardt Schroeder, explained in a televised address that 'the world stands on the eve of war. My question remains: does the level of threat posed by the Iraqi dictator justify war, which will result in the deaths of thousands of innocent men, women and children? My answer remains: no'.[225]

In terms of the Bush administration's own conclusion that, in fact, more good would result, it is worth considering for whom this good applied. Henry Shue points out that, in making the moral calculation, 'everyone counts: combatants, non-combatants, one's own, the adversary's, and those of neutrals—indeed, the entire international community'.[226] However, the administration's failure to prepare adequately for the chaos and carnage of the post-invasion period, its 'shock and awe' bombing strategy and General Franks' unsettling assertion that 'we don't do body counts'[227] might be construed as reflecting an underlying attitude which treated others' lives and values with greater disregard than American lives and values. Moreover, the flouting of Iraq's sovereignty and the undermining of the United Nations would clearly have repercussions for the whole international community and the basis of world order. That the United States would launch a unilateral pre-emptive strike (whether justified or not) further suggests that American interests were somehow privileged over the stated interests of other nationals.

1.2.6. Last resort

Just war thinking tends to begin from the premise that war is always a moral tragedy, and so every reasonable alternative to it ought to be exhausted. The demand of last resort is well supported by the moral and theological tradition of the just war as well as contemporary international law:

> War is never just another means that one can choose to employ for settling differences between nations. As the Charter of the United Nations Organization and international law itself remind us, war cannot be decided upon, even when it is a matter of ensuring the common good, except as the very last option and in accordance with very strict conditions . . . [228]

The concomitant notion of 'necessity' has abounded through centuries of just war writing, from Augustine's stipulation that 'it ought to be necessity, and not your will, that destroys an enemy',[229] through Calvin's description of 'being driven to it by extreme necessity' to Ramsey's proviso of 'hard necessity'.[230] For Vitoria, seeking a pretext for conflict was 'the mark of utter monstrousness' and so 'the prince should only accede to the necessity of war when he is dragged reluctantly but inevitably into it'.[231] The moral notion behind the requirement of last resort and the concept of necessity is the persistent conviction that 'to jaw jaw is always better than to war war' (Churchill); that it is 'greater to destroy war with a word than men with a sword' (Augustine).[232] The use of force is deemed to be *ultima ratio*, and 'the rough rule of thumb for statesmen and international laws is that the state that fails to exhaust the peaceful remedies available before resorting to war is *prima facie* an aggressor'.[233]

The requirement of last resort lends considerable support to the US Catholic bishops' suggestion that the just war tradition embodies a 'presumption against war'. Both James Turner Johnson and the theologian George Weigel are vehemently opposed to this 'presumption', which they see as leading to a 'functional pacifism', whereby 'the morally appropriate use of armed force is virtually inconceivable'.[234] Upon reflection, however, it is clear that the seven *jus ad bellum* tests are designed to render the destruction inherent to war not quite inconceivable, but indeed only rarely legitimate. The last resort criterion in particular requires that every non-military alternative is exhaustively considered (if not pursued), which assumes that avoiding war is better than war. Certainly, the challenge of last resort helps to block those seeking a pretext for war, which is absolutely abhorred in the western and Islamic just war traditions alike.

Interestingly, both Johnson and Weigel critique the 'presumption' by maintaining that it is a relatively 'new' development, which involves a 'misreading' of classical medieval and early modern Christian just war theory.[235] Yet, as they make their cases against the 'presumption', they simultaneously illustrate its widespread acceptance. Weigel, for example, cites as mistaken the interpretations of 'the overwhelming majority of American religious leaders and intellectuals', 'American and European politicians and commentators alike', 'European and American religious leaders and intellectuals', as well as 'the local congregational level'.[236] However, we have seen that, as a moral tradition, the just war tradition is not static but constantly, and necessarily, evolving—moreover, that evolution occurs with the existence of consensus. Weigel himself argues for the reopening and development of the concepts of defence against aggression, competent authority, and last resort in light of new weapons capabilities, terrorism, rogue states, and other contemporary challenges. Thus, because engaging with just war is not a solely historical enterprise, the (disputed)[237] claim that medieval and early modern Christian writers did not express a 'presumption against war' does not invalidate more recent expressions of it.

In any case, the robustness of the last resort idea was well illustrated by the Bush administration's characterizations of the invasion of Iraq. In November 2002, Rumsfeld spelled out US policy that 'military force should be . . . the last choice, not the first'.[238] Upon the invasion of Iraq, Powell underlined that 'war and force was not our first choice. We gave diplomacy every chance. . . . We did everything to avoid war'.[239] Bush too insisted 'the use of force has been and remains our last resort'.[240] Corroborating the claim of last resort was the argument that the Bush administration had 'tried every possible option'. Cheney pointed to '12 years of diplomacy, more than a dozen UN Security

Council resolutions, hundreds of UN weapons inspectors, thousands of flights to enforce the no-fly zones, and even strikes against military targets in Iraq'.[241]

Like most other just war criteria, last resort is subject to diverging judgements—in this instance, interpretations can vary over when the moment actually arrives. The Americans made two related arguments in furtherance of the case that invasion was the last resort in March 2003. Firstly, as Johnson points out, alternative avenues to war are to be pursued 'only if time permits'. Cheney argued that to wait would be to pander to Saddam Hussein because 'what he wants is time, and more time to husband his resources and invest in his ongoing chemical and biological weapons program, and to gain possession of nuclear weapons'.[242] Bush also invoked Munich, concluding on the eve of war that appeasement in the twenty-first century 'could bring destruction of a kind never before seen on earth'.[243] Thus, to pursue diplomatic options further was painted as especially dangerous. Secondly, the Bush administration defined resolution 1441 as the marker of last resort, and then maintained that Saddam Hussein had not complied with it. Resolution 1441 was deemed a 'decisive final chapter in an 11 year struggle'[244] and Bush decreed the consultations with the United Nations in early 2003 'the last phase of diplomacy'.[245] The draft resolution which the United States, United Kingdom, and Spain presented to the United Nations on 7 March 2003 then attempted to deduce that 'resolution 1441 . . . afforded Iraq a final opportunity to comply with its disarmament obligations under relevant resolutions'.[246] The suppositions of the draft resolution were rejected by the Security Council later that day.

Indeed, the assertion that the last chance had arrived and that Saddam Hussein had not taken it was precisely what was at issue in March 2003; the definition of last resort was the object of dispute. When the UN inspectors delivered their report on 7 March 2003, the German Foreign Minister inferred that 'peaceful disarmament is possible and there is a real alternative to war'.[247] While Powell interpreted the inspectors' report as 'a catalogue of non-cooperation', the Chinese Foreign Minister concluded that 'resolution 1441 has been implemented smoothly on the whole with progress made and results achieved'.[248] It was also the opinion of Dominique de Villepin, the French Foreign Minister, that 'significant evidence of real disarmament has been observed'.[249] Just as Russia declared itself to be 'firmly in favour of continuing and strengthening the work of inspectors',[250] Mexico stated it was 'convinced . . . every opportunity must be taken advantage of to resolve this matter peacefully'.[251] Thus, taking into account the alleged peril of waiting and Iraq's behaviour with regard to resolution 1441, a significant component of the international community, like the Pope, did not accept that the last resort had arrived.

The argument that further diplomatic means were fruitless in March 2003 did not benefit from the definitive last resort of January 1991:

The failure of the Geneva Talks, the continued intransigence of Saddam Hussein, the ongoing process of military build-up by Iraqi forces, the continuing systematic rape of Kuwait, the history of Iraq's relations with its own dissident population and its neighbours, and threats of violence by Iraq against those neighbours all provided ample reason to conclude that non-military means held little possibility of success, and that continuing atrocities in Kuwait necessitated action.[252]

Instead, the Bush administration's broader justification that the last resort had arrived seemed to rest, ultimately, on September 11. Douglas Feith stated in May 2004:

President Bush concluded in light of the 9/11 attacks that it was necessary to remove the Saddam Hussein regime by force. The danger was too great that Saddam might give the fruits of his WMD programs to terrorists for use against the United States. This danger did not hinge on whether Saddam was actually stockpiling chemical or biological weapons.[253]

Feith intimates that the last resort for America's enemies had arrived on September 11. This was a departure from the traditional just war demand that all non-military means are pursued vigorously before each conflict is commenced. This development owed much to the innovation of a 'post-9/11 necessity', which will be taken up extensively in Chapter 2.

1.2.7. Reasonable hope of success

For the just war, prudence requires that there be a reasonable hope of successfully realizing the just cause—that, in short, fighting is not hopeless. The neo-scholastics tended to refer to this criterion as 'certainty of victory', with Suarez making a distinction between offensive and defensive wars in this regard. He deemed the requirement of certainty of victory binding on all offensive wars but too constraining for defensive wars because the rule would mean that a weaker nation could never legitimately fight a stronger nation. Grotius remarked that even when a formal alliance or commitment is in place, no ally is 'bound to render aid if there is no hope of a successful issue'.[254] He quotes the Emperor Augustus that 'war ought not to be undertaken save when the hope of gain was shewn to be greater than the fear of loss'.[255] The idea is to avoid 'useless' and 'shameful bloodshed'.[256] What this amounts to is a serious judgement prior to war about whether it is, in Rumsfeld speak, 'doable'.[257]

In March 2003, the United States had every reason to be certain of military victory over Iraq's armed forces. The fact that the US Armed Forces continues to be the most powerful in the world with force projection capabilities unrivalled by any other single nation amply backed up Powell's caution to 'let there be no doubt about the outcome. We will drive Saddam Hussein and his regime from power'.[258] Bush observed that 'we're a no nonsense group of people who have got one thing in mind and that is victory'[259] and by May he felt himself in a position to declare 'in the battle of Iraq, the US and our allies have prevailed'.[260] For indeed, there was no question that the US-led coalition could and did trounce Saddam Hussein's forces.

Other questions arise, however, when the objectives which comprised the just cause are considered in turn. In terms of WMD, the United States was confident that it could defeat the Republican Guard and then seek out and destroy Iraq's illicit programmes. Provided Saddam did not unleash his chemical arsenal during the invasion (which, it appears, was a genuine worry), there was more than a reasonable hope that Iraq's WMD infrastructure would be dismantled. It turned out, however, that Powell's assured prediction that 'we will remove the shadow of Saddam's terrible weapons from Israel and the Middle East and we will keep them from the hands of terrorists'[261] was almost vacuously true because there were no WMD in Iraq. As considered above, this reality was put forward by many of the war's opponents prior to the invasion. But the success of ridding Iraq of WMD is the least controversial of the three elements of the just cause, because, whether the Bush administration believed Iraq possessed stockpiles or not, there was a reasonable hope that the WMD threat could be neutralized.

The case for reasonable hope of success was less forthcoming with regard to the second element of the just cause, which involved ending Iraq's support of terrorist groups like al-Qaeda. Cheney's prognosis that an Iraq invasion would mean 'extremists in the region would have to rethink their strategy of *jihad*'[262] was disputed before the invasion (e.g. Chirac: 'a war of this kind cannot help giving a lift to terrorism. It would create a large number of little bin Ladens'[263]) and challenged by events after it. The intensity of the insurgency in post-Saddam Iraq, especially in Sunni hotspots such as Ramadi and Fallujah, and the alarming number of Islamic resistance movements posting websites and broadcasting beheadings pointed to a proliferation of al-Qaeda-style ideologies and tactics in Iraq. One US government official anonymously conjectured that 'the way the administration has carried out its war—especially its attack on Iraq—may have sown dragon's teeth'.[264] This sentiment was echoed by Hans Blix, who told an Italian newspaper that the war 'had not put an end to terrorism in the world . . . on the contrary, the result of this iron-fisted approach has been to give it a boost'.[265] Spain's new Prime Minister, having won a surprising victory after the 2004 Madrid bombings, also declared that 'wars such as those which have occurred in Iraq only allow hatred, violence and terror to proliferate'.[266]

It is a contentious proposition that the Iraq war actively increased terrorist networks and their membership numbers, and it is difficult to verify. However, there are positive indicators that the al-Qaeda network remained alive and healthy in the period following the invasion—for example, the failure to capture Osama bin Laden; the al-Qaeda-connected bombings in Saudi Arabia, Morocco, Turkey, Spain, Jordan, London, Pakistan, Afghanistan, and Algeria; and, as early as one year after the war, the CIA director warned that 'the steady growth of Osama bin Laden's anti-American sentiment through the wider Sunni extremist movement, and the broad dissemination of al-Qaeda's destructive expertise ensure that a serious threat will remain for the foreseeable future, with or without al-Qaeda in the picture'.[267] Indeed, that threat did remain, with a series of loosely affiliated extremists massacring vast swathes of (largely Muslim) civilians, and the sectarian conflict which took hold in Iraq is said to have claimed tens of thousands of lives. As I have argued elsewhere, bin Laden himself appeared unable to halt the spiral of violence instigated in al-Qaeda's name.[268]

Of course, it remains a possibility that without the Iraq war the international terror situation would have become drastically worse. But such a claim can be challenged given that, in the first place, the Iraq war created a political power vacuum that would be used as a stomping ground for established and would-be Islamic extremists, and, secondly, the US-led pre-emptive strike added a new dimension of ill will towards America in the region. As Lakhdar Benchiba argues, if September 11 was recognized as an opportunity for the Algerian government to repair its international image, Bush's adventure in Iraq played the same role for militant Islamists in Algeria.[269] Osama bin Laden himself viewed the war in Iraq as 'a golden and unique opportunity',[270] and one al-Qaeda pamphlet relished the prospect that 'if the US is defeated this time—and this is what we pray will happen—the doors will be wide open to the Islamic tide. For the first time in modern history, we will have an advanced foundation for Islamic awakening and *jihad* close to the land of the two mosques and al-Aqsa mosque'.[271] Moreover, as Vali Nasr has pointed out, Sunni extremism was further fuelled by the fact that Washington 'snatched Iraq from the hands of "true" Islam and delivered it to the "heretical" Shias', in the form of a Shia-led government.[272]

This chapter has already noted that the case for the connection between Saddam Hussein and the perpetrators of 9/11 or al-Qaeda was wanting. The Bush administration was also urged to consider more fully the contingency that an Iraq invasion would either exacerbate such ties, if they believed them to exist, or outright create them. This concern was expressed by a range of actors prior to the war, including heads of state,[273] Church groups,[274] the intelligence community,[275] and regional experts,[276] and worked to cast doubt on the reasonable hope of successfully ending a link between Iraq and al-Qaeda.

The third element of the just cause, the 'liberation' of Iraqis from domestic tyranny, also appears problematic when considered in the light of reasonable hope of success. Cheney notoriously quoted the (neoconservative) academic Fouad Ajami that 'after liberation, the streets in Basra and Baghdad are sure to erupt in joy in the same way throngs in Kabul greeted the Americans'.[277] Instead, Basra city centre fell to al-Sadr's Mahdi Army, one fighter justifying his participation with the following: 'A year ago, the British came to Iraq to get rid of Saddam Hussein and we gave them the opportunity to develop Iraq. But in fact nothing has changed. Now there is no electricity, no water and even fewer jobs than before'.[278] Baghdad, too, became the most violent city in Iraq with devastating guerrilla attacks on Christian churches, market places, foreign embassies, and the UN headquarters, and on a single day in November 2004 'US forces were assaulted 66 times by gunfire, mortars, rocket-propelled grenades, roadside bombs or car bombs'.[279] Indeed, the so-called insurgency intensely took hold in Najaf, Mosul, Baiji, Baquba, Ramadi, Fallujah, and Sammarra, and in the period between May 2003, when Bush declared 'mission accomplished', and the time of writing, 97% of US fatalities were sustained.[280] Again, the Americans were forewarned that they would not be greeted as liberators by a significant percentage of the Iraqi populace, with Immanuel Wallerstein cautioning that 'the action could well become another Vietnam'.[281]

Of course, the Bush administration took great pains to indicate that the resistance in Iraq was not representative of the feelings of the average Iraqi, and that US forces were actually countering a 'collection of killers' comprised of 'Saddam loyalists and foreign terrorists'.[282] Nevertheless, it was evident that, owing to invasion, Iraqis were subjected to a very real and unprecedented security crisis. Rice talked of the war on terror being 'greatly served by the end of this source of instability in the world's most volatile region',[283] but Saddam Hussein's police state was anything but domestically unstable. In the years following the war, Iraqis were certainly rid of the Baath regime's violent political oppression, but to define them as 'liberated' might have obscured a significant humanitarian emergency on the ground. Thousands of civilians were deprived of electricity, education, and clean water while thousands of others met violent deaths,[284] and, upon the release of the Iraq Living Conditions Survey[285] in May 2005, the Iraqi Minister of Planning labelled the quality of life in Iraq as 'tragic'.[286] This bleak projection was made by the United Nations prior to the war, as a leaked draft document revealed.[287] Also prior to the war, the Care International aid worker Margaret Hassan, who was later executed by unidentified kidnappers in Iraq, warned the House of Commons that Iraqis were living through 'a terrible emergency' and could face a humanitarian catastrophe in the event of conflict.[288] Moreover, despite a series of elections, Iraq's political future remains uncertain.

These thousands of casualties and personal tragedies could be depicted as small fry in years to come if democratic institutions come to flourish in Iraq and its people readily describe themselves as liberated recipients of justice. However, there was, and continues to be, a vibrant debate over whether political 'freedom' can be successfully exported. The agenda of Bush's 'Greater Middle East Initiative' (the 'forward strategy of freedom in the Middle East'[289]) was offset by the scepticism of such diverse figures as Professor Eric Hobsbawm[290] and the Iranian Nobel laureate Shirin Ebadi.[291] United Nations Assistant Secretary-General and the supervisor of the Third Arab Human Development Report, Rima Khalaf Huneidi, took care to underline that 'it is most appropriate that [the renaissance that we seek] takes place by our own hands and in accordance with our own best interests, not at the mercy of the swords of others'.[292] Just as bin Laden noted that 'it is strange that they want to dictate democracy and Americanize our culture through their jet bombers',[293] Bush himself acknowledged that 'freedom, by definition, must be chosen, and defended by those who choose it'.[294] Incidentally, President Barak Obama left little ambiguity when he stated, in an address to Muslims in Cairo, that 'no system of government can or should be imposed upon one nation by another'.[295]

While it was reasonable for the Bush administration to presume it could decisively defeat the Iraqi defences and hunt down and destroy the alleged WMD stockpile, it seemed less reasonable to imagine that an invasion of Iraq would diminish the threat from terrorism born of Islamic extremism and it seemed less reasonable to maintain that a liberal democracy in Iraq could be ensured by invasion. Although reasonable hope of success is designed as a prudential test, Lackey argues that 'if the cause is just but cannot be achieved by war, then war for that cause is not a just war'.[296] Surely, the just war endeavours to extirpate counterproductive wars and the futile loss of life. It was, and remains, unclear whether advances against al-Qaeda-type terrorism and the political 'transformation of the Middle East' could be achieved by war in Iraq. It was always apparent that the US Armed Forces would triumph in the immediate military battle, but, in a dramatic turn around, Francis Fukuyama argued that certain neoconservative premises were 'utterly unrealistic in [their] overestimation of US power and our ability to control events around the world'.[297] Given that Iraq was targeted in the first place as part of the US's war on terror, the greatest worry was perhaps that, in the 2004 presidential election, bin Laden did indeed 'vote Bush'.[298]

1.3. CONCLUSION

This chapter sought to discuss the Bush administration's case for war in the light of the accepted just war criteria for *jus ad bellum*. In the seven preceding sections, each criterion was considered on its own terms, but there is an implication from the foregoing that applies generally. On the whole, the principal sources of controversy arose from the Bush administration's shift away from the modern, legalistic understanding of a just war based on reciprocal sovereignty and international institutions by making arguments based on the broader moral tradition of the just war. In contesting, for example, the ultimate war-making authority of the United Nations, the requirement of an act of aggression for a truly 'defensive' war and the need to exhaust utterly all non-violent alternatives, the Bush administration's arguments challenged robust norms about the justified resort to armed hostilities. Fundamental to this was an interjection of values such as 'liberty' and 'freedom' into the debate. This served to widen the moral and temporal scope of just war criteria and, in so doing, augmented the room for altercation. After all, underlying the evolution towards a more limited, legalistic conception of a just war was the attempt, spearheaded by Grotius, to make the just side objectively discernible.

John C. Ford wrote in 1945 that 'the practically unanimous view of American Catholicism, including that of the hierarchy, is that we are fighting a just war at present'.[299] By contrast, in 2003 the *National Catholic Weekly* surmised that 'with the exception of some Southern Baptist leaders and mega-church pastors, nearly all US churches are opposing war with Iraq'.[300] The Pope suggested the war would be 'a defeat for humanity',[301] while in the political arena traditional American allies joined the United Nations in standing steadfastly against invasion. In registering his opposition to the war, Jacques Chirac noted that 'a majority of world leaders' shared his view and underlined that France was 'not a pacifist country'.[302] The Canadian Prime Minister was greeted with a standing ovation in parliament when he pronounced that the war was 'not justified'.[303] Former President Jimmy Carter, emphasizing that he was no stranger to international crises, concluded that the Bush administration's actions were 'almost unprecedented in the history of civilised nations'.[304]

At the root of much of this clamour was the shared perception that the United States was not acting in self-defence. It is to this issue that we next turn.

2

Pre-emptive War on Iraq

While the Grand Mufti of Jerusalem wondered what Jesus would say to the concept of a pre-emptive strike, the New Zealand Council of Churches released a statement making plain their view on an impending invasion of Iraq: 'we state unequivocally: pre-emptive war is not a just war'.[1] Indeed, there was a notable difference between the US' case for war against Iraq and that of coalition members such as Britain and Australia. Whereas America's allies preferred to rely exclusively on Iraq's non-compliance with UN resolutions, the Bush administration presented a double-sided case that involved the detailing of Saddam Hussein's material breach of Security Council resolutions as well as the invocation of the doctrine of pre-emptive self-defence. Not only did this provide a qualitatively different grounding for the invasion of Iraq, it spurred a massive international discussion on legitimate conceptions of the right to self-defence.

The arguments put forward for pre-emptive war and responses to those arguments will be the focus of this chapter. This is a continuation of the discussion about the Bush administration's just cause in Iraq, started in Chapter 1.

The unanimous condemnation meted out by the international community to those responsible for the September 11 attacks was manifested in two Security Council resolutions which made a (rare) invocation of the 'inherent right of individual or collective self-defence'. Those references to 'self-defence' in resolutions 1368 and 1373 also served as the legal basis for the US-led intervention in Afghanistan, and both the United States and the United Kingdom wrote to the Security Council under Article 51 of the United Nations Charter.[2] However, when the United States sought to extend both the moral case and the legal mandate for 'self-defence' with reference to Iraq, the attempt prompted worldwide uproar. The war in Afghanistan was not without its critics, but America's claims to self-defence were given credence by the Taliban's deliberate harbouring of al-Qaeda[3] and concrete evidence that al-Qaeda was planning more attacks against the United States and its allies.[4] These conditions did not hold in Iraq, putting the Bush administration's claims to be acting in self-defence on far shakier ground.

Dick Cheney was certainly correct when he suggested that critics who claim the United States should not have acted because the threat from Saddam Hussein was not imminent 'are helping to frame the most important debate of the post-9/11 era'.[5] The pre-emption question was integral to the diverging perspectives on the legitimacy of the US-led war on Iraq, but it also revived a more philosophical discussion about the proper purposes and limits of the just war.

The issue provoked splits among nations, governments, international lawyers, just war theorists, and the Catholic Church:

> One eloquent, perceptive commentator recently described the neocons' new theory as corruption, rather than development, of dogma: 'there is some considerable irony in the Pope's biographer and trusted confidant, George Weigel, arguing against the Pope that a war on Iraq would be just according to new "developed and extended" just war principles, while the rebellious ultraconservative Society of St. Pius X, using old, undeveloped and unextended just war principles, argues that a war against Iraq would not be just'.[6]

The pre-emption debate was highly charged and greatly significant, with implications for morality and conceptions of right conduct as well as world order and international society. Pre-emption itself is a controversial doctrine, but even for those who accept its legitimacy under certain circumstances, its application to the case of Iraq specifically was cause for deep concern.

Condoleezza Rice observed that 'pre-emption is not a new concept'.[7] However, the same tradition which suggests that states do not have to accept passively the impact of an evident imminent attack also restricts states from doing whatever they please in order to prevent future threats from emerging. For as long as the concept of pre-emption has been in play, distinctions have been made between justified and unjustified instantiations of it.[8] To one theorist, the Bush administration's understanding of legitimate pre-emption 'represents an important *revision* in just war theory and the law of armed conflict'.[9]

Lawrence Eagleburger, who served as Secretary of State in 1992 when Dick Cheney was Secretary of Defense, believed his former colleague to be 'chest-thumping'. He argued that war with Iraq was only justified if there was evidence Saddam was about to launch an attack on the United States.[10] Here, Eagleburger singles out the concept of imminence, which is the cornerstone of the pre-emption controversy. This chapter aims to distinguish between different sorts of pre-emptive war, before going on to examine the crucial criterion of 'imminence' with regard to the Bush administration's arguments. It argues that the Bush administration's deliberate efforts to recast the concept of imminence aimed to deny the distinction between pre-emptive and preventive war. This was achieved with an appeal to the just war notion of 'necessity' at the *jus ad bellum* level (in summary form, necessity[AB]) which was, in turn, rooted in the 9/11 terrorist attacks.

2.1. NEW THREAT, NEW WAR, NEW WORLD

'September 11 had changed the strategic thinking, at least as far as I was concerned, for how to protect our country' (Bush, 26 March 2003).

In reflecting America's vulnerability to massive attack by an unconventional enemy in pursuit of nuclear technology, September 11 ushered in a 'new world' for the Bush administration. Cheney's observation that 'September 11, 2001 changed everything for this country'[11] was supported by the President's repeated reflection that 'none of us will ever forget that week when one era ended and another began'.[12] Wolfowitz, referring to an astronaut aboard the International Space Station on the day, recounted that 'even from space he could clearly observe a dramatically changed world beneath him'.[13]

The upshot of the dawn of this 'new era', 'new world' was that 'America is embracing a new ethic and a new creed: Let's roll'.[14] In other words, the United States was going to confront threats to its national security actively. Underpinning this approach was the belief that 'weakness and drift and vacillation in the face of danger invite attacks'[15]—indeed, 'if America shows weakness or uncertainty in this decade, the world will drift towards tragedy'.[16] For on that day 'we learned a lesson: the dangers of our time must be confronted actively and forcefully before we see them again in our skies and in our cities'.[17] This lesson brought with it a notable strategic implication: 'a good defense is not enough' (Cheney). In fact, 'the best defense is a good offense' (National Security Strategy) as 'the only path to safety is the path of action' (Bush).

As the war on terror unfolded, this morale-boosting language of 'action', which was translated into a forceful global strategy against the perpetrators of the September 11 attacks and their supporters, evolved into a specific and highly controversial interstate policy option. That is, when the doctrine of 'actively and forcefully confronting the dangers of our time' is applied to relations with a long-time conventional foe such as Iraq, it looks a lot like pre-emption.

2.2. PRE-EMPTION[1] AND PRE-EMPTION[2]

Theoretical discussions of the pre-emption issue suffer from a lack of definitional continuity. One writer's 'pre-emptive' war is another's 'preventive' one, and the notion of 'anticipation' further muddies the field. For example, Mary Ellen O'Connell's pre-emptive war concerns 'cases where a party uses force to quell any possibility of future attack by another state, even when there is no reason to believe that an attack is planned and where no prior attack has occurred'.[18] However, this definition of pre-emptive war is in fact taken to be preventive war by other commentators, such as David Luban and Neta Crawford. They treat pre-emptive war as forestalling imminent rather than distant threats. The term 'anticipation' is sometimes equated with preventive war,[19] at other times employed as an umbrella concept under which acceptable conditions for legitimate pre-emptive war are set out,[20] but in the nuclear case it can also hold the added connotation of surprising the enemy.

For Crawford, 'the distinction between immediate threats and long-term potential threats underpins the classical distinction between pre-emption and preventive war'.[21] Certainly, the crucial difference between the two is temporal: the imminence of the threat. And regarding imminence, the difference is also about certainty, as a state cannot be as certain of a future threat as it can be of an immediate one. The distinction is ultimately underwritten by different conceptions of necessity. This book will refer to military action against certain imminent threats as pre-emption[1] (P^1) and military action against potential long-term threats as pre-emption[2] (P^2). Luban notes that in international law the permissibility of our P^1 has not been controversial, and his article assumes that it can be assimilated into self-defence.[22] Indeed, P^1 is generally considered to bear a legitimacy that is denied to P^2.

The proposition that, in order to avoid committing the 'supreme crime' of aggression, a state must suffer an attack of which it has advanced knowledge is neither reasonable nor in tune with a meaningful understanding of the term 'self-defence'. Drawing upon the Wild West, Shue suggests that if the Good Guy sees the Bad Guy reaching for his six-shooter but is faster on the draw, it is legitimate for the Good Guy to employ pre-emptive counterforce by shooting the pistol from the hand of the Bad Guy; to require that the Good Guy only fire after the Bad Guy's bullet has left the barrel would entail 'a morality for suckers'.[23] As the United Kingdom maintained during the Security Council debate over the US bombing of Libya in 1986, 'the right of self-defence is not an entirely passive right'.[24] Indeed, referring to the UN Charter's clause that states have a right to self-defence 'if an armed attack occurs' (Article 51), the president of the International Court of Justice has argued that 'common sense cannot require one to interpret an ambiguous provision in a text in a way that requires a state passively to accept its fate before it can defend itself'.[25] More than being a matter of common sense, Shue argues that pre-emption may be militarily aggressive, but 'genuine pre-emption is not at all aggressive in the morally relevant sense'.[26] Hew Strachan describes how, for nuclear deterrence theorists, 'pre-emption was an attack in a war *initiated by the enemy.... It* was improvised and desperate. The key presumption was that, in political terms, the enemy had begun the process...'[27]

The very criteria that bestow P^1 with its status as 'genuine pre-emption' deny that status to P^2. A very narrow construction of the just war notion of 'necessity' underpins P^1, the intuition behind it famously expressed by US Secretary of State Daniel Webster in 1841: 'it will be for [the British Government] to show a necessity of self-defence, instant, overwhelming, leaving no choice of means, and no moment for deliberation'.

Writing in reply to the British ambassador's defence of its destruction of the *Caroline*, a private American steamer that was being used to ship recruits and arms to a group of anti-British rebels in Canadian territory, Webster articulated the conditions of a justified pre-emptive attack in order to demonstrate that none held in regard to the British action against the *Caroline*. He argued that the onus was on the British to prove the existence of a 'necessity, present and overwhelming' by showing that 'admonition or remonstrance... was impracticable or would have been unavailing' (principle of last resort); that there could be 'no attempt at discrimination between the innocent and the guilty' (principle of non-combatant immunity); that it would 'not have been enough to seize and detain the vessel' (principle of proportionality); that 'daylight could not be waited for' (imminence of threat/cost of delay). Although Webster recognized that a 'just right of self-defence always attaches to nations as well as individuals', he did 'not think that the transaction [could] be justified by any reasonable application or construction of the right to self-defence under the laws of nations'.[28]

Thus, Condoleezza Rice's invocation of Webster—'you know, Daniel Webster actually wrote a very famous defence of anticipatory self-defence'[29]—in order to support pre-emptive action against Iraq errs considerably from both the letter and the spirit of his remarks. Imminence understood as a necessity that is 'instant, overwhelming, leaving no choice of means and no moment for deliberation' defines the legitimacy of P^1 and its absence distinguishes cases of P^1 from cases of P^2. Moreover, this differentiation is consonant with the position of many international lawyers who interpret Article 51 of the UN Charter (which preserves the inherent right to self-defence if an armed attack occurs) as allowing self-defence against a certain attack before the blow is received. It is also well supported by modern state practice where, generally, a state need not wait to suffer an attack if it is certain an attack is coming. Legal expert Christopher Greenwood is quick to point out that

... practice also shows that the right of anticipatory self-defence is confined to instances where the armed attack is imminent. Not only was this limitation a central feature of the *Caroline* correspondence, it was the basis on which the Nuremburg Tribunal, while affirming the *Caroline* test, rejected the defence plea that the German invasion of Norway had been an act of anticipatory self-defence. It was also the basis for rejection of the Israeli claim in the reactor case.[30]

In his 1953 treatise on aggressive war, Cornelis Pompe included imminent threats in his definition of aggression, stressing that 'such an imminent threat can fulfil the requirement of aggression . . . to the effect that aggression leaves the State no other than military means to preserve its territory and independence'.[31] In this way, the imminence of the threat in P^1 allows the state which strikes the first blow to retain its moral status as the victim, coerced as it was by its counterpart's actions into waging a defensive war.

Nevertheless, the historical record reflects the general reluctance of states to depend publicly upon the doctrine of pre-emption for the recourse to force: 'arguments presented to the international community rarely rely on this logic'.[32] Christine Gray illustrates this point: during the 1962 Cuban Missile Crisis, the United States used regional peacekeeping under Chapter VII of the UN Charter to intercept Russia's missiles at sea forcibly; Israel chose to invoke Article 51 of the Charter in its case at the Security Council after launching strikes against Egypt, Syria, and Jordan in 1967, arguing that Nasser's blocking of the Straits of Tiran amounted to an act of war; Iraq first justified its invasion of Iran in 1980 with the language of pre-emption but quickly shifted its position in the United Nations by claiming to be reacting to a prior armed attack by Iran.[33] No doubt, states prefer to argue for an extended interpretation of armed attack in order to bring the use of force under Article 51 of the Charter (self-defence against an armed attack which has already occurred). Even for the international lawyers and theoretical commentators who acknowledge the legitimacy of P^1, the right conferred by 'the necessity of self-defence, instant, overwhelming, leaving no choice of means, and no moment for deliberation' is treated as exceptional.

Certainly, despite the general legitimacy of P^1, until very recently the international community has avoided dealing head-on with the pre-emption issue. The Security Council and General Assembly slammed specific attempts to plead pre-emptive self-defence,[34] but they hesitated in defining legal boundaries for terms such as 'imminence' and expressly acknowledging any right, however restrictive, for states to take pre-emptive action at all. In 2004, however, a UN high-level panel noted that 'a threatened State, according to long established international law, can take military action as long as the threatened attack is *imminent*, no other means would deflect it and the action is proportionate'.[35] In addition, the panel's report allowed for 'the *preventive* use of military force in the case of self-defence under Article 51'[36] if authorized by the Security Council under Chapter VII of the UN Charter. Arguing that the international community must concern itself with 'nightmare scenarios combining terrorists, weapons of mass destruction [WMD] and irresponsible states'—the very scenarios envisaged by the Bush administration—the panel insisted that the Security Council (alone) was authorized to take any necessary preventive action 'as the international community's collective security voice'.[37] Unilateral preventive action, as distinct from collectively endorsed action, is not legal.[38] While some commentators argue that Security Council authorization does not solve any of the important problems about the preventive use of force,[39] the point here is that where P^2 has been imagined as potentially legitimate in dealing with terrorists and/ or WMD, it is not considered to be the right of individual states.

It is true that the Bush administration's legal case for the invasion of Iraq centred on Iraq's failure to comply with its ceasefire obligations and its material breach of UN resolutions. Bush administration lawyers such as William Taft and Todd Buchwald vigorously argued that Security Council resolution 1441 did not require the Council to adopt any further resolution 'to establish the occurrence of the material breach that was the predicate for coalition forces to resort to force'.[40] However, even amid the legal reasonings of Taft and Buchwald and their interpretations of the text of resolutions appear striking references to pre-emption. In a rather circular manner, they cite President Bush's 'National Security Strategy' as 'the legal basis for the doctrine of pre-emption'.[41] For, as part of the broader moral argument for the Iraq war, members of the Bush administration deliberately referred to the doctrine and attempted to show that it was a perfectly legitimate policy option: 'Iraq has given the United States every reason to attack under the UN Charter, which allows pre-emptive action by nations facing an imminent threat'.[42] However, in directly referring to P^1, this official gets to the very core of the controversy of the decision to invade Iraq in March, 2003— namely, the question of whether an Iraqi attack on the United States was in fact imminent.

2.3. ADAPTING IMMINENCE

To the mind of one commentator, 'in its rush to convince Congress and the United Nations of the need to act quickly, the Bush administration has bandied about some very different concepts—pre-emption, preventive war, and Ms. Rice's "anticipatory self-defence" (a phrase Webster never used)—as if they were the same thing. Experts say they are not'.[43] Certainly, Bush failed to make a conceptual distinction between the sort of pre-emptive action taken in Afghanistan and that taken in Iraq,[44] the crucial contrast being that there was an imminent threat from al-Qaeda, which was openly afforded a sanctuary in Afghanistan. Moreover, in discussing potential pre-emptive action against Iraq, a friend apparently reminded Rumsfeld that 'in the sixteenth century, Sir Thomas More discussed pre-emption in his *Utopia*, that idea when you know there is going to be an attack that will come from a neighbour, you shouldn't just wait for it, you should go and do something'.[45] However, that part of the text to which Rumsfeld's friend presumably refers describes a situation of a certain imminent threat, where 'if a foreign prince takes up arms and prepares to invade their land, [the Utopians] immediately attack him full force outside their own borders'.[46] This situation is qualitatively different from the administration's resolve to '[take] anticipatory action to defend ourselves, even if uncertainty remains as to the time and place of the enemy's attack'.[47]

But far from failing to grasp the conceptual distinction between P^1 and P^2, the Bush administration's arguments for the Iraq war sought to deny the existence of such a distinction in the 'new world'. This was achieved by undermining the imminence criterion of P^1. Indeed, the 'National Security Strategy' plainly stated that 'we must adapt the concept of imminent threat to the capabilities and objectives of today's adversaries'.[48] In order to do so, two broad arguments were put forward.

Firstly, the disproportionately destructive nature of WMD was accentuated. The President urged that 'we face a threat with no precedent. Enemies in the past needed great armies and great industrial capabilities to endanger the American people'. This was no longer the case where 'weak states and small groups could attain a catastrophic power to strike great nations'.[49] And because such weapons are aimed at massacring innocents, the danger was depicted as 'the terrorist threat to civilisation'.[50] Given the gravity of the wanton destruction that WMD could inflict, the stakes in the war on terror were depicted as civilizational: 'this is civilisation's fight'.[51]

Secondly, the sudden carnage of 9/11 was invoked. Terrorism was presented as the new intervening variable, for the existence of WMD alone was not sufficient to 'adapt' imminence in the 'new world' since the nuclear stand-off was the mainstay of the past century's Cold War. Terrorism changed things because 'the whole thing that terrorists introduce is that you not only do not see the threat coming, but you do not know where it came from'.[52] Thus, the dreadful knowledge that for some, 'these are not weapons of last resort, but militarily useful weapons of choice', coupled with the surprise of the 9/11 attacks—'stop and think for a moment. Just when were the attacks of September 11th imminent?'[53]—required the administration to reconceptualize imminence. The attacks on New York and Washington were evidence that 'terrorists and terror states do not reveal threats with fair notice, in formal declarations',[54] and 'they showed what enemies of America did with four airplanes. We cannot wait to see what terrorists or terror states could do with weapons of mass destruction'.[55]

In this way, it was the overlap of technology and radicalism that required a shift in thinking about the concept of imminence, for it created a threat 'so potentially catastrophic—which can arrive with so little warning by means that are untraceable—that it cannot be contained'.[56] As a result of this grave and unconventional threat, 'it is too late if [threats] become imminent. It is too late in this new kind of war'.[57] According to Wolfowitz, 'anyone who believes that we can wait until we have certain knowledge that attacks are imminent has failed to connect the dots that led to September 11'.[58] Indeed, the 'lesson of 9/11' was whittled down by the President into a specific proposition: 'America must confront threats before they fully materialise'.[59]

By denying a meaningful distinction between P^1 and P^2 in the new era, the Bush administration attempted to use the relatively uncontested legitimacy of cases of P^1, while trying for a case that was prima facie P^2. In order to do so, the imminence criterion of P^1 was deliberately undermined. This was achieved with an argument about a broader, post-9/11 understanding of 'necessity', which emphasized the destructive nature of nuclear weaponry and the surprise of the September 11 attacks. In this way, the administration could publicly assert a unilateral right to pre-emptive self-defence with reference to Iraq in the absence of an ostensible 'imminent' threat.

2.4. RESISTANCE TO RECONCEPTUALIZATION

Generally, the Bush administration's worries about the nature of nuclear weaponry and the surprise manner of the September 11 attacks roughly reflect the two factors Greenwood puts forward as important in determining the imminence of an armed attack (which, he notes, did not exist at the time of the *Caroline* incident). The first is the gravity of the threat of an attack with WMD.[60] The second is the clandestine method of delivery of the threat.[61] These two material considerations could mean that an attack is reasonably treated as imminent in circumstances not applicable to attacks by conventional means, but Greenwood underscores that 'the requirement that the attack be imminent cannot be ignored or rendered meaningless'.[62]

Even given these features of the modern world, significant segments of the international community still did not accept that any threat from Iraq in 2003 was imminent and grave enough to permit the adaptation of the pivotal imminence criterion of P[1]. Security Council members Germany, France, Russia, and China did not think Iraq posed a clear and present danger and pushed for weapons inspections to continue, the German Foreign Minister famously following a speech by Donald Rumsfeld with the words: 'Excuse me, I'm not convinced'.[63] At home, Al Gore rejected the notion that an attack by Iraq was imminent and underlined that 'if [Saddam] presents an imminent threat we would be free to act under generally accepted understandings of Article 51 of the UN Charter which reserves for member states the right to act in self-defence'.[64] Resigning from his cabinet post Robin Cook told the House of Commons that '[the British People] do not doubt that Saddam Hussein is a brutal dictator but they are not persuaded he is a clear and present danger',[65] and the next day President Chirac insisted that 'Iraq does not represent today an immediate threat that would justify an immediate war'.[66] Professor Richard Dawkins, a signatory of the anti-war petition from Oxford's top academics, explained his own reasoning:

The first Gulf war was provoked by a specific aggressive act by Iraq. Not to have retaliated in Kuwait could legitimately have been compared to Chamberlain's appeasement of Hitler at Munich. Nothing of the kind applies to the present proposal for war. The timing gives the game away. It comes from America, not Iraq. . . . Bush is the aggressor.[67]

Greenwood himself noted that 'in so far as talk of a doctrine of "pre-emption" is intended to refer to a broader right of self-defence to respond to threats that might materialise at some time in the future, such a doctrine has no basis in law'.[68]

The religious establishment was similarly preoccupied with the issue of imminence. The US Conference of Catholic Bishops concluded that 'based on the facts that are known to us, we continue to find it difficult to justify the resort to war against Iraq, lacking clear and adequate evidence of an imminent attack of a grave nature'.[69] Swedish Church leaders wrote to their government urging that 'more time is needed',[70] and the Federation of Swiss Protestant Churches made clear that it did 'not consider the imminent threat to be of the required precondition to start a preventive war. When there is no imminent threat of attack but a probable yet vague insecurity, the universal standard of banning violence must be kept if international law is not to be undermined'.[71] Correspondingly, a Princeton professor of Systematic Theology argued in the *Christian Century* that 'the right to pre-empt an anticipated attack can be extrapolated from the self-defence principle if pre-emptive strikes meet a high standard of justification: the attack prevented must be imminent, not merely conjectured or vaguely feared in the long run'. He concluded that 'by just war standards . . . a pre-emptive attack against Iraq must be condemned'.[72] For the most part, therefore, the Bush administration's push to adapt imminence with regard to the threat from Iraq was unsuccessful, and the proposed invasion was widely viewed as a case of P^2.

Of course, attacking first in any conflict can be deemed intrinsically immoral. This deontological grounding was reflected in John F. Kennedy's pride that 'our arms will never be used to strike the first blow in any attack. This is not a confession of weakness but a statement of strength. It is our national tradition'.[73] International lawyers such as Gray and Brownlie provide a legal corollary for this, as there is also a school of thought in international law which holds that there is no right of self-defence until an armed attack has actually commenced. However, it has been considered in this chapter that, by and large, attacking first in the face of certain imminent attack by the adversary can be considered morally and legally legitimate: 'based on the practice of states and perhaps on general principles of law, as well as simple logic, international lawyers agree that a state need not suffer the actual blow before defending itself, so long as it is certain the blow is coming'.[74] This is distinguished from cases of P^2 involving a putative long-term threat. While there is a sound deontological impulse behind this distinction (e.g. the ostensible 'aggressor' state in P^1 may actually hold the moral status of the 'victim'), there are strong consequentialist reasons for rejecting P^2.

In the first place, there is the 'innumerable and fruitless wars' argument. Adopting P^2 would lead to a great many pointless wars fed by anxiety and fought on account of shifts in the balance of power. David Luban points out that this is rule consequentialist—that is, although performance of Action X could in some individual cases have the best consequences, adopting a rule allowing for the performance of Action X in all such cases would, on the whole, have bad consequences. At bottom, a moral or legal rule permitting P^2 legitimizes wars under conditions too close to the routinization of aggression. He suggests that allowing P^2 would 'reincorporate war launching into the repertoire of ordinary politics'.[75] The Conference of Catholic Bishops worried that 'to accept the notion that the pre-emptive use of force is justified in this case even absent an imminent threat of attack would create a dangerous moral precedent'.[76] Further, as part of the discourse surrounding the Iraq war, notable statesmen such as Henry Kissinger feared for the legal precedent the United States might set.[77]

Secondly, such a precedent bears down hard upon the 'security dilemma'.[78] A perceived potential threat from State X cannot be gauged with the accuracy of a certain imminent threat and, in preparing to meet the former, State Y might thereby create the very threat it so fears. Schelling and Halperin remarked about MAD (Mutually Assured Destruction) that 'hardly anything would be as tragically ironic as a war that both sides started, each in the belief that the other was about to, each compelled by its expectations to confirm the other's belief the attack was imminent'.[79] This tragic irony could be applicable to a situation where P^2 is normalized or legitimized even using conventional weaponry in the response.

Thirdly, P^2 creates unacceptable conflicts with other just war criteria. P^2 directly challenges conventional understandings of *jus ad bellum* concepts such as 'just cause', in terms of self-defence,[80] and 'last resort', in terms of pursuing every peaceful alternative to war.[81] And it is also in tension with the indispensable *jus in bello* guidelines. How can the proportionality of a pre-emptive attack be measured against a possible future attack? Fixing the boundaries of proper counterforce is highly problematic in cases without detailed proof of the nature of a specific threat. Webster's prescription that 'the act justified by the necessity of self-defense, must be limited by that necessity, and kept clearly within it' is rendered redundant by situations where the conception of necessity deals only with a future potential threat that has not materialized. In the absence of evidence of a particular threat against which the would-be victim must plan its pre-emptive response, the parameters of necessity and proportionality are inherently controversial. By contrast, the certain imminence of the concrete threat in P^1 provides the benchmark against which a proposed pre-emptive action can be assessed.

On the eve of the Suez crisis, a former lover of David Ben Gurion wrote him a letter arguing that 'there is no such thing as a preventive war. Preventive war only makes inevitable a war that might otherwise be prevented'.[82] Driving David Luban's doubts about P^2 is his belief that 'when a doctrine of just war justifies a great many wars that seem intuitively unjust ... we are entitled to scepticism about the doctrine'.[83] Surely, many world leaders and commentators expressed such scepticism about the justifiability of P^2. The Bush administration attempted to portray the war in Iraq as an instance of P^1 by recasting its pivotal imminence criterion. The international community was reluctant to allow this, maintaining for the most part that the Bush administration's action was an instance of the (illegitimate) doctrine of P^2.

2.5. CAPACITY AND INTENT

The imminence criterion of P^1 is predicated on compelling evidence for both the capacity and the intention to attack. Both are necessary for imminence; neither is by itself sufficient. We considered in Chapter 1 that the evidence about Saddam's WMD capabilities was hotly contested prior to invasion. This leaves only Saddam's intentions, but, in the words of one Democratic Congress-woman, by themselves 'intentions do not constitute a growing danger. It's hardly mushroom clouds, hardly stockpiles'.[84] However, it is worth consider-ing exactly what Saddam Hussein allegedly intended. It could have been one of three things:

2.5.1. To give WMD to al-Qaeda for use against the United States and/or its allies

There was no concrete proof prior to war that Iraq intended to arm al-Qaeda with WMD. Chapter 1 demonstrated that Cheney's assertions about 'over-whelming evidence [that] there was a connection between al-Qaeda and the Iraqi government'[85] were vigorously contested. The two premises of this proposition (that Saddam Hussein had WMD and that Saddam Hussein had ties to al-Qaeda) were consistently doubted.

2.5.2. To use WMD against the United States and/or its allies

This scenario was more likely than the previous. Undoubtedly, Saddam Hussein was exceedingly hostile and a menace to the international legal order. He displayed an alarming level of antipathy towards the United States for fifteen years prior to the 2003 invasion—in fact, he professed himself to be an enemy of America.[86] Saddam also had a history of capricious aggression, as exemplified by his invasion of Kuwait. Moreover, he had used chemical weapons in the past, against Iran as well as Iraqi Kurds, and he had publicly threatened to 'burn half of Israel',[87] a staunch ally of America.

Terence Taylor makes the point that 'given the unequivocally stated general intention and the clandestine nature of terrorist preparations, it can be argued that even a general threat could qualify as imminent in international law'.[88] That is, when dealing with al-Qaeda-type terrorism, it may be acceptable to proceed against the enemy without evidence for a specific plot at a specific time and/or place. However, this 'unequivocally stated general intention' applies to terrorists, not sovereign states.[89] The claim that a state is intending to soon launch an attack does seem to require some (relatively) specific proof. Imminence demands more than the fact that a state is an enemy. Iraq had not declared war on America,[90] but, whether deliberately or not, certain statements seemed to imply that it had: 'With those attacks, the terrorists and their supporters declared war on the United States. And war is what they got'.[91]

2.5.3. To develop WMD

This is the most strongly supported claim. Saddam Hussein certainly had hopes and plans to develop WMD. This was the conclusion of the UN Weapons Inspectors prior to the war, and the CIA's Duelfer Report[92] after the war. However, the *intention* to *develop* WMD is one logical step removed from the *intention* to *use* WMD, and two logical steps away from the *intention* and *capacity* to *use* WMD (Fig. 2.1).

Peculiarly, Bush responded to the Duelfer Report (which concluded, among other things, that there were no WMD in Iraq) by insisting that it 'raises important new information about Saddam Hussein's defiance of the world and *his intent and capability to develop* weapons'.[93] The intention and capability to develop WMD is a long way from the imminence of the threat of P^1. Administration spokesman Scott McClellan's reaction to the report represents the prevailing conflation of the use of weapons and the development of weapons:

> We all thought that we would find stockpiles, and that was not the case.... The fact that he had the intent and capability, and that he was trying to undermine the sanctions that were in place is very disturbing. And I think the report will continue to show that he was a gathering threat that needed to be taken seriously, that it was a matter of time before he was going to begin pursuing those weapons of mass destruction.[94]

Even taking into account the destructive nature of nuclear weapons and the clandestine method by which they could be employed, the intention and capability to 'pursue' WMD does not seem an adequate conceptualization of imminence.

Or does it? David Luban seeks to maintain that, in principle, a preventive war may be justified against a rogue state 'aiming to construct WMD', if that state's intentions are hostile, because if that state succeeds in constructing

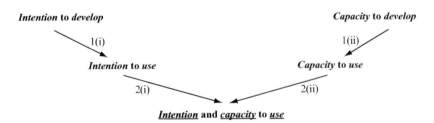

Figure 2.1 The logical difference between the intention to develop WMD and the intention and capacity to use WMD

WMD it may be too late to forestall a genocidal attack.[95] Luban invokes the notion of criminal conspiracy and emphasizes that the rogue state's plans must be backed up by at least significant and persistent overt actions to further the plan—he suggests that the alleged Iraq case would qualify (had it been true).[96] The adversary is morally liable to attack because it has created an emerging threat: 'the conspiracy to launch an eventual attack is itself a wrongful act, sufficient for a state to lose its immunity to preventive invasion'.[97] Critiquing Luban's thesis, David Rodin makes two important observations. Firstly, he points to the 'conspiracy paradox': planning a preventive war is itself a conspiracy to attack another state. Rodin notes that the US National Security Strategy explicitly affirms both the intention to attack and the active preparations for doing so, that is, a conspiracy to attack.[98] Thus, the rogue state might be entitled to a preventive war against the United States. Secondly, Rodin reminds us that preventive wars involve attacking and killing those who have not yet committed an act of wrongful aggression and have therefore not yet made themselves liable to attack. Here, Rodin reaffirms the fundamental importance of imminence: 'by requiring that self-defense cannot be undertaken until an unjust attack is imminent, the condition guarantees that those who are subject to defensive force are morally liable to it because they are currently engaged in an unjust aggressive attack'.[99]

The imminence of the threat in P^1 means that those that we kill have done something to forfeit their right to life, which is essential to the justifiability of wars of self-defence. Because the adversary in P^2 has not yet done anything to forfeit the right to life, if P^2 is ever legitimate, it cannot be on the grounds of self-defence. This does not, of course, mean that no action can be taken against the rogue state seeking WMD; that the only alternative is to wait for that state to acquire the WMD with which it plans to harm you in the future. Rather, the point is that different stages of threat require different sorts of responses. In a situation of self-defence, the state acting defensively is justified in using military force in response to the use of (or imminent use of) military force. In a situation where the aim is to prevent a rogue state from *acquiring* WMD with which it may later harm you, surely the logically (and morally) appropriate response would be to *prevent the rogue state's acquisition* of WMD. There exists a robust international weapons-control regime, which is designed to serve this purpose. Hence, in the run-up to the invasion of Iraq, the plea to 'give inspectors more time' was prevalent. In fact, given that the Iraqi regime did not possess WMD, it might be argued, if anything, that the Iraq war perversely proved the efficacy of the UN-mandated measures taken to prevent Saddam Hussein from acquiring WMD.

While the international community could be in no doubt that Saddam was hoping to develop WMD, many disputed that he was in possession of the weapons and therefore expressed deep scepticism about the appropriateness of a pre-emptive war. This was a collective nod to the just war teaching that another state's intention to augment its power or reach parity[100] is not itself a just cause for war. In setting out his argument that 'defence of life is permissible only when the danger is immediate and certain, not when it is merely assumed', Grotius quotes Cicero:

Who has ever established this principle, or to whom without the gravest danger to all men can it be granted, that he shall have the right to kill a man by whom he says he fears that he himself may later be killed?[101]

Warring in order to stop a state from attaining the capability to attack you in the future is P^2, and the justness of it is questioned. This is because ultimately, in Walzer's words, the hostility involved is 'prospective and imaginary'.[102]

2.6. CONCLUSION

The concern over which side 'fires the first shot' in war is a feature of modern international law, initiated by the Kellogg–Briand Pact and carried over into the UN Charter. In this sense, the aggressor–defender distinction is a relatively recent and, for that matter, very restrictive take on the just case. However, there is a broadly recognized idea that the 'defender' state may still retain its status as the victim of aggression even if it fires the first shot—an argument made by international lawyers as well as political theorists. Moral logic, just war thought, and state practice generally support the notion that leaving a victim no alternative but to suffer the first blow would make the right to self-defence diaphanous.

This chapter has sought to emphasize that the acceptability of this sort of reasoning turns entirely upon the imminence of a threat. Even those modern authors who are dubious about the applicability of Webster's dictum—O'Brien scorning the 'comic opera character of the affair', Walzer suggesting that it does not 'address itself usefully to the experience of imminent war'—provide developed understandings of imminence that are not satisfied by the situation between the United States and Iraq in 2003.[103]

The Bush administration's attempt to 'adapt the concept of imminence' was ill-received in a variety of quarters. Speaking with reference to Iraq, Cheney underlined that 'if the United States could have pre-empted 9/11, we would have, no question. Should we be able to prevent another, much more devastating attack, we will, no question'.[104] However, the horror of the surprise attacks on 9/11 notwithstanding, multifarious voices registered their opposition to pre-emptive war on Iraq. Howard Zinn contended that the administration's plans flagrantly violated both international law and common morality,[105] Filipino Bishops cautioned that 'employing pre-emptive military force against Iraq [was] bereft of any justifiable basis',[106] and the signatories of the Oxford University petition found 'the case for launching a pre-emptive war against Iraq unconvincing and morally questionable'.[107] After considering at length whether Iraq posed a clear and present danger which warranted pre-emptive military action, the General Synod of the Church of England advised the British government that 'to undertake a *preventive* war against Iraq at this juncture would be to lower the threshold for war unacceptably'.[108] In this way, the necessity[AB] argument, which posited the need for more expansive standards for understanding threat in the post-9/11 era, did not stave off the Iraq war's critics.

In terms of the just war tradition, the upshot of the foregoing is that the circumstances of P^1 were widely viewed as furnishing legitimate grounds for the pre-emptive use of force, whilst the moral and legal status of P^2 was confirmed as suspect, even in the post-9/11 era. This reinforces the lasting significance of 'self-defence' as the prevailing idea of a just cause because P^1 allows a state to maintain it is defending itself while P^2 does not. In addition, the accompanying debate reflected the salience of just war concepts ('necessity', 'proportionality', 'imminence', 'just cause', 'last resort'), however contested, in arguing about war.

Bush cast the war on terror generally[109] and the war in Iraq specifically[110] in terms of moral conflict. Although the American government was keen to be seen as 'fighting for the right', it has been shown that pre-emptive war based on an expansive conceptualization of imminent threat was inconsistent in key areas with popular conceptions of the right in the period surrounding the Iraq war. In his vehement defence of a possible invasion of Iraq, Thomas Nichols asserted that 'defiance of UN resolutions and recent Iraqi aggression illustrate the importance of the matter of justice and the relative unimportance of pre-emption and prevention'.[111] The foregoing has sought to challenge this dichotomy: in being integral to the concept of 'self-defence' and therefore just cause, the pre-emption question is inherently bound up with the matter of justice.

3

Jus in Bello, Guantanamo Bay, and the War on Terror

Clausewitz notoriously reasoned that 'attached to force are certain, self-imposed, imperceptible limitations hardly worth mentioning, known as international law and custom, but they scarcely weaken it'. However, the assertion that interjecting war with moderation must always lead to 'logical absurdity'[1] is borne out by neither the history of war nor the discourse surrounding it. As the Brussels Declaration of 1874 made plain, 'the laws of war do not recognise in belligerents an unlimited power in the adoption of means in injuring the enemy'.[2] For the *jus in bello*, that part of the just war tradition that applies to the conduct of armed forces, once conflict has begun, represents strong moral–theological impulses, underpinned by legal limits, concerning the way in which war is fought.

Relations between hostile states are currently regulated by a vast body of positive international law, 'the modern law of nations of which Vitoria was the expounder, Suarez the philosopher, and Grotius the systematiser'.[3] Grotius, for his part, observed 'throughout the Christian world a lack of restraint in relation to war such as even barbarous races should be ashamed of . . . it is as if, in accordance with a general decree, frenzy had openly been let loose for the committing of all crimes'.[4] If his inspiration was the no-holds-barred manner in which wars were being conducted in the sixteenth century, his treatises drew largely upon existing custom. Practices designed to moderate warfare are considered to be as old as organized fighting itself, and, as the notion of the sovereign state took hold in Europe, the principles of just warfare were expounded formally. The fourth Hague Convention held soldiers and civilians alike to be protected by the 'principles of the law of nations, as they result from the usages established among civilized peoples, from the laws of humanity, and the dictates of the public conscience'.[5] The latter half of the nineteenth century brought a slew of treaties and declarations and, despite its bloody unfolding, the norms and conventions of just warfare were strengthened and institutionalized during the course of the twentieth century. At the dawn of this century, Bush defended his plans for an Iraq invasion by stressing that the United States had found a way to wage war in a manner which spared civilians, avoided collateral damage, and targeted leaders and their means to fight.[6]

A crucial starting point for the just war theorist is that 'even in hell, it is possible to be more or less humane, to fight with or without restraint'.[7] On the just war understanding of warfare, it is not by its nature limitless; 'the fact of twilight does not mean you cannot tell night from day'.[8] Walzer draws attention to the 'set of articulated norms, customs, professional codes, legal precepts, religious and philosophical principles and reciprocal arrangements that shape our judgements of military conduct'.[9] This 'war convention' has been expounded, debated, and revised over many centuries. For Ramsey, *jus in bello* is the most remarkable part of the just war because the ordinary man can exert control over what he does in war, and the justness of his actions is more easily fathomable than that of the *jus ad bellum*: 'Christian ethics may attribute to ordinary men, and to their political leaders, a capacity to know more clearly and certainly the moral limits pertaining to an armed action a man or a nation is about to engage in, than they are likely to know enough to compare unerringly the overall justice of regimes and nations'.[10]

Of course, although a great deal of discussion on war's limitation is couched in ethical terms, such restraint has not always been the product of moral regard for fellow human. In the second century, Tertullian rejected violence because he thought it inherently idolatrous, as he did woodworking and astrology in particular.[11] The limited sovereign wars of the eighteenth century were also deliberately restricted for economic reasons, and deference to the laws of war has been commonly spoken of in terms of prudence. Douglas Feith pointed to this when he declared:

No country in the world upholds the Geneva Conventions on the law of armed conflict more steadfastly than does the United States. This is true not only because Americans recognise a moral obligation to be humane and because Americans are law abiding by nature and in practice. It is also true because no country in the world has a greater practical interest than the United States in respect for the laws of war.[12]

Still, the overwhelming impetus behind the development of *jus in bello* is the justice owed to the civilian, and indeed the soldier, as fellow human. Vitoria stated plainly that 'it would be heretical to say that it is licit to kill [the innocent]'[13] and Ramsey reminded that Christ also died for one's assailant.[14] General Orders 100 observed in 1863 that 'men who take up arms against one another in public war do not cease on this account to be moral beings, responsible to one another and to God'.[15]

Jus in bello relies heavily on both the judgement and the conscience of the individual soldier, applying as it does to the fog and pace of warfare in which actions are difficult to police. Geneva Protocol I, for example, enshrines the use of judgement by relativizing the definition of an appropriate 'military objective': 'limited to those objects which by their nature, location, purpose or use make an effective contribution to military action and whose total or partial destruction . . . in the circumstances ruling at the time, offers a definite military advantage'.[16] Grotius noted that 'law, even though without a sanction, is not entirely void of effect. For justice brings peace of conscience, while injustice causes torment and anguish, such as Plato describes, in the breasts of tyrants'.[17] The role of judgement and conscience has been emphasized because, ultimately:

What the legal instruments offer in real terms is no more than a reminder of the ideal aimed at, the hope that circumstances may exceptionally allow of its achievement, and a helpful broad array of principles, rules and practical advices as to how that may be made more likely.[18]

The striving for that ideal, however, has been institutionalized by modern armed forces with various military manuals[19] and promises that, whereas America in the war on terror 'faces an enemy who has no regard for the conventions of war or rules of morality . . . coalition forces will make every effort to spare innocent civilians from harm'.[20]

The constraints which the just war tradition places on warfare are generally discussed in terms of two principles: discrimination and proportionality. Section 3.1 will briefly engage with them in an exploration of some *jus in bello* issues raised by the US-led invasion of Iraq. This chapter will then turn to the long-term war on terror policy of detaining suspected terrorists in a US military facility known as Guantanamo Bay, described by one eminent international lawyer as making 'a mockery of our claim to stand for the rule of law'.[21]

3.1. DISCRIMINATION AND PROPORTIONALITY IN IRAQ

In the eleventh century, the Church attempted to limit warfare by banning fighting from sunset on Wednesday to dawn on Monday. This 'truce of God' was rarely respected and subsequently abandoned, a stark contrast to the persistent and demonstrably more resonant moral value of non-combatant immunity. The just war principle of discrimination, addressing itself to the issue of appropriate targets in war, requires that non-combatants are never directly attacked. Just as Vitoria barred the slaying of women, children, 'harmless agricultural folk', 'guests who are sojourning among the enemy', and the 'rest of the peaceable civilian population',[22] Protocol I Additional to the Geneva Conventions of 1949 decrees that 'the civilian population as such, as well as individual civilians, shall not be the object of attack'.[23] Ramsey maintains that in non-combatant immunity hangs the distinction between war and murder.[24]

The principle of discrimination rests upon the differentiation between men engaging in harm and men that are not. While this involves a purely practical assessment, such a distinction has moral force. This is because, as Walzer argues, immunity from attack is lost rather than gained: we are all immune to start with.[25] As we considered in Chapter 2, the soldier acts to lose his rights through posing a danger to others by bearing arms. Coates point out that in being the negation of 'nocere' (to harm), the 'innocent' are simply those who are doing no harm.[26]

Of course, the so-designated innocent can make huge contributions to the war effort, from forming the workforce in factories, the brainpower for specific strategies, or the political power behind the warring government. However, there exists no legal distinction between the rural peasant and the industrial engineer, between 'the politically impotent civilian population of a pre-industrial society and the democratically empowered civilian population of a highly developed one'.[27] The enemy's subjective *culpa* is fenced off and the combatant's objective attributes become the focus. By the laws of war, only soldiers can be targeted in an armed conflict. And, by extension, it is unlawful to harm the soldier once he lays down his arms.

It is clear from a moral point of view, however, that modern conflict, and especially urban warfare, puts considerable pressure on the principle of discrimination. This is due to both the nature of contemporary war (urban insurgencies, for example) and the development of weapons technology such as cluster bombs. As a result, W. V. O'Brien attempts to defend an understanding of discrimination that is not absolute but which balances 'the need to protect non-combatants with the need to recognise the legitimate military necessities of modern forms of warfare'.[28] However, as Richard Regan implies,[29] O'Brien's efforts seem somewhat superfluous. His reformulation of discrimination appears to do much of the same work as the already-existing principles of proportionality and double-effect.

Proportionality, as applied to *jus in bello*, refers to 'the balance to be struck between the achievement of a military goal and the cost in terms of lives'.[30] Originally, the principle was geared towards the limiting of means in warfare with, for example, the St Petersburg Declaration of 1868 prohibiting weapons that caused unnecessary suffering.[31] However, the First World War and the massive aerial bombardment of the Spanish Civil War demonstrated the dangers posed to civilians by allowable means. The principle evolved to require that the overall destruction inflicted be proportional to a legitimate military objective, which includes collateral damage to non-combatants and their infrastructure. Thus, for any proposed military operation, a commander and his advisers must weigh the potential concrete military advantage against the incidental loss of civilian life while bearing in mind what precautions are feasible.[32]

A related moral vehicle is the doctrine of double-effect, which dwells on the incidental aspect of the harm to civilians. Not entirely uncontroversial,[33] this idea emerged out of the moral deliberations of Catholicism. In his discussion on whether a Christian can lawfully kill a man in self-defence, Aquinas observed that 'nothing hinders one act from having two effects, only one of which is intended, while the other is beside the intention'. Aquinas sought to suggest that a man acting in self-defence does not directly intend to kill his attacker, but rather to preserve his own life. However, if 'he uses more than necessary violence, it will be unlawful'.[34]

Vitoria was the first to apply this reasoning to a discussion about *jus in bello*. He argued that it is 'occasionally lawful to kill the innocent not by mistake, but with full knowledge of what one is doing, if this is an accidental effect'.[35] Thus, in aiming to bring about a legitimate 'good' effect by attempting to accomplish a military objective, an action can also have a foreseen but unintended 'bad' effect such as harm to civilians. The action will be illegitimate, however, if the badness of the unintended effect outweighs the goodness of the intended one. Vitoria, with the doctrine of double-effect, is straightforwardly addressing O'Brien's concern about the immutability of non-combatant immunity: 'this is proven, since it would otherwise be impossible to wage war against the guilty, thereby preventing the just side from fighting'.[36] In this way, the moral imperative that non-combatants are never the *direct* object of attack can still be maintained.

This emphasis on the internal quality of actions in war renders it very difficult to engage in moral assessment. Where commanders might express their intentions and deliberations in private meetings, these are not accessible to the researcher. As George Weigel has argued, 'in the nature of the case, we can have less surety about *in bello* considerations than we can about certain *ad bellum* questions'.[37] Nonetheless, the more objective features of the US' conduct in the Iraq invasion prompted some scepticism about its respect for *jus in bello* principles.

The awesome manner in which the coalition commenced hostilities immediately cast doubt upon Bush's confident statement that 'the guilty have far more to fear from war than the innocent'.[38] In the opening days of the conflict, 3,000 bombs were dropped on Iraq, including in large cities such as Baghdad and Basra.[39] Three weeks into the US-led invasion, Amnesty International criticized the use of cluster bombs in heavily populated areas and drew attention to the fact that 'the rules of war prohibit the use of inherently indiscriminate weapons'. The report referred to scenes at one hospital where images of injured women, children, and babies cut in half were judged too awful to be aired on television by Reuters and the Associated Press.[40] Other allegations of attacks on civilians surfaced as the invasion progressed, from the killing of more than forty people at a wedding party in al-Qaim[41] to the bombing of crowded markets[42] and troops opening fire on civilian buses.[43] The director of operations for the International Red Cross angrily expressed his anxiety over the fact that 'every day seems to bring news of yet another act of utter contempt for the most basic tenet of humanity'.[44] The administration had also provoked condemnation of its behaviour while engaged in combat against legitimate targets, having admitted to using both depleted uranium[45] and napalm (under the new name of 'Mark 77 fire-bombs')[46] against Iraqi troops. Further, as the invading powers, the United States and its allies were responsible for protecting civilian infrastructure and ensuring the availability of essential services. However, the lack of water, electricity, and medical supplies was well documented, and it was said that thousands of children were dying from hepatitis, cholera, diarrhoea, acute respiratory infections, as well as a lack of access to basic medicines.[47] As order and security broke down, kidnappings[48] and killings[49] became commonplace.

While it is impossible to provide extensive details of the allegations levelled against the United States concerning violations of the laws of war in Iraq, it is worth focusing on the fate of one city in particular. The assault against Fallujah, codenamed 'Operation Phantom Fury', drew heavy criticism for almost all of its aspects. The Americans determined that key militants behind the post-invasion insurgency were hiding in Fallujah. Intense military operations were conducted there twice in 2004, in April–May and again in October–November. One military analyst advised that 'even if Fallujah has to go the way of Carthage, reduced to shards, the price will be worth it'.[50] In the second assault, the city's electricity and water were cut off,[51] its hospitals were stormed,[52] the Red Crescent was turned away,[53] thousands of civilians were made refugees, and in one week of fighting many of the 600 dead were said to have been women and children.[54] The UN High Commissioner for Human Rights called for an investigation into possible breaches of international law, 'including the deliberate targeting of civilians, indiscriminate and disproportionate attacks, the killing of injured persons and the use of human shields'.[55] One Congressman expressed his outrage at the November campaign, arguing that 'the means of attack employed against Fallujah are illegal and cannot be justified by any conceivable ends'.[56] Furthermore, the world looked on as video footage emerged of a 'wounded and unarmed'[57] Iraqi fighter being shot at point-blank range in a mosque by a US soldier, who was never charged.[58]

Also, the United States initially denied but eventually admitted using white phosphorous in Fallujah, a 'spontaneously flammable chemical' which burns the skin, sometimes down to the bone.[59]

It is worth noting that these events were not without strategic implications. Reuven Paz points out that 'following the American siege in Fallujah in November 2004 and the occupation of most of the city in early December 2004, it became increasingly difficult for Arab governments to silence the growing anti-Americanism and popular support for the mujahideen in Iraq'. He notes that, in November 2004, the Muslim Brotherhood began to voice its support for the war against American forces and a group of twenty-six senior clerics in Saudi Arabia issued a *fatwa* declaring that the struggle against America in Iraq was a (legitimate) *jihad*, with tacit support from the Saudi government.[60] At the time of writing, Fallujah continues to present a problem for stability in the Anbar province—despite a period of calm at the height of the so-called Sunni Awakening in 2008, the situation in 2009 is described as 'getting worse and worse'.[61]

In Iraq, the superpower's overwhelming military capability was demonstrated unambiguously. One commander indicated that this was somewhat intentional on the part of the Americans:

You said it, this is war. And we're going to prosecute the war not holding one hand behind our back. When we identify positively an enemy target, we're going to go ahead and take it out with every means we have available. I like to remember what Viscount Slim said during the Burma campaign. He said, 'Use a sledgehammer to crush a walnut.' And that's exactly what we will do.[62]

US heavy-handedness was lamented by some sectors of the media and many human rights groups, but also by its allies. In an interview with the *Telegraph*, one senior British Army officer explained:

My view and the view of the British chain of command is that the Americans' use of violence is not proportionate and is over-responsive to the threat they are facing. They don't see the Iraqi people the way we see them. They view them as *untermenschen*. They are not concerned about the Iraqi loss of life in the way the British are. Their attitude towards the Iraqis is tragic, it's awful. The US troops view things in very simplistic terms. It seems hard for them to reconcile subtleties between who supports what and who doesn't in Iraq. It's easier for their soldiers to group all Iraqis as the bad guys. As far as they are concerned Iraq is bandit country and everybody is out to kill them.[63]

The United States Conference of Catholic Bishops too expressed its 'deep concern' about 'overly aggressive tactics'.[64] In these ways, the American military's regard for the principles of proportionality and discrimination in Iraq was questioned by a variety of sources.

However, both the Bush administration and the military repeatedly insisted that 'we do everything in our power to keep our targeting as precision-based as it can be, always knowing that there is room for problems that could take place'.[65] Less than a month before one commentator suggested that the Iraq war was 'the deadliest campaign for non-combatants that US forces have fought since Vietnam',[66] Donald Rumsfeld congratulated the Commander of Centcom, Tommy Franks, for the supposed fact that 'there have not been large numbers of civilian casualties because the coalition took such great care to protect the lives of innocent civilians as well as holy sites. It's a remarkable achievement'.[67] At other times, the approach was more philosophical: in response to a specific incident in which seven civilians were killed at an army checkpoint, Centcom's Deputy Director of Operations explained that 'while we regret the loss of any civilian lives, at this point they remain unavoidable, as they have been throughout history'.[68]

In the end, it becomes unfeasible to settle upon the number of in-theatre violations which render a war 'unjust' or to determine how many badly fought battles impact upon the just cause. It is impossible to discern or stipulate a threshold. Nevertheless, it seems important to note the inconsistencies between the Bush administration's confident declarations about the cleanliness of its war and the facts which emerged from Iraq. Thus began a 2003 report by Human Rights Watch into the conduct of the war and civilian casualties:

U.S. President George W. Bush called the war in Iraq 'one of the swiftest and most humane military campaigns in history'. Yet thousands of Iraqi civilians were killed or injured during the three weeks of fighting from the first air strikes on March 20 to April 9, 2003, when Baghdad fell to U.S.-led Coalition forces.[69]

With talk of 'effects-based targeting' and Rumsfeld's claim that more than ninety per cent of the munitions used would be precision-guided, there had been great hopes that, with the Iraq war, the world could enter into an era where it was possible to prosecute a humanitarian war.[70] Others, however, were more doubtful. A few months before the invasion, one Canadian commentator argued that 'everybody hopes that Saddam can be overthrown at little cost in human life and without causing too much political chaos in the region, but the odds are against it'.[71] Early into its prosecution, to Bush's claim that Iraq was a clean war, Malaysian Prime Minister Mahathir Mohammad objected that 'it's a dirty war and you can see in the pictures that it's a dirty war'.[72]

During his (as it turned out, premature) 'Mission Accomplished' speech in May 2003, Bush continued to point to the invasion of Iraq as a model for the humane wars of the future:

With new tactics and precision weapons, we can achieve military objectives without directing violence against civilians. No device of man can remove the tragedy from war; yet it is a great moral advance when the guilty have more to fear from war than the innocent.[73]

Other onlookers, however, drew different conclusions about the implications of this technological advance. For example, Talal Asad:

What is certain is that by fighting the enemy at a distance, [the military] has been able to minimise its own casualties. Unchallengeable air supremacy and precision weaponry make virtual impunity of the pilot possible. Furthermore, domestic public opinion in liberal democracies is critical of excessive war casualties in its armies. This humanitarian concern means that soldiers need no longer go to war expecting to die but only to kill. In itself, this destablises the conventional understanding of war as an activity in which human dying and killing are exchanged.

Asad argues that this 'unequal killing' is made possible by a long-standing tradition of colonial warfare.[74] In any case, with tens of thousands of innocents killed in Iraq and oft-heard charges of 'crimes against humanity',[75] the moral advance trumpeted by Bush was not readily apparent. The tragedy, however, was glaringly so.

   We turn our attention now to one systematic strategy of the war on terror which was designed at the top of the administration and cannot thus be put down to the 'fog of war'. The US' detention and interrogation policies at Guantanamo Bay will be the focus of the remainder of this chapter. The purpose is not to detail specific allegations of brutal treatment made against the Americans, which have ranged from torture to the weaponization of Islam,[76] but instead to consider the issues in a general way and to suggest that the administration's defence of the facility relies on a *jus in bello* construction of 'necessity' (necessity[IB]). This is, in effect, a 'supreme emergency' argument which connects the laws of the *jus in bello* to the cause within the *jus ad bellum*.

3.2. SUPREME EMERGENCY IN THE WAR ON TERROR

'Evil is not to be done that good may come of it'

Romans 3:8

'Military necessity does not admit of cruelty'

Abraham Lincoln, *General Orders No. 100*, Article 14

In serving 'the cause of liberty'[77] with the war on terror, the Bush administration pursued a policy that was depicted as 'the gulag of our time' by

Amnesty International[78] and described as a 'monstrous failure of justice' by one UK Law Lord.[79] The notorious US detention centre at Guantanamo Bay, Cuba, where terrorist suspects were held indefinitely without access to trial and without the protections of the Geneva Conventions, was mired in scandal since its inception in 2001, with one UN report concluding that some of the practices carried out there 'must be assessed as amounting to torture as defined in article one of the Convention Against Torture'.[80]

It is the contention of this section that underlying the justifications offered by the 'defenders of freedom'[81] for such controversial *jus in bello* actions is a broad 'supreme emergency' rationale. In general, 'supreme emergency' thinking permits the just cause to encroach on the means employed in warfare. This section will demonstrate how Bush administration officials invoked the notion of moral crisis in the war on terror by representing America as the objectification of good locked in a zero-sum struggle with the embodiment of evil. This depiction works as a tacit explanation for the abrogation of the Geneva Conventions at Guantanamo Bay, as it is decreed that America must be defended at all costs: 'our nation faces a threat to our freedoms and the stakes could not be higher'.[82] Indeed, 'this is civilisation's fight'.[83]

3.3. THE SEPARATION OF *JUS AD BELLUM* AND *JUS IN BELLO*

Although Saint Ambrose, the popular fourth-century Bishop of Milan, argued that justice was binding even in war, it is said that 'he was prepared to use the devil's weapons as a means of realising the kingdom of God'.[84] The influential Swiss Protestant theologian Karl Barth denounced war as 'a flat betrayal of the gospel', and yet maintained that in those rare cases when war was sanctioned by God Christians were to fight joyfully and recklessly.[85] Saint Augustine too treated as exceptional the instances where a war is clearly warranted by God, but permitted ruthless and bloody fighting when He commanded it. The moral arbitrariness[86] and sheer brutality of the crusades and ideological warfare prompted the just war efforts to settle upon rules that were applicable to both sides regardless of the justification for resorting to war. Thus, just cause aside, *jus in bello* laws were binding in all conflicts against whatever kind of enemy: 'it follows that even in wars against the Turks we may not kill children, who are obviously innocent, nor women, who are to be presumed innocent at least as far as the war is concerned'.[87] Grotius grounds his discussion of the laws of war in natural law, which he affirms 'cannot be changed even by God himself'.[88]

In effect, the just war's two regimes of justice are to be applied separately. This idea is taken for granted in international law as well as by the publications of military establishments. Essentially, such a separation serves as a bulwark against the mercilessness of holy wars and the carnage of great ideological battles; the wrongs committed in the name of 'right'. However, history attests to the recurrently compelling logic of using the 'rightness' of the *jus ad bellum* to override *jus in bello* restrictions. Mark Osiel reported that many of the soldiers instructed to torture their captives during Argentina's Dirty War were reticent to do so until their priests assured them that they were fighting God's fight.[89] The most famous secular spokesman for this sort of reasoning was Winston Churchill during the Second World War, who sought to justify mining Norwegian waters[90] by focusing on the evil of the Nazis (and thus the relative 'good' of the Allies). Churchill underlined that 'we are fighting to re-establish the reign of law', and argued that 'we have a right, and indeed are bound in duty, to abrogate for a space of time some of the conventions of the very laws we seek to consolidate and reaffirm'.[91]

It is worth briefly noting that, in so far as *jus ad bellum* can ever be regarded as connected to *jus in bello*, it is because a true just cause necessarily *limits* the prosecution of the war. This is encapsulated by Paul Ramsey's eloquent expressions of the 'twin-born justification of war and the limitation which surrounded non-combatants with moral immunity from attack. . . . The same considerations which justify killing the bearer of hostile force by the same stroke prohibit non-combatants from ever being directly attacked with deliberate intent'.[92] This notion is present in Vitoria's writings too, as he buttresses non-combatant immunity with the observation that 'the foundation of the just war is the injury inflicted upon one by the enemy, as shown above, but an innocent person has done you no harm'.[93]

In this way, the just war tradition, as distinct from pacifism on one end of the spectrum and holy war on the other, sought to prevent the justice of a cause from impinging upon and permissively shaping a war's conduct. The laws of war were thus institutionalized in the twentieth century and reinforced by a body of international humanitarian law that is categorically independent of the grand agendas of actors. The invocation of supreme emergency, however, flies in the face of such a separation.

3.4. SUPREME EMERGENCY

For Brian Orend, supreme emergency is 'the most controversial, and consequential, amendment to just war theory ever proposed'.[94] This thesis of moral

philosophy was built around Churchill's usage of the term in the Second
World War. In seeking support for his proposal to violate Norway's neutrality,
Churchill argued that 'the letter of the law must not in a supreme emergency
obstruct those who are charged with its protection and enforcement'. In *Just
and Unjust Wars*, Michael Walzer observes that the phrase implicitly contains
a moral argument: 'that there is a fear beyond the ordinary fearfulness (and
the frantic opportunism) of war, and a danger to which that fear corresponds,
and that this fear and danger may well require exactly those measures that the
war convention bars'.[95] Walzer applies this reasoning to the Allies' conduct in
the Second World War, focusing on the British decision to resort to the 'terror
bombing' of German civilians as well as Truman's justification for the firebombing of Japanese cities and the eventual dropping of two atomic bombs.
Concluding that neither case conformed to the proper parameters of a
genuine 'supreme emergency',[96] Walzer does not rule out the possibility
of such mitigating circumstances in principle. He maintains that, in some
exceptional situations, a supreme emergency urgently overrides the *jus in bello*
dogma of non-combatant immunity.

Walzer's preoccupation with the 'immeasurably awful' consequences of
Hitler's mastery of Europe—indeed, the fact that Nazism was 'evil objectified'[97]—leads him to formulate the issue in the following way: 'should I wager
this determinate crime (the killing of innocent people) against this immea-
surable evil (a Nazi triumph)?'[98] Shue argues that what are threatened in
supreme emergencies are the general moral structures underlying civilized
society, 'principled society itself'. He teases out the inference at work:

> If the only way to ensure the long-term survival of the practice of honouring
> principles at all is to violate a fundamental principle (such as the immunity of non-
> combatants) in an isolated instance in order to defeat a ruthless enemy of principled
> conduct as such, one not only may but must violate the principle.[99]

Walzer is clear, however, that such a case would only count as legitimate in so
far as it corresponds with the two levels on which the concept of necessity
operates. That is, if the nature of the danger is unusual and horrifying, but
also imminent. Furthermore, Walzer stipulates that the violation of non-
combatant immunity in such instances must be guided by the restraints of
'usefulness and proportionality'.

Inhering in Walzer's treatment of the issue is a 'calculus'—a utilitarian
weighing-up of evils that involves not only numbers but judgements about
quality of life, civilization, and morality.[100] Incidentally, this does not sit well
with a discussion earlier in the book where he seems to eschew consequen-
tialism and endorse a deontological theory of human rights.[101] But Walzer
accepts the burden of this paradox. Although a statesman may be justified in

acting to protect his community's history and future, 'we cannot forget that the rights violated for the sake of the victory are genuine rights, deeply founded and in principle inviolable'.[102] In cases of supreme emergency we say 'yes and no, right and wrong'.[103]

The Bush administration has not, of course, provided any such philosophical reflection on the issue. No 'supreme emergency' argument has been made explicitly. Moreover, the Guantanamo Bay controversy does not involve the mass targeting of a large number of innocents. Nevertheless, this book seeks to suggest that implicit in the administration's justifications for refusing to apply the Geneva Conventions and subjecting detainees to tortuous acts is a similar appeal to the notion of moral crisis.

In the general logic of a 'supreme emergency', the separation between *jus ad bellum* and *jus in bello* is breached. The invoker of supreme emergency maintains that his just cause compels him to violate an otherwise inviolable *jus in bello* principle. The mechanism by which the separation is denied is through the insertion of ultimate values. The moral danger works to raise the stakes of defeat.

In the war on terror, generally it is said that there 'is no doubt that today America faces an existential threat'.[104] The threat is, moreover, value-laden. This requires an especially tough stance, for 'the only way to defeat terrorism as a threat to our way of life is to stop it, eliminate it, and destroy it where it grows'.[105] There can be little middle ground in such a conflict: 'They want to impose their way of life on the rest of us, and in pursuit of this goal, they are prepared to slaughter anyone who stands in their way. This is not a foe we can reason with, or negotiate with, or appease. This is—to put it simply—an enemy that we must vanquish'.[106] Thus, in Rumsfeld's words, 'they will either succeed in changing our way of life, or we'll succeed in changing theirs'.[107] In such a definitive battle, America must prevail because 'we have no other choice'.[108] This dichotomous way of posing the issue in turn affects how the war is conducted.

3.5. THE TORTURE PAPERS

When Senate Minority Whip Dick Durbin controversially described Guantanamo Bay as a 'death camp' in the style of Pol Pot, Hitler, and Stalin,[109] Senate Majority Leader Bill Frist accused him of 'heinous slander'. Certainly, Frist was correct to point out that the number of people killed at Guantanamo Bay is 'Zero. That's right: Zero people'.[110] Undoubtedly, however, elements of the international community were exercised by what they regarded as a qualitatively similar and systematic denial of human dignity. The notorious detention centre was dubbed 'a global experiment in inhumanity',[111] it was said to subvert the rule of law 'horrendously',[112] and the memoranda to which we turn have been described as 'an ethical train wreck'[113] and likened to the Nazis' 'punctilious legalisation of their final solution'.[114]

The 'torture papers' are a series of memoranda and reports authored by various departments of the Bush administration and their lawyers with the purpose of authorizing coercive interrogation techniques in Guantanamo Bay, Afghanistan, and Iraq.[115] A host of issues are thrown up by these documents, including, but not limited to, the constitutional question of whether Congress can rightfully interfere in the president's direction of war matters;[116] the jurisdictional matter of whether *habeas* claims filed by inmates held on US-controlled territory in Cuba can be heard in American courts;[117] the legal-cum-ethical theme of 'advice for hire' and the fact the memoranda were seen as 'advocacy document[s] for a pro-torture conclusion';[118] the political issue concerning the way in which dissenting voices within decision-making circles were marginalized and systematically isolated.[119] Indeed, it was argued that the memoranda contributed to a 'torture culture' that led to the infamous horrors committed in Iraq's Abu Ghraib prison, involving 'numerous incidents of sadistic, blatant and wanton criminal abuses',[120] which included brutal beatings, allegations of rape,[121] sodomy with phosphoric lighting,[122] and, at one Afghanistan air base, homicide.[123] These other abuses, however, occurred in a situation where the US administration deemed the Geneva Conventions to be applicable. There was no similar determination with reference to Guantanamo Bay, where the inmates, dubbed 'unlawful combatants', were held beyond the Conventions' reach. This cast something of a shadow over such moralistic assertions as Condoleezza Rice's: 'as we defend the deepest principles we hold against terror and tyranny, we must live up to those principles ourselves'.[124]

3.6. PARADIGM SHIFT

In his capacity as counsel for the White House, Alberto Gonzales advised that 'the nature of the new war' implied a 'new paradigm [which] renders obsolete Geneva's strict limitations on questioning of enemy prisoners and renders quaint some of its provisions'.[125] It is worth pointing out, as Philippe Sands does, that Vice-President Cheney's lawyer, David Addington, is believed to be the real author behind this written advice.[126] Assistant Attorney General Jay Bybee also acknowledged the 'novel nature of this conflict',[127] emphasizing that the Geneva Conventions were intended to cover traditional wars.[128] In a memorandum addressed to the Vice-President, the Secretary of State, the Secretary of Defense, the Attorney General, Chief of Staff to the President, Director of the CIA, Assistant to the President for National Security Affairs, and the Chairman of the Joint Chiefs of Staff, President Bush accepted this 'new paradigm'. Noting that it was 'ushered in not by us but by the terrorists', he urged that it required 'new thinking in the law of war'.[129]

The 'unique nature of the war on terrorism'[130] was double-sided. Firstly, the novelty was strategic. Faced with the 'radicalism of this unprecedented enemy',[131] counterterrorism operations entailed foiling plots to 'covertly attack innocent civilian populations without warning',[132] which in turn placed a high premium on the ability to quickly obtain information. Indeed, Bybee suggested that 'it may be the case that only successful interrogations can provide the information necessary to prevent the success of covert terrorist attacks upon the United States and its citizens'.[133]

Secondly, a moral indictment was levelled against the enemy which 'demonstrated a ruthless disregard for even minimal standards of civilised behaviour'.[134] Gonzales later defended his infamous position by underlining that America faced an enemy which 'most importantly does not fight according to the laws of war'.[135] Apart from suggesting a tit-for-tat approach to the issue, these statements seem to imply that such adversaries were not morally deserving of the Geneva Conventions' protections, not even the minimal protections of Common Article 3 (which are, of course, not restricted to prisoners of war (POWs)). Speaking about the prisoners held in Guantanamo, the Secretary of Defense admitted: 'I do not feel even the slightest concern over their treatment. They are being treated vastly better than they treated anybody else over the last several years and vastly better than was their circumstance when they were found'.[136] Bush was equally dismissive when he faced similar questioning: 'Remember . . . the ones in Guantanamo Bay are killers. They don't share the same values we share'.[137]

Derided by one international lawyer as 'the Brave New World of Osama bin Laden and al-Qaeda',[138] the postulation of an unparalleled warfare entailed for members of the Bush administration a 'paradigm shift'.[139] While others were 'imprisoned in old categories, old rules', Berenson points to legal advisers within the administration who were not:

There was certainly a sense that there was a group of people, a group of lawyers in the executive branch who really were the political appointees most directly accountable to the president, who understood the new threat, who understood the new paradigm, who understood the imperative to be forward-leaning and to be aggressive in trying to protect American national security and American civilian life.[140]

Such insight led to the adoption of two related and politically divisive policy moves.

3.6.1. 'Paradigm shift': illegal combatants

Although he acknowledged that 'since the Geneva Conventions were concluded in 1949, the United States has never denied their applicability to either US or opposing forces engaged in armed conflict, despite several opportunities to do so',[141] Gonzales insisted the war on terror mandated innovation. Adopting terminology not recognized by the Geneva Conventions, the United States labelled its Guantanamo detainees 'unlawful combatants'.[142] This was intended to lift them beyond the reach of Convention (III) Relative to the Treatment of Prisoners of War, which was both signed and ratified by the United States. The administration's lawyers argued that al-Qaeda did not 'receive the protection of the laws of war' because it failed to satisfy all four elements of the eligibility requirements for treatment as POWs;[143] because as a non-state actor it was not a high contracting party to the conventions; and because of the non-conventional nature of the conflict.[144] Although the Taliban presented 'a more difficult legal question', not least because Afghanistan had been a state party to all four Geneva Conventions since September 1956, the lawyers determined Afghanistan a 'failed state'. This was because it lacked the essential attributes of statehood.[145] Moreover, due to the fact the Taliban was 'functionally intertwined with al Qaeda', this put the two 'on the same footing' with regard to the Geneva Conventions.[146] Indeed, this feature of the Taliban rendered it 'more akin to a terrorist organisation that used force . . . for terrorist purposes'.[147]

While international lawyers and human rights organizations[148] disputed all this legal reasoning, the administration's own State Department registered its scepticism. Powell referred to the 'factual errors' of the aforementioned recommendations and argued that failing to apply the Geneva Conventions would provoke negative international reaction, undermine support among America's allies, and possibly prompt international legal charges. Powell warned this would 'reverse over a century [*sic*] of US policy and practice in supporting the Geneva Conventions and undermine the protections of the law of war for our troops'.[149] The Chairman of the Joint Chiefs of Staff, General Richard Myers, also reportedly insisted to Donald Rumsfeld that 'it is our military culture. . . . We train our people to obey the Geneva Conventions, it's not even a matter of whether it is reciprocated—it's a matter of who we are'.[150]

Certainly, as State Department lawyer William Taft argued, the United States had extended Geneva protection to the Vietcong during the Vietnam

War,[151] as it did when dealing with an enemy that fell short of the four Geneva requirements in Panama, Somalia, Haiti, and Bosnia.[152] Nonetheless, the Bush administration maintained that the provisions of the Geneva Conventions were wholly inappropriate when confronted with the extraordinary enemy in the war on terror:

There's a lot of things that prisoners of war are entitled to which don't make sense if you have dangerous terrorists. . . . Oh, for example, you're allowed to cook your own food, which would, I assume, would [*sic*] mean you get knives and things like that. You're allowed to have recreation, intellectual pursuits, including scientific research. The idea of the Geneva Conventions is a very sort of charming one: once you're removed from the fighting you, as an honourable warrior, don't fight anymore, but you're to be treated with a lot of respect due to your position as a warrior. And you get a long list of things you would have normally gotten back at home.[153]

Gonzales, too, seemed to downplay what an abrogation of Geneva entailed, pointing to provisions such as advances of monthly pay, athletic uniforms, and scientific instruments.[154] Strikingly, there was little mention of Common Article 3, which rejects the inhuman treatment of all human beings, regardless of legal status ('persons taking no active part in the hostilities, including members of armed forces who have laid down their arms and those placed *hors de combat* by sickness, wounds, detention, or any other cause').[155] Given that the administration's legal advisers were branded by one Professor of Law and Philosophy as 'the torture lawyers',[156] the worry was indeed that, in addition to being held indefinitely without access to a fair trial,[157] the absence of Geneva protections would expose America's detainees to mental or physical violence.

3.6.2. 'Paradigm shift': torture

'Guys, wake up, smell the coffee, take your gloves off'

Marshall Billingslea[158]

As well as Common Articles Two and Three of the Geneva Conventions, the lawyers' memoranda are extensively preoccupied with the United Nations Convention Against Torture and Other Cruel, Inhuman or Degrading Treatment or Punishment (1984) and America's domestic corollary, known as the 'Torture Statute'.[159] Both explicitly proscribe torture,[160] as does Article Five of the Universal Declaration of Human Rights (1948), Article Seven of the International Covenant on Civil and Political Rights (1966), Article Seventy-Five of Protocol I Additional to the Geneva Convention (1977),[161] and Article Seven of the Rome Statute of the International Criminal Court

(1998).[162] The United Nations Economic and Social Council point out that 'the prohibition on torture moreover enjoys *jus cogens* status'.[163] Like non-combatant immunity from direct attack, the ban on torture is a first-order principle that is non-derogable: 'no exceptional circumstances whatsoever, whether a state of war or a threat of war, internal political instability or any other public emergency may be invoked as a justification for torture'.[164]

The memoranda operate on the assumption that 'since the detainees are not enemy prisoners of war, the Geneva Conventions limitations that would ordinarily govern captured enemy personnel interrogation are not binding on the US personnel conducting detainee interrogations at GTMO [Guantanamo]'.[165] This is coupled with a reappraisal of the definition of torture. Bybee advances what is, in his own words, 'an aggressive interpretation as to what amounts to torture'.[166] He argues that US law regards 'severe pain' as amounting to an emergency medical condition, and that any such pain must reach a high level, 'a level that would ordinarily be associated with a sufficiently serious physical condition or injury such as death, organ failure, or severe impairment of body functions in order to constitute torture'.[167] He ventures that 'torture is not the mere infliction of pain or suffering on another but is instead a step well removed',[168] concluding that 'only the most egregious conduct' could be penalized.[169] Luban points out that Bybee based his organ-failure definition of torture 'on a Medicare statute that has nothing whatsoever to do with torture' and that this portion of the Bybee memorandum, perhaps more than any other, involved defective legal analysis.[170]

To one former Judge Advocate General at Guantanamo Bay, Bybee's advice 'define[d] away torture as we understood it'.[171] The lawyers' efforts and arguments took on a number of guises, from employing versions of the doctrine of double-effect,[172] to underlining that the United States is immune from prosecution by the International Court of Justice.[173] Relevant to the purpose here, however, is the manner in which a supreme emergency logic renders first-order principles contingent on other values or circumstances that tie into the *jus ad bellum*. The Bush administration accomplished this by (*a*) weighing up values and (*b*) privileging self-defence.

Reiterating that the ban on torture is limited to only the most extreme forms of harm, Bybee sets out two possible legal defences for interrogators who have 'arguably crossed the line'.[174] The first of these is 'necessity', which he also refers to as the 'choice of evils'. Bybee quotes LaFave and Scott that 'sometimes the greater good of society will be accomplished by violating the literal language of the criminal law' and highlights how this reasoning could be successfully maintained 'under the current circumstances'.[175] Bybee calls to mind the attacks of 9/11 and argues that 'a detainee may possess information that could enable the United States to prevent attacks that potentially could equal or surpass the September 11 attacks in their magnitude'. 'Clearly', he continues, 'any harm that might occur during an interrogation would pale into insignificance compared to the harm avoided by preventing such an attack, which could take hundreds or thousands of lives'. While the argument Bybee sets out is a legal defence, he also makes a moral claim. That is, contra the Convention Against Torture's explicit stipulation that 'no exceptional circumstances whatsoever' can justify torture, Bybee suggests that the prohibition against torture is not absolute. He assesses it against a competing good: the prevention of a possible terrorist attack. Indeed, he refers to his analysis as a 'calculus',[176] which was, incidentally, replaced with the word 'rationale'[177] when his advice was incorporated into a different report.

The second defence examined by Bybee is that of 'self-defence'. He suggests that 'under the current circumstances' of the war on terror, an interrogator accused of torture could claim that he was acting to protect thousands of US civilians—that is, 'in defence of another'.[178] Further, argues Bybee, this would be supported by the fact that 'the nation itself is under attack and has the right to self-defence'. Thus, the defendant could claim 'he was fulfilling the Executive Branch's authority to protect the federal government, and the nation, from attack. The September 11 attacks have already triggered that authority'.[179] In this way, the justification for torture was based upon the administration's just cause for resorting to war: defence of America.

3.7. THE LIMITS OF SELF-DEFENCE

Not only does this way of thinking jar with Vitoria's maxim that 'it is never right to commit evil, even to avoid greater evils',[180] it can be seen to contravene the spirit of the laws of war. Surely, the *jus in bello* developed as a sphere of justice expressly separate from the just cause. Moreover, as was discussed in Chapters 1 and 2, all modern just wars are supposed to be fought in self-defence. Therefore, if violations of the laws of war can be justified because a nation is fighting in self-defence, all just wars would be entitled to set the laws of war aside.

Of course, there are grounds upon which to contest the premise of Bybee's argument, which is that aggressive interrogation can yield information crucial to self-defence. Cicero observed in the first century BC that torture forces even the innocent to lie, which is an idea institutionalized in many modern armies. US Army *Field Manual 34-52* instructs that the use of force in interrogations is 'a poor technique, as it yields unreliable results, may damage subsequent collection efforts, and can induce the source to say whatever he thinks the interrogator wants to hear'.[181] The charge that a morally dubious policy is also unwise or ineffective is reminiscent of Britain's 'supreme emergency' in the Second World War. Churchill's policy of terror bombing the German population was opposed by many British officers who could not countenance deliberately targeting civilians, the Blitzkrieg notwithstanding. According to Walzer, these officers did not want to imitate Hitler.[182] Moreover, as Alex Bellamy points out, 'targeting non-combatants has very little effect on the immediate ability of the enemy to inflict the impending calamity'.[183] Bombarding German civilians—and firebombing Japanese ones—was not conducive to the Allies' triumph in the war. It was, in short, pointless.

Similar conclusions have been drawn with reference to Guantanamo Bay. Philippe Sands contends that 'the US Army Field Manual was set aside, but the cruelty that followed did not produce meaningful intelligence'.[184] Indeed, the Federal Bureau of Investigation (FBI) had consistently voiced opposition to the use of aggressive interrogation techniques at Guantanamo, with agents variously arguing that '. . . we often discussed DoD techniques and how they were not effective or producing Intel that was reliable';[185] '[the FBI] voiced its strong objections regarding the efficacy of a fear-based approach';[186] '. . . reports from those knowledgeable about the use of these coercive techniques are highly sceptical as to their effectiveness and reliability';[187] '. . . every time the FBI established a rapport with a detainee, the military would step in and the detainee would stop being cooperative';[188] 'these tactics have produced no intelligence of a threat neutralization nature to date . . .'[189]

One of Bellamy's general worries about the doctrine of supreme emergency is that it makes 'fundamental rights conditional . . . secondary to utilitarian considerations'.[190] This turns rights into privileges, conferred by the opposing military so long as such rights are not inconvenient to their victory. But even if the idea of a supreme emergency allowing for certain *jus in bello* violations is upheld in principle, it is not clear whether America's position with respect to al-Qaeda would constitute such a looming catastrophe. Brian Orend seeks to maintain that supreme emergencies are 'real', as witnessed by the Native Americans, the Turkish Armenians, the European Jews, the Rwandan Tutsis, and the Albanian Kosovars. But Orend points to the fact that the United States is a hyper-power whose military defeat is not close or imminent.[191] What's more, the threat in a supreme emergency must be qualitatively grave enough to imply either genocide or the destruction of an entire civilizational structure. Walzer defends his decision to discuss supreme emergency in the context of Nazism because 'here was a threat to human values so radical that its imminence would surely constitute a supreme emergency; and this example can help us understand why lesser threats might not do so'.[192] With this in mind, the menace of al-Qaeda has not, at the time of writing, implied a similar impending doom.

Nonetheless, the Bush administration sought to maintain that, in the war on terror, the United States finds itself face-to-face with a comparable foe. Herein lays the moral logic for privileging self-defence. Wolfowitz made the explicit comparison in July 2004,[193] which Bush echoed to a wider audience in a 2005 speech,[194] implying the Iraq war was 'the modern-day moral equivalent' of the struggle against the Nazis.[195] The Bush administration did not shrink from dubbing al-Qaeda evil—indeed, in announcing the war on terror, the President vowed to 'rid the world of evil-doers'.[196] More than a matter of national defence, the war on terror was presented as 'a conflict between good and evil',[197] and countless references were made to the 'evil forces of terror'[198] and 'the struggle against evil'.[199] The United States, on the other hand, was presented as 'the greatest force for good on this earth'.[200] Again, this way of setting up the conflict worked to raise the cost of defeat. America's triumph was imperative, a universally desirable end that simultaneously worked as a justification for controversial means.

3.8. CONCLUSION

This chapter has shown that *jus in bello* involves a constant series of decisions that are relative to the situation in which they are taken and the information available at the time. Accordingly, the chapter focused on one *jus in bello* policy that was implemented at the very top of the American administration over an extended period of time, in offices far removed from the zone of combat. At Guantanamo Bay, hundreds of suspected terrorists were denied Geneva protections and held for years without trial, in a manner described by the Italian political philosopher Giorgio Agamben as '*homo sacer*': creatures legally dead while biologically still alive.[201] As one interrogator told Detainee 063, the purpose of Camp X-Ray (at Guantanamo) was to leave its inhabitants 'unable to feel like a human being'.[202]

Though Douglas Feith referred to the POW protections extended to irregular fighters which were added to the Geneva Conventions in 1977 as 'law in the service of terror',[203] others argued that failure to confer the rights of the Conventions to suspected terrorists at Guantanamo Bay was 'a shocking affront to the principles of democracy'.[204] While former president Jimmy Carter labelled the facility 'a disgrace to the USA',[205] one American Army captain explicitly shunned justifications which relied on al-Qaeda's moral quality: 'when did al-Qaeda become any type of standard by which we measure the morality of the United States?'[206] The Chief Air Force JAG likewise insisted that 'the use of the more extreme interrogation techniques simply is not how the US armed forces have operated in recent history. We have taken the legal and moral "high road" in the conduct of our military operations regardless of how others may operate'.[207] Adding to the comparisons of Guantanamo Bay with 'the most egregious symbols in the history of mankind', a British Archbishop noted that 'in Uganda President Amin did something similar, he did not imprison suspects because he knew that in prison, the law would apply to them so he created special places to keep them. . . . This is a breach of international law and a blight on the conscience of America'.[208] In a similar way, the American National Council of Churches reminded that both domestic and international law reflected the biblical mandate to 'do unto others as we would have them do unto us', and they both uphold 'as core principles the right of due process and the humane treatment of all prisoners, even in times of war'.

Indeed, the Churches' statement also pointed out that torture 'denies the preciousness of human life and the dignity of every human being by reducing its victims to the status of despised objects, no matter how noble the cause for which it is employed'.[209] However, in contravention of this latter notion, that the just cause is irrelevant to the way in which a war ought to be conducted, the Bush administration used the overall objectives of the 'war on terror' to justify 'rethinking' the laws of war. This *jus in bello* formulation of 'necessity' advocated that certain absolute rules (the right of *habeas corpus*, the ban on torture) ought to be weighed against al-Qaeda's alleged extreme evil and the imperative of defending America in a war in which an entire 'way of life' was at stake. As we have seen, this move represented a challenge to the independence of the *jus in bello* as a sphere of justice, and it was itself challenged in sharp moral terms by a diversity of voices in the international arena.

In 1960, Robert Tucker argued that American foreign policy goals were historically depicted as the ends of humanity itself.[210] The 'war on terror' is no different in this regard:

We stand for the permanent hopes of humanity, and those hopes will not be denied. We're confident, too, that history has an author who fills time and eternity with his purpose. We know that evil is real, but good will prevail against it.[211]

Tucker suggested that this could account for the US' demonstrated lack of restraint in warfare. Similarly, Ralph Potter noted that the American tradition is to shy away from war unless for an incontrovertibly just cause, 'but once drawn into war in response to the wickedness of enemies, we have shown a disinclination to be bound by the fine distinctions of the *jus in bello*'.[212] Potter also observed that when state power is applied to promote righteousness rather than merely to restrain specific acts of injustice, the *jus in bello* is eroded and the single criterion of just cause is applied in a utilitarian fashion. That is, 'the crusading mentality appears'.[213]

Such is the chief motivation for barring the values of the *jus ad bellum* from nullifying *jus in bello* protections. Hence, the emergence of the just war in contrast to holy war. James Turner Johnson proclaims:

> The principal intention of just war thought is to serve as a source for guidelines in making *relative* moral decisions. The era for which it is meant to serve is history—our own time of moral grays and shadows, not the apocalyptic time of stark light and darkness.[214]

In 2006, Condoleezza Rice asserted that 'if you're relativist about right and wrong then you can't lead'.[215] However, this apparent Manichaeism seems antithetical to the conduct of a just conflict. *Jus in bello* norms developed to protect men *qua* men, irrespective of whether they are acting on behalf of right or wrong.

*

This chapter concludes the first part, in which it was shown that the Bush administration's plans for an invasion of Iraq and its practices at Guantanamo Bay collided with important ideas about just warfare, both historically and in the present day. In particular, the necessity[AB] argument attempted to reconceptualize the necessity of a defensive war against Iraq to fit the context of a new and covert enemy seeking WMD. By appealing to the moral necessity of defeating the threat posed by the Guantanamo detainees, the necessity[IB] argument used the just cause to qualify fundamental *jus in bello* rules. In the second part, to which we now turn, it will be shown that al-Qaeda's arguments for war confronted accepted norms of warfare in the *jihad* tradition. Chapter 4 will examine Osama bin Laden's argument for just cause, which is based on an appeal to the juristic principle of 'reciprocity'. Chapter 5 will consider further issues of al-Qaeda's *jus ad bellum*, before Chapter 6 demonstrates how a *jus in bello* version of 'reciprocity' underpins the justification for killing American civilians.

Part II

Jihad and Al-Qaeda

4

Jihad and Al-Qaeda's Just Cause

Having declared a *jihad* against the United States five years previously, nine-teen members of the al-Qaeda organization hijacked four commercial airliners on 11 September 2001 and managed to crash two of them into the towers of the World Trade Centre in New York City and another into the Pentagon. The fourth plane did not reach its target of Capitol Hill, instead plummeting into a Pennsylvanian field where all on-board were killed. The overall death toll of up to 3000 people was overwhelmingly civilian. The 9/11 Commission labelled the surprise attack 'an event of surpassing disproportion . . . it was carried out by a tiny group of people, not enough to man a full platoon. Measured on a governmental scale, the resources behind it were trivial.'[1] For Osama bin Laden, this 'brave and beautiful operation'[2] was a consummate *jihadi* action waged in the name of Muslims worldwide. 'We are following our Prophet's mission', he explained to a Pakistani newspaper on 12 November 2002. 'This is a defensive *jihad* to protect our land and people'.[3]

With the exception of a few demonstrations of solidarity with bin Laden,[4] Muslims across the world were horrified by the attacks. While the Grand Mufti of Bosnia affirmed that 'there is not one normal man on this planet who can justify what happened in New York and Washington',[5] the Chief of Intelligence in the Palestinian territories declared that 'Tuesday's outrages ha[ve] smitten the conscience of humanity'.[6] Similarly, the leaders of a variety of Islamic groups issued a joint communiqué conveying their condolences to the families of the victims and made clear that, 'appalled by yesterday's killings, explosions, destruction, and attacks on innocent civilians, these leaders denounce very firmly and strongly these incidents that contravene all human and Islamic values'.[7] Among the signatories were names often heard in conjunction with radical Islam, such as the founder of Hamas, Sheikh Ahmed Yasin, and controversial Egyptian cleric, Sheikh Yusuf al-Qaradawi. The leader of Jamaat-i Islami, Pakistan's premier Muslim party, expressed his sorrow at the incident and condemned it. In the Islamic Republic of Iran, candle-lit vigils were held for the victims of the attacks and a minute of silence was observed before the start of a World Cup qualifier match against Bahrain. Chants of 'death to America' were also 'noticeably not heard at the Friday prayers at Tehran University'.[8] The Iranian president, Mohammad Khatami, stated that the attacks 'can only be the job of a group that have voluntarily severed their own ears and tongues, so that the only language which they could communicate would be destroying and spreading death'.[9] The attacks were even publicly deplored by the Taliban government of Afghanistan, the state which was said to harbour al-Qaeda, as Mullah Abdul Sala Zaeef asserted that 'we strongly condemn the attacks and condemn those who have carried out these blasts'.[10]

Further, much of the denunciation was framed in Islamic terms. One London-based daily wondered 'what *jihad* are they calling for and for whose sake and what purpose?', concluding that 'it had nothing to do with Islam and it did not render any service to religion or Muslims'.[11] Al-Nahda, Rashid Ghannoushi's Islamic reform party in Tunisia, put out a statement declaring that it 'unreservedly condemns the terrorism...behind these unjustifiable barbarous acts, which cannot be attributed to Muslims'.[12] Sheikh Usmanu Sharbutu, Ghana's chief Imam, labelled the strikes as 'inhuman, unethical, and unIslamic',[13] while a local Imam in Burkina Faso conjectured that 'anyone who understands Islam will be stunned to see a terrorist act committed in the name of Islam'.[14] The former head of Pakistan's Inter-Service Intelligence agency,[15] Hameed Gul, underlined that 'such events are not *jihad*, and killing innocent people cannot be described as *jihad*'.[16] Sheikh Mohammad Hussein Fadlallah, founder of Hizballah and spiritual leader of the Shias in Lebanon, affirmed that 'the attacks on America are not compatible with *sharia* law',[17] and reasoned that 'if some Muslims are responsible for this then they have wronged Islam as a set of human values, as a movement, and as a society'.[18] Hizballah's Secretary General, Hasan Nasrallah, concurred with Fadlallah's verdict, stressing that the attacks contradicted Islam and the Quran, 'which do not permit this barbarity'.[19] Such was al-Qaeda's moral isolation that one of Chechnya's key separatist leaders admitted: 'I do not rule out that we had links, but I can say that as of now our units no longer have any ties with bin Laden'.[20]

The Head of the Higher Committee of the Yemeni Reform Group told the newspaper *Al-Quds Al-Arabi* that

What took place in the cities of New York and Washington is a major crime and horrible terrorism that makes one shiver and which is rejected by all religions. No one but the devil can think up such an act which we along with every Muslim and anyone with a human conscience condemn and reject.[21]

Osama bin Laden, on the other hand, represented the attacks as legitimate warfare in the form of *jihad*. The statements of Osama bin Laden and his deputy, Ayman al-Zawahiri, are laden with moral and Quranic justifications for the reasons for resorting to war, the means employed, and the chosen targets. The following three chapters will explore those arguments and assess their consistency with the Islamic just war tradition of *jihad*, which includes contemporary Muslims' voices.

This chapter will deal with the specific *jus ad bellum* issue of just cause. Bassam Tibi is adamant that

the western distinction between just and unjust wars linked to specific grounds for war is unknown in Islam. Any war against unbelievers, whatever its immediate ground, is morally justified. Only in this sense can one distinguish just and unjust wars in Islamic tradition. . . . The usual western interpretation of *jihad* as a 'just war' in the western sense is, therefore, a misreading of the Islamic concept.[22]

One of the principal aims of this chapter is to dispute Tibi's supposition and to suggest that a just cause (beyond fighting unbelievers) is considered to be an urgent requirement for the waging of *jihad*. This is true of Islamic theory both historically and in the present day. Firstly, however, this chapter will provide a brief overview of the *jihad* tradition in Islam and propose that it be understood as a continually evolving ethic which morally enjoins war within limits.

4.1. JIHAD AS JUST WAR

Many key writings on *jihad* are infused with the spirit of the *hadith* (oral tradition)[23] which says that the 'true believers are those who strictly observe their moral code when they kill'. Ibn Taymiyyah, the renowned medieval jurist, argued in the thirteenth century that 'lawful warfare is essentially *jihad*'.[24] He wrote of 'permissible hostility'[25] and counselled that 'the commendable way to fight is with knowledge and understanding, not with the rash impetuosity of one who takes no thought and does not distinguish the laudable from the blameworthy'.[26] Quoting a series of Quranic injunctions 'regarding fairness and lack of animosity in the *jihad*', he concludes by referring to two verses which deal with both the manner in which war is conducted and the reasons for going to war: 'do not allow hatred of any people to incite you not to act fairly—that is closer to your duty' (5:8). 'Fight in God's cause those who fight you; but do not provoke hostility, for God does not love aggressors' (2:190).[27] In warning soldiers of 'going too far in the opposite direction and becom[ing] over-aggressive',[28] ibn Taymiyyah further suggests that the way in which a war is prosecuted can affect the justice of resorting to war in the first place.

Similarly connecting the *jus in bello* to the *jus ad bellum*, Sayyid Qutb argues that 'aggression also entails exceeding the moral and ethical limits set by Islam for fighting a just war'. In *Fi Dhilal al Quran*, he touches upon 'the code that governs war in Islam' and offers a selection of Islamic principles and conventions as proof of 'the nature of the Islamic approach to just war, hitherto unknown to human society'.[29] Al-Qaeda founder Abdullah Azzam refers to 'this rule of defence or *jihad*'[30] and demonstrates some preoccupation with the rules of warfare when he notes that issues such as 'the distribution of booty and treatment of prisoners of war' arose among the regiments of his *mujahidin*.[31] To twentieth-century scholars such as Majid Khadduri and the international lawyer Hasan Moinuddin, *jihad* is quite plainly 'the *bellum justum* of Islam'.[32]

Sayyid Abu Ala Mawdudi defines *jihad* as 'struggle in the way of God'. In his *tafsir*, a methodical exposition of the Quran's message, Mawdudi suggests that 'this attribute of God [the readiness to pardon] should be reflected in the behaviour of the believers as well....When the believers resort to armed conflict, they should do so not for the sake of quenching their thirst for vengeance but in the cause of God's religion'.[33] Thus, rather than being about holy war to enforce conversion, the notion of '*jihad fi sabil Allah*' (*jihad* in the way of God) can be understood as fighting for a just cause within limits. Indeed, Uthman Dan Fodio, the eighteenth-century *mujahid* of West Africa, advised his soldiers to avoid any actions that would compromise the spiritual value of the *jihad*. In an online *fatwa*, Sheikh Yusuf al-Qaradawi, whose 'appeal across the Muslim world is unparalleled',[34] reminds his readers:

In *sharia*, with all its sources—the Glorious Quran, the *sunna*, the consensus of the Muslim jurists—aggression and violation of human rights are completely forbidden....
In Islam, *jihad* is not to kill others or to deny their existence or their rights to live and develop their life. It is only a means of protection against any aggression or injustice.[35]

In this way, the fact of a Muslim's servitude to God can serve to limit—as opposed to enhance—the reasons for going to war and the zeal for punishing his enemies.

Of course, the historical record testifies to a number of belligerent and bloody wars fought under the banner of Islam. While the religion was still young the military successes of the Prophet's successors resulted in an empire that was as large as that of the Romans. Accordingly, 'one can say that during the first several centuries of Islam the interpretation of *jihad* was unabashedly aggressive and expansive'.[36] Such expansionism was entailed by two theoretical features of Islam. In the first place, the message of Islam is universal and addressed to all humanity. Thus, Islamic theory confers a duty to extend the borders of the faith with the end of achieving permanent peace—indeed, if any other territorial entities are recognized at all, it is only temporarily in apprehension of the inevitable triumph of Islam. A true Islamic state is, therefore, necessarily expansionist.

Secondly, and implicit in the foregoing discussion, is the union between religion and politics. In direct contrast to the Christian idea that the Kingdom of Christ is not of this world, the notion of '*din wa dunya*' is integral to the Quranic image of the polity. Sayyed Hassan Nasrallah proclaims that 'Islam is not just a simple religion that is limited to worship and religious observances... it is the answer to all the general and specific concerns of mankind'.[37] To Ayatollah Fadlallah, 'the separation between religion and state is like an amputation of a concept from itself'.[38] Islam is more than merely man's relationship to God—'it is a total way of life'.[39] Qaradawi notes that 'Islam is creed and legislation, religion and state, worship and leadership, prayer and *jihad*', emphasizing that 'Islam does not accept the rule "leave to Caesar what is Caesar's and to God what is God's"'.[40] Ayatollah Khomeini, too, bemoaned 'the ignoramuses' who consider 'Islam separate from government and politics', reminding that 'the Holy Quran and *sunnah* of the Prophet contain more rules regarding government and politics than in other matters'.[41] Ibn Taymiyyah observed that religion suffers without the coercion of the state while, without the discipline of revealed law, the state becomes tyrannical.

These aspects of the Islamic message combined with the tradition of tribal warring in the Arabian Peninsula,[42] the urgent need for unity and the exigencies of survival to result in a burst of furious, and remarkably successful, expansionism. But even under such circumstances, as Khadduri explains:

> The object of war was the achievement of an ultimate religious purpose and not the annihilation of the enemy; an invitation to accept Islam must therefore precede fighting. Muslim commanders were advised to negotiate if the enemy agreed to do so as an alternative to fighting. Even if Islam were not accepted, and the unbelievers agreed to pay tribute (if they were scripturaries), a peace treaty would become the basis of temporary relations. Unnecessary damage in the prosecution of war was disapproved of and practices such as killing noncombatants, mutilation, and treacherous acts were prohibited.[43]

Moreover, as the empire grew, going to war became less about fighting to spread the new religion, and more centred on conventional *raison d'état*: conflicts were begun by Caliphs for personal reasons, peace treaties were concluded with non-Muslim states, and, of course, Muslims began fighting each other.[44] What is more, the peaceful propagation of the faith proved hugely successful and 'people of the book', Jews and Christians, were tolerated in exchange for a poll tax, *jizya*, and limited rights of citizenship (the taking of a tributary tax was also the practice of the Byzantines and the Persian

Sasanians). Abdulaziz Sachedina points out that, though Islam's imperial wars were regarded as *jihad* by Sunni Muslim scholars, such wars were political 'with the aim of the expansion of Islamic hegemony and without the Quranic goal of religion being entirely God's'.[45]

It was under these highly politicized circumstances, where *jihad* was formulated as offensive warfare to extend the Islamic polity, that the key 'classical' juristic works on *jihad* were devised. However, even while a morally dubious just cause was in operation (fighting polytheism), war was considered a legal situation and *jus in bello* norms were developed, including commandments that would not look out of place today: 'there is no disagreement about the rule that it is forbidden to slay women and children provided that they are not fighting, for the women in that case [of fighting] may be slain'.[46] In addition, the concept of right authority was robust and the Muslim practice of issuing a notice of attack and then offering the enemy the chance to convert or live as a protected minority preceded the Hague rules on commencing hostilities by thirteen centuries. Furthermore, a more sophisticated conception of just cause was later developed, such that, by the late thirteenth century, ibn Taymiyyah construed the just war as the war for self-defence. After all, the Islamic tradition is in a state of permanent progression and it is not, as some would maintain, frozen into its classical manifestation.

As with the just war tradition of the West, interpretations of *jihad* in Islam have been intimately bound up with history. Despite Islam's universal mission to convert all of humanity, the ebb in the empire's fortunes required a rethink of the understanding of *jihad* as permanent war. Indeed, after twenty years of conquest in Europe, the Umayyad advance was curbed by the Franks at Poitiers in 732, and the push into Asia did not go farther east than India (Islam did not spread to the Malay world until much later). Thus, at an early stage the Muslims had to deal with and implicitly recognize non-Muslim states, climaxing with the Ottoman Empire's entry into the Concert of Europe in 1856. With the Mongol invasions in the thirteenth century, the ideology of conquest was quickly replaced by urgent theorizing about the duties of self-defence.

In the modern era, the impact of historical change upon abstraction can be seen with ideational reactions to imperialism. The crisis of colonialism brought an important calibration in the understanding of *jihad* as self-defence, as nineteenth-century 'modernists' like Mohammad Abduh construed the fact of colonial occupation as a form of aggression. In the twentieth century, the close connection between conceptions of *jihad* and local enemies further focused onto the repressive regimes that flourished in the wake of decolonization. With their literalist interpretations of the Quran and *sharia*, Islamic 'fundamentalists' lay blame for their authoritarian governments and the moral decay of society on secular nationalism and the neglect of the sacred duty of *jihad*. In the 1980s and 1990s, 'Islamist' movements in countries like Egypt and Algeria had declared war upon such governments, embroiling vast swathes of civilians and foreign tourists in their campaigns against 'western-backed' tyranny. In contrast to the bygone era of Islamic expansionism, by the end of the twentieth century *jihad* was primarily an inward thrust against the un-Islamic enemy at home. This cursory (and hugely incomplete) overview aims to suggest that the concept of *jihad* interacts with the specifics of history. It has mutated and been manipulated to suit the vagaries of time and place.

The *jihad* tradition, then, is neither static nor superficial, encompassing as it does a diversity of moral and legal[47] sources, voices, and responses to the needs of the community. It is a normative framework with a moral content which is deeply rooted in history. The evolution of tradition is enhanced in Islam by the absence of an ecclesiastical hierarchy. As Bruce Lawrence notes:

> *Jihad* is an especially complex category: not only does it have scriptural and juridicial usages, but its invocation as a Muslim duty has been contested within Islam. Moreover, those who contest it have equal claim to being devout Muslims.[48]

In arguing that Islam is a living tradition, John Kelsay points to '*sharia* reasoning', an Islamic field of discourse which is the principal mode by which Muslims attempt to forge links between the wisdom of previous generations and the challenges posed by contemporary life: 'those engaged in *sharia* reasoning cite texts, which are interpreted in connection with particular instances in the story Muslims tell about the beginnings and subsequent development of their tradition.'[49] It is a practice which has involved, over the centuries, a balance between continuity and creativity. Yet it is, in addition, an essentially open practice: the attempt to discern divine guidance in particular contexts through the interpretation of sources inevitably yields disagreement.[50]

Just as conceptions of *jihad* differ between time and place, within specific movements there is constant contestation over the boundaries of warfare in the name of Islam. For example, the Salafist Group for Preaching and Combat (GSPC) was, from the late 1990s onwards, implicated in a number of terrorist activities and massacres in Algeria. However, in 2002 it saw fit to issue a statement criticizing a *fatwa* by radical Palestinian cleric Abu Qatada, which deemed it legitimate to target the children of apostates. As considered in the introduction, there is, therefore, evidence of a normative consciousness in the most brutal of *jihadi* trends. This is also suggested by the Gama'at Islamiya's self-awareness following the 1997 massacre at Luxor: three days after claiming responsibility for the slaying of the 58 foreign tourists, the militant Egyptian group put out a second communiqué emphasizing that it would never deliberately target foreigners. It would seem that, irrespective of whether the ethical sentiments are internalized or not, there are moral standards that even terrorist groups feel the need to grasp for.

This chapter will suggest that al-Qaeda, too, feels itself constrained by the moral bounds of the *jihad*. The remainder of this chapter examines al-Qaeda's presentation of just cause, and upholds that it is rooted in the idea of self-defence. We will, accordingly, see how the *jus ad bellum* argument for reciprocity ('reciprocity[AB]') is set up by bin Laden. The claim of reciprocity for *jus in bello* ('reciprocity[IB]') will be taken up in Chapter 6.

4.2. JUST CAUSE

Osama bin Laden is all too often depicted as a fundamentalist and a salafist attempting to revive the *jihad* of the classical era. In reality, whatever his ultimate ambitions, his statements explaining the case for war against America are thoroughly modern—that is, they rely for the most part on the idea of resisting unprovoked aggression. Indeed, bin Laden is quite clear that 'he who commences hostilities is the unjust one'.[51] Under pressure from an *Al-Jazeera* journalist, he wondered: 'what is wrong with resisting those who attack you? All religious communities have such a principle, for example these Buddhists, both the North Koreans and the Vietnamese who fought America. This is a legal right . . . this is reassurance that we are fighting for the sake of God'.[52] The main argument of this section is that, although he must inevitably draw upon broader, religious elements of the *jihad* tradition to make an intelligible case against America, bin Laden actively seeks the legitimacy of defensive war by moulding his basic argument into the self-defence paradigm.

At various junctures both bin Laden and his deputy have recognized that this strategy is most in tune with Muslim opinion. In 1998, bin Laden acknowledged with strange candour that 'the real reasons why some—indeed all—of the Gulf states supported the Afghan *jihad* was that they saw it as self-defence. For they were themselves participants in the battle. After the Russians were defeated these states turned their backs completely and began—to my great regret—to publicly denounce the *jihad* and the *mujahidin*'.[53] Zawahiri demonstrates a similar realization. Writing a letter to Abu Musab al-Zarqawi,[54] to whom the internecine slaughter which developed in post-invasion Iraq was attributed, Zawahiri cautioned that 'the Muslim masses—for many reasons, and this is not the place to discuss it—do not rally except against an outside occupying enemy, especially if that enemy is firstly Jewish and secondly American. . . . The sectarian factor is secondary in importance to outside aggression'.[55]

Certainly, there is a robust tradition in Islam of limiting just war to defence against aggression. Rudolph Peters observes that 'by the end of the nineteenth century the idea that *jihad* is defensive warfare became current in the Middle East'.[56] This was due to the influence of Egyptian 'modernists' such as Mohammad Abduh and Rashid Rida, as well as Sayyed Ahmad Khan and Cheragh Ali in South Asia (with the latter complaining that 'all of the European commentators do not understand that the Koran does not teach a war of aggression, but had only, under the adverse circumstances, to enjoin a war of defence').[57] In the First World War, the Ottomans issued a *fatwa* calling for Muslims to join the fight against the Allies based on the fact that 'their warships and armies attack[ed] the Seat of the Islamic Caliphate and the Imperial Dominions'.[58] This emphasis was carried through into the twentieth century with Islamic scholars such as Mohammad Abu Zahra of al-Azhar who inferred that 'the Prophet fought only to repulse aggression'[59] and the prominent Shia cleric Murtada Matahhari who argued that 'the Quran has fundamentally defined *jihad* not as a war of aggression, of superiority, or of domination, but of resistance to aggression'.[60]

The defensive tendency was arguably strengthened by the colonialism endured by millions of Muslims, for the *jihad* tradition was mobilized for purposes of liberation. There was little question, therefore, of launching an offensive war to conquer other lands. As we have seen, after decolonization *jihad* was primarily invoked with reference to rebelling against secular tyrannical rulers at home, where 'oppression' was routinely elided with 'aggression' (e.g. Qutb: 'all victims of aggression and oppression have the right and duty to defend themselves and destroy their enemies').[61] When Iraq invaded Iran in 1980—which, interestingly, Saddam justified with the concept of 'legitimate preventive defence'[62]—the fledgling Islamic Republic's response was to declare a *jihad* 'in defence of Islam and the Muslims'.[63] However, it was the Israeli occupation of Palestine and the Soviet invasion of Afghanistan in 1979 which served to cement the conception of *jihad* as defence. In both cases a pan-Islamic consciousness was galvanized in support of the perceived Muslim victims. The rhetoric of resisting aggression abounded as the Islamic actors in both settings sought to use the language of defending Muslims against external attack in order to explain their *casus belli*.

The construction of *jihad* as self-defence is not confined to 'modernism', or indeed the modern era. Ibn Taymiyyah, who is, in Sunni circles, 'accepted as an authentic spokesman of Islam',[64] argued that 'we may only fight those who fight us when we make God's religion victorious' and took great pains to paint the Mongols as 'aggressors'.[65] In the sixteenth century, as the people of Malabar embarked upon an often suicidal *jihad* against their Portuguese colonizers, Zayn al-Din al-Ma'abri justified the action by underscoring that

Muslims had been attacked and slain in their own country, their trade had been badly damaged, and their mosques destroyed.[66] An early Sayyid Qutb upheld, in 1945 and prior to his imprisonment by Nasser, that 'when Islam commands war against infidel peoples, the command refers only to defensive war which is aimed at stopping aggression'.[67] Reflecting the political quietism of Twelver Shia, Nasr al-Din Tusi permitted Muslims to fight without the presence of the Imam only 'if they fear for their lives and if their borders are being attacked by enemies'.[68] Twelvers believe that offensive war is only permissible on the authority of the twelfth Imam, who went into occultation in the seventh century, for he alone can ensure that such a war is right. Thus, the Assassins, a millenarian Shia sect which waged a terror campaign against the religious establishment between the eleventh and thirteenth centuries, 'made extra-ordinary efforts to demonstrate that they acted defensively'.[69] Contemporary Shias, like Fadlallah, continue to counsel that '*al jihad al ibtida'ie* (offensive war) is not feasible before the reappearance of the twelfth Imam'.[70] Hence, Nasrallah explains Hizballah's war against Israel with the affirmation that 'the resistance is a reaction to the aggression'[71] and the conviction that 'we have to defend our country, so the reasons of our cause are justified'.[72]

Palestinian suicide bombings against Israelis, too, are justified by Hamas hardliners with the conviction that 'in the end, we believe [it] will stop their aggression against us' (Abdul Aziz Rantissi).[73] Whereas once its rallying call was for the return of the strict enforcement of the *sharia*, the reconstituted Taliban in Afghanistan, since 2002, also constructs its ideology based on the foundational claim that its cause consists of defending Afghans against NATO aggressors.[74] Meanwhile, across the border in Pakistan, the militant group Lashkar e-Taiba opened its 2008 conference to the sounds of the 'jihadi tarana' (*jihad* anthem), which describes *jihad* as 'the protection of the *umma*'.[75]

We will see that, in suggesting that al-Qaeda's war is defensive, bin Laden simultaneously relies upon and reaffirms a manifestly mainstream tradition of Islamic *jihad*. The understanding of just cause as self-defence is, in turn, echoed by those Muslims who denounce bin Laden and describe his *jihad* as aggressive. In other areas of the 'war on terror', too, the circumscription of just cause to cases of self-defence was articulated. For example, in the run-up to the US-led invasion of Afghanistan after 9/11, a senior Taliban official stated that '*jihad*, or holy war, would only be declared if America invaded Afghanistan or any other Islamic country'.[76] Likewise, the deputy chairman of Indonesia's Council of Ulemas observed that '*jihad* will only be done when the US has really attacked Afghanistan. If it has not, it will not be done'.[77]

4.3. RELIGIOUS DIFFERENCE AS GROUNDS FOR WAR

The Quran itself sends contradictory messages on the grounds for war—the first verse revealed in connection with *jihad* at 2:190 ('fight in the cause of Allah those who fight you, but do not transgress limits; for Allah loveth not transgressors')[78] can be offset against later belligerent verses such as 9:5 ('but when the forbidden months are past, then fight and slay the polytheists [*al-mushrikin*] wherever ye find them, and seize them, beleaguer them, and lie in wait for them in every stratagem of war'). This led to the controversy of 'abrogation' (*naskh*) in Islamic scholarship, whereby some maintained that the earlier 'verses of peace' were abrogated by the later 'verses of the sword'. In arguing that the provisions of the bloodier verses superseded those of the preceding peaceful ones, such jurists were not, it is worth noting, operating under the assumption that Allah had revealed contradictory messages—what was being abrogated was not the texts themselves but the legal rulings embedded in the texts.[79] The theory of abrogation has been shunned, however, by scholars, like those belonging to the nineteenth-century modernist movement, who emphasize that the Prophet's years in Mecca far outnumbered his years in Medina (after the Muslims emigrated from Mecca to Medina the tone of Quranic verses on *jihad* changed as it was presented more aggressively).

In the early period of Islam, the operative assumption was that all polytheists were hostile and must be subdued; that *shirk* was, by its nature, reprehensible and inexorably aggressive. But while Imam al-Shafi upheld the doctrine that polytheists could be fought on account of their unbelief, Abu Hanifa and ibn Malik never intimated that war could be waged for such reasons and stressed that tolerance should be shown unless the inhabitants of the *dar al-harb* (abode of war) came into conflict with *dar al-Islam* (abode of Islam).[80] As the tradition evolved, there emerged a distinct trend in *jihad* theorizing which correlates with the Augustinian notion that just wars are based on the wrongdoing of the opposing party. Consider ibn Taymiyyah, for example:

... it is necessary to have legal sanctions to protect religion and worldly interests against the wrong of the wrongdoer. As the exalted one said, 'sanction is given to those who fight because they have been wronged; God is indeed able to give them victory' (22:39). Thus He makes the fact that 'they have been wronged' the legitimate reason for punishing them by fighting them.[81]

Therefore, by the medieval period, the relevant feature of the polytheist invader was not the fact that he was polytheistic but the fact that he was invading. Indeed, opponents of abrogation employed a method known as *jam'* (harmonization) to argue that the verses outlining peaceful relations with non-Muslims provide the general rule in Islam, while the verses calling for fighting unbelievers represent cases in which an aggression had been committed against the Muslims.

In his commentary on verse 2:193 ('but if they desist let there be no hostility except to those who practise oppression'), Mawdudi points out that 'what is meant here by "desisting" is not the abandonment of unbelief and polytheism on the part of the unbelievers but rather their desistence from activity hostile to the religion'.[82] In this spirit, Fadlallah underlines that Hizballah's position against Israel 'does not emanate from an anti-Semitic complex; we are Semites ourselves. Even the Quran speaking negatively about the Jews did not refer to them as a race. The Quran meant certain practices and behaviours on their part'.[83] Though Jews are demonized in much anti-Israeli rhetoric, Fadlallah publicly draws attention to the objective crux of the conflict with Israel: 'the problem has nothing to do with Jews or non-Jews. It is simply a matter of returning the land to its rightful owners'.[84] When he argues that 'fighting is for the defence of the Muslims against the aggression of atheists',[85] Abdullah Azzam too suggests that the relevant characteristic of the unbeliever is his belligerent behaviour.

This current is complemented by an aversion towards religious compulsion in the Islamic tradition. While there were, no doubt, practical reasons behind such an impulse during the days of empire—namely, the income from the tax (*jizya*) levied on Jews and Christians in exchange for the right to practise their own faith[86]—there is a significant moral sanction in play. The attitude expressed in Quranic verse 2:256, which reads 'there is no compulsion in religion', is reinforced by the celebration of diversity at 49:13: 'O mankind! We created you male and female and made you into nations and tribes, that ye may know each other (not that ye may despise each other)'. Hence, Qutb inferred that 'forced religious conversion is the worst violation of a most inviolable human right. It is a much more heinous offence than murder'.[87] Tusi also directed that *jihad* for the purpose of religious conversion was a 'pernicious error',[88] and the prominent contemporary Islamic reformer Mohammad Shahrour argues that 'attacks on others in order to spread Islam is a deformed historical concept of *jihad*'.[89] Accordingly, Hamas' vision for an Islamic state involves making the land of Palestine safe for all religions.[90]

In Islam's early years, certainly, the conduct of some Arab conquerors gave rise to the depiction of Muslims as warriors wielding the Quran in one hand and the sword in the other, offering the vanquished a stark choice between Islam or death. The command to 'convert or die' was seen by some Muslims as an outgrowth of the Quranic right to propagate the religion. But Patricia

Crone argues that 'the stereotype is misleading'. In terms of Islamic theory, the question of whether defeated infidels should be forced to convert depended on what type of infidels they were. The *jizya* was offered to Christians and Jews, as fellow 'people of the Book', but the classification of pagan idolaters was more tricky. The Prophet was said to have confronted the Arab Pagans he encountered with the demand to embrace the religion or perish, but he accepted *jizya* from (Iranian) Zoroastrians in eastern Arabia. As a result, Shafi jurists argued from Mohammad's eradication of Arab idolaters to mean that all pagans, whatever their ethnicity, had to choose between Islam and death, while Maliki and Hanafi jurists upheld that non-Arab pagans should be offered *jizya* as the Zoroastrians were. In terms of Muslim practice, once a war was over, the institution of *jizya* promised the defeated peoples, pagans included, protected status and peace, and 'the conquered population at large rarely seems to have been given a choice between conversion and death....One should not think of *jihad* as something conducted along the lines of Charlemagne's forced conversion of the Saxons'.[91] M. Cherif Bassiouni, too, argues that after the threat to the Islamic nation's existence abated the propagation of Islam by peaceful means became the rule and not the exception.[92]

At first glance, Osama bin Laden appears to break with the tradition which emphasizes the aggressive aspect of the unbeliever's actions when declaring war upon him. Instead, he gives the impression of hating Jews and Christians on account of their religion alone. He talks of '*jihad* against world unbelief',[93] '*jihad* against the enemies of God',[94] 'the blessed strikes against global unbelief and its leader America',[95] and 'the duty of *jihad* to reassert the authority of God's word'.[96] This is more in line with radical fundamentalist groups such as Egypt's Tanzim al-Jihad, which assassinated President Sadat based on accusations about failing to apply *sharia* and concluding alliances with unbelievers.[97] Occasionally, bin Laden's implacable hatred is laid startlingly bare. For example:

Every Muslim, from the moment they realise the distinction in their hearts, hates Americans, hates Jews and hates Christians. This is part of our belief and part of our religion. For as long as I can remember I have felt tormented and at war, and have felt hatred and animosity for Americans.[98]

As an aside, it is worth noting that bin Laden made this statement in response to the allegation by a journalist that al-Qaeda had been funded by the CIA during the Afghan war against the Russians. His response is very defensive in tone. He tries a number of ways of accounting for the alliance, in the end settling upon an Islamic justification: 'when the Muslims were fighting the Byzantines during the fierce war between the Byzantines and the Persians, no one in their right mind could say that the Muslims were fighting as agents of the Persians'. Zawahiri is also eager to stress that 'the truth that everyone should learn is that the United States did not give one penny in aid to the *mujahidin*'.[99]

Bin Laden does demonstrate a religious loathing for his enemies. However, in the context of his entire case for war, the fact of America's Christianity is principally emphasized in conjunction with its alleged bellicosity. He argues that 'these people [jihadis] are resisting global unbelief that has *occupied our lands*'[100] and speaks of 'the brutal crusader *occupation* of the peninsula'[101] underlining that 'it is not acceptable in such a struggle that the crusader should *attack and enter my land* and holy sanctuaries and plunder Muslims' oil'.[102] Abu Ghaith, too, describes 'this disbelieving American beast which *wants to dominate violently* the world',[103] while Zawahiri refers to 'the kingdom of Satan that is *waging war upon us*'.[104] A comprehensive survey of bin Laden and Zawahiri's statements indicates that they centre their arguments on the fact of American and/or Israeli aggression.

4.4. AL-QAEDA'S DEFENSIVE JIHAD

Al-Qaeda's *jihad* is formulated as 'a defensive *jihad* against the American enemy'.[105] Bin Laden maintains that 'we ourselves are the victims of murders and massacres. We are only defending ourselves against the United States'.[106] In a letter addressed to the American public he states plainly that 'as for the question why are we fighting and opposing you, the answer is very simple: because you attacked us and continue to attack us'.[107] Similarly, Zawahiri urges his fellow Muslims to 'eject the enemies from our homes and seize our rights with the power of *jihad*'[108] and describes 9/11 as 'that resistance which reached its peak with the two blessed battles of New York and Washington'.[109] He gives a message to the American people in the run-up to the 2004 US Presidential elections: 'Elect whoever you want, Bush, Kerry or Satan himself. We don't care. We care about purifying our country of the aggressors and resisting anyone who attacks us'.[110]

For bin Laden and Zawahiri, al-Qaeda's defensive *jihad* is perfectly in line with Islamic teaching. Zawahiri explains that 'resistance is a duty imposed by the *sharia*',[111] and bin Laden reminds that 'the highest priority after faith is to repel the invading enemy'.[112] He is careful to underline that his command to 'kill the Americans and their allies—civilian and military' is 'in accordance with the word of God Almighty: fight the idolaters at any time if they first fight you'.[113] Again, he quotes the Quran in the context of a defensive message: 'those who have been attacked are permitted to take up arms because they have been wronged—God has the power to help them to victory (22:39)'.[114] He elaborates that 'it is commanded by our religion and intellect that the oppressed have a right to respond to aggression: do not expect anything from us but resistance, *jihad* and revenge'.[115] In fact, *jihad* is portrayed as a natural and instinctive reaction as 'these living beings [Muslims] have been given an inner sense that rejects any intrusions by outsiders. . . . If an armed person enters a chicken's home with the aim of inflicting harm to it, the chicken would automatically fight back'.[116] Abu Ghaith uses a similar metaphor: 'does the prey not have the right, when it is bound and being dragged to its slaughter, to escape? Does it not have the right, as it is being slaughtered, to lash out with its foot? Does it not have the right, after it is slaughtered, to attack its slaughterer with its blood?'[117]

Bin Laden draws upon the authority of ibn Taymiyyah repeatedly with respect to just cause, and each of these references deals with 'unconditionally fighting the attacking enemy',[118] 'repel[ing] the invading enemy',[119] 'repelling the aggressive enemy',[120] and 'fighting to repel an enemy'.[121] Indeed, bin Laden compares members of the American administration directly to the Mongols:

This Rumsfeld, the butcher of Vietnam, is responsible for the deaths of two million, as well as injuries to many others. As for Cheney and Powell, they have reaped more murder and destruction in Baghdad than Haluga the Tartar.[122]

This argument for moral equivalence between the United States and the attacking Mongols is similar to the comparison touched upon in Chapter 1, where Bush equated his invasion of Iraq with the Allies' stand against Hitler. These examples appear to be the gold standards of self-defence within their respective traditions. It is worth noting, in addition, that bin Laden makes a cross-traditional appeal to the Hitler case, exclaiming suddenly in an interview: 'did not the Europeans resist the German occupation in World War Two?'[123]

4.4.1. Reciprocity[AB]

In effect, al-Qaeda's self-defence arguments appeal to the principle of reciprocity at the *jus ad bellum* level. Bin Laden formulates this himself, stating that 'the road to safety begins with the cessations of hostilities and reciprocal treatment is a part of justice'.[124] That is, because the United States is 'attacking' the Muslims, the Muslims have a right to respond: 'it is well known that every action has a reaction. If the American presence continues, and that is an action, then it is natural for reactions to continue against this presence. In other words, explosions and killings of American soldiers will continue'.[125] Sayf al-Adil, an important al-Qaeda military leader, described the primary objective of 9/11 as retaliation against the United States for its aggression in the Muslim world.[126] The invocation of reciprocity allows al-Qaeda to emphasize that it is not the aggressor, because 'what is happening in occupied Palestine, and what happened on September 11 and March 11 are your goods returned to you. It is well known that security is a vital necessity for every human being. We will not let you monopolise it for yourselves'.[127] In this way, bin Laden and Zawahiri appeal to the idea of fairness because 'what America is tasting today is but a fraction of what we have tasted for decades'[128] and 'you have created rivers of blood in our countries so we blew up volcanoes of rage in your countries'.[129] It is imperative that 'as they kill us, without a doubt we have to kill them until we obtain a balance in terror. This is the first time in recent years that the balance of terror has evened out'.[130]

Thus, bin Laden uses reciprocity to appeal to both fairness and fear, as 'the time has come to settle accounts. Just as you kill, so you shall be killed; just as you bomb, so you shall be bombed. And there will be more to come'.[131] Bin Laden argues for a direct correlation between US aggression towards Muslims and further attacks against US interests, opining that 'whoever encroaches upon the security of others and imagines he will himself remain safe is but a foolish criminal'.[132] The Americans have, in a sense, forfeited their right to security through their actions, because 'a criminal or robber who enters the countries of others in order to steal should expect to be exposed to murder at any time'.[133] For bin Laden, this is profoundly rational: 'by what logic does your blood count as real and ours as no more than water?'[134]

This notion of reciprocity, of 'reacting in kind',[135] serves to define al-Qaeda's just cause very narrowly, in terms of resisting aggression. Contained within this argument, therefore, are the conditions for the cessation of hostilities—to wit, stop attacking us and we'll stop attacking you. Bin Laden observes that 'whichever state does not encroach upon our security thereby ensures its own'.[136] He counsels the US public that 'if you could avoid perpetrating these injustices, you Americans would be on the right path towards the security you enjoyed before September 11. This is what I can say about war and its reasons'.[137] With the foregoing statements, bin Laden implies that al-Qaeda's resort to war is a paradigmatic case of self-defence. At bottom, 'it's a very simple equation that any American child could understand: live and let others live'.[138]

Given that America had not launched any invasion of bin Laden's country (be it Saudi Arabia, Sudan, or Afghanistan)[139] before 11 September, the theory of bin Laden's defensive war did not sit easily with the reality of the international situation. As a result, it was incumbent upon bin Laden to qualify 'aggression' in two critical ways.

4.4.2. Qualification 1: the expansive conception of 'self'

Bin Laden must employ an expansive conception of the territorial entity that is being defended against attack. To that end, he draws upon the universalism of the Islamic message to demarcate the relevant unit: the entire Islamic *umma*. The concept of statehood, as distinct from the society or community, is not to be found in the Quran. Moreover, the Quran advocates racial equality and the Prophet did not recognize ethnic differences among the believers. While pan-Islamism is not a Ladenese innovation in itself, its mobilization by a *jihadi* group as grounds for war is certainly distinctive. Causes like those of the Palestinians and the Afghanis had stirred pan-Islamic sentiments, no doubt, but this was in *response* to the occupation of Palestine by Israel and the invasion of Afghanistan by the Soviets. For al-Qaeda, the aggressive act itself is rooted in pan-Islamism. America, it is argued, has invaded the *umma*.

Bin Laden takes his pan-Islamic cue from al-Qaeda's founder, Abdullah Azzam, who lamented in 1984 that 'unfortunately, when we think about Islam we think nationally. We fail to let our vision pass beyond geographic borders that have been drawn up for us by the *Kuffar*'.[140] Bin Laden follows his mentor in mobilizing the vocabulary of a popular *hadith* by decrying aggression 'against even a hand's span of Muslim land'.[141] Azzam had urged the whole *umma* to rally in protection of 'this organ which is exposed to the onslaught of a microbe'.[142] However, Azzam's main concern was recruiting for the Afghani resistance against the Soviet invasion—a definite act of aggression that had already occurred at a specific time and place. Bin Laden's agenda, on the other hand, is to establish the act of aggression in the first place.

Bin Laden told the International Conference of Deobandis in April 2001 that 'I write these lines to you at a time when every single inch of our *umma's* body is being stabbed by a spear, struck by a sword, or pierced by an arrow'.[143] This is surely an implicit reference to the *hadith* which describes 'the believers, in their love, mutual kindness, and close ties [as] like one body; when any part complains, the whole body responds to it with wakefulness and fever'. Accordingly, al-Qaeda's leader later painted '9/11 [as] merely a response to the continuous injustices inflicted upon our sons in Palestine, Iraq, Somalia, Southern Sudan and places like Kashmir'.[144] Indeed, bin Laden's list is sprawling. In his 'Declaration of *Jihad*' against America in 1996 he makes the point that Muslim blood is regarded as cheap by referring to a series of 'massacres' in Lebanon, Tajikistan, Burma, Kashmir, Assam, the Philippines, Fatani, Ogaden, Somalia, Eritrea, Chechnya, and Bosnia-Herzegovina. In 2001, he reiterates that 'every day, from east to west, our *umma* of 1200 million Muslims is being slaughtered in Palestine, in Iraq,[145] in Somalia, Western Sudan, Kashmir, the Philippines, Bosnia, Chechnya and Assam'.[146]

Needless to say, not one of these cases involves the flagrant American aggression upon which bin Laden rests his rationale of self-defence. This will be considered further in Section 4.4.3. The point here is that bin Laden seeks to manipulate 'the unity of Islam, which neither recognises race nor colour, nor does it pay any heed to borders and walls'[147] to imply that the United States has waged war on the Muslims. Al-Qaeda's case for war is not intended to be an indictment of US foreign policy as underhanded and irresponsible—it is quite clear that bin Laden seeks to portray his cause as a traditional case of self-defence: 'we ... advise you to pack up your luggage and get out of our lands'.[148] However, in attempting to construct his just cause as narrow (that is to say, defence against aggression), bin Laden falls back on broader ideas about religious difference. In conceptualizing the 'self' that has been attacked, bin Laden employs a religious demarcation: the Islamic *umma*.

4.4.3. Qualification 2: the expansive conception of 'attack'

Bin Laden must resort to religious idioms again when defining the US's aggressive actions. His main bone of contention is with 'the invasion by the American and western Crusader forces of the Arabian peninsula and Saudi Arabia, the home of the noble Ka'ba'.[149] Apparently, 'the US transgressed in its aggression until it reached the *qibla* of the Muslims in the whole world'.[150] He speaks repeatedly of 'this bare-faced occupation',[151] but, since US troops were not occupying Saudi Arabia and instead kept a military presence there on the invitation of the regime, he must explain their aggression religiously: 'the Noble sanctuary is attacked and the direction of prayer for 1200 million Muslims is attacked'.[152] Thus, the US 'attack' is ultimately figurative, for 'the sacred symbols have been looted'[153] and the Holy territories are 'defiled'[154] as American troops roam the lands which are 'the cornerstone of the Islamic world, place of revelation, source of the Prophetic mission and home of the Noble Ka'ba'.[155]

The 'occupation' of Saudi Arabia is not limited, however, to the Christian military presence in the lands of Islam. Though he favours religious imagery, bin Laden also refers to US support for the Saudi monarchy and its regional policies: 'America has occupied the holiest parts of the Islamic lands, the Arabian peninsula, plundering its wealth, dictating to its leaders, humiliating its people, terrorising its neighbours and turning its bases there into a spearhead with which to fight the neighbouring Muslims'.[156] The concern with Saudi Arabia on bin Laden's part is logical, given that it was his country. In short, he can appear less like an interloper, or an opportunist latching onto some other people's cause. However, it has been considered that bin Laden must, in addition, draw upon other 'Islamic' causes to bolster his claim of outright aggression.

We considered the litany of conflicts in which the United States was said to have manifested its aggression, but all of these claims do not stand up to scrutiny. It is difficult to divine how America might be held to account for issues like the Burmese ethnic cleansing or the Eritrean independence struggle, and the charge that America 'supported the Serbs massacring the Muslims in Bosnia'[157] is contradicted by the fact that the US intervention in 1995 swung the balance of power back in favour of the Muslims. The flimsiness of bin Laden's argument is crudely apparent when he lists the aforementioned massacres in the 'Declaration of *Jihad*' and must conclude, with a relatively anticlimactic flourish, that the United States 'has prevented the dispossessed from arming themselves'. In order to gloss over the fact that no flagrant aggression has been committed (arguably, at least, until the 2003 invasion of Iraq), he resorts to rhetorical flourishes that emphasize the religiosity of the Americans: 'the evident Crusader hatred in this campaign against Islam';[158] 'the Crusader hordes that have spread like locusts';[159] 'the Romans [that] have gathered under the banner of the cross to fight the nation of beloved Mohammad'.[160]

The most cogent of bin Laden's illustrations is the example of Palestine. As Bruce Reidel has remarked, 'the Palestinian cause is the centrepiece of al-Qaeda's narrative of Western Crusader aggression against the *umma*'.[161] Bin Laden's case is again imbued with religious terminology, as he frequently speaks of striving to 'liberate the al-Aqsa mosque'[162] and makes reference to America 'helping Israel build new settlements in the point of departure for our Prophet's midnight journey to the seven heavens'.[163] In fact, because of the Israeli–Palestinian conflict, and the US support for Israel, bin Laden can posit the existence of a 'Zionist-Crusader alliance'[164] and 'a neo-Crusader-Jewish campaign'.[165] In this way, the United States, as Israel's steadfast ally and superpower backer, can be implicated in the killing of hundreds of thousands of Muslims: 'the Zionist-American alliance was mowing down our sons and our people in the blessed land of al-Aqsa, at the hands of the Jews but with American planes and tanks'.[166] In explanation for the 9/11 attacks, he wondered how 'the poor mothers of Palestine [can] bear the murder of their children at the hands of the oppressive Jewish policemen with American support, American aeroplanes and tanks? Those who distinguish between

America and Israel are true enemies of the *umma*.[167] Zawahiri maintains that some 22,497 tons of weapons, equipment, and ammunition were airlifted to Israel during the 1973 Arab–Israeli war, and maintains that 'this tipped the balance of military power in favour of Israel'.[168] Hence, bin Laden and Zawahiri assert that America is directly responsible for harm against Muslims through its unholy alliance with Israel.

In the end, al-Qaeda must enlist religious criteria to demarcate the 'self' that is being attacked as well as the actions which constitute an invasion. Prior to the war on Iraq in 2003, bin Laden had little to work with in suggesting that the United States had launched an unprovoked assault (after the US-led invasion, however, al-Qaeda allies in Iraq like the Abu Hafs al-Masri Brigades could more easily affirm that 'if an enemy enters a single inch of the Muslims' land, then it becomes the Muslims' duty to fight until they get the enemy out').[169] By throwing together a host of international injustices framed in Islamic terms, bin Laden avoided having to pin down any single act of aggression, and could instead claim that there was an overall war against Islam: 'Bush has declared in his own words "Crusade attack". The odd thing about this is that he has taken the words right out of our mouth'.[170]

Upon close examination, bin Laden's double qualification on aggression appears to play upon two important elements of the *jihad* tradition. Indeed, it could be said that there are two lines of thought which serve as precedents for al-Qaeda's war in defence of Islam against the worldwide subjugation of Muslims: *jihad* in defence of religion and *jihad* against oppression.

4.4.4. Defending religion and resisting oppression

Firstly, bin Laden appeals to the custom permitting *jihad* in defence of religion. It has been commonly argued that Muslims can fight those who obstruct the practice or propagation of the faith. Defending religion is an important condition for peace, as is evident in the writings of 'modernists' as well as twentieth-century 'radicals' or 'fundamentalists'. Hasan al-Bana, the Muslim Brotherhood's founder, argued that *jihad* was made incumbent 'not as a means of aggression nor as a vehicle for personal desires but in order to protect the proclamation [of Islam] as a surety for peace'.[171] Qutb, his disciple, staunchly advocated freedom of belief and argued that Muslims could defend themselves in the face of 'suppression of religious freedom'.[172] As such, the protection of religion is often subsumed under 'self-defence'. For example, Al-Azhar's current Grand Imam maintains that '*jihad* was legitimized to enable people to defend themselves, their religion, property and honour'.[173] His predecessor, Sheikh Mahmoud Shaltout, contended in 1948 that *jihad* was confined to repelling aggression, protecting the Islamic mission, and defending religious freedom.[174] It is worth noting that the link between *jihad* and the protection of religion also served to circumscribe the cause for conflict. In British-controlled India, Sayyed Ahmad Khan urged his followers to be obedient subjects and decreed that *jihad* only became obligatory when the colonial authorities actively obstructed practices of worship.

Secondly, bin Laden's case for war refers to the close connection between *jihad* and the battle against political tyranny. He argues for a defensive *jihad* in the face of oppression—a line of thought which is certainly consistent with some modern articulations of justified *jihad*. Mawdudi, writing on behalf of the Muslim minority in pre-partition India, defined *jihad* as 'war waged solely in the name of Allah and against those who perpetrate oppression as enemies of Islam'.[175] In the Arab world's decolonization movements, this association was mobilized to great effect, as with the Algerian mantra: 'Islam is my religion, Arabic is my language, Algeria is my country'.[176] The Iranian revolution against the Shah, which marked a dramatic rupture in the Shia tradition of political quietism, revived the fight against state injustice that was begun by Ali and Hussein.[177] Moreover, Islamist groups such as the Muslim Brothers in Egypt, Hamas in the Palestinian territories, and Hizballah in Lebanon cut their teeth supplying welfare services to struggling communities neglected by the authorities. Even Mohammad Shahrour, a modern reformer and tireless critic of Islamic fundamentalism, upholds that '*jihad* is justified in only two cases: to defend the homeland or to fight for freedom and justice'.[178] Thus, *jihad* has been entwined with social justice at home; it is not completely confined to justice between states.

However, it becomes clear that the constructions of *jihad* in defence of religion and to throw off oppression were designed to deal with local, 'national', situations. As *jihad* was revived in the nineteenth and twentieth centuries, its mandate was largely domestic—it was marshalled in the face of colonial administrations and unrepresentative regimes which sought to suppress Islam. Yet, in bin Laden's arguments, these two local concerns subtly underpin the justification for *international* war; they inform both of his qualifications on 'aggression'. Essentially, he must seize upon general notions of oppression and religion under threat to establish that Muslims have a right to fight back. But, bin Laden's claims err substantially from the purposes for which such understandings about *jihad* were devised. *Jihad* in defence of religion referred to situations in which Muslims were persecuted for their beliefs, and their rights of worship were infringed. *Jihad* to resist oppression was intended to throw off the yoke of brutal governments, and, in any case, it has been hotly contested as a justification for war by those who would go to any lengths to stave off *fitna*.[179] At bottom, bin Laden's arguments do not properly conform to either of these traditions of *jihad*. It is unsurprising, then, that the 9/11 attacks were widely perceived as illegitimate and aggressive.

4.4.5. Bin Laden as aggressor

In his famous *fatwa* of February 1998, which announced the creation of the World Islamic Front, bin Laden describes, among other things, 'the brutal Crusader occupation of the Peninsula', America's 'excessive aggression' against the people of Iraq, the 'occupation of Jerusalem', and the fact America serves 'the interests of the petty Jewish state'. What's more, his argument goes, 'they are trying to repeat the horrific massacres'. He concludes that 'all these American crimes and sins are a clear proclamation of war against God, his messenger, and the Muslims'.[180] Other voices from within the Islamic tradition, however, vigorously denied that any such proclamation had been made.

To Qaradawi's mind, on 9/11 bin Laden was 'the aggressor'.[181] A well-known advocate of suicide bombing in the Palestinian territories, Qaradawi draws a firm distinction, commenting that 'the difference is huge. What happens in Palestine is self-defence. But in 9/11 they were not fighting an invasion'.[182] The Grand Imam of al-Azhar, Mohammad Tantawi, similarly described 9/11 as 'an abominable aggression'. He stated that the attacks were 'an inhuman crime that no religion, law, or sound mind approves, because they constitute an aggression against male and female and Muslim and Christian civilians who have nothing to do with wars'.[183] A group of Arab NGOs also referred to the assaults on New York and Washington as an 'aggressive attack against American civilians',[184] and a statement released by Hizballah deemed the perpetrators to have 'committed aggression and terrorism'.[185] Egyptian Mufti Nasr Farid Wasel declared that 'Islam and Muslims do not approve of the September 11 aggression on the United States',[186] while an Egyptian newspaper noted that 'true Islam stresses that we must stand by those who fight for their usurped lands and defend their countries, themselves and their sacred shrines, because their cause is just. . . . But what bin Laden says is self-propagandistic and manifests his isolation and apprehensions'.[187] Sheikh Abdul Aziz al-Sheikh, Saudi Arabia's pre-eminent cleric, decreed in response to the attacks that 'those who kill non-Muslims with whom Muslims have treaties will never see paradise'.[188]

The Palestine conflict can be considered the linchpin of bin Laden's position that an aggressive Crusader assault had been waged against the *umma*. But the leadership of Hamas, the popular Islamic movement from within the territories, underlined after 9/11 that 'the Hamas strategy consists of fighting against the Zionist occupier in Palestine. . . . We are not looking to extend the conflict outside of Palestine'.[189] Likewise, Jerusalem Grand Mufti Ikrema Sabri indicated that bombings were not acceptable outside of Israel.[190] In this way, the 9/11 attacks elicited condemnation that was over and above horror at the mass targeting of civilians—the argument that the United States had already launched an attack was shunned and the hijackers were regarded as the aggressors.

Thus, bin Laden's arguments for self-defence employed criteria that were unacceptably broad to the minds of others within the Islamic tradition. Though artful, the expansive conceptualizations of 'self' and 'attack' did not amount to a convincing case for the resort to war. In fact, al-Qaeda's own arguments often moved away from the defensive line towards talk of a 'clash of civilizations'. However, we shall see that this position is pursued in furtherance of the case for self-defence, rather than despite it.

4.5. MANICHAEISM

One potential and compelling counter to my argument is bin Laden's stated belief in the ineluctable conflict between Islam and the West. There is, no doubt, a stark Manichaean element to the pronouncements of al-Qaeda. Bin Laden claimed that the entire world was split into two camps 'one of faith, with no hypocrites, and one of unbelief'.[191] Wondering why nations such as Germany and Australia had joined the US coalition against al-Qaeda, bin Laden concluded that the West was 'reviving the Crusades. Richard the Lionheart, Barbarossa from Germany and Louis from France—the case is similar today, when they all immediately went forward the day Bush lifted the cross'.[192] He explained on 3 November 2001 that

this war is fundamentally religious in nature . . . those who try to hide this clear and evident reality, which the entire world knows to be true, are deceiving the Islamic nation and trying to deflect attention from the real nature of the struggle. This reality is established in the book of God Almighty and in the teachings of the Prophet. We cannot ignore the enmity between us and the infidels, since it is a doctrinal one . . . So the issue is one of faith and doctrine, not of a 'war on terror'.[193]

Moreover, he contends that 'this clash of civilisations is a very clear matter, proven in the Quran and the traditions of the Prophet'.[194] Accordingly, 'the conflict between right and falsehood will continue until judgement day'.[195]

However, such proclamations sit in marked contrast to the argument for 'reciprocity', which implies that the conflict is a clear matter of defence in the face of ongoing aggression. For example, when asked on 12 November 2001 whether he was against the American people, bin Laden affirmed he was not and that al-Qaeda was only defending Muslims. He went on to observe that 'many in the west are polite and good people. The American media are inciting them against Muslims but some of these good people are against the American attacks. . . . So good people are everywhere'.[196] Further, in April 2004, he offered a peace proposal to the people of Europe 'which is essentially a commitment to cease operations against any state that pledges not to attack Muslims or intervene in their affairs'.[197] Such overtures contradict, somewhat, his more bloody presumption of an eternal and inevitable battle between the west and Islam: 'your reprimand to the Crusaders should be just as the poet said, "all there is between you and me is the piercing of kidneys and smiting of necks"'.[198]

At times, Zawahiri also subscribes to the 'clash of civilizations' theory, declaring that 'we must never lay down our arms'[199] and 'the greatest battle of Islam in this era will happen according to what appeared in the *hadiths* of the Messenger of God about the epic battles between Islam and atheism'.[200] However, in claiming that al-Qaeda is merely defending Muslims against ongoing attacks, he suggests that America has a choice in the matter by opting to either treat Muslims with respect 'or as if our lives and property are available for you to invade'.[201] In the same way, Abu Ghaith outlines 'a conflict between the good and evil', but he elaborates that this is contingent upon America's actions: 'as long as America insists on this oppressive and unfair policy against the Muslims . . . we won't stop attacking them anywhere in the entire world'.[202]

The 'clash of civilizations' component of al-Qaeda's thought is noticeably more pronounced after the 11 September attacks. Though the reasons for this are inaccessible, one possible account might involve the rhetoric employed by the Bush administration in response to the attacks. That is, Bush's use of the word 'Crusade' and his declaration of an ultimate battle between good and evil was treated as confirmatory evidence of the need for Muslims to defend themselves. As such, al-Qaeda's Manichaeism is ultimately employed to confer even more legitimacy upon the self-defence argument: 'Bush admitted that there can only be two kinds of people. . . . So the world today is split into two parts, as Bush said "either you are with us or you are with terrorism". Either you are with the Crusade or you are with Islam. Bush's image today is of him being in the front of the line, yelling and carrying the big cross'.[203] Abu Ghaith echoed this when he observed 'they have announced explicitly that this is a Crusader war so the banner is clear and henceforth there is only the trench of faith or the trench of unbelief'.[204] It would seem that bin Laden wants to maintain that civilizations must clash because the West will always attack. He is insistent that America 'carries the unspeakable Crusader hatred for Islam'[205]—thus, 'this third world war was started by the Crusader-Zionist coalition against the Islamic nation'.[206]

CONCLUSION

The recognition of an inevitable civilizational conflict is a supporting, secondary argument to that of self-defence. As was considered earlier in the chapter, the relevant feature of the 'global Crusader' is the fact of his invasion. Moreover, any inevitability of such a war rests on the fact that the 'global Crusader' will never desist from his aggressive ways. Therefore, al-Qaeda's defensive argument is not undercut by Manichean statements describing a definitive battle between Islam and the West; it is supported by them.

Al-Qaeda's quest for a defensive *jihad* is a strong testament to the durability of the tradition which says that Muslims must only fight when they are attacked. In his impressive survey of the *jihad* tradition, Rudolph Peters remarks:

... modernist authors underline the defensive aspect of *jihad* and hold that *jihad* outside Islamic territory is only permitted when the peaceful propagation of Islam is being hindered or when Muslims living among unbelievers are oppressed. Fundamentalist writers, on the other hand, do not depart to a great extent from the classical doctrine and emphasise the expansionist aspect.[207]

This chapter, however, suggests that al-Qaeda falls outside of the dichotomy between 'modernist' and 'fundamentalist' *jihad*: though it is an organization comprised of 'fundamentalists', its cause for war against the United States and its allies is categorically modern.

Bin Laden and Zawahiri are certainly keen to indicate that, in prosecuting their war, they are inside the Islamic fold. In describing al-Qaeda, bin Laden underscores:

We are the children of an Islamic Nation, with the Prophet Mohammad as its leader; our Lord is one, our Prophet is one, our direction of prayer is one, we are one *umma*, and our Book is one. . . . We aren't separate from the *umma*. We are the children of an *umma*, and an inseparable part of it.

When the interviewer goes on to ask what bin Laden has to say about the strong criticism levelled against him by Arab states, bin Laden responds by reiterating: 'I assure you that we are a part of this *umma*'.[208] Though al-Qaeda bombers are dubbed 'extremist lunatic fringes, as crazy as those crazies in America who go to the post office and shoot people at random',[209] its leaders are desperate to represent their cause as authentically Islamic. As a result, rather than ignoring centuries of tradition on Islamic *jihad*, al-Qaeda's ideologues try, however unsuccessfully, to engage it.

This chapter has resisted bassam Tibi's assumption that 'the distinction between just and unjust war is alien to Islam'.[210] The classical period of expansion certainly lacked a meaningful just cause, but the *jus in bello* evolved at that time, and we have seen that a more restrictive just cause was developed in subsequent centuries. Indeed, at the dawn of the twenty-first century, two hugely influential clerics associated with both Sunni and Shia radicalism each suggested bin Laden might be 'tried by an Islamic court consisting of Muslim *ulema*' for the war he waged upon America on 11 September.[211]

5

Jus Ad Bellum in Al Qaeda's Jihad

This chapter continues the discussion of al-Qaeda's *jus ad bellum*. Chapter 4 argued that, although inconsistent with reality, al-Qaeda elaborates its just cause in terms of self-defence. In bin Laden's worldview, 'Uncle Sam' was engaging in 'reckless transgressions'.[1] America is rendered a legitimate target not because al-Qaeda hates freedom—'perhaps [Bush] can tell us why we did not attack Sweden, for example?'[2]—but because 'America heads the list of aggressors against the Muslims'.[3] While this argument sought the legitimacy of a narrow case of defensive war, it was ultimately dependent upon dubious conceptions of aggressive actions and the relevant entity under attack. As a result, prominent Muslim figures eschewed bin Laden's claims and cast al-Qaeda as the aggressor on 9/11.

Chapter 4 also indicated that the *jihad* tradition is comprised of a multivalent body of thought with diverse roots. Bin Laden is certainly aware of the existence of such a tradition:

We are now in the fifteenth century of this great religion, whose complete and comprehensive methodology has clarified the dealings between one individual and another, the duties of the believer towards God, and the relationship between the Muslim country and other countries in times of peace and war. If we look back at our history we will find that there were many types of dealings between the Muslim nation and the other nations in peacetime and wartime, including treaties and matters to do with commerce. So it is not a new thing that we need to create. Rather, it already exists.[4]

Moreover, he tries to position his case for war inside it. This chapter will examine that case by considering three further aspects of al-Qaeda's *jus ad bellum*: right authority, last resort, and reasonable hope of success.

5.1. RIGHT AUTHORITY

Proper authority in waging *jihad* was designed as the decisive test of a conflict's legitimacy. The authority question was central to classical theories of *jihad* which maintained that war could only be lawful if declared by a rightful ruler who is responsible for assessing the war's moral mandate. As with the medievalists of just war theory, the predominating concern was to arrogate the use of justified coercion exclusively to the state apparatus, thus guarding against rebellion and thuggery. In Sunni political theory, the caliph served as the executive head of government but, unlike Mohammad, he had no prophetic functions and his legitimacy was derived from implementing Islamic law and obedience to Allah. For Shia, on the other hand, the rightful leader of the *jihad* was imbued with spiritual attributes which rendered *jihad* in his absence a technical impossibility. The Hidden Imam is believed to have special qualities that enable him to mediate between the human world and Allah's kingdom. In this vein, Tusi argued that 'it is imperative that the Imam should be the one to commence *jihad* against unbelievers. After all, the Imam is endowed with the knowledge of the will of God, and he is infallible. Only he can guarantee that the *jihad* will not lead to the nullification of the cause for which it is undertaken'.[5] Although Shiism and Sunnism assume very different traits in the leader of lawful *jihad* (the former divine, the latter pragmatic), both sought to limit violence to the authoritative enforcement of God's law against outsiders.

Such a circumscription of the right to declare *jihad* has never been without controversy. From the violent challenge to the caliphate mounted by the Khariji sect in the seventh century to the problem of fighting the ostensibly Muslim Mongol usurpers in the thirteenth century, the authority doctrine has been put under pressure. However, it was the end of the Ottoman Empire and the corresponding collapse of the caliphate in 1924 that presented Muslims with the most dramatic crisis of authority. Consider Qaradawi:

The most serious problem of the Muslims and their minorities scattered all over the world is that our Muslim *umma*, expansive and large in numbers as it is, has no leadership that can order it to move, stop, cry or keep silent, or turn right or left ... We have lost the caliphate and we have found no other system to replace it, so we have lived without any leadership of any kind ... We Muslims have neither a caliph to obey nor a 'Pope' to listen to. We are like orphans turned away from every door they knock at.[6]

Spurred by similar existential anxiety, Islamic groups emerged that were self-consciously political. The Muslim Brothers, for example, 'formed their society in Egypt in order to reclaim Islam's political dimension, which had formerly resided in the person of the caliph'.[7] That other, more fanatical Muslim organizations have proliferated in the century since the caliphate's demise is unsurprising, given that the arena was, by its nature, unregulated, and Islam gradually became 'objectified'.[8] As Tilman Seidensticker has pointed out, the lack of central religious authority is a factor of primary importance in several waves of attacks in the Islamic world, and 'the most influential (re-)thinkers of Islam in the last century were autodidacts'.[9]

5.1.1. Jihad as an individual duty

Right authority in the *jihad* tradition hangs on a pivotal distinction developed by classical Islam. The early jurists decreed that, in contrast to offensive wars which require the caliph's sanction, defensive *jihads* do not require the authority, nor even the existence, of a central Islamic sovereign: 'defensive warfare remained legitimate whether there was an Imam or not according to all'.[10] In addition, an offensive *jihad* is a collective obligation 'which is imposed upon the community considered as a whole and which only becomes obligatory for each individual in particular to the extent that his intervention is necessary for the realisation of the purpose envisaged by the law'.[11] That is, if a section of the Muslim community comes forward to discharge this collective duty (*fard kiffayah*), the remainder of the community is absolved of responsibility. However, 'this concession vanishes for the citizen of an Islamic state when it is attacked by a non-Muslim power. In that case everybody must come forward for *jihad*.[12] A defensive *jihad*, then, entails an individual duty (*fard ayn*) incumbent upon all Muslims and it can be waged in the absence of the caliph.

This distinction and its concomitant implications for authority have formed a robust and enduring part of lawful *jihad*. Just as Khomeini adhered to the principle that defensive war does not require religious leadership,[13] ibn Taymiyyah noted that 'if an enemy attacks the Muslim community fighting them is a duty on all those who are directly attacked as it is a duty of others that are not attacked to aid them'.[14] In furtherance of the *mujahidin's* resistance against the Soviets, Abdullah Azzam was particularly attentive to this issue. He acknowledged that '*jihad* in the days of the companions and successors [of the Prophet] was mostly *fard kiffayah* because they were embarking on new conquests',[15] but the situation in 1987 rendered *jihad* *fard ayn* on every Muslim. Azzam argued that the weight of tradition was unequivocal in this regard:

In this condition [the *kuffar* entering a land of the Muslims] the pious predecessors, those who succeeded them, the *ulama* of the four *madhabs* (Maliki, Hanafi, Shafi, Hanbali), the *muhadithin*, and the *tafsir* commentators are agreed that in all the Islamic ages, *jihad* under this condition becomes *fard ayn* upon the Muslims of the land which the *kuffar* have attacked and upon the Muslims close by. . . . And if the Muslims of this land cannot expel the *kuffar* because of lack of forces, because they slacken, are indolent, or simply do not act, then the *fard ayn* obligation spreads in the shape of a circle from the nearest to the next nearest. . . . This process continues until it becomes *fard ayn* upon the whole world.[16]

Though the judgement that Afghanis were not by themselves able to ward off the aggressors was made 'according to our modest experience and knowledge',[17] Azzam holds the principle itself to be beyond contention. He emphasizes further that no scholar has ever maintained that the absence of a community of Muslims under a single caliph cancels the obligation of *jihad* for the defence of the Muslim lands.[18]

Osama bin Laden observed that Allah 'made it possible for us to aid the *mujahidin* in Afghanistan without any declaration of *jihad* but instead through the news that was broadcast by radio stations that the Soviet Union invaded a Muslim country'.[19] This right of self-defence, obvious, automatic, and in need of no formal backing by a Muslim ruler in the urgent case of Afghanistan accentuates the fact that bin Laden's *jihad* against America was in substantially more need of justification. It is not surprising, therefore, that it was incumbent upon al-Qaeda to declare a *jihad* against the Crusader–Zionist alliance in the first place.

In line with what was considered in Chapter 4, al-Qaeda's defensive *jihad* is not in need of the caliph's authority. This is because, in the words of Abu Ghaith, '*jihad* has become an obligatory duty for all Muslims. The Muslim lands are occupied'.[20] Bin Laden is keen to point out that this 'does not mean that bin Laden alone has to endure this, but that it is a duty on all of our *umma . . . jihad* is today obligatory for all of us'.[21] However, though self-defined 'vanguard' groups like al-Qaeda are eager to represent the concept of the *jihad* of individual duty as a popular uprising of sorts, historical precedents assumed that even situations of *fard ayn* would be led by recognized leaders: 'the appeal to fighting as an individual duty appears as a summons to Muslim rulers in neighbouring provinces to come to the aid of their co-religionists in Syro-Palestine'.[22] When he makes such statements as 'I say that *jihad* is without doubt mandatory for all Muslims',[23] bin Laden reaches out to Muslim individuals *qua* Muslim individuals, rather than as members of politically organized communities. This subversion of established patterns of authority is distinctive to modern radical Islamism.

Yet, an ambiguity arises from the fact that, on the one hand, al-Qaeda's *jihad* is cast as requiring no authority while on the other hand, al-Qaeda's own, self-defined authority is invoked. The problem is compounded by the fact that bin Laden himself is neither a Muslim head of state nor a trained Islamic scholar. Accordingly, the *fatwa* by the 'World Islamic Front against Jews and Crusaders', a legal edict prescribing *jihad* against civilian and military American targets, is countersigned by three other Muslim figures.[24] This is in marked contrast to the 'Declaration of *Jihad*', issued two years earlier in 1996, which is signed by bin Laden alone. Indeed, the *Al-Quds Al-Arabi* journalist Abdel Bari Atwan was told by bin Laden's media adviser that he could not record their interview because bin Laden was afraid of making grammatical or theological mistakes, which could be used against him.[25] The son of a Saudi businessman who did not complete his Bachelor's degree in Economics, bin Laden faces something of a credibility problem in matters of Islamic authority.

Bin Laden addresses this with two main tactics. In the first place, as suggested above, he trades on the authority of other trained Islamic jurists. Publicly,[26] he venerates the 'great Islamic decisions' of Mullah Omar, for example, and justifies his position by stressing that 'it is a well known fact that America is against the establishment of any Islamic state—the Commander of the Faithful [Mullah Omar] has declared this on more than one occasion'.[27] He also defers to the authority of radical Saudi clerics:

> ... Sheikh Hamud bin Abdallah bin Uqla al-Shu'aybi, may God bless his life, who is one of the greatest scholars of Saudi Arabia; he urges the duty of fighting the Americans and fighting the Israelis in Palestine, making attacks on their blood and wealth permissible. There also appears a *fatwa* from Sheikh Sulayman al-Ulwan ... in which he denounced those who say that fighting is invalid.[28]

In this way, bin Laden buttresses his case for *jihad* by referencing more authoritative voices from within the community of (radical) scholars.[29] In addition, however, bin Laden accentuates and relies upon his own Islamic credentials.

5.1.2. Bin Laden's Islamic credentials

Broadly, there are three ways in which bin Laden sets up his own authority: as an Islamic scholar himself, as a leader who wields both the pen of the sage and the sword of the soldier, and through parallels between his situation and that of the first Muslims.

5.1.2.1. *Bin Laden as scholar*

Selectively[30] citing Prophetic traditions and passages from the Quran, bin Laden seeks to come across as a scholar capable of interpreting Islamic law and systematically balancing juristic evidences. Indeed, his conclusions are presented as deductions derived from Islamic sources, as is the 1998 command to kill American soldiers and civilians which is said to be 'in accordance with the words of God Almighty: 'fight the idolaters at any time if they first fight you'; 'fight them until there is no more persecution and until worship is devoted to God'; 'why should you not fight in God's cause and for those oppressed men, women and children who cry out: Lord, rescue us from this town whose people are oppressors! By Your grace give us a protector and a helper!'[31] Certainly, in the manner of an *alim*, he feels himself capable of weighing in on a variety of legal issues, deciding that it is permissible for Muslims to fight alongside Iraqi Baathists[32] during the US-led invasion of 2003: 'there is no harm in such circumstances if the Muslims' interests coincide with those of the socialists in fighting the Crusaders . . . just as the Muslims' struggle against Byzantium suited the Persians but did not harm the Prophet's companions'.[33] On other occasions, he boldly eschews the employment of Islamic precedents and makes categorical pronouncements based on his own Islamic authority, as when he deems that any Iraqi cooperating with America in any way immediately becomes an apostate and an infidel.[34]

When bin Laden released his 1998 *fatwa* announcing the formation of the 'World Islamic Front', Bernard Lewis acknowledged that the statement was 'a magnificent piece of eloquent, at times even poetic Arabic prose'[35] (indeed, owing to his 'distinctive monotone' and 'clever rhymes', bin Laden was renowned as a wedding poet during the 1990s).[36] Yet it is worth noting that, as compared to other self-appointed *jihad* ideologues, bin Laden's style is more limited. Mohammad Abd al-Salam Faraj, author of the manifesto of Anwar Sadat's assassins, 'attempts to convince Azhar-trained readers and others, with learned quotations from the volumes of the Prophetic Traditions and from the commentaries on these volumes, that Muslim scholars agree that duties of leadership cannot be executed by an unbeliever'.[37] In the same way, Abdullah Azzam offers juristic opinions punctiliously corroborated by *hadiths* and numerous references indicating consensus among the four schools of Islamic jurisprudence. Bin Laden's analyses, on the other hand, and eloquent as they may be, tend to be driven by his political points. He does not quote Islamic scholarship at length and does not loyally function within the *ulema* tradition. However, though his manner of argumentation is ultimately polemical in nature, he does, nonetheless, aspire to adopt the mantle of a learned scholar who can speak authoritatively on normative Islamic issues.

5.1.2.2. *Bin Laden as warrior*–mujtahid

But bin Laden emphasizes that, unlike his critics, he is not an arm-chair *jihadi*. In the great tradition of ibn Taymiyyah and Abdullah Azzam, he depicts himself as a warrior–scholar leading the *jihad* by example. Azzam, who held a Master's Degree in *Sharia* from al-Azhar and a PhD in *Usul al-Fiqh*, spent many years in the Afghan trenches. He was keen to emphasize that his judgements about the *jihad* came in the context of 'living my eighth year amongst the *mujahidin*'.[38] Indeed, he carefully articulated his belief that

the life of the *umma* is connected to the ink of the scholars and the blood of the martyrs. What is more beautiful than to write the history of the *umma* with both the ink of the scholar and his blood, such that the map of Islamic history becomes coloured with two lines: one of them black, and that is what the scholar writes with the ink of his pen; and the second red, and that is what the martyr writes with his blood. And more beautiful than this is when the blood is one and the pen is one, so that the hand of the scholar, which expends the ink and moves the pen, is the same hand that expends his blood and moves the nations. So history does not write its lines except with blood. Glory does not build its lofty edifice except with skulls. . . . Empires, noble persons, states and societies, cannot be established except with examples.[39]

Ibn Taymiyyah, a professor of Islamic law at the age of nineteen, also played a prominent role in fighting the Mongols. The editor of one of his works compiled by the Saudi Ministry of Education notes that 'ibn Taymiyyah did not carry out *jihad* with the pen alone: he also fought with the sword'. He was instrumental in rallying the Muslim people against the Tartars and, it is believed, turning the tide against them in war.[40]

Bin Laden is keen to follow this model. In the words of ibn al-Khattab, he is 'one of the major scholars of the *jihad*, as well as being a main commander of the *mujahidin* worldwide'.[41] To counter the opinions of 'many scholars [who] say that now is not the time for *jihad*', bin Laden insists that ibn Taymiyyah 'makes it clear in this regard that he who issues a juridical decree regarding *jihad* is he who has knowledge of the legal aspects of religion, who has knowledge of *jihad* and when it should be waged. In other words, *he should wage jihad himself*'.[42] At another stage he explicitly uses his status as a scholar on the frontlines to directly undercut his detractors, wondering 'how can you obey those who never fought for God, while remaining true to the duty of *jihad*? Are you not thinking?'[43]

5.1.2.3. *Bin Laden as approximation of the Prophet*

Of course, the ultimate warrior–thinker is the Prophet Mohammad. Islam's founder was said to have participated in twenty-seven military campaigns, deputizing fifty-nine others.[44] There are, however, additional ways in which parallels between bin Laden and Mohammad are tacitly drawn. To begin with, bin Laden paints an interesting gloss on the fact that he was expelled by the Saudi government and then pressured to leave by the Sudanese, suggesting that 'when a Muslim migrates repeatedly he is doubly rewarded'.[45] Here, bin Laden is explicitly invoking the central Islamic concept of *hijra*, which holds the symbolic resonance of Mohammad's flight from Mecca, and over the centuries has acquired the moral and political connotations of an escape from 'evil' to 'good' or from 'injustice' to 'justice'.[46] Indeed, bin Laden punctuates his statements with such phrases as 'when I emigrated from my country to defend you'[47] and '[Allah] blessed us with this gift of emigration'.[48] The reference to al-Qaeda as 'this group of emigrants who wage *jihad*'[49] endeavours to explain its members' outlaw status in terms of extreme piety. Ultimately, bin Laden is casting al-Qaeda in a role similar to that of the first Muslim community who embarked upon a physical-cum-metaphysical movement away from Mecca to Medina because they had been persecuted for their beliefs.

Bin Laden's use of the Arabic language is frequently archaic, evoking the era of early Islam by favouring Quranic vocabulary. He commands his followers to 'launch the raid'[50] and explains his presence in Afghanistan with the observation that 'by the grace of God there became a safe base in Khurasan, high in the peaks of the Hindu Kush'.[51] Moreover, he talks of 'spreading our message in Hijaz and Najd for more than twelve years',[52] implying a Prophetic role for himself, and observes that 'by the grace of God Almighty I have brought happiness to Muslims in the Islamic world'.[53] After railing against the clerics who have been co-opted by the Saudi regime, he remarks 'how similar are these years to the years the Prophet told us about'.[54] Further, he lists the names and nationalities of fallen al-Qaeda fighters, providing the impression of a shepherd closely connected with his flock.[55] He stresses his pious lineage by noting that his father 'built the mosques of the holy sites where the Ka'ba is' and renovated the Dome of al-Aqsa for no profit,[56] and he points out that he was named after one of the Prophet's venerable companions, Osama bin Zeid.[57] Robert Fisk commented that 'with his high cheekbones, narrow eyes and long brown robe, Mr bin Laden looks every inch the mountain warrior of *mujahidin* legend'.[58]

In this way, bin Laden's implied authority emanates from the fact that he is a spiritual leader who has changed his life for the Islamic cause, waging *jihad* with the pen in one hand and the sword in the other. Bin Laden's personal authority combines, however, with the suggestion that the duty to lead the *jihad* against America has, in some way, defaulted to him.

5.1.3. Authority by default

In the absence of a caliphate, the responsibility to lead *jihad* rests with the clerics and the Islamic heads of state. As has been noted, even fighting as an individual duty should be executed under the command of established Islamic leadership (after all, Saladin may not have been the caliph, but he was a publicly recognized regional commander). However, bin Laden makes it clear that neither the religious establishment nor the wicked, secularized governments are capable of discharging their obligations, leaving the duty of *jihad* unfulfilled.

5.1.3.1. *The ulema have abandoned the duty of jihad*

Bin Laden is aggrieved by what he terms 'the scholars of evil and the writers for rent'.[59] He maintains that the 'judeo-Crusader alliance undertook to kill and arrest the righteous scholars and hardworking preachers',[60] and that the remaining *ulema* have aligned themselves with tyrannical regimes for personal gain. Bin Laden lambastes 'the *ulema* and preachers of evil'[61] and rails against 'the Imams of the religion who bear false witness every morning and evening and lead the nation astray . . . for a handful of coins'.[62] He also claims that other 'clerics are prisoners and hostages of the tyrants. Some of them told me: "We cannot speak the truth [because we are civil servants]"'.[63] When asked his opinion on Sheikh Tantawi's *fatwa* against al-Qaeda, bin Laden asserts that 'no official scholar's juridicial decrees have any value as far as I'm concerned'. He further upholds that the curriculum of Al-Azhar has been interfered with by America.[64] 'Imagine!' he exclaimed in 2003. 'The offices of the Clerics Authority [in Saudi Arabia] are adjacent to the royal palace, and the building of the Fatwa Authority of Al-Azhar is adjacent to Hosni Mubarak's Palace of the Republic'.[65]

Like ibn Taymiyyah, bin Laden recognizes that he is at odds with the *ulema* of his day, but he puts this down to the fact that the religious establishment has been co-opted and corrupted by unjust regimes. In a sense, then, the authority to declare *jihad* has devolved to bin Laden because 'these important and famous people have only been unwilling [to wage *jihad*] because they knew what was in their interest . . . for these pious, righteous men were afflicted by this disease, the disease of holding back from *jihad*'.[66]

5.1.3.2. *The rulers have abandoned the duty of jihad*

His most vitriolic criticism, however, is reserved for the region's regimes—in particular, the House of Saud. Bin Laden speaks of the Arab rulers' 'inability to protect the land',[67] the fact they 'have lost the power to do anything against this barefaced occupation'[68] and he conjectures that 'the virility of the rulers in this region has been stolen'.[69] For bin Laden, 'the question strongly raised is: are the governments of the Islamic world capable of pursuing this duty of defending the faith and *umma* and renouncing allegiance to America?'[70] However, the regimes' 'general incapacity'[71] is not construed as resulting from benign incompetence. Nor is it a matter of personal malice ('the rulers of the Arabs who have laughed at our *umma* for more than a century'[72]). On the contrary, al-Qaeda upholds that the rulers have committed acts that place them outside of Islam—that is, they are declared to be apostate.

With this, al-Qaeda invokes the hugely controversial doctrine of *takfir*. In order to become apostate, a Muslim must commit an action that shows him to have knowingly abandoned Islam. Thus, bin Laden argues that 'these rulers have betrayed God and his Prophet and they have gone beyond the pale of the religious community'.[73] The leaders in the Arab world have 'engage[ed] in the major unbelief which takes them out of the fold of Islam in broad daylight and in front of all of the people'.[74] He decides that 'certain actions by the ruler are in fact some of the cardinal sins in our *sharia* that should not be tolerated'[75] and underlines that 'we are not talking merely of a debauched and a depraved ruler, but one who is an apostate and a collaborator with the infidels'.[76]

Pronouncing a fellow Muslim *kafir* is a deeply divisive issue in Islam, particularly as the condemned man's blood becomes forfeit and he is sentenced to death. Ibn Taymiyyah's presumption to judge a Muslim's 'Muslim-ness' serves as the benchmark for most modern-day invocations of the doctrine. Given that the Mongols had converted to Islam, and that Ghazan Khan in particular was said to be a serious and devout Muslim, the onus was on ibn Taymiyyah to prove that the Tartar dynasty was not truly Muslim and could therefore be fought. He accomplished this by emphasizing that they did not strictly apply the *sharia*—the Mongols favoured Genghis Khan's Yasa Code—arguing that 'any community or group that refuses to abide by any clear and universally accepted Islamic law . . . must be fought until they abide by its laws. This applies even though they make the verbal declaration'.[77] Though the medieval jurist 'was reluctant to use the term *takfir*,[78] the heirs of his literalist and puritanical conception of Islam employed it with considerably more abandon. During Nasser's crackdown on the Muslim Brothers, Sayyid Qutb described Egyptian society as being in a state of '*jahiliyya*' (pre-Islamic ignorance), which implied that its members were no longer genuine Muslims. But, Gilles Kepel argues that Qutb died before he could fully explain his theory, leaving it unclear if the accusation of *takfir* applied to Nasser's regime only and whether the remedy involved preaching rather than condemnation.[79]

Qutb's flirtation with the doctrine of *takfir* marked a departure from the Muslim Brotherhood mainstream—indeed, it became a key issue in the formation of more fanatical movements. The terrorist cell Jama'at al-Muslimin (more commonly known as Takfir wa Hijra),[80] 'an extremist fundamentalist group which repudiated Egypt's entire social system and even viewed Muslim clergy as heretics under whose auspices it was unlawful to pray',[81] was established in Nasser's notorious Abu Za'bal prison by a handful of disaffected Muslim Brothers who refused to support the 1967 war against Israel because it was led by their apostate president.[82] *Al-Farida al-Ghaiba*, Faraj's justification for Sadat's assassination, cited ibn Taymiyyah's *fatwas* against the Mongols in support of the obligation to fight a regime which had refused to implement the *sharia*, shunned the duty of *jihad*, and openly manifested unbelief by entering into alliances with infidels.[83] The Groupe Islamique Armé in Algeria denounced all of its opponents as *kafir*, and took to beheading or slitting the throats of leading intellectuals and politicians, as well as moderates within its own ranks.

Until Qutb's revival of the doctrine, *takfir* was seldom used in Islamic history and heresy trials in the classical era were extremely rare. This is due to the inherent danger of shedding Muslim blood, and the Prophet himself is said to have erred on the side of caution: one *hadith* states that the Muslims killed a man in battle who had declared the *shahada* as the knife was held up to his throat. When the Prophet learned of the incident, he was incensed. The killers objected that the man had made the profession merely to save his skin, but the Prophet replied 'did you open his heart and look inside it?' The Kharijis, a puritanical sect which emerged in the early years of Islam, were violently promiscuous in their usage of *takfir* (owing to their belief that committing sin immediately eradicated belief) and they have been regarded as dangerous extremists by both Sunnis and Shia ever since. The matter of *takfir* is sensitive to the extent that it is held to be the sole prerogative of the religious establishment which has, for the most part, shied away from using it. In refutation of the case laid out in *Al-Farida al-Ghaiba*, Sheikh Jad al-Haqq of al-Azhar decreed that a Muslim can be declared an apostate only if he denounces the *sharia* in its entirety, and he reminded that, in any case, questions of belief or unbelief are to be decided by the *ulema*.[84]

Despite being a huge influence on Qutb, Mawdudi was a staunch opponent of *takfir*, declaring that 'probably nothing else has done the Muslims as much harm as this has done'. He argued that it was 'a crime against society' and that it 'tore Islam to pieces' because it caused different sects to proliferate, each condemning the other, and split the *umma* asunder. Pronouncing the verdict of *takfir* 'is in fact to oppose God Himself', because no one but He can know whose heart has faith and whose heart does not.[85] More recently, Sir Mohammad Zafrullah Khan argued that an apostate's life was made forfeit by the Quran only when he was fighting the Muslims—to punish simple apostates on account of their unbelief alone 'renders altogether nugatory the freedom of conscience and belief that is so emphatically guaranteed by Islam'.[86] While not against the pronouncement of *takfir* in theory, the Saudi clerical establishment subjects it to severe restrictions, with Sheikh Abdulrahman al-Sudays citing 'a long list of religious scholars, including the authoritative ibn Taymiyyah . . . and the reformer Saudi Imam Muhammad bin Abd al-Wahab, founder of the Wahabi movement, as saying that a Muslim can only be repudiated on the basis of a unanimous opinion by the *ulema*'.[87]

Bin Laden, conversely, asserts that there are two spheres of action in which the Middle East's rulers generally—and the Saudi dynasty particularly—have actively shown themselves to be *kuffar*. In the first place, they do not properly apply the *sharia*. The regime, apparently, has 'desecrated its own legitimacy' through its 'suspension of the rulings of Islamic law and replacement thereof with man-made laws'.[88] Bin Laden reminds that 'these are the people who sapped the energies of the *umma* from the righteous men and followed human desires; these are the ones who followed democracy, the religion of ignorance'.[89] Such rulers demand that they are obeyed by the people, 'which is tantamount to worshipping them rather than God', and they 'think that Islam consists of mere words uttered . . . but do not know that these words have requirements'.[90]

Secondly, 'by being loyal to the US regime the Saudi regime has committed an act against Islam. And this, based on the ruling of the *sharia*, casts the regime outside the religious community'.[91] Thus, through its alliance with America, the House of Saud has turned its back on Islam: 'these rulers have contravened this testimony [the *shahada*] from its very root through their client status'.[92] Al Qaeda makes clear, however, that it is not quibbling over doctrinal issues—rather, the matter is one of the gravest importance to the security of the *umma*. Some regimes in the Arab and Muslim world 'have turned themselves into tools of occupation of the greatest House in the universe [the Ka'ba]'[93] and 'the government in Riyadh has entered into a global alliance with Crusader unbelief, under the leadership of Bush, against Islam and its people . . . helping the infidel to take the land of Muslims and control them is one of the ten acts contradictory to Islam'.[94] In short, 'they have accepted the rule of the cross'.[95] Zawahiri asserts that the Egyptian government has likewise 'weakened and kneeled down before the invading crusader'.[96] The Arab rulers are termed 'the new al-Ghasasinah'[97] and, in bin Laden's analysis, 'the [Saudi] regime has gone so far as to be clearly beyond the pale of Islam'.[98]

Urging his fellow Muslims to oust their tyrannical leaders, bin Laden is clear that 'religious terms should be used when describing the ruler who does not follow God's revelation and path, and champions the infidels by extending military facilities to them . . . they should be called infidels and

renegades'.[99] With their apostasy, the Arab rulers have defaulted on their duty
to implement the *sharia* and defend the *umma*, thus contravening a social
compact between sovereign and people: 'leadership is a covenant between the
leader and his subjects'.[100] Referencing ibn Taymiyyah, he observes that
obedience is not absolute but conditional on the ruler's integrity.[101] Defying
such traitors is posited as integral to the Islamic tradition:

> The scholars of Islam have agreed that authority cannot be given to an infidel, so if he
> becomes one his authority is thereby revoked and it is obligatory to remove him by
> force.... Therefore it is not we who say that the infidel leader has overstepped the
> bounds of his authority; it is the consensus of the Imams who say so.[102]

Indeed, bin Laden is sensitive about parallels drawn between al-Qaeda and the
Kharijis, noting that '[the regime] has accused the *mujahidin* of following the
path of the Kharijis, but they know that we have nothing to do with such
a school of thought'.[103] As such, it is important for bin Laden to stress that
Islam itself provides the scales by which the actions of rulers are assessed.[104]

In the end, bin Laden wants to maintain that the Muslims have been
betrayed by their *kufr* leaders through their apostatic collusion with the
Crusader–Zionist alliance, and he speaks of the need 'to fill the vacuum
caused by these religiously invalid regimes and their mental deficiency'.[105]
Al-Qaeda, then, is presented as the group willing to bear the burden,[106] and
protect the Muslims' interests in accordance with a true understanding of
Islam. Hence, Sayf al-Adil, an al-Qaeda military leader, identified one of the
three objectives of the 9/11 attack as signalling the emergence of a new
virtuous leadership dedicated to opposing the Zionist–Anglo-Saxon–Protestant coalition.[107]

With these arguments, al-Qaeda suggest that the *ulema* and the Arab
leaders have forfeited their obligations as defenders of the community and
guardians of Islamic justice (not by coincidence, a hallmark of the *kafir* is his
reluctance to wage *jihad*). While the *ulema* are suffering from the 'disease of
holding back from *jihad*', the region's rulers 'work on burying *jihad* alive'.[108]
The duty of *jihad* has been defaulted—indeed, neglected—in a sequence of
evasion. While the rulers pander to the Crusaders ('they have provided
evidence they are implementing the schemes of the enemies of the
umma'),[109] the *ulema* are beholden to the rulers ('I advise the Muslims not
to listen to these disingenuous scholars that work for *kufr* regimes and only
issue fabricated *fatwas*').[110] Proper Islamic authority has vanished.

Bin Laden's double-pronged approach to the authority question creates a
mutually reinforcing dynamic between his own, self-defined Islamic authority
and the *ulema* and rulers' lack thereof: he employs his own authority in
determining that the establishments have abandoned the duty of *jihad*, and

it is this very same determination which provides him with the authority to be a vanguard of the Muslims. With his arguments, however, bin Laden flies in the face of Islamic orthodoxy on the question of legitimate authority for *jihad*.

Al-Qaeda's audacity in this regard was a major source of Islamic censure after the 9/11 operations. In condemning the attacks, Hasan Nasrallah 'called on the Islamic movements, authorities, and jurisprudence centres to regulate the *fatwa* on *jihad* and martyrdom so that it will not be abused',[111] and Malaysian Islamist Anwar Ibrahim wondered 'who hijacked Islam?' in an article for *Time* magazine.[112] Given that al-Qaeda was almost universally viewed as the initiator of aggression against the United States, bin Laden's personal authority was the subject of intense scrutiny. Mullah Omar, the supreme leader of the Taliban, had argued in June 2001 that 'any *fatwa* issued by Osama bin Laden declaring *jihad* against the US and ordering Muslims to kill Americans is null and void. Osama bin Laden is not entitled to issue *fatawa* as he did not complete the mandatory 12 years of Quranic studies to qualify for the position of mufti'.[113] Similarly, Deobandi cleric Maulvi Waris Mazhari asserted that 'the classical scholars of Islamic jurisprudence have clearly laid down that only the amir or leader of an established state can issue a declaration of *jihad*. Private individuals or groups do not have the right to do so; self-styled *jihad* has no legitimacy'.[114] This is supported by the Egyptian Mufti's ruling that 'the one with the authority to declare *jihad* is the Imam who has under his command a regular army capable of waging a war of regular armies. . . . The one with the flag in our day is the president of the state, in every one of the [Muslim] countries'.[115] In his denunciation of al-Qaeda as relying on inventions in religion, the Saudi Sheikh al-Hawashi also underlined that *jihad* is not permissible without rulers.[116] Sheikh Tantawi dismissed bin Laden's call to *jihad* simply by pointing out that *jihad* in Islam becomes a duty only in self-defence.[117]

In the nine years since the 2001 attacks, scepticism about bin Laden's authority has only intensified. This is directly linked to the indiscriminate manner in which his *jihad* continues to be waged, as those slaughtered in al-Qaeda's name have tended to be civilians—and, crucially, most of the time they are Muslims too. The reality on the ground, which amounts to grave harm against Islam and the *umma*, immediately casts into doubt the qualifications of al-Qaeda's leaders to manage a *jihad* and make judgements about its proper course. Thus, as a flurry of important Islamic *radicals* renounced their support for al-Qaeda in 2007 and 2008, they laid emphasis on the group's authority deficit. Sayyed Imam al-Sharif, a former colleague of Zawahiri in the Egyptian Islamic Jihad group and a principle ideologue of jihadism, has made clear that 'all of them— bin Laden, Zawahiri, and others—are not religious scholars on whose opinion you can count. They are ordinary persons'.[118] Bin Laden's former mentor, the

Saudi Sheikh Salman ibn Fahd al-Odah, was equally dismissive, describing his co-national as 'a simple man without scholarly credentials'.[119] The Libyan Nu'man bin Othman, a former brother-in-arms of bin Laden and veteran of the Afghan war against the Soviets, also made a high profile turnaround, wondering on a BBC programme: 'why should I believe I have a duty or obligation towards al-Qaeda? You need to convince me and the other Muslims how you established your authority. I'm talking about Islamically'.[120]

In 1991, Ayman al-Zawahiri distributed a leaflet attacking the blind head of the Egyptian group Gama'at Islamiya (a rival to his Islamic Jihad organiza-tion) on the grounds that a rightful leader, according to the *sharia*, should have all his five senses intact.[121] By contrast, al-Qaeda's leadership of the war against America has come in for far more substantive criticism. That a layman like bin Laden would presume to direct a *jihad*, defensive or otherwise, on behalf of the *umma* is the biggest challenge al-Qaeda poses to the Islamic tradition. This challenge is especially acute since, through the globalization of his *jihad*, bin Laden's authority has become at once far-reaching and fragmented. As al-Qaeda 'franchises' have sprung up in Muslim countries, imported in service of local and sectarian ends in places such as Iraq, Afghanistan, and Pakistan, the Muslim death toll has soared, and, seemingly, bin Laden has been unable to stop the intra-Muslim bloodshed.[122] Thus, it makes sense to concur with Faisal Devji that almost incalculable in its effects is the global *jihad*'s 'democratisation of Islam, accomplished by its fragmen-tation of traditional forms of religious authority and the dispersal of their elements into a potentially endless series of re-combinations'.[123]

5.2. LAST RESORT

The *hadith* which says, 'the most ugly names are *harb* (war) and *murrat* (rebellion)', reflects the Islamic trend which depicts violence, however neces-sary, as an evil. The Quranic idea that 'fighting is prescribed for you, though it be hateful to you' is heavily emphasized in more modern texts of the tradition. Qutb, for example, considers fighting to be 'a necessary evil that ultimately may result in something good'.[124] Mawdudi counsels that 'force should be used only when it is unavoidable and only to the extent that it is absolutely necessary',[125] the latter part of the statement hinting at the *jus in bello* principle of proportionality which will be taken up in Chapter 6. Fadlallah is a firm believer in the proposition that coercion will never solve a disagree-ment—'violence breeds violence'—and upholds that 'should the aggressor be a human being and it is possible to avoid their aggression by any means at one's disposal, even by fleeing, it is permissible to do it unless it leads to the breach of the sanctity and dignity of the intended victim'.[126] He holds steadfastly to the principle of last resort, advising that violence ought to be seen as a 'kind of surgical operation that a person should use only after trying all other means, and only when he finds his life imperilled'.[127] The *fiqh* expert Taha Jabir al-Alwani uses the same therapeutic analogy, preaching that 'fighting in the perspective of Islam is like a surgery sought only as the last resort'.[128] Qaradawi affirms that 'Islam considers peace and prevention of war as a blessing'[129] and Nasrallah, who cannot be mistaken for someone soft on the Israelis, espouses his belief in dialogue: 'we tell anyone who wants to talk to us to present us with a plan'.[130]

Though there can be no doubt that the concept of martyrdom and waging the justified *jihad* have been glorified intensely in the Islamic tradition, fighting as an end in itself is decidedly un-Islamic. War is a state of affairs that a Muslim has been forced into. This was even true of the classical era of offensive *jihad*, where the enemy was presented with two options for avoiding hostilities before the commencement of combat: 'the *jihad* must be preceded by an "invitation to Islam", and only failure to accept the new faith or pay the poll tax in the case of Scriptuaries would precipitate fighting with the enemy'.[131] The Muslims could maintain, then, that the decision to resort to war was forced upon them by the adversary's intransigence. This 'invitation to Islam', it is said, was a practice observed faithfully by the Prophet Mohammad and his early successors. In fact, Mohammad is believed to have spent his final days dictating letters to the rulers of the great empires of his day, summoning them to Islam.[132] The invitation became a legal attitude in classical Islam and was underpinned by the belief that each among the enemy's ranks was a potential convert to Islam.

Al-Qaeda, with unintended irony, does extend such an invitation to the United States: 'the first thing we are calling you to is Islam . . . it is the religion of showing kindness to others, establishing justice between them, granting them their rights and defending the oppressed and the persecuted'.[133] But, its conception of the last resort criterion goes beyond the classical variant which offers the enemy something of a false (not to mention archaic) choice. As the vanguard of a defensive *jihad*, al-Qaeda justifies the resort to hostilities, its timing, and the necessary use of violence.

5.2.1. Justification of resort: warnings have been issued

In 1997, bin Laden directed an examination of the causes of the 1993 World Trade Centre bombing towards the US administration. Denying that he had any connection with its mastermind, Ramzi Yousef, he continued:

But I say if the American government is serious about avoiding the explosions inside the US, then let it stop provoking the feelings of 1.25 billion Muslims. Those hundreds of thousands who have been killed or displaced in Iraq, Palestine and Lebanon do have brothers and sisters who will make of Ramzi Yousef a symbol and a teacher. The US will drive them to transfer the battle into the United States. Everything is made possible to protect the blood of the American citizen while the bloodshed of Muslims is permitted everywhere. With this kind of behaviour, the US government is hurting itself, hurting Muslims and hurting the American people.[134]

This analysis of the objective situation in the Middle East is complemented by warnings about al-Qaeda operations specifically: 'we also advise you to pack your bags and get out of our lands. We only desire this for your goodness, guidance and righteousness, so don't force us to send you back as cargo in coffins'.[135]

Indeed, in terms of 9/11, bin Laden was adamant that the United States had been warned for years, and 'you could see this, if you were so inclined, in the interview with Scott Macleod in *Time* magazine in 1996, as well as the one with Peter Arnett on *CNN* in 1997, and with John Weiner in 1998. You could see it in the events in Nairobi, Tanzania, and Aden; you could see it in my interviews with Abdel Bari Atwan and with Robert Fisk'.[136] In fact, he informed Western reporters in the summer of 2001 that the United States can 'expect a major blow'.[137] Though he refused in 1998 to take responsibility for the embassy bombings in Tanzania and Kenya, he explained that 'we have repeatedly issued warnings over a number of years'.[138] With regard to the Bali bombings, he comments that 'we warned Australia beforehand not to take part in the war in Afghanistan, as well as about its disgraceful attempts to separate East Timor, but it ignored the warning until it woke up to the sound of explosions in Bali'.[139] In his 'message to the British' after the attacks in London of 7 July 2005, Zawahiri remarks that 'the lion of Islam, the *mujahid* Sheikh Osama bin Laden . . . before offered you a truce if you would leave the lands of Islam'.[140]

Bin Laden had, for sure, presented a peace proposal to America's European allies, based on the fact that opinion polls show 'that most people in Europe want peace'. Al-Qaeda offered to cease operations against any state which vowed not to attack Muslims or intervene in their affairs. While this gesture served to exalt bin Laden's self-image as a jurist and legitimate Islamic statesman—'it will come into effect after the departure of its last soldier from our lands, and it is available for a period of three months from the day this statement is broadcast'—it was also designed to meet the Islamic test of last resort before further violence was employed.[141]

5.2.2. Justification of timing: the situation is now urgent

The Muslims, it is argued, are in a desperate situation, and *jihad* is the only way out of it. The stakes are said to be existential, for '[*jihad*] is a pressing need for our nation's life, glory and survival. Although our enemy lies, our religion tells the truth when it stipulates: you fight so you exist'.[142] Bin Laden stresses that global circumstances and America's actions have forced al-Qaeda's hand: 'the Israeli forces are occupying our land and the American forces are sitting on our territory. We no longer have any choice but *jihad*'.[143] Zawahiri further maintains that 'there is no solution without *jihad*. The spread of this awareness has been augmented by the failure of all other methods that tried to evade assuming the burdens of *jihad*'.[144] Bin Laden concurs that 'the Americans and the Jews will not stop their aggression and will not cease their oppression against us except with *jihad*'.[145] He asks on another occasion, 'is there any other way to repel the infidels?'[146]

5.2.3. Justification of means: violence is the only language understood by the United States

There is an abiding reason, however, why all other means have failed. This is because 'America does not understand the language of manner and principles, so we are addressing it using the language it understands'.[147] In bin Laden's assessment, 'they evidently won't wisen up without the language of beatings and killings.... They will not come to their senses until the attacks fall on their heads and until the battle has moved inside America'.[148] Zawahiri, too, speaks of 'the need to inflict the maximum casualties against the opponent, for this is the language understood by the west',[149] and Abu Ghaith concurs that 'America does not know the language of dialogue! Or the language of peaceful coexistence! America is kept at bay by blood alone'.[150] In a bid to do the United States a favour,[151] bin Laden explains when 'the plan of striking the towers' occurred to him so that Americans can 'reflect on it'. He pins down the critical event to the Israeli invasion of Lebanon in 1982—which, he maintains, was supported by the United States—and, more specifically, to the Israel Defense Forces' (IDF) bombings of high-rise residential blocks in West Beirut. The distressing scenes of blood, torn limbs, and women and children massacred affected him tremendously, for 'it was like a crocodile devouring a child who could do nothing but scream. Does a crocodile understand any-thing other than weapons?'[152] As the Muslims are confronted by such a 'crocodile', peaceful means are, by definition, futile.

In a sense, then, al-Qaeda is appealing to the West's own (morally bankrupt) worldview and its own *modus operandi* in global politics:

> ... the west, led by the US, which is under the influence of the Jews, does not know the language of ethics, morality and legitimate rights. They only know the language of interests backed up by brute military force. Therefore, if we wish to have a dialogue with them and make them aware of our rights, we must talk to them in the language that they understand.[153]

Thus, the element of 'reciprocity' is apparent once more, not only because 'President Bush was the one who started the war',[154] but because the sole means of communicating with 'America, the tyrant, which has destroyed all human values and transgressed all limits and which only understands the logic of power and war',[155] is to fight fire with fire and resort to force.

In this way, al-Qaeda argues that before 9/11 the Americans had been warned, the Muslims' backs were against the wall, and there was but a single means left of effectively repelling the assault: *jihad*. However, this argument is, by necessity, general. No single act of American aggression is pointed to as the trigger for the resort to force—indeed, no such act had occurred. Yet each of the claims for last resort is contingent on the premise that the United States was, in fact, committing aggression. In a related way, no meaningful peaceful alternative was presented to the Americans. This was because America, along with the rest of the world, utterly disputed the proposition that it had somehow started an aggressive war against any Muslims. As a result, al-Qaeda's claim of using force as the final option goes the way of the argument of self-defence: al-Qaeda is described as the aggressor. Like the host of other Muslim leaders considered in Chapter 4, Sheikh Abdulkadir Orire of Nigeria explained that 'a Muslim or a Muslim government is not allowed to start aggression. If you are attacked, you should only defend yourself. . . . So any happening now should not be associated with Islam'.[156]

5.3. REASONABLE HOPE OF SUCCESS

'Cast not thyself by thine own hands into destruction'
(Quran 2:195)

There is a strong prudential current underlying the *jihad* tradition, which is made manifest with the stipulation that victory be very likely. Mohammad's refusal to fight the pagans who were persecuting the believers in Mecca is commonly explained by the fact that the Muslims were vastly outnumbered at the time.[157] Indeed, in order to safeguard the pilgrimage to the Ka'ba, Mohammad later signed the ten-year Treaty of Hudaybiyya with the Meccans, which is considered a seminal precedent for peace between Muslims and non-Muslims. Thus, Shaybani directs that Muslims can accept a peace agreement with non-Muslims for a specified number of years without them having to pay the tax, 'provided the Imam has considered the situation and has found that the inhabitants of the territory of war are too strong for the Muslims to prevail against them and it would be better for the Muslims to make peace with them'.[158] Al-Tabari also considers at length the conditions under which Muslims can make peace with polytheists, and cites Abu Hanifa as allowing the Muslims to submit to a truce in which *they* must pay an annual sum to the polytheists, if the enemy's forces are superior.[159] Khadduri points out that in Shia Islam 'under no circumstances...should the Imam risk a *jihad* if he considers the enemy too powerful for him to win a victory, namely, if the enemy is at least twice as powerful as the Muslims'.[160] This threshold was evident in Sunni Islam too, as ibn Rushd surmised that the maximum number of enemies against which a Muslim is obliged to stand his ground is double his own troops.[161]

Modern Islam also reflects a preoccupation with the realistic prospect of realizing the just cause. Sayyed Qutb warns that 'Islam...sets out to make real preparations that are within the capability of Muslims so that victory becomes achievable. It does not raise the sights of the Muslim community towards that sublime horizon without making sure that it has firm ground upon which it can stand'.[162] In contrast to the Islamic Jihad group, the Jama'at al-Muslimin in Egypt ('Takfir wa Hijra') invoked the experience of the Prophet in Mecca and denied that *jihad* was presently obligatory based on the unfavourable balance of power.[163] In fact, *jihadi* ideologist Sayyed Imam al-Sharif claims that he warned Zawahiri's Islamic Jihad group in the 1990s that the Egyptian government was too powerful and that its insurgency would fail (he argues too that *jihad* is not required if the enemy is twice as strong as the Muslims and opines that 'those who have triggered clashes and pressed their brothers into unequal military confrontations are specialists neither in *fatwas* nor in military affairs').[164] Similarly, Fadlallah advises the Shia that 'if there be a possibility that you are not going to overcome the aggressor, you are not required to engage them'.[165]

That 'reasonable hope of success' is a staple of the Islamic tradition is unsurprising, given that Islamic theory cannot readily accommodate the concept of a Muslim defeat: if the Muslims were to lose, it would cast doubt as to whether Allah was on their side. So, the reasonable hope of success criterion draws attention to the objective conditions of combat, and allows Muslims to explain any losses in terms of poor judgement by commanders.

Zawahiri, for example, peppers his memoirs with excuses for failed Islamist operations against the Egyptian government: the attempted coup at the Military Technical College in 1974 failed because 'it did not take into consideration the objective conditions and the need to prepare well for it',[166] and the 1981 armed rebellion in Asyut was doomed to fail because 'it was an emotional uprising that was poorly planned'.[167] To avoid risking a defeat for Allah's cause, Muslims must, therefore, be scrupulous in picking their fights.

Though he commonly provides the impression of being a fanatical ideologue enslaved by the alleged justice of his cause, bin Laden does give some deference to the prudential requirements of the *jihad* tradition. In 1993, he explained quite bluntly that 'the situation in Bosnia does not provide the same opportunities as Afghanistan. A small number of *mujahidin* have gone to fight in Bosnia-Herzegovina but the Croats won't allow the *mujahidin* through in Croatia as the Pakistanis did with Afghanistan'.[168] In terms of the prospects of success for al-Qaeda's *jihad* operations, he argued in 1998 that

in some countries it might have been shown to some people that the necessary conditions [for *jihad*] are in place, but after a while they gain experience and know-how and realise that this is in fact not the case; in this instance they are charged with pardon and forgiveness... it is true that *jihad*, as long as it is an individual duty, is sometimes impossible, but real preparation requires good numbers and equipment.

After invoking his authority as a warrior scholar—vis-à-vis his critics among the *ulema* who have no experience of fighting—bin Laden then decrees that 'we are certain that our *umma* today is able to wage *jihad* against the enemies of Islam'.[169]

This certainty occasionally relies upon the spiritual support of Allah—'don't be afraid of their tanks and armoured personnel carriers, these are artificial things'[170]—but it also refers to a sense of moral superiority. He counsels his followers not to 'let their numbers frighten you for their hearts are empty and they are falling into military and economic disarray'[171] and observes that the American troops 'are utterly convinced of their government's tyranny and lies and they know the cause they are defending is not just'.[172] However, the principal theme dwelt upon in furtherance of the idea that al-Qaeda will triumph is the myth of the insurmountable superpower.

5.3.1. The myth of the superpower

Zawahiri is adamant that 'with the available means, small groups could prove to be a frightening horror for the Americans and the Jews'.[173] Bin Laden quotes Khalid ibn Walid, commander of the victorious, yet outnumbered,

Muslims who fought the Byzantines at Yarmuk in AD 636, to the effect that 'armies do not triumph by having large numbers. They are only conquered by their own defeatism'.[174] The 9/11 hijackers were also reminded in their 'Spiritual Manual'—a handwritten document found in Mohammad Ata's luggage which prescribes prayers and rituals for each stage of the attack—of the Quranic verse which states 'how often a little company has overcome a numerous company, by Allah's leave!'(2:249).[175] In fact, the document ends by advising the operatives that, upon seeing 'the crowds of unbelievers', they should recall the 10,000 strong enemy against which a small contingent of Muslims triumphed at the Battle of the Trench in AD 627.[176] For al-Qaeda's persistent claim is that, despite its enormous military and economic prowess, the US superpower does not exist. Three main arguments are put forward in support of the proposition that the 'Crusaders' can be overcome.

5.3.1.1. *The mujahidin's triumph over the Soviets in Afghanistan*

Bin Laden consistently maintains that, with the Afghan war against the Soviets, 'the myth of the superpower was destroyed'.[177] The Muslims had 'crushed' this 'atheist power', which was, allegedly, 'the strongest power known to humanity in modern history'[178] with 'the largest land army in the world'.[179] In the decade-long conflict, the *mujahidin* 'gained expertise in guerrilla and attritional warfare in our struggle against the great oppressive superpower, Russia, in which we and the *mujahidin* ground it down for ten years until it went bankrupt and decided to withdraw in defeat'.[180] In fact, bin Laden takes credit for the demise of the Soviet Union altogether and considers it to be a cautionary tale: 'there is a lesson here. The Soviet Union entered Afghanistan late in December of 1979. The flag of the Soviet Union was folded once and for all on the 25th of December just 10 years later. It was thrown into the waste basket. Gone was the Soviet Union forever'.[181] Moreover, it is said that, in the Soviet Union's collapse, 'the US ha[d] no mentionable role, but rather the credit goes to God and the *mujahidin* in Afghanistan'.[182]

It is additionally held that at the hands of the *mujahidin* the very concept of the superpower was decimated. Fighting with few supplies, 'they managed to destroy the myth of the largest military machine ever known to mankind and utterly annihilate the idea of the so-called superpowers'.[183] It is not just that the Soviet Empire became 'a figment of the imagination',[184] but that the superpower theory itself was exposed as false. Indeed, 'after our victory in Afghanistan and the defeat of the oppressors who had killed millions of Muslims, the legend about the invincibility of the superpowers vanished. Our boys no longer viewed America as a superpower'.[185]

Furthermore, the argument goes, 'we believe that America is much weaker than Russia'.[186] Since the Soviet Union was destructible, the (less powerful) United States can, *a fortiori*, be smashed in battle. All of this adds up to the belief that 'the defeat of America is something achievable—with the permission of God—and it is easier for us—with the permission of God—than the defeat of the Soviet empire previously'.[187]

5.3.1.2. *US weakness in Somalia*

The experience of combat between US Rangers and militants in (Muslim) Somalia is repeatedly held up as a shining example of American cowardice. Due to drought and devastating civil conflict, a famine had gripped the East African country in 1992. In the face of attacks on humanitarian aid convoys by militias and armed gangs, UN peacekeeping forces were dispatched to ensure the delivery of supplies and to work to achieve a ceasefire. The United Nations Operation in Somalia was joined by a US-led Unified Task Force, which codenamed the mission 'Operation Restore Hope'. After twenty-four Pakistani peacekeepers and six US soldiers were slain in the summer of 1993, the American government dispatched specialist Army Rangers to mount a manhunt for General Mohammad Aidid, prominent warlord and leader of one of the main factions, who was said to be responsible for the killings. On 3 October the Rangers attempted to apprehend Aidid by launching a helicopter raid on a Mogadishu hotel. Two Blackhawk helicopters were shot down by Aidid's forces and a sixteen-hour gunfight ensued. In addition to more than 500 Somali dead, 18 Rangers were killed, 84 Rangers were wounded, and one Blackhawk pilot was captured.[188] In response to an outcry by the US public and the Congress, March 1994 was set as a deadline for US withdrawal (after which the United Nations lost confidence and departed under US protection in February 1995).

According to al-Qaeda, that operation exposed the United States as 'a paper tiger'.[189] Bin Laden claims that America killed 13,000 Muslims in Somalia, 'but then the lions of Islam, the Afghan Arabs and their brothers, leapt on them and rubbed their face in the mud, killing many of them, destroying their tanks and downing their planes'. Though the claim that al-Qaeda was in any way involved in the Battle of Mogadishu has never been substantiated,[190] he goes on to describe how 'America and her allies fled in the dark of the night, without disturbing anyone'.[191] In fact, bin Laden appears to relish the image of harried American forces stealing away in the shadows of the night, dragging their dead: 'when only eight [*sic*] of them were killed they packed up in the darkness of night and escaped without looking back';[192] 'after a few blows [the US] forgot about all those titles and rushed out of Somalia in shame and disgrace, dragging the bodies of its soldiers'.[193]

Apparently, al-Qaeda's 'brothers in Somalia' had relayed their surprise at the 'weakness, frailness and cowardliness of the American solider'.[194] Bin Laden himself articulated the implications of the abortive operation to an American journalist in 1997:

> After a little resistance, the American troops left after achieving nothing. They left after claiming that they were the largest power on earth. They left after some resistance from powerless, poor, unarmed people whose only weapon is their belief in God Almighty, and who do not fear the fabricated American media lies. . . . We learned from those who fought there that they were surprised to see the low spiritual morale of the American fighters in comparison with the experience they had with the Russian fighters. The Americans ran away from those fighters who fought and killed them, while the latter stayed.[195]

This, al-Qaeda claims, is cause for considerable optimism in terms of the hopes of success for their own *jihad* against America.

5.3.1.3. *Al-Qaeda's own experience with the United States*

Furthermore, bin Laden maintains that the infirmity of the United States has already been proven at the hands of al-Qaeda. He pointed out that, by 1997, 'there were several attempts to arrest me or to assassinate me. This has been going on for more than seven years. With God's grace, none of these attempts succeeded. This is in itself proof to Muslims and to the world that the US is incapable and weaker than the picture it wants to paint in people's minds'.[196] Past successful operations against the United States are also proffered as proof of America's vulnerability. The killing of US marines in Lebanon is invoked,[197] as is the bombing of the *USS Cole*, the operations in Kenya and Tanzania, the explosions at Riyadh and Khobar, and, of course, 9/11. He reminds Bush, 'the White House goof', that 'you received the deep backstab in Aden and again you were slapped in the middle of your sanctuary in New York and Washington, and that is all sheer success from Allah to the brigades of good deeds from the children of our Muslim *umma*'.[198]

Thus, he reassures the *umma*: 'O you people, don't let America and its army frighten you, for by God we have struck them and defeated them time and again. They are the most cowardly people in battle'.[199] Indeed, in a message to the people of Iraq he dwells at length on al-Qaeda's own experience of engaging US forces in Afghanistan during the (now infamous) battle of Tora Bora:[200]

In that great battle, the forces of faith triumphed over all the evil forces of materialism by remaining true to their principles.... Despite the unprecedented scale of this bombardment and the terrible propaganda, all focusing on one small, besieged spot, as well as the hypocrites' forces, which they got to fight us for over two weeks, non-stop, and whose daily attacks were resisted by the will of God Almighty, we pushed them back in defeat every time, carrying their dead. Despite all this, the American forces dared not storm our positions. What clearer evidence could there be of their cowardice, of their fear and lies, of the myths about their alleged power.... We suffered only 6% casualties in the battle.... Neither smart nor stupid bombs can penetrate well-disguised trenches in anything better than a random way.[201]

The account also juxtaposes the Americans' B-52 bombers, modified C-130 planes, bunker busters, and cluster bombs against the small group of 300 *mujahidin* huddled in their trenches at temperatures as low as minus ten degrees.

This 'David-and-Goliath'-like tale is used as a heartening confirmation of the ineffectualness of the alleged superpower's super power. According to Abu Ubeid al-Qurashi, through 'fourth-generation' warfare the superiority of the theoretically weaker party has already been proven, nation states have been defeated by stateless nations, and 'the Islamic nation has chalked up the most victories in a short time in a way it has not known since the rise of the Ottoman Empire'.[202] In addition to suchlike grandiose claims, bin Laden thumbs his nose at the Americans for their inability to apprehend him, paraphrasing a US Senator that 'the American Enduring Freedom Operation in Afghanistan has changed to the Failure and Enduring Frustration Operation'.[203]

5.3.2. Assessing Bin Laden's analogies

These three strands of historical reference combine in support of the proposition that the superpower is mythical and the United States is far from invincible. Accordingly, al-Qaeda's *jihad* is presented as winnable. However, since the practical component of the case is integral to the normative position as a whole, it is important to subject these lines of argumentation to critical evaluation. After all, the ideological vision of a just war in Islam is heavily bound up with pragmatic concerns about its viability. In the end, each constituent of bin Laden's rationale for 'reasonable hope of success' is not without its problems.

To begin with, the usefulness of the analogy with the Soviet Union could be questioned. It appears to be flawed in two major, and related, respects. Firstly, though the *mujahidin* did put up an effective resistance in Afghanistan, this cannot be confused with the collapse of the USSR. The war in Afghanistan was but one feature of the Soviets' economic and military overstretch which hastened the fall of the empire. In the years before the Afghanistan invasion, the centrally planned Soviet economy had stagnated, unable as it was to compete in a global market based on innovation and the free flow of goods, capital, and information. According to John Lewis Gaddis, the Soviets 'faced not only external exhaustion but also a simultaneous internal crisis occasioned by a ... tectonic force: the inability of command economies to cope with the growing demands of post-industrial societies'.[204] In addition, from the late-1970s the United States stepped-up its 'proxy' competition with the Soviets, backing a range of the USSR's foes in a number of third-world conflicts, with a military capability that far outstripped that of its communist rivals.[205] The increasing spread of cultural and informational contacts, the dramatic personal role of Gorbachev,[206] and the abandonment of the belief in Leninist ideas about the international class struggle were also crucial factors in bringing the Cold War to an end.[207] The *mujahidin's* resistance in Afghanistan did not cause the dissolution of the USSR; indeed, the withdrawal from Afghanistan in 1989 was itself occasioned by the overall strain of the Soviet Union's imperial excesses and the domestic disasters of the communist system.

Secondly, it could be argued that America's economic, military, technical, and, indeed, geopolitical strength is non-comparable to that of the Soviet Union in its heyday. The United States is not weaker; it is stronger. After the Cold War, America emerged as the sole superpower while commentators heralded the dawn of the unipolar era—'US pre-eminence is unprecedented'[208]—and other states began to acknowledge American *hyperpuissance.*[209] While the Soviet Union could lay claim to having the largest army in the world at the time of its intervention in Afghanistan, its technology and power projection capabilities were already eclipsed by the scientific advances being made in the West and, as considered above, communism was failing economically and politically. When al-Qaeda attacked the United States in 2001 the situation was in marked contrast:

The United States is far from a normal state; no country in modern history has ever held such overwhelming power across so many dimensions. It not only possesses the single largest, wealthiest and most dynamic market for every good and service imaginable, but it is also home to the world's strongest military forces. Its culture is incredibly dynamic, as it opens its doors to the best and brightest from every continent. ... Balancing against the United States is not a likely outcome, since in economic terms there is no good alternative to the American order, while in military terms it spends as much on defence as the rest of the world combined. From all this, one can only conclude that the American century has just begun.[210]

For all of bin Laden's boasting about inflicting damages of 1 trillion dollars,[211] the 9/11 attacks did not visit any economic doom upon America. But, for sure, some lapses have been suffered since then. Ironically,[212] the 'war on terror' policy of invading Iraq cost the United States hundreds of billions of dollars,[213] and forced the administration to finance its budget deficit by borrowing from Japan and China. Nonetheless, America continues to enjoy a pre-eminent role in the world—economically, militarily, and culturally— and any comparisons with the Soviet Union's situation in the 1980s cannot be reasonably countenanced.

There are similar weaknesses in bin Laden's invocation of 'Operation Restore Hope'. He refers to Somalia as a precedent for the US predisposition to cut-and-run when the going gets tough. However, the US intervention in Somalia was humanitarian in nature. The famine was said by the director of the American Office of Foreign Disaster Assistance to be 'the greatest human-itarian emergency in the world'. Indeed, Nicholas Wheeler argues that the administration of George Herbert Walker Bush decided to intervene for three reasons: because of the personal humanitarian impulses of the President and his senior advisers; because it was perceived as a relatively risk-free and short-term operation, without any great danger of body bags coming home; and finally because of Bush's desire to deflect attention away from his inaction over Bosnia and thus prove that his vision of a 'new world order' was not empty rhetoric.[214] After the eighteen Rangers were killed, undoubtedly, the United States packed its bags and withdrew. But, this is evidence of the low American casualty threshold in regard to operations of humanitarian inter-vention[215] rather than dealing with strategic political or economic threats— for which the 1991 Gulf War against Saddam Hussein is a far more appropri-ate example. In fact, while the UN Secretary General wanted the United Task Force to go on to disarm the warring factions, the United States expressly insisted that its mission was limited to ensuring the delivery of food aid. In sum, American action in Somalia in 1993 was entirely humanitarian and not about American security—and the conflict with al-Qaeda is certainly the latter—so it cannot serve as an honest or relevant precedent.

In terms of al-Qaeda's own successful terrorist operations against the United States and its allies, it is true that they have been designed in a way that masterfully manipulates the drastic imbalance of power through 'mar-tyrdom', and such plans have been deftly executed. Bin Laden and his deputy have certainly managed to evade capture, and it would seem that the *muja-hidin* have settled upon an effective mode of engaging the US military which involves 'dragging the enemy forces into a protracted, exhausting, close combat, making the most of camouflaged defence positions in plains, farms, hills and cities' as well as urban warfare.[216] However, though it would seem that al-Qaeda's leadership is able to function 'on the run' and mass terrorist violence continues to be committed in al-Qaeda's name, it is questionable whether al-Qaeda's stated objectives are being realized.

Bin Laden argued that 'the [9/11] attacks benefited Islam greatly'.[217] However, the Imam of Mecca, winner of 'Islamic Personality of the Year' in 2005, cautioned that those who consider 'bloodshed as a way of reform ... do not consider the grave dangers to the future of Islam and Muslims, especially Muslim minorities around the world'.[218] Indeed, the attacks did not only precipitate an anti-Muslim backlash in America in the weeks after 9/11,[219] they led directly to two overwhelming interventions in the Islamic world by the United States and its allies in Afghanistan and Iraq. If bin Laden's just cause was to spur the United States to 'pack its bags and get out of the Muslim lands', it would seem that Western involvement in the region has become even more entrenched with scores of Muslim lives either taken or tainted by the violence and instability. One Thai Muslim intellectual noted in the days after 9/11 that violence 'is unwise politically and will probably result in further consequences beyond common imagination as already evident in the beginning exodus of old and young Afghans from Kabul, and the attacks on oil and vandalism against Muslims around the world'.[220] Similarly, the leader of the Copts in Egypt warned that al-Qaeda sympathizers 'fail to estimate the reaction of their unwarranted glee. They must realise, of course, that the other party will seek revenge and with this glee they hurt themselves and their country'.[221] In Fadlallah's analysis, 'beside the fact that they are forbidden by Islam, these acts do not serve those who carried them out but their victims, who will reap the sympathy of the whole world'.[222]

In addition to the thousands of Muslim lives lost in the US military response to 9/11, there were a series of other ramifications. Islamic reformist movements suffered a significant setback by the attacks and the resultant rhetoric of the 'war on terror'. Regimes facing challenges by domestic Muslim groups could appeal to this discourse to delegitimate their opponents' claims and dismiss them as 'terrorists'—or even step-up the use of force against them.[223] The Palestinian cause, too, was hurt by the 'war on terror'. One Jordanian newspaper told bin Laden that 'these acts will not return the Palestinian people to their country or restore a part of their rights',[224] and Yasir Arafat stated bluntly that 'Osama bin Laden has damaged the Palestinian cause more than any other being'.[225] Though the 'Roadmap to Peace' was introduced in June 2002,[226] the Palestine issue was, in practice, placed on the back-burner as the more urgent military and humanitarian situations in Afghanistan and Iraq exhausted the West's time, resources, and political will. Further, 9/11 brought war and turmoil to millions of civilian Muslims, not only through the US-led invasions conceived as part of the 'war on terror', but through the wave of sectarian and insurgent terrorism perpetrated by local groups in Iraq and Afghanistan (whether instigated by al-Qaeda or not). Thus, a few successful attacks against Western targets notwithstanding, the majority of Islamic terrorism's victims post-9/11 have been the Muslims of bin Laden's cherished *umma*.[227]

Thus, just as the three arguments for the myth of the superpower are problematic, so is the overarching contention that al-Qaeda's *jihad* is winnable. However, as was considered in regard to the Bush administration in Chapter 1, there remains the counterargument that the foregoing discourse constitutes short-term setbacks on the long road to liberty. Certainly, Zawahiri emphasizes the long-term perspective when he assesses whether the Egyptian *jihad* movement has failed or succeeded: 'this is a goal that could take several generations to achieve. The Crusaders in Palestine and Syria left after two centuries of continued *jihad*'.[228] However, the acute regional turmoil in the Middle East, coupled with the near-instant and overwhelming adverse consequences for Muslims worldwide (both normatively, in terms of the 'terrorist' discourse, as well as physically, in terms of war and persecution), does work to cast doubt on the contention that bin Laden is in fact ridding the Islamic world of the West's interference.

It is precisely the notion that bin Laden's *jihad* is destined for failure which forms the centrepiece of the recent criticism levelled against al-Qaeda from Islam's more radical quarters. For those who are otherwise sympathetic to bin Laden's Islamist agenda, the pragmatic component of the Islamic *jihad* tradition becomes crucial in their defection. They refer to the scores of maimed or murdered Muslims, the prisons packed with Muslim youths, and the rising Islamophobia in the West, to call into question the legitimacy of al-Qaeda's *jihad*. Salman al-Odah, for example, the puritanical Saudi preacher once lionized by bin Laden, asked him in a televised address: 'how much blood has been spilled? How many innocent children, women, and old people have been killed, maimed and expelled from their homes in the name of "al-Qaeda"?' Al-Odah, who was jailed for his opposition to US forces in the Kingdom in the 1990s and supported *jihad* against American troops in Iraq in 2003, wondered what is to be gained from the destruction of entire nations, who stands to benefit from turning countries into battlefields, and 'what have all these long years of suffering, tragedy, tears and sacrifice actually achieved?'[229]

Sayyed Imam, who refers to 9/11 as 'a catastrophe for Muslims',[230] also made most of his arguments against attacking the West and fighting regimes in Muslim countries based on practical considerations: the imbalance in forces, the incapacity of the *mujahidin*, and the general inability of popular movements to bring about regime change throughout Egypt's history. *Jihad*, under such conditions, entails 'more damage than benefit'. The preconditions for success do not exist, victory is not likely, it is impossible to differentiate between combatants and non-combatants, thus pursuing armed struggle creates 'vast harms ... while not achieving the hoped for benefit'.[231] Nu'man bin Othman argues, in fact, that he and some other jihadist leaders warned bin Laden, in 2000, that his global *jihad* was doomed: 'we made a clear-cut request for him to stop his campaign against the United States because it was going to lead nowhere. But they laughed when I told them that America would attack the whole region if they launched another attack against it'.[232]

The lack of a reasonable hope of success in al-Qaeda's goals has led many commentators to speculate that the group actually views conflict as an end in itself—that it lauds violence for the sake of violence and practices, in Gunaratna's terminology, 'apocalyptic terrorism'.[233] Olivier Roy, for example, upholds that in the final analysis, 'neo-fundamentalists'[234] like al-Qaeda have no political goal—rather, they wage *jihad* in pessimistic revolt for an elusive ideal world.[235] Indeed, it is understandable that such conclusions are drawn: the unrealistic nature of al-Qaeda's ambitions does cast significant doubt upon its commitment to a restrictive, defensive, just cause. However, the analysis of Chapters 3 and 4 has sought to suggest that, its dubious outcomes notwithstanding, bin Laden has taken great pains to depict al-Qaeda's *jihad* as morally and legally legitimate by positioning it within the Islamic tradition.

5.4. CONCLUSION

In 1993 bin Laden recounted to a journalist how, under bombardment by the Russians in Afghanistan only thirty meters away from him in battle, 'I was so peaceful in my heart that I fell asleep'.[236] This sense of serenity (*sakina*, divine tranquillity) and certitude about having God on his side is transferred into the conflict with the Americans, but this chapter has seen that bin Laden does not make the case by relying solely on grand faith-based statements about good versus evil. Instead, he offers a series of sometimes intricate arguments that connect with the *jihad* tradition and endeavour to present al-Qaeda's cause as limited, just, necessary, and practical.

Despite his best efforts, however, the legacy of bin Laden's case for the resort to war is that of innovation. For right authority, he deftly contrives that the duty to lead a *jihad* has defaulted to him from the corrupted clergy and the regimes comprised of 'secular, apostate opportunists'.[237] For violence as last resort, he offers three broad arguments (warnings have been issued, Muslims face an existential crisis, killing is the only language understood by the West), which hinge entirely on the false premise that the United States has launched an outright assault against the Muslims. For reasonable prospect of success, he disingenuously urges his followers that the historical record reveals the superpower to be surmountable and, ultimately, imaginary.

But it is only on one count that bin Laden seeks to actively 'reinvent tradition', and that is in regard to the authority question. With the remaining *jus ad bellum* issues considered in Chapters 3 and 4—just cause, last resort, and reasonable hope of success—bin Laden engages in what is more accurately described as a reinvention of reality. He holds fairly firm to the principles involved, but his description of the world in each of these cases— that the United States had aggressed against the Muslims for just cause and last resort, and that American power is mythical for reasonable hope of success—fails to correspond to reality. Accordingly, this thesis must concur with Devji that the most significant, lasting effect of al-Qaeda's *jihad* is the fragmentation of traditional forms of Islamic authority. Otherwise, with the stipulation of only warring for self-defence, the precept of violence as last resort, and the practical criterion of hope of success, bin Laden remains surprisingly true, in principle, to the main tenants of the *jihad* tradition.

6

Jus in Bello, Suicide Bombing, and Killing Civilians

In November 1996, bin Laden observed proudly that the Afghan *jihad* was 'unstained with any blood of innocent people, despite the inhuman Russian campaign against our women, our children, and our brothers'.[1] By contrast, the surprise attacks of 11 September targeted and massacred thousands of US civilians. The ensuing outrage was articulated in moral and humanitarian terms, but diverse Muslim reactions to the attacks also expressed their dismay that the carnage was sustained in the cause of their religion. Indeed, the practice of indiscriminate killing is associated with the pre-Islamic period of *jahiliyya*[2] and the deviant Khariji sect was infamous for its slaughtering of women, children, and prisoners of war. Islam, on the other hand, embodies a strict ethical code on the permissible and the impermissible in warfare. Certainly, under certain circumstances, a Muslim has the right to resort to hostilities, but this right can only be exercised 'on the condition that the conflict be a clean one'.[3]

This chapter explores issues raised by al-Qaeda's conduct during its war against the West in the light of Islamic ideas about *jus in bello*. Since 1993, civilians have been al-Qaeda's chosen targets with suicide attacks in New York, Kenya, Tanzania, Saudi Arabia, Tunisia, Bali, Morocco, Iraq, Turkey, Spain, Jordan, England, Algeria, Pakistan, and India, but the main focus of this chapter will be the September 2001 assault upon America. Bin Laden shows deference to the Islamic tradition that 'victory is not only a question of winning, which is how most people see it, but of sticking to your principles',[4] yet his own tactics in the war against America lie in significant tension with the robust *jus in bello* principles of Islam. Section 6.1 will briefly set out that Islamic *jus in bello* tradition, while Section 6.2 will consider the highly controversial issue of suicide bombing. Finally, Section 6.3 will concentrate on the systematic al-Qaeda policy of taking civilians as targets, thus overturning the forceful Islamic provision for non-combatant immunity.

6.1. *JUS IN BELLO* IN ISLAM

In the early days of Islam, the Muslim jurists determined that the *dar al-harb*, which was vilified for the very reason that it did not conform to Islam's ethical and legal standards, was not a moral no-man's-land. There was a legal obligation to respect the rights of non-Muslims in war, civilians and combatants alike.[5] The Muslims had inherited a vast source of custom from the city-states of pre-Islamic Arabia, which had constructed diplomatic codes of conduct and laws of war dealing with POWs, arbitration, alliances, spies, armistice, and so on. (This, of course, undercuts the aforementioned narrative which depicts the period of *jahiliyya* as unmitigated barbarism. The Kharijis, too, quickly evolved into the much more moderate Ibadi sect, which established a strong presence in Oman and parts of Africa.) The Quran itself was an enormous influence in this regard, according, as it did, pride of place to the showing of mercy and the idea of 'commanding the good and forbidding the evil'. Verse 5:8, for example, advises Muslims to 'let no rancour towards others cause you to incline to wrong and depart from justice. Be just: that is closer to piety'. In his practice and sayings, the Prophet, too, conveyed the notion that 'the noblest in the field of war are the people of faith'.

Consequently, the early Muslims established a body of international law which regulated relations with other states in times of war and peace. In terms of the laws of war, this dealt with diverse matters ranging from the distribution of booty,[6] to the damage allowed to be inflicted on the enemy,[7] to the treatment of prisoners of war.[8] Given that all Muslim scientific endeavours were underpinned and subservient to the Quran—'history [developed] primarily to explain the allusions in the Holy Book, philology (including poetry) to explain the exact sense of the words used in it, astronomy and physical geography to find out the direction of the Ka'ba to turn towards, as also the timing for the daily religious services, grammar to standardise the text and diction of the Holy Writ, and so on'[9]—Islamic international law was steeped in the ethical values of the Book.

In this way, legality was reinforced by morality and spirituality to compel that a true Muslim conducts himself justly in warfare. Qutb emphasizes that the main secret of the early Muslims' victories lay in their faith and obedience to God, for to have 'ignore[d] God's commands and the Prophet's instructions would have deprived them of the only force that could ensure victory'.[10] Similarly, Mawdudi maintained that:

It is characteristic of the believers that they faithfully observe the limits prescribed by God in all matters, whether these relate to doctrine or modes of worship, to ethics and morality or society, culture, economics or political life, or to the laws of war and peace. They act both individually and collectively in strict conformity with the limits set by God. . . . The Muslims are warned that God's command to be stern towards and fight against the hypocrites should not mean disregard of moral and humanitarian considerations. For, regardless of what they do, Muslims are always required to act within the limits prescribed by God. Transgression of these limits will render them undeserving of God's support.[11]

Moreover, after the true believers are victorious in battle, they must 'adopt a general attitude of forgiveness and tolerance towards the vanquished rather than subject them to revenge for the wrongs they committed in the past'.[12]

The medieval Sunni jurist Ibn Taymiyyah warned against 'iniquitous, unjust and immoral conduct on the part of the soldier'[13] and observed that 'courage does not reside in physical strength. . . . The strong and valiant is he who controls himself when provoked to anger and so does the right thing'.[14] In fact, in a manner which suggests a link between *jus in bello* conduct and the *jus ad bellum*, he expresses deep concern about a Muslim soldier 'going too far in the opposite direction and becoming over-aggressive'.[15] This notion implies that the Muslims' just cause can be tainted by unethical, un-Islamic behaviour on the battlefield. Sheikh Mohammad Hussein Fadlallah also evidences anxiety in this regard, cautioning Muslims not to 'use unwarranted excessive force and turn aggressors themselves'.[16] As was noted in Chapter 3's discussion on western *jus in bello*, the relevant connection between the two spheres of justice in war is that the just cause serves to *limit*, rather than impassion, the prosecution of a war: 'once the aggressor is checked and backs off, it is not permissible to chase them [*sic*] up; should you carry on engaging them after they have backed off or fled and caused them any injury in the process, the *victim turned aggressor* should stand to compensate them any loss they may have sustained'.[17]

The principle of discrimination—'Islam does not permit aggression against innocent people'[18]—will be taken up extensively later on in this chapter, but it is worth noting in addition the existence of the principle of proportionality. That is, the destruction allowable to a Muslim army must be proportional to its limited military objectives. Khadduri explains the impulse behind this in classical Islam:

In Muslim legal theory, the objective of war is neither the achievement of victory nor the acquisition of the enemy's property; it is rather the fulfilment of a duty—the *jihad* in Allah's path—by universalising the Islamic faith. The jihadists, accordingly, were advised to refrain from the shedding of blood or the destruction of property unnecessary for the achievement of their objective.[19]

Consequently, and to different degrees, the jurists set about banning the slaying of flock, the felling of trees, and the destruction of beehives.[20] In more recent writings, the damage permitted in combat is linked with the modern objective of stopping aggression. Qutb, for his part, was insistent that 'there should be no excessive retribution'. Instead, based on Quranic verse 2:194,[21] 'the Muslims are instructed to retaliate in a measured way and within the limits dictated by the type and extent of the initial aggression'.[22] For Fadlallah, 'precaution is called for in every sphere of self-defence and the means used to achieve it ... lest one should be excessive so much so that he could be overstepping the boundaries of the legitimate right'.[23]

Contained in Osama bin Laden's statements are explicit appeals to the proportionality concept. Before 9/11, he warned that 'the American forces should expect reactions from the Muslim world which are proportionate to the injustice these forces inflict'.[24] In the wake of the attacks, and after the United States had responded by leading an invasion of Afghanistan, he employed the principle in criticism of America's *in bello* conduct: 'America, in her hatred for the Taliban and for the Muslims, drops bombs weighing seven tons on our brothers in the front lines. That is equivalent to seven thousand kilograms, or seven million grams, even though seven grams is more than enough for one person'.[25] Thus, in addition to his (predictable) argument that the United States had no business being in Afghanistan, bin Laden drew upon the *jus in bello* norm of proportionality to heap more derision upon the illegitimate intervention. The proportionality idea is entrenched to the extent that it was utilized by some Muslims against bin Laden, as, for example, one Indonesian surmised the need to 'formulate a more proportional stance in response to various developments at home and overseas, which have affected Muslims and Islam'.[26]

A related concept, the doctrine of double-effect, was considered in Chapter 3 with regard to the Western just war tradition of *jus in bello*. This is the idea that, in aiming to bring about a 'good' effect by attempting to accomplish a military objective, an action can also have a foreseen but unintended 'bad' effect such as harm to civilians. The action becomes illegitimate if the badness of the unintended effect outweighs the goodness of the intended one. Initially articulated by Aquinas in relation to killing a man in self-defence, this line of reasoning was applied to discussions about *jus in bello* by Vitoria in the sixteenth century. Its existence in the Islamic tradition, however, can be traced back to the classical period. And, interestingly, it developed out of the concern over killing fellow Muslims held hostage by the fighting. Hence, Shaybani argues that if the Muslims are laying siege to a city and its people are using Muslim children as shields, the Muslims may attack the enemy with arrows and mangonels, but 'the warriors should aim at the inhabitants of the territory of war and not the Muslim children'.[27] He goes on to say that it would be permissible to strike them with swords and lances as long as the children were not intentionally aimed at. In *Al-Hidayah*, al-Murghinani recognized that 'it is impossible in shooting to distinguish precisely between [the children or Muslim captives] and the infidels'—nevertheless, he argued, 'the person who discharges the weapon must make this distinction in his intention and design by aiming at the infidels and not the others, since thus much is practicable'.[28] Imam al-Shafi, too, upheld that provided that the intention was to kill the unbelievers, the Muslims could fire at close range even if this led to the killing of Muslim captives placed among them.[29]

In the thirteenth century, a *fatwa* by ibn Taymiyyah also maintained that 'if with the *kuffar* there are pious people from the best of mankind and it is not possible to fight these *kuffar* except by killing them, then they are to be killed as well'. In fact, in 'Defence of the Muslim Lands', this *fatwa* is cited as support for Abdullah Azzam's advice to his comrades in Afghanistan: 'if the *kuffar* use Muslim captives as human shields in front of them in an advance to occupy a Muslim land, it remains an obligation to fight the *kuffar* even if this leads to the killing of Muslim captives'.[30] Azzam's protégé, bin Laden, in turn uses this logic in justifying the Muslim death toll on 9/11. When asked how he could possibly approve of an event in which hundreds of Muslims were slain, bin Laden creatively equates Muslims living in the United States with human shields:

This is a significant issue in Islamic jurisprudence. According to my information, if the enemy occupies an Islamic land and uses its people as human shields, a person has the right to attack the enemy. In the same way, if some thieves broke into a house and took a child hostage to protect themselves, the father has the right to attack the thieves, even if the child gets hurt.[31]

At another stage, and in rejecting comparisons between al-Qaeda and the Kharijis, he makes clear that 'if some Muslims have been killed during the operations of the *mujahidin* then we pray to God to take mercy on them; this is a case of accidental manslaughter and we beg Allah's forgiveness for it and we take responsibility for it'.[32] This issue will be taken up in greater depth later in the chapter. Here, it is sufficient to note that the doctrine of double-effect and the accompanying notion of 'accidental manslaughter' form a distinct part of conversations about justified *jihad*.

In addition to broad moral principles, the Islamic tradition addresses itself directly to specific *jus in bello* questions ranging from prisoners of war (POWs) to the status of irregular combatants. The fate of any prisoners taken in battle was in classical Islam left up to the discretion of the caliph who had the legal option of executing them, enslaving them, conducting a prisoner exchange, releasing them for ransom, or setting them free. A tradition dating back to the first Muslim community, however, shirked the option of execution. After the Battle of Badr, the Muslims found themselves in possession of seventy prisoners and, while the famous military commander ibn Khattab exhorted that they be decapitated immediately, the Prophet followed Abu Bakr's advice to ransom them and set them free. Abu Bakr had argued morally that the prisoners were 'our kith and kin', and instrumentally that these seventy souls were potential Muslims who could one day be guided by Allah to Islam. Shaybani thus instructed that 'the prisoner of war should not be killed, but he may be ransomed or set free by grace',[33] and ibn Taymiyyah noted that 'the *sharia* enjoins fighting the unbelievers but not the killing of those who have been captured'.[34] Yet both simultaneously acknowledged that execution was an option if the caliph determined that such a course would be advantageous to the Muslims.

Contemporary, radical treatments of the POW issue lay great stress on the fact that the caliph could choose between alternatives to establish the legality of executing prisoners. Yusuf al-Ayyiri, the prolific al-Qaeda ideologist killed by Saudi security forces in 2003, insisted that the choice was to be made between execution, amnesty, ransom, or enslavement, depending on which course would bring the greatest benefit to Muslims. Ayyiri penned his treatise, 'A Guide for the Perplexed on the Permissibility of Killing Prisoners', in response to the outcry over the Chechen execution of Russian prisoners in 2002.[35] Before him, Sayyid Qutb favoured killing captives because it gave strength to the Muslims and weakened their enemies, and he rejected the possibility of taking ransom, as it amounted to the sinful quest for material gain.[36] Mawdudi, too, warned against the 'greed for ransom', but he allowed for the possibility of execution only in exceptional cases. Mawdudi was also insistent that 'no precedent has been found when a prisoner might have been mistreated in [the Prophet and his Companions'] time'.[37] Certainly, the humane treatment of prisoners is prescribed by the Quranic verse which states 'and they feed, for the love of Allah, the indigent, the orphan, the captive' (76:8).

Early on, it was incumbent upon the believers to fashion a policy on the treatment of Muslim rebels. Just as the first caliph, Abu Bakr, was compelled to fight those who would not pay the *zakat*, so Ali's reign as fourth caliph was riven with challenges from other Muslims. The primary goal being reconciliation between Muslims, rebels were not to be treated as criminals and force was to be used against them only if the rebels themselves were evidencing the intention of fighting. Once violence was resorted to, leniency was emphasized—no destructive weaponry was to be used, the wounded were not to be killed, no property was to be confiscated, enslavement was banned, and the rebels were entitled to an Islamic burial. This framework of law, known as Ahkam al-Bughat, depicted the situation of civil conflict as objective and legal, rather than political. A group of naysayers could be defined as legitimate rebels if it adhered to three criteria: *khuruj*, an act of resistance to the caliph; *ta'wil*, adherence to an interpretation of an Islamic source arrived at through *ijtihad*; *shuaka*, possession of numerical power as well as organization and leadership. This classical Islamic categorization foreran the Geneva Convention provisions, considered in Chapter 3, which afford protections to irregular forces if they wear distinctive insignia, carry arms openly, respect the laws of war, and act under responsible command. In being accorded a legitimacy of sorts, genuine insurgency was distinguished from common outlawry and, in contrast to the West, which treated rebellion with extreme hostility prior to the French Revolution and its break of the Church's grip, Islam always possessed a form of relativism. Khaled Abou El-Fadl maintains that both government and insurgents stood as equal before God, 'a type of argument [which is] unique, especially in a religious context where truth is supposed to be absolute and uncompromising'.[38]

In this way, Islamic thinking on *jus in bello* is comprised of broad moral principles, with divine sanction, as well as specific legal judgements. As with the West, *jihad* theorizing has emphasized the *jus ad bellum* and *jus in bello* to varying degrees at different junctures in history. The early jurists, who were very much engaged in statecraft, were more preoccupied by proper conduct than with the justification for going to war in the first place, supposing as they did that warring to extend the borders of Islam possessed holy warrant. As the imperial tide turned against the Muslims, *jus in bello* matters assumed secondary importance in favour of more pressing questions about just cause and *jus ad bellum*. This might partly explain why, for example, deliberations about the doctrine of double-effect were for a long time frozen in the seventh-century debate about killing Muslims used as human shields, and have only recently been analytically extended to cover harming enemy civilians. However, while Sohail Hashmi notes that 'in current Muslim discourse on war and peace, *jus in bello* issues receive very little attention', he also observes that 'relevant and interesting discussion[s] of right conduct in war [occur] in the context of specific conflicts'.[39] As such, the 9/11 attacks seem as good a context as any in which to explore these discussions.

The remainder of this chapter will consider the controversy thrown up by al-Qaeda's means (suicide bombing) before turning to the principle of discrimination and al-Qaeda's justifications for its chosen targets (civilians).

6.2. SUICIDE BOMBING

In addition to the moral-theological emergencies of committing aggression and killing civilians, the 9/11 operation immediately confronted Islam with another normative question: the legitimacy of suicide attacks. The contentiousness of the issue is born of the fact that suicide is considered an egregious sin in Islam.

Verse 4:29 states plainly 'and do not kill thyselves', which is supported by the spirit of the commands not to cast thyself by thy own hands into destruction (2:195) and never to give up hope of Allah's mercy (12:87). A slew of authoritative *hadith* support the injunction against suicide, such as 'the one who strangles himself will be strangling himself in the Fire, and whoever stabs himself will be stabbing himself in the Fire', and, by the eighth century, at the latest, Muslim jurists and preachers had come to condemn suicide as a grave offence. In the words of a tenth-century scholar, 'such an act is detested by the intellect, considered sinful by tradition and shunned with horror by nature; for the generally known injunctions of the religious laws and the consensus of all in each generation and region show that suicide is forbidden and that nothing should be done which might lead to it'.[40] An eighteenth-century *fatwa* judged suicide as a more serious crime than murder, and, a century later, the German Orientalist Theodor Noldeke noted that Islam was 'a religion amongst the followers of which suicide is almost absolutely unknown'.[41] Indeed, it is said that in the 1980s, members of the *mujahidin* fighting the Soviets in Afghanistan asked the Tamil Tigers if they would supply suicide bombers in exchange for money, offensive as suicide was to both Islam and the Afghan code of honour.

Shahada (martyrdom), by contrast, is often expressed as a valiant Islamic aspiration. Though martyrdom and suicide share the essential characteristic of knowingly walking into one's own death, the distinction between them entails the difference between heaven and hellfire. Mohammad Ata, widely regarded as the lead hijacker, left a note which stated that he wanted to go to heaven as a martyr,[42] as did Ahmad al-Ghamidi of the Washington flight, who pre-recorded a video message declaring 'O God, I sacrifice myself for your sake, accept me as a martyr'.[43] But while Osama bin Laden upheld that 'these people fought the great unbelief with their hands and their souls and we pray to Allah to accept them as martyrs',[44] Ayatollah Fadlallah decided that the hijackers 'did not die in the course of *jihad*. . . . They were merely suiciders'.[45]

6.2.1. Martyrdom in Islam

In a striking parallelism, both Christian and Muslim doctrines of martyrdom emerged out of the concept of a martyr as a witness. In fact, in all but one[46] of its usages in the Quran, the word '*shahid*' is not used to denote 'martyr' but, instead, 'witness'. Brian Wicker argues that the witness's manner of living and dying gradually became proof of his reliability, and the notion of martyr attached to the person who was willing to be killed for his faith. In this way, 'the concept of witnessing to the faith originated in a non-violent context, but later, as a result of persecution of the faithful, became specialised into dying for it'.[47] In Islam, this transformation did not occur until the eighth century. However, though the concept had identical origins in the two traditions, it quickly evolved in different directions: Christianity deemed that martyrdom could never be achieved in warfare, while Islam considered war as the most laudable context for martyrdom. As the classical jurists promoted an expansionist understanding of *jihad*, so they conceptualized martyrdom 'almost exclusively in a military sense and a hortatory genre developed around the merits of falling on the battlefield'.[48]

Indeed, one modern commentator noted that '*shahid* is the warrior who was killed by the enemy in battle, not the one who killed himself'.[49] As such, the idea of the unflinching, unfeasibly brave Muslim charging into battle with a very high chance of dying (known as *inghimas*) has its corollary in other representations of the martial ideal, from Hollywood depictions of Sir William Wallace to the legend of the Spartan King Leonides' courageous 'last stand' against a gigantic Persian army at Thermopylae. Hence, when a child living in the slums of Gaza stated in a documentary '*mumkin astashhad bukra*' (I could be martyred tomorrow), he was describing the ever-present possibility of being killed by the Israelis.[50] However, what the Palestinian situation calls to mind is the recently conceived close connection between martyrdom and suicide bombing. And, it is worth emphasizing that 'this form of *jihad*, in which the body is used as a weapon, is a recent development in the annals of Islamic warfare, even if the concept of holy war and martyrdom is as old as the religion itself'.[51]

Martyrdom has held particular resonance for the Shias, who have a specialized genre of literature known as *maqtal* relating the biographies and glories of their martyrs. The sacrifice of the third Imam, Husayn,[52] in the face of Umayyad tyranny continues to be marked today by the mourning festival of Ashura.[53] Another crucial figure in the symbolic topography of Shiism is Husayn's father, Ali. After suffering a mortal blow from his Khariji assassin, he is reported to have rejoiced in his own death with the words 'by the Lord of the Ka'ba I have succeeded'. The cultural significance of this martyrdom motif was instrumentalized to great effect by the Islamic ideologues of the 1979 revolution in Iran (on one occasion, for example, Khomeini compared the death of an eighteen-year-old killed by the Shah's troops to the children who died with Husayn at Karbala).[54] Although, historically, the Sunnis demonstrated greater caution towards the place of martyrs, due to the worry that such veneration could amount to *shirk* (the association of something with

God, other than God Himself), in the modern period the concept of martyr-dom has been similarly popularized. Anti-colonial movements adopted the lexicon of martyrdom to describe their struggles and their fallen comrades (which continues today in Palestine), there is a burgeoning Sufi martyrdom literature, and the term 'martyr' is even extended to such situations as being stampeded to death on the Haj.

Crucially, Sunni-orientated *jihad*s have embraced the concept of martyr-dom, which has increasingly taken the form of self-killing in the process—that is, the '*shahid*' commits to death before the operation and dies along with his intended victims in its execution. This weaponization of the human body emulates the campaign waged by the Tamil Tigers in Sri Lanka since the 1970s, whose 'martyrdom' is framed in nationalist and ethnic terms, rather than religious ones. For sure, 'in Sunni Islam examples of suicide attacks are rare prior to the 1990s',[55] but since 1994 suicide bombings have been the primary tactic adopted by, for example, the Palestinian resistance movement.[56]

Unlike the Japanese kamikaze pilots in the Second World War, whose cultural and religious traditions conceive of suicidal practices like hara-kiri as honourable, suicide *jihad*is would appear to be acting against the weight of their tradition. As noted above, suicide is forbidden in Islam. At the same time, however, the concept of martyrdom was valorized by the classical jurists who pointed to Quranic verses such as 'think not of those as dead who are killed in the way of Allah—nay, they are alive with their Lord, and they have provision' (3:169). This verse had been revealed as the Muslims grieved for their losses after the battle of Uhud.[57] But if the defeat at Uhud prompted the seminal Quranic verse on martyrdom, the victory at Badr[58] inspired a series of *hadith*s which glorify the warrior fearlessly plunging himself into his enemy's ranks. One relates how, in order to please Allah, Mu'adh ibn Afra went so far as to remove his armour and charge determinedly into the fray. Another concerns Umayr al-Humam, who was leaning against a wall eating some dates while listening to a rousing speech by Mohammad. He said suddenly, 'really, now! Nothing stands between me and paradise apart from fighting?', upon which he threw down the dates, took up a sword, and fought until he was killed. Needless to say, great show is made of these 'precedents' in the attempts made at theologically justifying suicide bombing.

6.2.2. Some theological justifications of suicide bombing

Wicker, Azzam, and Bishop note that 'Hamas has never sought to find a theological argument for the use of suicide bombings, relying instead on the popular acceptance among the Palestinians of the legitimacy of such attacks and the 'martyrdom' of its perpetrators'.[59] Indeed, Khaled Misha'al speaks of the tactic in instrumental terms—'it is an effective form which our people resorted to because of their limited options... the more forms of terrorism and aggression the occupation forces carry out against us, the more right our people have to look for alternatives'[60]—and Abdulaziz Rantissi invokes the example of Jesus Christ.[61] Other Muslims, however, have appealed to Islam directly in an endeavour to present suicide bombing as a legitimate part of their religious tradition. This is usually done in three ways: by emphasizing the Islamically legitimate intentions of the bomber, by relying upon 'The boy and the king' *hadith* as precedent, and by reviving the classical tradition of the fighting martyr.

6.2.2.1. *Intention*

Ayman al-Zawahiri's defence of 'martyrdom operations' (suicide bombing) begins by according central place to the agent's intention (*niyya*). He asserts that suicide is prohibited in Islam, but determines that the 'deciding factor is the intention—is it service to Islam [martyrdom] or is it out of depression and despair?'[62] An article which appeared in the Australian *Nida'ul Islam* magazine also distinguished suicide from the death of a 'martyr' in a suicide bombing by invoking the moral device of intentionality. The author, Abu Ruqaiyah, argued that 'it is important to know that suicide is forbidden because of its evil objectives, such as impatience, desperation or any other bad and evil objects.... On the other hand, the one who contributes his life to the cause of Allah, Islam and Muslims, his doing is sacrificial; he gives his life away for Islam and Muslims, which is the highest sacrifice'. Thus, because the suicide bomber is driven by his faith and Allah's cause, he is distinguished from the ordinary suicider, whose motivations are 'Islamically pointless, meaningless and intentionally suicidal'.[63]

Yusuf al-Ayyiri, the hugely influential al-Qaeda theorist, adopted a similar scheme. In a document, entitled 'The Islamic Ruling on the Permissibility of Martyrdom Operations', written for the Chechen *mujahidin*, he likewise emphasized the bomber's self-sacrificial intentions:

The name 'suicide operations' used by some is inaccurate, and in fact this name was chosen by the Jews to discourage people from such endeavours. How great is the difference between one who commits suicide—because of his unhappiness, lack of patience and weakness or absence of *iman* and has been threatened with Hellfire—and between the self-sacrificer who embarks on the operation out of strength of faith and conviction, and to bring victory to Islam, by sacrificing his life for the uplifting of Allah's word![64]

The distinction being promulgated here possesses some parallels with Emile Durkheim's conceptualization of egoistic versus altruistic suicide. While the former is the product of excessive individuation and a detachment from society, the latter results from insufficient individuation and strong social integration. The altruist kills himself 'not because he assumes the right to do so but, on the contrary, *because it is his duty*'.[65] Ayyiri sums up the intention argument succinctly when he states that unlike suiciders who kill themselves on account of a lack of faith, the *mujahid* in a 'martyrdom operation' is driven by the strength of his faith.[66]

6.2.2.2. *The boy and the king*

Justifications of suicide bombing regularly rely on the *hadith* of the 'boy and the king', which is an outgrowth of the 'Companions of the Pitt' story in the Quran (85:4–8).

The tradition concerns a young trainee sorcerer who one day slays an attacking beast using the strength of his belief in Allah, inculcated in him by a monk, rather than his supernatural skills. The king finds out about this, and the fact that the boy is also able to cure the sick, and orders his guards to compel the boy to renounce his faith, or else kill him. But when the henchmen march the boy to the top of the highest mountain, Allah intercedes by shaking the mountain so that they all fall down, just as when the boy is taken by boat to the middle of the sea, Allah sends a wave to capsize it so that all but the boy are drowned. Finally, the boy advises the king that the only possible way to kill him would be for the King to crucify him on a tree in front of the people, string an arrow to the quiver, and say 'in the name of Allah, Lord of the youth', and then fire. The king assembles a great crowd and does just as the boy recommended, and the arrow hits the boy straight in the temple. The crowd, converted by the accuracy of the boy's prediction, begins to chant, 'we believe in the Lord of the youth, we believe in Allah'. But the King is so incensed that he conveys these new converts to a burning ditch and forces them to either renounce their religion or jump into the fire. One woman holding her young son becomes very frightened by the flames and thinks of recanting, but the child looks up at her and says 'mother, go on, for you are in the right'.

Ayman al-Zawahiri uses this story to demonstrate that 'the youth killed himself through his own will and choice by showing the King the way to kill him', yet in the Quran and the *hadith*, the boy is never regarded as 'evil or suicidal'. Rather, the *hadith* shows, according to Zawahiri, that 'it is permissible for a believer to destroy himself for the good of the religion'.[67] The Ayyiri document used by the Chechens, and many other Islamist websites, also infers that 'the Boy ordered the King to kill him in the interest of the religion, and this indicates that such a deed is legitimate, and not considered suicide'.[68] Bin Laden himself surmises that 'there is a clear moral in the *hadith* of the youth, the king, sorcerer and monk—of people offering themselves up for the proclamation that "there is no God but Allah"'.

It is, perhaps, significant that this story, almost completely ignored in Islamic history, has only achieved recent prominence for the precedent it allegedly sets. But, as Raymond Ibrahim points out, Quranic verses should be the foundation of a legal argument, with *hadiths* serving the secondary role of exemplification.[69] Moreover, there seems to be a fundamental distinction between the boy's death and that of the suicide bomber: the boy did not die by his own hand, not to mention the fact that he did not kill anyone else— rather, he was crucified and then killed for his belief in Allah, *by the king*.

6.2.2.3. *The fighting martyr*

Theological justifications of suicide bombing claim that there is plenty of Islamic precedent for suicidal behaviour in war. Appeals are made to the scores of warriors who engaged the enemy while facing certain death and are glorified in the *hadith* for their actions. Zawahiri devotes considerable effort to providing 'examples from the unadulterated *sunna* and the biographies of the companions regarding *mujahidin* placing themselves in peril and thus being killed by their enemies'. Abu Ruqaiyah, too, cites a series of Quranic verses and *hadith*, including the case of Umayr al-Humam, to suggest that 'it is Islamically legitimate to fight the enemy to death'.[70] He emphasizes, though, that a Muslim must be sure that he will actually inflict casualties on the enemy (thus, as with 'reasonable hope of success', pragmatic considerations are again integral to discussions on the just *jihad*). Ayyiri also sets out Islamic pre- cedents which are 'clear evidence of the virtues of *jihad* operations in which it is most likely that one will die' and concludes that 'nothing has appeared to contradict sacrificing one's life for raising Allah's word'.[71]

However, as became clear with the alleged precedent of 'the boy and the king', these revered martyrs, crucially, were slain *by the enemy*. In Zawahiri's pamphlet, for example, each account of the martyr held up as a precedent for suicide bombing actually ends with the statement, 'he slashed away til he was slain', or 'the man plunged himself into the ranks of the enemy, fighting "til he was slain"'. Ayyiri, though, explicitly recognizes that 'there is one difference between the martyrdom operations and their classical precedent, namely that in our case the person is killed by his own hand, whereas in the other he was killed by the enemy'.[72] This discrepancy is addressed with the argument that in plunging into enemy ranks without hope of escape, a *mujahid* is contributing to his own death, and contributing to one's own death is just like killing oneself. In fact, the Muslim who is killed in 'martyrdom operations' 'is better than the one who is killed fighting in the ranks, for there are gradations even among martyrs'.[73]

By asserting a moral distinction between the intentions of the suicider and those of the martyr, reinterpreting the somewhat obscure *hadith* of 'The boy and the king', and reinventing the tradition of the fighting martyr, theological justifications of suicide bombing endeavour, in Zawahiri's words, to 'demonstrate the legality of martyrdom operations'. But Zawahiri also acknowledges that 'many disputes have revolved around its legitimacy, both from the people of Islam themselves and their foes'.[74] It is to recent disputes about suicide bombing that this chapter will turn, after briefly considering the place of the 'cult of martyrdom' within Islam.

6.2.3. The cult of martyrdom

It is intriguing, and hopefully worth noting, that the 'cult of martyrdom' upon which al-Qaeda draws, and to which it contributes, engages with aspects of Islam which are associated with the very sects that al-Qaeda, as a puritanical Sunni organization, denounces. In the first place, as was pointed out by Navid Kermani in 2002, the cult of martyrdom possesses a distinctively Shia quality. Kermani argues that the 9/11 hijackers' 'way of thinking does revert back to certain forms of Islamic religious tradition but to the Shite beliefs which they regard as heretic'. The cult of martyrdom, he observed, only developed in opposition to the Islamic majority, and many of its spiritual and ritual elements are 'alien to the nature of Sunni Islam, such as the idea of redemption, the need for repentance, the practice of flagellation and the idea of an imitation of suffering'. As such, al-Qaeda's bombers are borrowing from a past which is not even their own.[75]

Secondly, Sufi elements are clearly at work. Most Sunni extremists are implacably hostile to Sufism, a branch of Islam which combines the teachings of the Quran with mystical and esoteric elements, and which is often demonized as a backward and heretical cult that venerates the dead. Yet, the hijacker's 'Spiritual Manual', for example, prescribes an almost cultic recitation of prayer aimed at inducing a trance-like mental state. Moreover, during the Afghan war, Abdullah Azzam famously related a series of martyrdom narratives. He would speak of the bodies of martyrs as sweet-scented, protected from decay and radiating light, and he would describe martyrs still holding on to their weapons after death and continuing to cause damage to the enemy. David Cook argues that Azzam's powerful reformulations of martyrdom have set the standard among radical Muslims, but he remarks, too, that 'these stories resemble nothing so much as the type of stories to be found among various Sufi cults of saints and martyrs'.[76] It is inevitably curious, therefore, that al-Qaeda's suicide bombers dynamically engage with those Islamic traditions which they endeavour to define themselves against.

6.2.4. Recent 'martyrdom' debates

In a bid to be seen as inside the Islamic fold, Ayyiri's document observes that 'the [suicide bombing] issue is at worst a disagreed issue among scholars, such that we cannot be criticised for following legitimate scholarship'.[77] Though the sin of suicide renders the subject a closed book for the arch-conservative clerical establishment, there certainly exists an Islamic debate on the matter.

Sheikh Mohammad Nasr al Din al-Albani, one of the foremost Islamic scholars of the twentieth century, declared that 'all suicide missions in our current time are unsanctioned deeds that are all to be considered *haram* (prohibited) ... these suicide missions are not Islamic, period!' He recognized that in past generations small groups of Muslims would confront much larger contingents of the enemy, but he upheld that there is no such thing as an Islamic suicide in the absence of proper Islamic authority. Only the caliph is qualified to barter with the lives of Muslims. As a result, suicide bombings were 'solely individualised acts that do not have a positive consequential result that is benefiting to the Islamic call'.[78] Saudi Arabia's Mufti, Sheikh Abdul Aziz al-Sheikh, has likewise affirmed that the enemy must be killed in 'ways which do not violate Allah's law'. He explained that 'I do not know any guiding principle of Islamic law favouring it [suicide bombing], nor do I know that it is part of the *jihad* for the sake of God. I'm afraid that it amounts to suicide'.[79]

Sheikh Tantawi, the Grand Sheikh of Al-Azhar, has also condemned suicide bombings in the Palestinian territories and maintained that the *sharia* is against terrorism. However, Tantawi's grounds were somewhat different from the foregoing: 'we reject and condemn the attack on innocent civilians in the name of the *sharia*'.[80] That is, he bases his censure on the *targets* of the bombings and invokes the principle of discrimination (to be discussed in the next section). Indeed, on another occasion, Tantawi stated that 'the actions of martyrdom undertaken by the Palestinians are in self-defence and are a sort of martyrdom as long as they are intended to kill fighters, not women and children'.[81] For Tantawi, then, the suicidal means itself is not Islamically off-limits, so long as non-combatant immunity is respected.

A few influential Muslims go farther than Tantawi. A graduate of Al-Azhar himself, Sheikh Qaradawi claims that Israeli society in its entirety is militarized such that there are no civilians there: 'an Israeli woman is not like women in our societies, because she is a soldier'.[82] Responding to Tantawi's objection to 'martyrdom operations' which are not directed at military installations, he wondered, 'how could the Grand Imam prohibit the killing of assailants? How could he consider them innocent, defenceless civilians?'[83] The argument here echoes that of the nineteenth-century Anarchist, Emile Henri, who maintained that there were no innocent bourgeoisie:

> The building where the Carmaux Company had its offices was inhabited only by bourgeois; hence there would be no innocent victims. The whole of the bourgeoisie lives by the exploitation of the unfortunate, and should expiate its crimes together. So it was with absolute confidence in the legitimacy of my deed that I left my bomb before the door to the Company's offices.[84]

Thus, for Qaradawi as for Henri: 'Il n'y a pas d'innocents'.

Qaradawi stated that hundreds of Islamic scholars shared his opinion. For sure, twenty-eight Al-Azhar clerics signed a communiqué opposing Tantawi's position outright. During his tenure as Mufti of Egypt, Ahmad al-Tayeb agreed that 'Israel is an aggressor and martyrdom operations are legitimate as they seek to defend Muslim rights and holy sites'.[85] The leaderships of the two principal Shia groups in Lebanon, Amal and Hizballah, also stressed their full support for 'the quality martyrdom operations' and for the Palestinians' right 'to resist the occupation by all means and methods'.[86] Sheikh Ali Gum'a, who replaced al-Tayeb as Egypt's Mufti, similarly emphasized the Palestinians' defensive just cause and, after Qaradawi, the combatant status of every Israeli: 'the one who carries out martyrdom operations against the Zionists and blows himself up is, without a doubt, a *shahid* because he is defending his homeland against the occupying enemy who is supported by superpowers such as the US and Britain. The Zionists themselves do not differentiate between civilian and military personnel. They have set the entire people to military service'.[87]

But if Palestinian suicide bombings against Israeli civilians are considered by some to be genuine 'martyrdom operations', the status of the al-Qaeda attacks is certainly more suspect. None of the maverick clerics in favour of the Palestinian missions supported 9/11. Qaradawi, the public champion of the legitimacy of suicide bombing as part of the Palestinian resistance, was avowedly against the attacks. We saw in Chapter 4 how he depicted al-Qaeda as aggressors and we will see later in this chapter how he registered his abhorrence at the targeting of US civilians. Speaking to *Al-Sharq Al-Awsat*, Qaradawi reiterated his belief that 'describing martyrdom operations as suicide is wrong. They are martyrdom operations, because a person sacrifices himself for the cause for which he is fighting'. When the journalist suggested that this conflicted with his views on 9/11, he maintained that 'there is [no] conflict because the two situations [are] entirely different'.[88] In an interview with the *Guardian*, considered in Chapter 4, Qaradawi declares again that 'the difference is huge. What happens in Palestine is self-defence. But in 9/11 they were not fighting an invasion'.[89] Al-Tayeb, too, is pressed by an interviewer on the *prima facie* inconsistency between his support of Palestinian suicide bombers and his condemnation of 9/11. The questioner notes, 'you said that what happened on September 11 was a crime. Aren't the Palestinians doing the same thing?' Al-Tayeb responds in the same vein as Qaradawi: 'No. The situation is completely different. What the Palestinians are doing is self-defence, defence of their religion and their homeland. They are responding to the killing and to a barbaric enemy. This situation is different than what happened in America'.[90]

Flying in the face of the Islamic prohibition on suicide, the modern phenomenon of 'martyrdom operations' is more than a strategic challenge to the West. In its empowerment of individuals and small groups with weapons of war, suicide bombing directly undercuts the political leadership of the Middle East and the conservative brand of Islam espoused by the state-centred Muslim establishment. Indeed, many of those who objected to Al-Sheikh's equation of suicide bombing with suicide implied that his verdict was motivated by political considerations and that his objective was to reassure America.[91] However, even in the context of this emerging defiance of the religious and political 'powers that be', the 9/11 suicide bombings were deemed illegitimate. Once again, the Palestinian situation was brought to the fore and held up as an authentic case of self-defence. Because of the Palestine–Israel conflict, in some radical quarters the discussion on suicide bombing is shifting away from a stress on the taboo of suicide towards an emphasis on the rights of Muslims to defend themselves. As a result, and on account of the dubiousness of its 'defensive' just cause, al-Qaeda's action on 9/11 was even deplored by these firebrand clerics.

A few famous advocates of Palestinian 'martyrdom operations' notwithstanding, it is worth stressing that suicide bombing is a recently devised tactic 'which 1,500 years of Islamic theology would view as heretical'.[92] A number of prominent clerics continue to unequivocally oppose it, from the entirety of the Wahhabi establishment to the chief cleric of Bangladesh[93] to former Iranian president Mohammad Khatami.[94] In addition to the issue of suicide, Islamist suicide bombings have often also raised the question of killing civilians. Condemning operations in Israel, for example, the Grand Imam of Mecca affirmed that attacking 'people of the Book' was 'not allowed under the Islamic *sharia*' and he urged Muslims to protect Christian and Jewish civilians and their properties.[95] To be sure, civilian immunity is a staple and integral part of Islamic thinking on just war, and moral opposition to the 9/11 suicide bombings was almost always expressed with reference to the principle of discrimination. That principle will be the subject of the remainder of this chapter.

6.3. CIVILIANS AS TARGETS FOR AL-QAEDA

Osama bin Laden explained to an American journalist in March of 1997 that 'we have focused our declaration on striking at the soldiers in Saudi Arabia . . . even though American civilians are not targeted in our plan, they must leave'.[96] By February 1998 he commanded that 'to kill the Americans and their allies—civilian or military—is an individual duty incumbent upon every Muslim in all countries'.[97] In less than a year, al-Qaeda's *modus operandi* had been dramatically altered, climaxing with the massacre of 3000 American civilians in 2001. This section will first outline that non-combatant immunity is a strong principle of the Islamic *jihad* tradition, evidenced starkly and urgently by the cataclysmic attacks of 9/11. The discussion will then turn to bin Laden's own arguments for overturning the immunity of US non-combatants. We shall see that bin Laden himself subscribes to the principle of discrimination and employs it in levelling virulent criticism against America's policies—we will also see that his acceptance of the principle leads him into an unclear and uncomfortable moral position.

6.3.1. Non-combatant Immunity in Islam

Advocating the systematic murder of civilians is a source of insurmountable tension for groups which model their behaviour, and especially their aspirations, along Islamic instructions. Surely, in the words of the Mufti of Saudi Arabia, 'Islam strictly forbids the killing of women, children and innocent people'.[98] Numerous sayings are attributed to the Prophet which unequivocally prohibit the killing of women and children (e.g. 'do not cheat or commit treachery, nor should you mutilate or kill children, women or old men'), and Abu Bakr was reported to have commanded the first Syrian expedition to 'neither kill a child or aged man or woman'.

Accordingly, 'the jurists agreed that non-combatants who did not take part in fighting, such as women, children, monks and hermits, the aged, blind, and insane, were excluded from molestation'.[99] Indeed, Shaybani recounts in great detail the chain of transmission of the tradition of civilian immunity, upholding that 'the Apostle of God prohibited the killing of women . . . the Apostle of God said: "you may kill the adults of the unbelievers, but spare their minors, the youth"'.[100] Ibn Rushd surmised that:

There is no disagreement about the rule that it is forbidden to slay women and children provided that they are not fighting, for then women, in [that] case, may be slain.[101] This rule is founded on the fact that, according to authoritative traditions, the Prophet prohibited the slaughter of women and children and once said about a woman who had been slain: 'she was not one who would have fought'.[102]

In the Iran–Iraq war, Khomeini made great show of his unwillingness to harm civilians, and, while praising one successful raid, he noted that the Revolutionary Guard could have inflicted far more damage 'were it not for their Islamic commitment and their desire to protect the innocent and their fear of destroying property belonging to the brotherly Iraqi nation'.[103] Speaking about the US invasion of Iraq in 2003, Sheikh Qaradawi decided that those killed fighting the American forces were martyrs, yet he underlined that 'the issue is not with the Americans who are peace-loving, but with their arrogant government'.[104]

As noted earlier in this chapter, many Islamic thinkers judge overreactions, in terms of disproportionate damage or slaying non-combatants, to be acts of aggression themselves. Consider Qutb:

Aggression implies attacks on non-combatants and peaceful, unarmed civilians who pose no threat to Muslims or to their community as a whole. This includes women, children, the elderly, and those devoted to religious activity, such as priests and monks of all religious and ideological persuasion. Aggression also entails exceeding the moral and ethical limits set by Islam for fighting a just war.[105]

Interestingly, Qutb arrives at this injunction during his commentary on the Quranic verse 2:190 (translated in Qutb's *tafsir* as 'fight for the cause of God those who wage war against you, but do not commit aggression. Indeed, God does not love aggressors').

Ibn Taymiyyah, too, ultimately decides in favour of an absolute non-combatant immunity principle based on 2:190:

But those who do not constitute a defensive or offensive power, like the women, the children, the monks, old people, the blind and the permanently disabled should not be fought, as is agreed upon by the majority of Muslims, unless they carry on a kind of fighting with words (conducting anti-propaganda) or with certain actions. . . . Some jurists maintain that all should be fought (and put to death) because they are infidels, except the women and the children as they constitute part of the booty. The former view, however, is the true one, since we should only fight those who fight us if we really want the religion of Allah to be victorious. Allah, be He exalted, has said in this respect: 'and fight in the way of Allah those who fight you but be not aggressive, surely Allah loves not the aggressors' (2:190).[106]

Using the same verse, the famous Shia cleric Murtada Mutahhari extracts the protection of civilians in a corresponding way. He quotes 2:190 and then explains:

So you who have faith, fight those who are fighting you, because they do so, but do not violate the limit. What does not violating the limit mean? Naturally its obvious meaning is that it is those who are fighting us that we are to fight, meaning that we are to fight with a certain group of people and that group is the soldiers that the other side has sent, the military men.

People who 'are not in a state of combat' are not to be interfered with.[107]

As seen in Chapter 4, verse 2:190 is a seminal Quranic statement about the justification for resorting to war. By grounding a *jus in bello* precept in the discussion about *jus ad bellum*, non-combatant immunity is thus established with direct reference to just cause—for, if Muslims are only to fight those who make war against them, by definition, civilians cannot be fought. Certainly, 'the ethical constitution of legitimate war in Islam dictates that it is prohibited to kill anyone except those who are fighting. In this legitimate war, fighting is restricted to face-to-face confrontation between Muslims and the armies of the aggressors'.[108] This parallels the current in the Western just war tradition, considered in Chapter 3, which describes the 'twin-born' justification of war and its limitation. It was influentially elucidated by Paul Ramsey, who suggested that 'the same considerations which justify killing the bearer of hostile force by the same stroke prohibit non-combatants from ever being directly attacked with deliberate intent'.[109] For Ramsey, 'what justified also limited!' In a significant Islamic tradition, too, justification and limitation are twinned.

Consequently, some of the Islamic reaction to the 9/11 attacks explicitly invoked the terminology of aggression against civilians. Just as the Grand Sheikh of Al-Azhar stated that 'in the name of *sharia*, we reject and condemn the aggression on innocent civilians',[110] so the Secretary General of Nigeria's Jamaatu Nasril Islam explained that 'as our religion commands us, we don't become aggressive, we don't kill innocent men even in war. We are to protect everybody except those who are military men who want to kill us'.[111] In the same way, the communiqué issued by a variety of Islamic groups, some of them associated with radicalism, underlined that 'the rule of Islam proscribes all form of aggressions against the innocent'.[112] Thus, by the moral logic of some Muslims, bin Laden's decision to target civilians impacted directly upon his just cause. The content of his *casus belli* was made irrelevant, for the murder of civilians was enough to render al-Qaeda an aggressor.

Indeed, almost all of the Islamic uproar at the 9/11 attacks took its starting point from the deaths of civilians. One Jordanian Muslim leader accentuated that Muslims 'strongly oppose and condemn such despicable acts, especially when the innocent are targeted' and articulated his country's 'deepest sorrow at this calamity that has befallen the American people'.[113] Muslim statesmen from all over the world publicized their horror at the civilian dead, as Mohammad Khatami sent out his 'deep sympathy ... to the American nation',[114] Megawati Sukarnoputri described the assault as 'brutal and indiscriminate',[115] and Muammar Gaddafi indicated his readiness to send aid to the American people. In Albania, the National Assembly passed a resolution which considered 'the terrorist acts on innocent civilians and symbols of democracy ... a flagrant violation of the most fundamental right of the individual, the right to life',[116] while in Senegalese political circles the attacks were labelled, by turn, 'barbarity against innocent targets', 'inhuman, savage and despicable', and 'acts that every religion and morality condemns'.[117] In Azerbaijan, the leader of the reformist wing of the People's Front of Azerbaijan noted that 'there is no doubt that these events have no precedent among terrorist acts. I think these crimes were committed against humanity'.[118]

Many reasoned that, by virtue of their targets, the attacks could not be associated with Islam. Turkey's Mufti, Mehmet Nuri Yilmaz, affirmed:

Terrorism means intimidation, inflicting fear, and killing. Our religion is Islam. Even the name Islam is adequate to prove that our religion has nothing to do with terrorism. Islam means peace. How can threats, intimidation, and fear coexist with peace? As a matter of fact, the Koran orders to struggle against terrorism.[119]

A statement issued by a group of leading Palestinian intellectuals, including Mahmoud Darwish and Hanan Ashrawi, defined the assault as an 'unspeakable crime' and 'terror that can attach to no religion in particular, no colour in particular, and no cause in particular; even if the cause in whose name the outrage was carried out were a just one ... the murder of innocent civilians can never be elevated to the status of a legitimate act'.[120] Still another Palestinian National Council member referred to 'this ugly criminal act ... this abominable terrorist act'.[121] Later, in one of many sessions triggered by the crisis of targeting innocents in the name of Islam, the Islamic Jurisprudence Assembly of the Muslim World League concluded that terrorist acts 'constitute an attack on religion'.[122]

Among more radical Islamists, too, indignation at the mass killing of civilians was manifest. A spokesman for the Islamic Salvation Front, an opposition Islamist group in Algeria, declared:

This ignoble act of violence cannot, under any condition, be accepted. Whatever the reasons that these people may give for this, it cannot be acceptable. It is an act that must be repressed. It is an ignoble act that neither our religion nor the laws governing countries nor the rules of humanity can accept. . . . There is a very big difference between terrorism and Islam.[123]

The armed Palestinian Group Islamic Jihad noted that the attacks were a consequence of America's policies in the Middle East but avowed that 'we are against the killing of innocent people'.[124] Likewise, and despite dubbing America 'the arch Satan', which makes 'satanic choices' in foreign policy, a controversial Egyptian Muslim writer stressed that 'Islam does not sanction the killing of innocent people, regardless of their beliefs or nationalities'.[125] In a similar way, the founder of the Islamist group Al-Muhajiroun, Sheikh Omar Bakri Mohammad, suggested that bin Laden was acting in self-defence, yet he nevertheless underlined that 'killing innocent civilians [is] unacceptable to Islam but if they were targeting military installations or military personnel or machinery directly at war with Muslims then we must be supportive'.[126] He noted, too, that 'even the most radical of us have condemned this. I am always considered to be a radical in the Islamic world, and even I condemn it'.[127] When Sheikh Ahmad Yasin was asked his reaction to seeing the television pictures of the event, Hamas's spiritual leader noted that he felt 'very sad. I do not like seeing innocent people suffer'.[128] Sheikh Yusuf Qaradawi, who, as we have seen, clings to the contentious belief that there are no civilians in Israel, repeatedly deplored the 9/11 attacks, encouraged Muslims to donate blood to the victims, and dubbed the killing of civilians 'a heinous crime in Islam'. He strenuously reaffirmed that 'even in times of war, Muslims are not allowed to kill anybody save the one who is indulging in face-to-face confrontation with them'.[129]

In this manner, while the 9/11 attacks constituted evidence, for some, of the lack of a principle of discrimination in Islam,[130] the very crisis of the attacks compelled Muslims to rearticulate the principle's existence. The targeting of civilians provoked near-unanimous condemnation of the hijackings and explosions, even from those otherwise sympathetic to al-Qaeda's allegedly 'defensive' just cause. Bin Laden, on the other hand, sought to confront that line of criticism straightforwardly, before the attacks as well as in their aftermath. His statements indicate a sustained preoccupation with this particular constituent of al-Qaeda's philosophy, replete as they are with attempts to legitimize the murder of ordinary Americans.

6.3.2. Bin Laden's arguments

Though bin Laden has never devised a comfortable ideological position, he makes three principal arguments in support of his call for the murder of non-combatants. The remainder of this chapter will consider those arguments. The first argument seeks to deny the innocence of US civilians based on the inclusiveness of the democratic political system. The second, more prevalent strand constitutes the *jus in bello* argument from reciprocity (reciprocity[IB]). It acknowledges that the victims of al-Qaeda operations are innocents, but justifies their deaths with the fact that scores of innocent Muslims are being killed by the United States. The final argument draws on a version of the doctrine of double effect to assert that those innocent people who fall during al-Qaeda operations are not intentionally slain—that they are, in effect, collateral damage.

6.3.2.1. *Argument 1: democracy negates innocence*

On several occasions, bin Laden reasons from the fact of America's democratic form of government to the legitimacy of targeting its civilian citizens in war. In fact, in May 1998, bin Laden warned the people of the West that if they 'do not wish to be harmed inside their very own countries, they should seek to elect governments that are truly representative of them and that can protect their interests'.[131] Several months later, and after the bombings of US embassies in Kenya and Tanzania, bin Laden continued on this theme:

A target, if made available to Muslims by the grace of God, is every American man. He is an enemy of ours whether he fights us directly or merely pays his taxes. You might have heard those who supported Clinton's attacks against Iraq formed three-quarters of the American population. A people that regards its president in high favour when he kills innocent people is a decadent people with no understanding of morality.[132]

In this statement, bin Laden refers to the joint US–UK bombing of Iraq in December 1998 for its failure to comply with UN weapons inspections. Thus, he calls upon the democratic institution of taxation, measures of account-ability, and popular moral support for the president to cancel protections for US civilians. However, at this stage, bin Laden confines the reversal of non-combatant immunity to grown men.

Owing to the indiscriminate nature of the attacks on New York and Washington, in which many elderly people, women, and children lost their lives, it was incumbent upon bin Laden to modify his stance after 9/11. To that end, he points to taxation and popular participation and representation to deny the innocence of the attacks' victims:

The American people should remember that they pay taxes to their government and that they voted for their president. Their government makes weapons and provides them to Israel, which they use to kill Palestinian Muslims. Given that the American Congress is a committee that represents the people, the fact that it agrees with the actions of the American government proves that America in its entirety is responsible for the atrocities that it is committing against Muslims.[133]

That is, on account of the participatory political system of the United States, the American populace is actively engaged in harming the *umma*. Civilians are complicit in the deaths of Muslims—moreover, their political system directly empowers them, should they choose, to transform their government and end the 'atrocities' being meted out in their name. He continues on this theme in his 'Letter to the Americans' in October, 2002, explicitly justifying aggression against US civilians for three reasons: 'the American people have the ability and choice to refuse the policies of their government, and even to change it if they want'; 'the American people are the ones who pay the taxes which fund the planes that bomb us'; 'the American army is part of the American people'.[134] Thus, he makes an inference from government by the people to the peoples' non-immunity in war.

The principle of non-combatant immunity aside, this argument goes against the Quran's articulation of personal responsibility. The verse 'no bearer of burdens can bear the burden of another' (17:15) can be seen as a clear rejection of the notion of collective responsibility. Indeed, when he upheld in 1996 that al-Qaeda only kills soldiers, bin Laden himself quoted the verse 'then fight in Allah's cause, thou art held responsible only for thyself, and rouse the believers' (4:84).[135] In any case, alongside the suggestion that the fact of democracy creates collective responsibility in war, is a second, much more common argument.

6.3.2.2. *Argument 2: Reciprocity*[JB]

A recurrent Ladenese tack is the *jus in bello* argument about reciprocity. Put simply, because the United States is attacking Muslim civilians, al-Qaeda is permitted to attack US civilians: 'so we kill the kings of disbelief and the kings of the Crusaders, and the civilians among the disbelievers, in response to the amount of our sons they kill—this is correct in both religion and logic'.[136] America's disdain for civilian immunity is said to be true in general, as well as with specific and ongoing regard to the Muslim people.

The proposition that America targets civilians is proven generally by its track record in warfare. According to bin Laden, 'throughout history, America has not been known to differentiate between the military and the civilians or between men and women or adults and children'.[137] Indeed, 'the name of the American government and the names of Clinton and [George H. W.] Bush directly reflect in our minds the picture of children with their heads cut off before even reaching one year of age'.[138] Zawahiri, too, notes the American 'disregard for all taboos and disrespect for the customs of wars and conflicts'.[139] The favoured example in furtherance of this claim is America's use of the atomic bomb against Japan in the Second World War, 'when it would not be possible for those bombs to hit only military troops. Rather, these bombs were dropped on entire nations, including women, children, and elderly people'.[140] When pressured about his own failure to respect the principle of discrimination, bin Laden repeatedly appeals to the cases of Hiroshima and Nagasaki over the years. In 1996 he pointed to 'the premeditated dropping of the H bombs on cities with their entire populations of children, elderly, and women'[141]; in 1998, he observed that 'those who threw atomic bombs and used weapons of mass destruction against Nagasaki and Hiroshima were the Americans. Can the bombs differentiate between military and women and infants and children?';[142] in 2001 he noted that 'hundreds of thousands, young and old, were killed in Japan, the most distant land—but this is not a war crime, just an issue to be looked into'.[143]

Further, bin Laden avows that, in this day and age, the Muslims specifically are bearing the brunt of America's disrespect for non-combatant immunity. Over the years, the US government is said to have targeted 'Muslim civilians and execut[ed] more than 600,000 Muslim children in Iraq by preventing food and medicine from reaching them'.[144] He stated in 2001 that 'until this point, a million innocent children have been killed in Iraq although they had done nothing wrong . . . we do not hear anyone protesting or lifting a finger to stop it'.[145] In Palestine, too, 'everyday . . . children are killed' such that 'no one, not even animals, would put up with what is going on there'.[146] Through its stalwart alliance with Israel, the United States is complicit in the killing of Palestinian non-combatants. Furthermore he says,

The mention of the US reminds us before everything else of those innocent children who were dismembered, their heads and arms cut off in the recent explosion that took place in Qana.[147] This US government abandoned even humanitarian feelings by these hideous crimes. It transgressed all bounds and behaved in a way not witnessed before by any power or any imperialist power in the world.[148]

It is clear, though, that America could only ever be indirectly responsible for the UN sanctions regime against Iraq as well as Palestinian casualties under occupation—the primary actors being the United Nations and Israel. With the advent of the coalition war against Afghanistan, however, bin Laden could begin to finger the United States directly for its use of 'cluster and napalm

bombs which are supposedly banned internationally'[149] and point to American 'war crimes in Afghanistan in which densely populated innocent civilian
villages were destroyed'.[150]

There are two upshots to this indictment against the United States—one
moral, the second practical. Firstly, bin Laden is vividly illustrating his
recurring point about America's moral hypocrisy:[151] 'it is very strange for
Americans and other educated people to talk about the killing of innocent
civilians. I mean, who said that our children and civilians are not innocents,
and that the shedding of their blood is permissible?'[152] American values
altogether are systematically undermined, because 'in what creed are your
dead considered innocent but ours worthless? By what logic does your blood
count as real and ours as no more than water?'[153] Secondly, and in terms of
practical implications, bin Laden concludes that 'the world is governed by the
law of the jungle'.[154] The adversary's gloves are off—'America has no
shame'[155]—and 'I write these lines to you at a time when even the blood of
children and innocents has been deemed fair game'.[156]

Thus, the reciprocity[IB] argument states that Muslims ought to target
US civilians because Muslim civilians are so targeted: 'the Americans started
it and retaliation and punishment should be carried out following the principle of reciprocity, especially when women and children are involved'.[157] The
reciprocity idea is applied straightforwardly, because 'we treat others like they
treat us. Those who kill our women and our innocent, we kill their women
and innocent, until they stop doing so'.[158]

Unfortunately for bin Laden, there is little precedent for this sort of analysis
in the tradition of Islamic *jihad*. Where the principle of non-combatant
immunity is elucidated, its mandate is universal and without condition. For
sure, Islamic law has a principle of *qisas* (talion), in which the punishment is
supposed to be equal to the offence—this is often used in Islamic states as
justification for sentencing murderers to death. However, *qisas* is an institution of personal vengeance and it is 'forbidden to kill any one other than the
guilty one'.[159] Indeed, *qisas* 'can only be applied after definite proof of guilt
. . . [and] only when the next of kin (*wali*) of the slain man or owner of the
slain man, if he was a slave, demands it'.[160]

Thus, Sayyid Qutb explicitly shuns the argument which brings in the
notion of reciprocal punishment to flout Islamic standards of warfare. At
one stage of his *tafsir* he notes that 'these principles had to be observed even
with those enemies who had persecuted [the Muslims] and inflicted unspeakable atrocities on them'.[161] Later, he reaffirms that 'Islam maintains its own
high moral principles and does not recommend resort to the same obscene
methods used by its detractors. It simply directs the Muslims to stand up to
those who offend against them, and reserves the right to appropriately and

publicly punish them'.[162] Qutb's position is reflected widely by contemporary Muslims. For example, Sheikh Wahbeh al-Zuhili, the head of *fiqh* at Damascus University, contends that the principle of reciprocity was embraced by Islam to establish standards of fairness and impartiality, but 'if the fundamental ethical and moral principles are breached, Muslims should not do the same'.[163] Another *fiqh* expert, Sheikh Ahmad Kutty, argues that even in the case of retaliation in war time, there are ethics that a Muslim must honour. He maintains that while fighting and retaliating Muslims must always act within the permissible limits prescribed by the *sharia*, holding steadfastly to their values and ethics so that they retain the moral high ground.[164]

Indeed, in al-Tabari's seminal *Book of Jihad*, 'most of the opinions expressed by the jurists and their reasoning in deducing certain rules...do not show any reliance on the principle of reciprocity'.[165] Interestingly, in Mohammad Qalahji's *Dictionary of Islamic Legal Terminology* the definition given for 'reciprocity of treatment' is that 'a person possesses rights in the same way that he possesses duties',[166] which is somewhat distinct from the limitless right of tit-for-tat arrogated by bin Laden.

6.3.3.3. *Argument 3: collateral damage*

As noted earlier, the 'doctrine of double-effect' morally differentiates between intended outcomes on the one hand and foreseen but unintended outcomes on the other, such that a serious harm can be considered a permissible side effect of promoting a good end. Bin Laden invokes this distinction about intentions in justification for the large civilian death toll on 9/11, arguing that 'the targets of September 11 were not women and children. The main targets were the symbol of the United States: their economic and military power. Our Prophet Muhammad was against the killing of women and children'.[167] Zawahiri also appealed to the distinction, upholding that only the *intentional* killing of women and children is prohibited in Islam and, so, it can sometimes be permissible to bombard the enemy in areas where there is reason to believe that civilians are also present. Zawahiri makes clear, however, that such a course of action is only allowable as a last resort, when no other means of attacking the enemy is available.[168] As considered in Chapter 5, al-Qaeda's claim of last resort is repeatedly made by pointing to the 'massacres' against civilians committed all over the Islamic world, confronting Muslims with an existential crisis. Hence, in *The Exoneration*, Zawahiri's rebuttal to Sayyed Imam's criticisms of al-Qaeda, he stated barefacedly that he has never condoned the killing of innocent people nor claimed that the *jihad* was free from error.

The claim that the *mujahidin* do not directly intend to kill civilians with their attacks is the one which al-Qaeda's leaders rely upon most in justifying specifically Muslim civilian casualties. As considered earlier in this chapter, bin Laden has declared that the killing of Muslims during al-Qaeda attacks amounts to 'accidental manslaughter'. This notion is also elaborated, on other occasions, by declaring that Muslim civilians are being used by their occupiers as human shields. Bin Laden says his understanding of Islamic jurisprudence indicates that 'if the enemy occupies an Islamic land and uses its people as human shields, a person has the right to attack the enemy'.[169] In 1998, he determined that the Americans had attacked the Islamic world and were using 'the children of Osama bin Laden' as shields. But, he continued, 'if we abstain from firing on the Americans lest we should kill these Muslims (used by them as shields)',[170] it would be impossible to repel the invaders. Zawahiri quotes the thirteenth-century Maliki scholar Mohammad ibn Ahmad al-Qurtubi to the effect that 'it is permissible to slay the human shield . . . Allah willing, if the advantage gained is imperative, universal and certain'.[171]

The author has argued elsewhere that, as al-Qaeda franchises have proliferated, the assertion that Muslims are only killed unintentionally in lawful operations conducted against the invader is increasingly difficult to defend.[172] Despite repeatedly planting bombs in crowded areas populated solely by Iraqi and Jordanian civilians (hotels, mosques, and marketplaces, for example), Abu Musab al-Zarqawi 'sw[ore] that they [Muslim civilians] were not the chosen targets'.[173] The Algerian leader of Al-Qaeda in the Islamic Maghreb, Abdelmalek Droukdal, has likewise insisted that 'we are not insane to target our Muslim brothers. . . . Mistakes may occur in the war but they are unintentional'.[174] However, given that such bombings take place in local contexts in which there is no invader positioned directly behind the Muslim, the plea of 'accidental manslaughter' or 'collateral damage' is necessarily weak. The Muslim appears to be the direct object of attack precisely because he is the *only* object of attack.

Indeed, each of the three arguments justifying non-combatant deaths has been openly criticized from within the *jihadi* community. Ayatollah Fadlallah, of Hizballah, argued shortly after 9/11 that US citizens could not be held accountable for the actions of their government as they were insufficiently informed of their state's foreign policy. In an 'open' Internet meeting with Ayman al-Zawahiri held in a radical Islamist forum—whereby questions were typed to al-Qaeda's deputy leader online which he answered in a general way through an audio posting—one Saudi contributor asked whether there were any means by which the goals of the *jihad* could be accomplished without violence. 'Please', he added in pre-emption of the commonly put reciprocity argument, 'don't use as a pretext what the Americans or others are doing.

Muslims are supposed to be an example to the world in tolerance and lofty goals not to become a gang of revenge seekers'.[175] Expressing his opposition to suicide bombing, and also quoting al-Qurtubi, Sheikh Abu Basir al-Tartousi noted that the collateral damage/human shield claim could only be sustainable if certain stringent conditions were met (among them that the only way to repel the enemy's assault is from the direction of the human shield and that it is not possible to put off killing the enemy). The question that arises, continued Tartousi, is whether suicide bombings 'conform to the preceding conditions and limitations, such that one might justify them legally through the case of the [human] shield?'[176]

6.3.3. Having it both ways

The elusiveness of an Islamic justification for the killing of innocents is well represented by bin Laden's ambivalent, even paradoxical, approach to the issue. At times he levels accusations against the United States, without a hint of an appreciation of the irony. In late 1998, he admitted that 'God, praise and glory be to him, has prohibited the killing of women and children unless the women are active fighters'.[177] In December 2001, he stated that 'history knows that one who kills children, even if rarely, is a follower of Pharaoh'.[178] In October 2004, he noted that 'the mass butchering of children is the worst thing that humanity has ever known'.[179]

At other times, however, bin Laden's precarious moral position forces him to contradict himself within short spaces of time. Consider the interview with John Miller in 1998:

We, however, differentiate between the western government and the people of the west. If the people have elected those governments it is because they have fallen prey to the western media. . . . We do not have to differentiate between military or civilian. As far as we are concerned, they are all targets, and that is what the *fatwa* says. . . . Our retaliation is directed primarily against the soldiers only and against those standing by them. Our religion forbids us from killing innocent people such as women and children. This, however, does not apply to women fighters.[180]

Again, in an interview with *al-Jazeera*, his standpoint appears muddled: 'they preach one thing and do another; we differentiate between men and women, and between children and old people. . . . Every American is our enemy, whether he fights directly or whether he pays taxes'.[181] Maintaining at first that al-Qaeda protects women and children and then intimating that there are no American civilians, bin Laden argued in 2001 that 'our Prophet Mohammad was against the killing of women and children. . . . The American people should remember that they pay taxes to their government and voted for their President'.[182] This prevarication arises out of bin Laden's great difficulty in squaring his command to murder civilians with his oft-heard acknowledgement—boast even—that civilians are not legitimate targets in Islam.

Pressed on the issue of killing innocents by Taysir Alluni, bin Laden touches upon three distinct, and somewhat incongruous, justifications in quick succession. First, bin Laden puts forward the reciprocity argument which makes al-Qaeda's observance of non-combatant immunity contingent upon the enemy's observance of it:

Alluni: So you say that this is an eye for an eye? They kill our innocents, so we kill theirs?

Bin Laden: Yes, so we kill their innocents—this is valid both religiously and logically. But some of the people who talk about this issue, discuss it from a religious point of view. . . . They say that the killing of innocents is wrong and invalid, and for proof, they say that the Prophet forbade the killing of women and children, and that is true. It is valid and has been laid down by the Prophet in an authentic tradition . . .

Alluni: That is precisely what I'm talking about! This is exactly what I'm asking about!

Bin Laden: . . . but this forbidding of killing children and innocents is not set in stone, and there are other writings that uphold it.[183]

To establish that the civilian immunity principle is 'not set in stone', bin Laden references four medieval writers, among them ibn Taymiyyah and al-Qurtubi.

It seems that there are only two of ibn Taymiyyah's arguments that bin Laden could be referring to. In the first place, we have seen that ibn Taymiyyah allows for the Muslim soldiers to kill civilians used as human shields. Secondly, he considered it legitimate to target monks if they leave their monasteries and contribute to the enemy's war effort, if only in a spiritual capacity.[184] But, on reflection, neither of ibn Taymiyyah's qualifications on civilian immunity can be faithfully extended to entail the legitimacy of targeting women, children, and the elderly *en masse*. In addition, while al-Qurtubi considered verse 2:190 (fight those who fight you but do not transgress limits) to be abrogated by later verses, this abrogation does not appear to apply *in toto*. He opined that the Muslims could fight even those polytheists who did not fight them—that is, he permitted offensive warfare—but he still upheld the condition of non-combatant immunity, which he organized into six categories: women, children, monks, the chronically ill, old men, hirelings, and agricultural workers. Al-Qurtubi's *tafsir* makes plain that 'it is not permitted to kill anyone who does not fight or help the enemy'.[185] Moreover, his discussion of *qisas* (talion) is elaborated with reference to limits:

... if anyone wrongs you, you may take your right according to how you were wronged, and if someone insults you, you may respond with what he said but may not go beyond what he said. But you are not permitted to lie about him even if he lies about you. Disobedience may not be countered by disobedience.[186]

In this way, even when reciprocating another's actions, al-Qurtubi maintains that moral absolutes are not to be infringed. Given that he formulates non-combatant immunity as an absolute, it seems that, by extension, no behaviour on the part of another can negate its protections: disobedience may not be countered by disobedience.

Secondly, in the same interview with Taysir Alluni, bin Laden employs an argument of an entirely different nature. He makes the appeal to a version of the doctrine of double-effect by suggesting that the deaths of civilians were not intended but merely incidental to a legitimate military objective:

Bin Laden: ... those young men, for whom God had cleared the way, didn't set out to kill children, but rather attacked the biggest centre of military power in the world, the Pentagon, which contains more than 64,000 workers, a military base which has a big concentration of army and intelligence ...
Alluni: What about the World Trade Centre?
Bin Laden: As for the World Trade Centre, the ones who were attacked and who died in it were part of a financial power. It wasn't a children's school! Neither was it a residence.[187]

Finally, bin Laden makes the factual claim that most of the victims of 9/11 were men and that al-Qaeda did not, in fact, kill many women and children:

Bin Laden: And the general consensus is that most of the people who were in the towers were men that backed the biggest financial force in the world, which spreads mischief throughout the world.[188]

Not only is bin Laden trying to imply that al-Qaeda did not target women and children, and thus salvage some semblance of faithfulness to the principle of non-combatant immunity, he further intimates that the targeted men were combatants of sorts, through their involvement in America's 'mischief-spreading' economic might.

In this way, and in the space of a few minutes, bin Laden proffers three qualitatively different sorts of explanations for targeting civilians. The first reasoned that American civilians can be killed because Americans kill Muslim civilians; the second suggested that civilians were not the actual targets on 9/11; the third upheld that the dead were mostly men who were combatants in some way.

In the end, bin Laden vilifies America for its policy of targeting civilians, and yet he uses that vilification in order to morally justify doing exactly the same thing—namely, targeting civilians. Hence, there is a pronounced overall conflict in bin Laden's approach to the matter of murdering non-combatants: on the one hand he seeks to deny the innocence of US civilians and, on the other hand, he wants to maintain that, unlike the West, Muslims hold steadfastly to the principle of civilian immunity. Thus, like Bush on the issue of UN authority for the war in Iraq (where he acted in contravention of the will of the United Nations by declaring the United States to be upholding the will of the United Nations), bin Laden wants to have it both ways. And, just as Bush's uneasy position reflected the widely shared importance of the vestige of UN authority for waging war in the West, so bin Laden's awkward stance is testimony to the centrality of the non-combatant immunity principle in Islam.

6.4. CONCLUSION

Bin Laden once laid claim to the honourable notion of not fighting dirty in Afghanistan, despite the behaviour of the Soviets. In his war with America, not only does he advocate an extremely dirty fight, but he justifies that recommendation precisely because of the behaviour of the Americans. The turnaround is marked, bringing with it doctrinal disarray for bin Laden. This chapter has shown that in order to criticize America's behaviour, he must assert the principle of non-combatant immunity, but then he uses the principle of non-combatant immunity with respect to Muslims to fashion an argument which overturns the principle of non-combatant immunity with respect to Americans.

We have seen that bin Laden's predominating case for aiming at American civilians was the reciprocity[IB] argument: because you kill our innocents we can kill yours. To the American people he explains, 'your religion does not forbid you from committing such acts, so you have no right to object to any response or retaliation that reciprocates your own actions'.[189] With this idea, and in parallel to his just cause, bin Laden can again imply that al-Qaeda never initiates but merely responds, thus forging a union between the *jus ad bellum* and *jus in bello* in an overarching discourse of defensive reciprocation.

The trouble is that non-combatant immunity is a staple constituent of the Islamic tradition which is, in its recurring formulations, absolute. In fact, it could be deemed unfeasible to invoke the *jihad* tradition and simultaneously call for the murder of innocents—without either flagrant misrepresentation or metaphysical muddle, that is. Just as the issue has beset bin Laden, leading him into the paradox of asserting non-combatant immunity and contradicting it at the same time, so it has plagued other radical Islamists. Muntasir al-Zayatt, for example, spokesman and sometime lawyer for the Gama'at Islamiya in Egypt, withdrew his support for the group in 1997 with the explanation that 'the cause to which I have devoted myself is no longer clear.... If violence is sometimes justified, it has no justification if it is no longer rooted in logic and sound argument and turns into an indiscriminate act conducted against innocent people as just happened at Luxor'.[190]

Such is the robustness of civilian immunity in Islam that many of the Muslims sympathetic to al-Qaeda's cause could only reconcile their support for bin Laden with the events of 9/11 by denying that he was in fact the culprit. In rejecting the notion that either bin Laden or any Islamic group was responsible for the attacks, Algeria's Salafist Group for Preaching and Combat (GSPC) stated that 'Islamist organisations do not target, in their actions, innocent civilians'.[191] In the same way, the Chairman for the Council for the Defence of Afghanistan and Pakistan, Sami el-Haq, explained to a reporter that 'we condemn these acts. The Taliban's clerics' council has also condemned them because human life is very precious and to kill it is not just. But the controversy is over who is responsible for these acts'.[192] In the service of more than one purpose, then, the principle of non-combatant immunity was re-established by Muslims in response to 9/11. For sure, the actions taken by Muslims on that day can be held up as proof that there is no idea of non-combatant immunity in Islam. Yet, in the Islamic discourse surrounding those actions, we have seen the moral boundary described once more, and the discrimination principle articulated anew.

Conclusion

From its inception, the 'war on terror' was described by its protagonists in moral terms. After nineteen al-Qaeda hijackers slammed their planes into buildings of great symbolic significance in two of America's major cities, the Mayor of New York declared that 'there [was] no moral equivalent for this [terrorist] attack'.[1] While the Bush administration considered the United States to have been struck by 'the evil forces of terror',[2] Osama bin Laden explained that the young Muslim hijackers who sacrificed themselves represented the conscience of the *umma* 'which sees that it is imperative to take revenge against evildoers and transgressors and criminals and terrorists'.[3] Indeed, the US administration operated on the premise that 'the larger war we face is a war of ideas',[4] and al-Qaeda recognized that 'we are in a media battle in a race for the hearts and minds of our *umma*'.[5] As such, the battlefield was closely and continually drawn with reference to ideas.

This book began from the observation that ideas, and especially moral ideas, were given top billing in the 'war on terror'. Yet, after placing the Bush administration and al-Qaeda's moral claims under scrutiny, it was suggested that, in important ways, Bush and bin Laden's arguments involved revisions of the Western and Islamic just war traditions. In addition, it was shown that contemporary Muslims and the heirs of the Western tradition also appealed to just war concepts to oppose Bush and bin Laden's cases for war. In the war on terror, then, important just war standards have been reiterated and established once more, by Bush and bin Laden's critics, but also by Bush and bin Laden's arguments which relied, however unsuccessfully, on core just war principles. The implications of this will be addressed in three areas of conclusion—on moral traditions, on just war, and on the 'war on terror'—before a final note on the ideology of al-Qaeda.

1. ON MORAL TRADITIONS

It has been possible to speak of the just war and *jihad* traditions with an appeal to consensus and descriptions of support in the literature behind the ideas and concepts of those traditions. Certainly, normative traditions do stabilize to a certain degree such that variations upon them can be—and in the 'war on terror', were—contested. However, in the final analysis traditions are not rigid, for at the heart of the intersubjective condition of traditions is their mutability. It has become clear that when placed under pressure, two seemingly contradictory features of tradition are presupposed: stability and contest. Traditions are stable to the extent that they can be appealed to in the first place, but those that make the appeal can themselves contest interpretations of the tradition, as well as invite contestation from others within the tradition. As noted in the Introduction, traditions only exist in the conversation between interpretations of meaning; in the nexus between some consensus and the argument which seeks to challenge it.

Thus, the fact that Bush and bin Laden did not eschew the role of morality in politics (and instead offered justifications which connected with central moral ideas) is as much a commentary on tradition as it is on international politics. By invoking and engaging with some key tenets of just warfare, Bush and bin Laden's (at this juncture, controversial) claims make clear that the ideational content of traditions is never fixed. Further, the opposition examined in this book notwithstanding, it is very possible that Bush and bin Laden's descriptions of the just war and *jihad* traditions could take root over time, not least because of the moral and legal precedents that may have been set. That is, Bush and bin Laden could act as 'norm entrepreneurs', agents who have strong notions about appropriate or desirable behaviour in their communities and actively pioneer new standards of appropriateness.[6] As Quentin Skinner has argued, 'an ideologist changes one part of an ideology by holding another part fast; by appealing to and so reinforcing convention'.[7] In the end, traditions can be as fragile as the judgements made about them.

2. ON JUST WAR

Three broad conclusions on just war can be brought out. Firstly, in addition to considering just war and *jihad* theories throughout the centuries, a great deal of this book has involved looking at arguments about just wars made at the beginning of the twenty-first century. As a tradition of thought, then, just war is alive and relevant; it is both used and useful. Indeed, the specific and enduring focus of this particular tradition on justice in warfare is a vast conceptual resource—not just instrumentally, for those who wish to present their wars as just, but through the indispensable capacity it provides for making judgements on the morally inappropriate/appropriate use of force.

In a sense, the just war tradition sidesteps foundational questions about justice, and the debate on moral relativism versus universalism: it becomes possible to look at the dialogue of actors and make an assessment on whether what is said fits in with the framework that is appealed to. Though an inevitable degree of moral judgement is involved on the part of the assessor, the just war tradition provides an important opportunity for controlled research to be conducted in a highly specific and organized sphere of justice.

Secondly, Islamic *jihad* is just war, not unbridled conflict for the sake of religious conversion. It is only 'holy' war to the extent that the moral limitations it enjoins are justified with reference to scripture. As such, 'the doctrine of *jihad* [is] a counterpart to the western notion of just war theory';[8] 'the notion of a just war is . . . an aspect of the foundational narrative of Islam'.[9] This argument has been put forward by referencing writings on *jihad* through the ages, but Osama bin Laden's own conception provides equally compelling evidence. Al-Qaeda's ideologues recognized that to proclaim a *jihad* against unbelievers, on account of their unbelief alone, would be a non-starter. Instead, a nuanced case was constructed, which relied on notions like self-defence, necessity, last resort, practicability, and the (albeit questionable) idea of reciprocity. That even the most fanatical trends in Islam imagine justified *jihad* in this way is testament to the fact that *jihad* is legitimized with the moral language of limits; it is appreciated in ways altogether more complex than the misnomer, 'holy war'.

Thirdly, there is a notable degree of overlap on the principles of just wars in the traditions of the West and Islam. To begin with, and in a fundamental way, the norm of self-defence as the only just cause for war is as pronounced in the *jihad* tradition as it is in the West. So resonant in Islam is the language of resisting the aggressor that al-Qaeda falls in line with such diverse figures as ibn Taymiyyah, Ayatollah Khomeini, Sheikh Jabir Al-Sabah, and Hamas in resting his case for war upon it. In fact, a possible explanation for why bin Laden was slow to take explicit responsibility for the 9/11 attacks was that he was waiting for the Americans to invade a Muslim country—waiting for a more permissive normative environment in which the United States could more readily be depicted as an attacker.[10] Prima facie, of course, there is a tension between the 'self' to be defended in the West and in Islam. The territorially delineated nation state has been difficult to reconcile with Islamic political theory, which privileges the more mythical community of the *umma*, and it has been viewed as a concept devised to perpetuate colonialism and the submission of Muslims. However, the integrity of the sovereign state is currently being challenged by sub-national groups as well as super-national systems of federalism and expressions of solidarity with the victims of the state (in terms of tyranny, genocide, or poverty), such that Western political theorists are actively reimagining the ideal order.[11] Though an admittedly simple starting point, in the widely accepted norm that aggression is a moral crime lies the possible basis for a cross-traditional consensus on justified and legal warfare.

In addition, while this book did not aim to achieve a strict point-by-point comparison between the Bush administration and al-Qaeda's arguments, there were four other criteria considered in the context of both traditions. Although it was not within the remit of this book to develop such correlations, these basic areas of overlap could serve as touchstones in the search for an inter-traditional agreement on the legitimate use of force in international relations. Firstly, the principle of non-combatant immunity was shown to be a staple of just war and *jihad* in Chapters 3 and 6, respectively. Secondly, the requirement of last resort was central in each tradition such that both Bush and bin Laden made great efforts to answer it. Thirdly, though the definition of right authority is distinct between the two traditions (with *jihad* theory revolving around the question of the caliph), it is worth noting that numerous Muslim statesmen explicitly invoked the United Nations as the proper authority and avenue with which to deal with the perpetrators of the 9/11 attacks: Iran's Foreign Minister 'welcomed a UN-led anti-terrorism campaign';[12] Sudanese President Omar al-Bashir called for 'a global battle against terrorism free of double standards and under the auspices of the UN';[13] the Yemeni authorities said they would 'join an international coalition against terrorism but that it must be led by the United Nations';[14] both religious and civilian leadership in Egypt advocated 'an integrated international method to deal with terrorism within the framework of international legitimacy'.[15]

Finally, both bodies of thought contain the pragmatic stipulation that there be a reasonable hope of successfully realizing the just cause and that fighting not be futile. Indeed, it is worth underscoring the significance of this consequentialist criterion to the unravelling of the 'war on terror'. Grave doubt has been cast upon the Bush administration's project to install liberal-democratic polities in the Middle East by way of warfare. Given the horrific cycles of violence which unfolded after the US-led invasion of Iraq, and the seeming inability of coalition forces to control the situation, we might tentatively conclude that Bush's 'forward strategy of freedom' has been largely discredited. At the same time, in the light of the predominantly Muslim death toll from al-Qaeda-related bombings, a series of radical Muslims have condemned al-Qaeda's *jihad* for its unrealistic goals, its adverse consequences and its ultimate wastefulness. This backlash can be interpreted, at least in part, as a repudiation of entrepreneurial, 'self-styled' *jihad*. As noted in Chapter 5, condemnation of widespread Muslim bloodshed has been linked to questions about a layman's abilities to lead the just and legal *jihad*. Moreover, as with

Western scepticism about the wisdom of warring to install democracy, this inherently pragmatic criticism serves as a rejection of ideologically driven warfare—limited, as it is, in neither time nor space.

3. ON THE 'WAR ON TERROR'

The first part of this book suggested that the most controversial elements of the Bush administration's two policies (the pre-emptive strike on Iraq and the treatment of detainees at Guantanamo Bay) were justified using reworked notions of 'necessity'. For the pre-emptive strike against Iraq, it was said that in the post-9/11 world, the necessity of a defensive war must be understood more widely so as to allow for the disproportionately destructive nature of weapons of mass destruction (WMD) and the unconventional nature of the new enemy. With regard to Guantanamo Bay, the overwhelming necessity of the just cause was again brought in to play, this time to describe a situation of emergency in which the provisions of the Geneva Conventions served as obstacles to the victory of civilization. Robert Holmes notes that 'however much we wrap our rationalisation in the language of necessity, we choose to do these things. And as with all our choices, these are subject to moral assessment'.[16] Indeed, this part of the book also demonstrated that Bush's plea of necessity was morally assessed and often opposed by his contemporaries, who argued that war in Iraq, torture, and detention without trial were, in fact, categorically *un*necessary to the articulated objectives of the 'war on terror'.

Part II argued that bin Laden's most contentious policies, just cause for the *jus ad bellum* and overturning the principle of discrimination for the *jus in bello*, were underpinned with appeals to the principle of 'reciprocity'. In asserting a just cause, al-Qaeda suggested it was only acting in self-defence, and its deliberate targeting of American non-combatants was justified with the allegation that the American government targets non-combatants: 'Thus, if we are attacked, then we have the right to strike back. . . . And whoever kills our civilians, then we have the right to kill theirs'.[17] However, it has been shown that bin Laden's rendering of 9/11 as self-defence was largely abhorred by his fellow Muslims, and the intentional killing of civilians was explicitly depicted as anathema to the *jihad* ethic. Indeed, Sohail Hashmi notes that 'strict reciprocity has never been established as a principle of the Islamic ethics of war: wanton disregard for humane treatment of combatants and non-combatants by the enemy does not permit Muslim armies to respond in kind'.[18]

That the Bush administration and al-Qaeda utilize similar ideological devices and represent comparably rigid worldviews is a point commonly made in general terms,[19] but in this much more specific area of just war arguments, close parallels are unmistakable. For example, both employed expansive understandings of just cause. As noted above and demonstrated in Chapter 2, the Bush administration upheld that the Iraq invasion was conducted in self-defence—a proposition which required an expansive conception of threat, owing to the destructiveness of WMD and the stealth of the enemy. This finessed the distinction between pre-empting an imminent attack, largely regarded as legitimate in the just war tradition, and the more dubious doctrine of preventive warfare. Moreover, the Bush administration's overarching just cause was defined as spreading 'liberty' to the region as a bulwark against future extremism. At a juncture when the tradition is legalistic and largely understood as permitting only very limited warfare in the face of an objective act of aggression, this broad moral goal rested on values which are ultimately subjective.

Al-Qaeda's leaders, too, insisted that theirs was a war of self-defence and that 'the Islamic nation should know that we defend a just cause. The Islamic nation has been groaning in pain for more than eighty years under the yoke of joint Jewish-Crusader aggression'. The battle had merely been 'transferred into the US heartland'.[20] However, as we saw in Chapter 4, in order to maintain the claim of victimization through aggression, bin Laden qualified 'aggression' so that the territorial entity that was being attacked was defined as the entire *umma*, and aggressive actions were described as symbolic attacks on the sanctity of Islam and its holy sites. As with the Bush administration's recourse to broad moral terminology, bin Laden's qualifications fell back on general, religious criteria. They did not demarcate a specific act of aggression. And, as a result, a series of Muslim leaders rejected his claim of self-defence and cast al-Qaeda as the aggressor on 9/11.

The war-making authority of each of these actors was also contestable— indeed, it was hotly contested. That bin Laden presumed the duty to lead a *jihad* had defaulted to him from the region's rulers and the clerical establishment was as provocative as Bush's claim to be unilaterally upholding the will of the United Nations (against its own will). Equally suspect were the claims, on both sides, that war was waged as a last resort. The Bush administration argued legally that UN Security Council resolution 1441 was the technical marker of last resort, and prudentially that appeasement was especially dangerous given the involvement of WMD, yet these two issues—the meaning of the UN resolution and the existence of WMD in Iraq—were the very subjects of heated international dispute. Bin Laden maintained that warnings had been issued, that Muslims faced an existential crisis, and that violence is the only language understood by the United States, but these propositions were entirely contingent on the imagined premise that the United States had, in fact, started an aggressive war against some Muslims. For 'reasonable hope of success', also, the prospects were questionable on both accounts. Bush was warned of the dangers of instigating a political vacuum in the Middle East, and it was difficult to imagine that the world would be safer[21] after the invasion of a Muslim country, at a time when, ideologically, the region was on the brink of being 'set on fire'.[22] Likewise, there was scant hope that bin Laden's *jihad* would benefit Muslims by subjecting them to the ire of a superpower reeling from a cataclysmic attack committed in the name of Islam.

It might be upheld that these corresponding deviations from the mainstream consensus on justified warfare go some way to explaining the existence of the 'war on terror'. Far from a clash between civilizations,[23] war was begot by the Bush administration and al-Qaeda acting at odds with the just war tenets in their own civilizations. There is reason to say that each betrayed its own tradition, and the world has been caught up in the fallout.

The problem began with aggression. The instability ushered in by the 'war on terror' was rooted in two critical events: the 9/11 attacks and the invasion of Iraq. Each was legitimized with the language of self-defence, yet each met the genuine requirements of self-defence only superficially. As a result, in each case the aggrieved party ('the Americans', 'the West', 'the Iraqis', 'the Muslims') could, in turn, plead self-defence, and a cycle of 'defensive' bloodletting was generated.[24] And if the analysis here is correct in placing aggression at the centre of the problem, this has little to do with Islam or Christianity or Western culture. Though the victims of aggression might define themselves using religious terminology (explicitly by al-Qaeda, and more implicitly in the case of the Bush administration), the content of these religions as value systems or 'ways of life' has no bearing whatsoever on the fact of the conflict. In fact, religion becomes relevant in only one, crucial way: both the Islamic and Christian-based just war traditions reinforce the modern, secular framework that makes aggression an international crime.

The problem of 'mutual aggression' was compounded by egregious behaviour in the conduct of warfare. Just as al-Qaeda targeted US innocents by virtue of their nationality alone, the one common characteristic of all Guantanamo inmates, held indefinitely and without access to trial, was that they were Muslim. Again, the issue was not that either or both traditions were in some way incomplete, deficient, or demonic. Islam has a strict and morally absolute principle of non-combatant immunity, and the Geneva Conventions were spearheaded by the United States ('US law classifies torture and cruel treatment forbidden by common Article 3, along with grave breaches of Geneva, as war crimes carrying a potential death sentence'.[25] Indeed, on 22 January 2009, Barack Obama deemed Common Article 3 applicable to all persons in US custody, anywhere in the world and signed an executive order to close Guantanamo Bay.) The Western and Islamic traditions contain robust rules in each of these areas. The problem, as before, was rather that the Bush administration and al-Qaeda decided to violate the organic provisions of their own civilizations.

In the 'war on terror' we may have proof, then, that prudence and morality make similar demands. Certainly, it seems unwise to meet a wrong received with (what looks to a lot of people like) another wrong. To respond to an aggressive attack with an attack that itself suggests aggression, can serve to perpetuate and actively promote the existence of conflict. Self-defence, after all, is a resonant and universally shared moral impulse, and almost all cultures and traditions claim it as a right. Likewise, to behave badly in warfare because the enemy has broken the rules does more than surrender the moral high-ground or expose your own people to similar treatment: such behaviours can become political acts that aggravate the enmity already existent in war and work to protract and expand it.

Indeed, it is not insignificant that breaking one's own rules in warfare is often accompanied by discourses about 'good' versus 'evil'. Ultimately, such narratives involve sophisticated attempts to dehumanize the adversary systematically. What better examples of dehumanization at work than images of manacled men kept indefinitely in cages on the presumption that they are guilty of terrorism, and office workers, commuters, and children blown up on account of their citizenship. But, as noted in Chapter 3, the sanction that underwrites the moral and legal stipulations of the *jus in bello* is deliberately and categorically indifferent to the moral virtue of the enemy and his cause. Moreover, if the notion of 'evil' unabashedly informs a conflict, especially if it occurs on both sides, war is no longer limited, but zealous and seemingly endless: 'we will rid the world of evildoers' (Bush, September 16, 2001); 'the way to stop the infidels' evil is *jihad* for the sake of God' (Osama bin Laden, 14 February 2003).

There is a debate, in just war theory, about whether both sides of a conflict can be just. Some writers, such as Saint Augustine and Paul Ramsey, suggest that this is possible. Others, among them Suarez, Vitoria, and Michael Walzer, assert that only one side can be just. But, certainly, all implicitly recognize that both sides can be unjust. It is not for the author to make judgements about the overall justice of each 'side' in the 'war on terror'; for sure, some would say this is the responsibility of the International Criminal Court, while many others would maintain that such judgements are only for God. Instead, this book has endeavoured to demonstrate that both the Bush administration and al-Qaeda embarked on wars that were viewed as highly controversial from within their own traditions—that fact alone can account for the occurrence of the 'war on terror', without recourse to explanations which accentuate fundamental differences between 'the West' and 'Islam'. In fact, it has been shown that these two civilizations share in common mature moral traditions on justified warfare, traditions which were put under pressure by the Bush administration and al-Qaeda.

4. ON AL-QAEDA

In opposition to commonplace portrayals of Osama bin Laden as a nihilistic holy warrior, this book has argued that his case for war is certainly more subtle. Though, ultimately, bin Laden may be a religious fanatic who believes in aggressive warfare against unbelief, he speaks to his larger Muslim audience using reasonable and reasoned moral arguments which depict his *jihad* as just, limited, and necessary. In this way, bin Laden can maintain that al-Qaeda is very much within the Islamic fold, and he can attempt to maximize his appeal beyond the few thousand professional *jihadis* training in desert camps to the millions of moderate Muslims across the globe.

Nonetheless, al-Qaeda's stated objectives, however insincere, are frequently misunderstood in the West. The Bush administration has been at the forefront of this confusion, intent as it was on characterizing al-Qaeda as an enemy 'whose only goal is death'[26] and the 'war on terror' as 'a war to save civilisation itself'.[27] While this misrepresents bin Laden's messages to the world—'so the situation is straightforward: America won't be able to leave this ordeal unless it pulls out of the Arabian peninsula, and it ceases its meddling in Palestine, and throughout the Islamic world. If we gave this equation to any child in any American school, he would easily solve it within a second'[28]—it also constructs barriers for those wishing to understand, contextualize, and successfully counter al-Qaeda's *jihad* ideology. Indeed, Michael Scheuer has argued, based on experience as head of the CIA's Osama bin Laden unit from 1996 to 1999, that the agency was obsessively focused on factual questions about the man himself, such as whether he had serious kidney disease—'we spent more time studying that than listening to what he said'.[29]

In reality, bin Laden and Zawahiri offer arguments which are, firstly sophisticated, and, secondly broadly consonant with secular values. In terms of sophistication, the preceding chapters have shown that much more than exhortation to commit violence against Christians and Jews in opposition to their creeds or 'ways of life', al-Qaeda's spokesmen draw upon refined just war concepts in setting out a modern case for legitimate war. In the words of Talal Asad, 'it is worth bearing in mind that terrorists themselves often talk about what they do in the language of necessity and humanity'.[30] In a general way too, bin Laden and Zawahiri evince more developed thinking than is commonly supposed. Bin Laden, for instance, allows himself to be put under considerable pressure from journalists, and he sometimes provides highly nuanced answers to difficult questions:

> Taysir Alluni: In connection to Afghanistan, you have said that you will defeat America in this country. Don't you think that the existence of the al-Qaeda organisation on the land of Afghanistan is making the Afghan people pay a high price?
> Bin Laden: Well, this view is partial and incomplete, and only from one perspective.[31]

Moreover, in explaining why it is that people tend to side with the United States, he offers a philosophy of human nature (which is, incidentally, very similar to 'realist' theories of international relations): 'there is a strong instinct in humans to lean towards the powerful without knowing it'.[32]

Al-Qaeda's leaders are also very much in touch with the culture of, and happenings in, the West: bin Laden references a lecture by 'a British diplomat at the Royal Institute for International Affairs',[33] while Zawahiri quotes a character from one of Disraeli's novels[34] and cites 'an English proverb [which] says, the person who is standing among the leaves of the tree might not see the tree'.[35] On Western combat doctrine, too, al-Qaeda's strategists are notably well versed as such figures as Abu Ubeid al-Qurashi cite a diverse literature which ranges from Clausewitz, Mao, and Giáp to Peter Paret, Thomas X. Hammes, and Vincent J. Goulding Jr. In addition, bin Laden invokes the Bush administration's own behaviour in the West (appealing to the norms of the West) as supporting evidence for his denunciations. For example, he rails against America for having 'destroyed nature with your industrial waste and gases, more than any other nation in history. Despite this, you refuse to sign the Kyoto agreement so that you can secure the profit of your greedy companies and industries'.[36] He notes on another occasion that 'while millions of Americans are homeless and destitute and live in abject poverty, their government is busy occupying our land and . . . helping Israel build new settlements'.[37] In this way, al-Qaeda's discourse does not rely on a simplistic or fundamentalist worldview. Instead, it often involves quite complex commentaries on 'right' and 'wrong', and on the state of the world.

Secondly, al-Qaeda's war is ultimately framed in secular terms. Though the resurrection of the caliphate and universal adoption of the *sharia* are no doubt desired, the use of violence is justified in a distinctly secular idiom. The claim of self-defence—of being driven to war by ongoing aggression— underwrites almost all of al-Qaeda's rhetoric and characterizations of its *jihad*. This assertion is not informed by religion but, instead, reason: 'is it in any way rational to expect that after America has attacked us for more than half a century, that we will then leave her to live in security and peace?'[38] Indeed, Stephen Holmes notes with reference to the lead 9/11 hijacker, Mohammad Ata that 'the grievances he loudly and frequently articulated against the United States and the Muslim autocracies that the United States supports were almost entirely secular'.[39] In a sense, the struggle against the hegemonic oppressor, a cornerstone of Marxist, nationalist, and anti-colonial movements in the twentieth century, is globalized to great effect by al-Qaeda at the turn of the twenty-first. Such confrontation has found fertile ground in the Middle East because it 'is merely echoing the rejectionist views of Nasser which were very popular in the 1960s and 1970s'.[40]

John Esposito describes how many Islamist movements ended up siding with the staunchly secular Saddam Hussein during the Gulf War in 1990, despite having been long-time beneficiaries of Saudi and Kuwaiti support. They 'respond[ed] not to the man but to his message: the failures of Arab governments and the excesses and corruption of the oil-rich states, the liberation of Palestine from Israeli control, and freedom from western inter-vention and dependency/occupation'.[41] It is not insignificant that these same (largely unresolved) issues top the playbill in al-Qaeda's war against the West—it is only in this broader discursive sense that Saddam Hussein and Osama bin Laden can be associated. And, as evidenced by the availability of bin Laden t-shirts in German markets, there is a dimension of this symbolic championing of the dispossessed which finds favour worldwide.

In an interview promoting his book, *Faith, Reason, and the War against Jihadism: A Call to Action*, George Weigel, a prominent commentator on religious issues in the United States, stated that 'moral reason doesn't have much to do with *jihadism*, which is built on a foundation of irrationality'.[42] It is difficult to see, however, how an effective 'call to action' against *jihadism* might be based upon such a premise. The material presented here would suggest, by contrast, that al-Qaeda both defines and empowers itself with moral reasoning. Indeed, to deny that bin Laden possesses a moral project would be to deny ourselves the most powerful weapon in the campaign against al-Qaeda: it is precisely because bin Laden invokes the Islamic *jihad* tradition and simultaneously pushes its moral boundaries that the main source of vulnerability for al-Qaeda is created. Firstly, because many of his arguments are gravely flawed, and have increasingly been pointed out as such by even radical Muslims. And secondly, because, in the end, and particularly with the slaughter of Muslim civilians, bin Laden fails to live up to his own moral standards, thus exposing his agenda and worldview as ultimately bankrupt. Contra Weigel, it is on account of the profoundly moral founda-tions and pretensions of *jihadism* that it will decline and disappear as a force in international relations.

However, this is not to deny the importance of counterterrorism policies. Rather, the point is that the content of *jihadi* discourses ought to be kept at the forefront of the campaigns waged against them. Bernard Lewis suggested more than a decade ago that 'in devising strategies to fight the terrorists, it would surely be useful to understand the forces that drive them'.[43] This understanding is crucial, no matter how irksome or offensive it may be to give weight to narratives which are opportunistic, fictitious, and removed from reality. Indeed, failure to do so may help that fiction to become reality. If, for example, it is said that the United States is a tireless and shameless aggressor, a unilateral pre-emptive attack on Iraq based on highly disputed evidence becomes bad policy in a war against al-Qaeda (allowing, as it does, for bin Laden to crow that the United States' presence in Iraq 'is a blatant occupation in every sense that this word conveys to me'[44]). If it is alleged that the United States is persistently willing to massacre innocents and commit war crimes in furtherance of its own strategic interests, sticking to international guidelines and keeping civilian casualties in theatre to an absolute minimum would undermine such claims. And if it is upheld that America is waging a war against Muslims, it becomes unwise to conflate two causes (Iraq and al-Qaeda) which are only ostensibly linked because both involve errant Arab Muslims, and to detain Muslims indefinitely without trial amidst allegations of torture and practices which deliberately weaponize Islam. On seminal just war issues such as these, morality and prudence are aligned.

Notes

INTRODUCTION

1. Stephen Frederic Dale, 'Religious Suicide in Islamic Asia: Anticolonial Terrorism in India, Indonesia and the Philippines', *The Journal of Conflict Resolution*, vol. 32, no.1, March 1988, p. 48.
2. Navid Kermani, 'A Dynamite of the Spirit: Why Nietzsche, Not the Koran, Is the Key to Understanding the Suicide Bombers', *TLS*, 29 March 2002, p. 14.
3. See for example 'The President's Agenda for Long-term Growth and Prosperity', 15 July 2002 available at http://www.whitehouse.gov/news/releases/2002/07/20020715.html and 'Vice President's Remarks at 30th Political Action Conference', 30 January 2003, at http://www.whitehouse.gov/news/releases/2003/01/20030130-16.html. Unless otherwise stated, official pronouncements by the President, Vice President, National Security Adviser, and other White House staff are contained in the George W. Bush White House News archives, which can be found at http://georgewbush-whitehouse.archives.gov.
4. Bush, 'Operation Iraqi Freedom: President's Radio Address', 5 April 2003.
5. Michael Walzer, 'So, Is This a Just War?', *Dissent Magazine*, web exclusive, posted March 20, 2003, reprinted in Michael Walzer, *Arguing About War*, 2004, p. 160.
6. Richard Norton-Taylor, 'Law Unto Themselves', *Guardian*, 14 March 2003.
7. 'Executive Committee Statement Against Military Action in Iraq', 18 February 2003, available at http://www.wcc-coe.org/wcc/what/international/exco03-iraq.html.
8. David Earle Anderson, 'Not a Just or Moral War: The Churches' Pre-Emptive Response to Bush's Iraq Plans', *Sojourners Magazine*, January–February 2003.
9. World Islamic Front *fatwa*, February 23, 1998, reprinted in Bruce Lawrence, *Messages to the World: The Statements of Osama bin Laden*, 2004, p. 61. In this particular *fatwa* he quotes Allah's words to 'fight the pagans all together as they fight you all together'. Unless otherwise indicated, citations of Osama bin Laden's speeches will refer to the Lawrence collection, for the sake of consistency and because it is a convenient and generally well-translated compilation. The author was, however, careful to check controversial vocabulary in its original Arabic, and key statements extraneous to Lawrence's book but nonetheless judged to be significant, have also been referenced.
10. For example, he cites 5:32 that 'who so ever kills a human being . . . it shall be as if he killed all mankind and whosoever saves the life of one, it shall be as if he had saved the life of all mankind' and quotes the Prophet's saying 'a believer remains within the scope of his religion as long as he doesn't kill another person illegally'.
11. See 'Sheikh Yusuf Al-Qaradawi Condemns Attacks Against Civilians: Forbidden in Islam', 13 September 2001.

12. Al-Sheikh argued that 'hijacking planes, terrorising innocent people and shedding blood constitutes a form of injustice that cannot be tolerated by Islam, which views them as gross crimes and sinful acts'. See 'Reactions to Terrorist Outrages in America', *Saudi Arabia Information Source*, 15 September 2001.

13. The Ayatollah stated that 'killing of people in any place and with any kind of weapons . . . is condemned. It makes no difference whether such massacres happen in Hiroshima, Nagasaki, Qana, Sabra, Shatilla, Deir Yessin, Bosnia, Kosovo, Iraq or in New York and Washington'—Untitled, *Islamic Republic News Agency*, 16 September 2001. The Iranian President, Muhammad Khatemi, suggested the attacks were perpetrated by a 'cult of fanatics'.

14. The *Ikhwan* issued a statement condemning 'such activities that are against all humanist and Islamic morals'. See 'Condemning Aggression', *Al Ahram*, no. 551, 13–19 September 2001.

15. Rohan Gunaratna, *Inside Al-Qaeda: Global Network of Terror*, 2002, p. 10.

16. Answering questions posed to him by some of his followers in a camp in Afghanistan, May 1998. Transcript available at http://www.pbs.org/wgbh/pages/frontline/shows/binladen/who/interview.html.

17. Testimony to joint SSCI/HPSCI hearing, 26 September 2002, quoted in Thomas E. Ayers, 'Six Floors of Detainee Operations in the Post-9/11 World', *Parameters*, vol. 35, Autumn 2005, p. 33.

18. In 'Manual for a "Raid"', *The New York Review of Books*, vol. 49, no. 1, 17 January 2002.

19. Sandhya Jain, 'Post 9/11: Clash of Civilisations', *The Pioneer* (Delhi), 10 September 2002.

20. Paul van Tongeren, 'Ethics, Tradition and Hermeneutics', *Ethical Perspectives*, vol. 3, no. 3, 1996, p. 180.

21. Alasdair MacIntyre, 'Social Science Methodology as the Ideology of Bureaucratic Authority', in Kelvin Knight (ed), *The MacIntyre Reader*, 1998, pp. 58–9. He argues that 'what objectivity requires in the study of such subject matters is an awareness of the contestable and argumentative character of what is going on'.

22. Cecilia Lynch, 'Dogma, Praxis and Religious Perspectives on Multiculturalism', in Fabio Petito and Pavlos Hatzopolous (eds), *Religion in International Relations: The Return from Exile*, 2003, p. 59.

23. Scott Thomas, 'The Global Resurgence of Religion and the Study of World Politics', *Millennium*, vol. 24, no. 2, 1995, p. 294.

24. 'Religion and International Conflict', in K. R. Dark (ed), *Religion and International Relations*, 2000, p. 13.

25. James Piscatori, *Islam in a World of Nation-States*, 1986, p. 13.

26. See Lawrence Rosen, 'Orientalism Revisited: Edward Said's Unfinished Critique', *Boston Review*, January/February 2007.

27. Kelsay, *Arguing the Just War in Islam*, 2007, p. 4.

28. Edward Shils, *Tradition*, 1981, p. 15.

29. Terry Nardin, 'Ethical Traditions in International Affairs', in Terry Nardin (ed), *Traditions of International Ethics*, 1992, p. 21.

30. Robert Jackson, 'Dialectical Justice in the Gulf War', *Review of International Studies*, vol. 18, 1992, p. 336.

31. Nicholas J. Wheeler, 'The Humanitarian Responsibilities of Sovereignty: Explaining the Development of a New Norm of Military Intervention for Humanitarian Purposes in International Society' in Jennifer M. Welsh (ed), *Humanitarian Intervention and International Relations*, 2004, p. 32.

32. One Romanian editorial noted soon after 9/11 that al-Qaeda had 'staged a planetary show, and it is very likely that they will try to do it again. They multiplied horror, pity, and fear, as Aristotle said, on a global scale. But their greatest propaganda success . . . is having created a wave of solidarity with those that are wronged, around their crimes'. Zoe Petre, 'Whom Are We Fighting Against?', *Ziua*, 21 September 2001.

33. In Kai Alderson and Andrew Hurrell (eds), *Hedley Bull on International Society*, 2000, p. 44.

34. See Reus-Smit, *The Moral Purpose of the State*, pp. 33–6.

35. Quentin Skinner, 'Some Problems in the Analysis of Political Thought and Action' in James Tully (ed), *Meaning and Context: Quentin Skinner and His Critics*, 1988, p. 115.

36. Quentin Skinner, 'Language and Social Change', in Tully, *Meaning and Context*, p. 132.

37. Neta Crawford, *Argument and Change in World Politics: Ethics, Decolonisation and Humanitarian Intervention*, 2003, p. 128.

38. Michael Walzer, *Just and Unjust Wars: A Moral Argument with Historical Illustrations*, 2000, p. 19.

39. Jay S. Bybee, 'Standards of Conduct for Interrogation Under 18 USC 2340-2340A' (Memo 14), 1 August 2002, reprinted in Karen J. Greenberg and Joshua L. Dratel (eds), *The Torture Papers: The Road to Abu Ghraib*, 2004, p. 207.

40. Bakr Uwaydah, 'We Want to Know', *Al-Sharq al-Awsat*, 4 October 2001.

41. *Ibn Taymiyyah Expounds on Islam: Selected Writings of Shaykh al-Islam Taqi ad-Din Ibn Taymiyyah on Islamic Faith, Life, and Society*, Mohammad Abdul-Haqq Ansari (ed), 2000, p. 544.

42. Olivier Roy, *The Failure of Political Islam*, 1994, pp. 7–12.

43. See Ernest Nys, *Les Origines de Droit International*, 1894, p. 2 and Mohammad Hamidullah, *Muslim Conduct of State*, 1945, pp. 63–5.

44. Hamidullah insists that in Islam we see the very first exposition of international law and that the works of Ayala, Vitoria, Gentili, and Grotius 'are but echoes of these Arabic works on *jihad* and *siyar*'.

45. Sayyed Qutb, *Fi Dhilal al-Quran (In the Shade of the Quran)*, vol. 30, M. A Salahi and A. A. Shamis (eds), 1979, p. 184.

46. See George Joffe, 'Democracy, Islam and the Culture of Modernism', *Democratization*, vol. 4, no. 3, 1997, pp. 133–51.

47. Cheragh Ali, *A Critical Exposition of the Popular Jihad* (Calcutta: Thacker, Spink and Co., 1885), p. 88.

48. John Kelsay and James Turner Johnson (eds), *Cross, Crescent and Sword*, 1990, p. xvi.

49. Kelsay in James Turner Johnson and John Kelsay (eds), *Just War and Jihad*, 1991, p. xvi.

50. Andrew Vincent, *Modern Political Ideologies*, 1992, p. 20.

51. The doctrine advocating 'the closure of the door of *ijtihad*' was set forth by Islamic jurists in the tenth century, stipulating that the content of God's will was now finally established and that the use of independent reasoning was fully exhausted. Thus, *ijtihad* gave way to *taqlid* (imitation) as jurisprudential exercises were confined to the detailed analysis of established rules and 'extracting the last ounce of implication from original principles' (N. J. Coulson, *A History of Islamic Law*, 1964, p. 81).This doctrine was never universally accepted, however, and ibn Taymiyyah famously claimed for himself the right of *ijtihad* in the thirteenth century, as did more modern jurists such as Mohammad Abduh and Mohammad Iqbal.

52. James Piscatori, *Islam in a World of Nation-States*, 1986, p. 9.

53. James Turner Johnson, *Just War Tradition and the Restraint of War*, 1981, p. 349.

54. 'GU Professor William O'Brien Dies', *Washington Post*, 19 July, 2003, p. B6.

55. Nicholas Rengger, 'On the Just War Tradition in the Twenty-First Century', *International Affairs*, vol. 78, no. 2, April 2002, p. 355.

56. Spencer Ackerman, 'Is Al-Jazeera the Next PBS?', *The New Republic*, 1 May 2006.

57. Quoted in Anthony Shadid, 'Maverick Cleric is a Hit on Arab TV', *Washington Post*, 14 February 2003.

58. Maha Azzam, 'Al-Qaeda: The Misunderstood Wahabi Connection and the Ideology of Violence', Royal Institute of International Affairs Briefing Paper No. 1, February 2003.

CHAPTER 1

1. President George W. Bush, 'President Delivers State of the Union Address', 28 January 2003.

2. Senator Edward M. Kennedy, 'Eliminating the Threat: The Right Course of Action for Disarming Iraq, Combating Terrorism, Protecting the Homeland, and Stabilising the Middle East', 27 September 2002.

3. James Turner Johnson, *Can Modern War Be Just?*, 1984, p. 11.

4. Johnson understands moral values as they are known through identification with historical communities, so he takes a 'moral tradition' to represent the continuity through time of such communal identification. See his *Just War Tradition and the Restraint of War*, 1981, pp. ix–x. Von Tongeren puts his description of a moral tradition negatively by suggesting that without such a tradition we would not know what we are obliged to do. See 'Ethics, Tradition and Hermeneutics', *Ethical Perspectives*, 1996, vol. 3, no. 3, p. 175.

5. St Thomas Aquinas, *Summa Theologica*, Fathers of the English Dominican Province (transl), 1981, vol. 2, p. 1359.

6. William V. O'Brien, *The Conduct of Just and Limited War*, 1981, p. 2.
7. John Helgeland, Robert J. Daly, and J. Patout Burns, *Christians and the Military: The Early Experience*, 1985, p. 91.
8. Hugo Grotius, *De Jure Belli ac Pacis Libri Tres*, Francis W. Kelsey (transl), 1925, vol. 1, chapter 2, section 7, p. 65. For Grotius' case 'that war is not in conflict with the law of the gospel', see pp. 63–70.
9. Quoted in Sydney D. Bailey, *Prohibitions and Restraint in War*, 1972, p. 18.
10. Paul Ramsey, *The Just War*, 1968, p. 144. Ramsey's own justification for the use of force springs from the fact that 'Jesus taught that a disciple in his own case should turn the other cheek, but he did not enjoin that his disciples should lift up the face of another man for him to be struck again on his other cheek'. In this way, it can be justifiable to rescue God's children from tyranny.
11. James Turner Johnson, *Morality and Contemporary Warfare*, 1991, p. 51.
12. See Johnson, *Just War Tradition and the Restraint of War*, pp. 122–3.
13. '[they] galvanised them into action, elevated and firmed them up, illumined and sensitised the justices of men to produce severer restrictions upon the form of human conflict which the Christian or any truly just man can ever believe justified'. Ramsey, *The Just War*, p. 145.
14. See Johnson, *Can Modern War Be Just?*, for the caution against historical positivism about morals, p. 12–13.
15. Jean Bethke Elshtain (ed), *Just War Theory*, 1992, p. 4.
16. Johnson, *Just War Tradition and the Restraint of War*, p. 190.
17. Published during the American Civil War in 1863, this document enshrined the rights of the Confederate forces to be treated as legitimate belligerents despite the fact that they were taken to be 'rebels' by the North. It was principally prepared by the lawyer, Francis Lieber, and then revised by a board of officers. As well as considering the treatment of non-combatants and prisoners of war, the document expresses general just war principles such as 'the ultimate object of all modern war is the renewed state of peace' (article 29) and 'modern wars are not internecine wars in which the killing of the enemy is the object' (article 68).
18. Elshtain, *Just War Theory*, p. 2.
19. Michael Walzer, *Just and Unjust Wars: A Moral Argument with Historical Illustration*, 1977, p. 19.
20. O'Brien, *The Conduct of Just and Limited War*, p. 5.
21. Ibid., pp. 71–87.
22. Ralph B. Potter, *War and Moral Discourse*, 1969.
23. Neta Crawford, 'Just War Theory and the US Counterterror War', *Perspectives on Politics*, vol. 1, no. 1, March 2003.
24. *The Fog of War: Eleven Lessons From the Life of Robert S. McNamara* (2003), directed by Errol Morris, distributed by Sony Pictures Classics.
25. 'It was not as though there was no alternative at the time. Hans Blix, the chief UN weapons inspector, and UN Secretary General Kofi Annan had both pressed for more time before the final decisions were taken. And much of the rest of the world, both governments and their peoples, were saying, "Let's get this

208 *Notes*

investigation sorted before we start blowing up human beings"'. George Solomou, 'Why I'll Refuse to Fight in this Immoral War', *Independent*, 21 January 2005, p. 37.

26. Ibid.

27. The Geneva Conventions require that the laws of war be studied by the armed forces and disseminated as widely as possible. See 'Geneva Protocol I Additional to the Geneva Conventions of 12 August 1949' (article 83), reprinted in Adam Roberts and Richard Guelff (eds), *Documents on the Laws of War*, 2000, p. 470.

28. United States Conference of Catholic Bishops, *The Challenge of Peace: God's Promise and Our Response*, 1983, p. 30.

29. Ramsey, *The Just War*, p. 187.

30. Francisco di Vitoria, *De Indis Relectio Posterior, Sive de Jure Belli* (1539), reprinted in Anthony Pagden and Jeremy Lawrance, *Vitoria: Political Writings*, 2001, p. 315.

31. Johnson, *Morality and Contemporary Warfare*, p. 41. Aquinas' paradigmatic statement of the *jus ad bellum*, which represented the consensus of Scholastic theology and the canon law of his time, singled out just cause, right authority, and right intention as the 'three things necessary' for a war to be just. See *Summa Theologica*, vol. 2, pp. 1359–60.

32. There is the argument that all modern warfare is, by the nature of the weaponry employed, inevitably disproportionate. For example, see Robert Holmes, *On War and Morality*, 1989, pp. 146–82.

33. Suarez thought the requirement of certainty of victory too much, as (*a*) it is almost impossible to realize, (*b*) it may be in the interests of a state not to await such certitude, and (*c*) it automatically precludes a weaker state declaring war on a stronger.

34. Following Ramsey's usage in *The Just War*, p. 131.

35. Six as opposed to seven because in Guthrie's schema, right intention and goal of peace are treated as one. Lord Guthrie of Cragiebank, 'The Just War: Ethics in Modern Warfare', lecture delivered at Las Casas Institute, Oxford, 21 January 2009.

36. Thomas Hurka, 'Proportionality in the Morality of War', *Philosophy and Public Affairs*, vol. 33, no. 1, 2005, p. 35.

37. Quoted in Bob Woodward, *Plan of Attack*, 2004, p. 8.

38. Quoted in Julian Borger, 'Bush Aiming at Wrong Target, US Critics Fear', *Guardian*, 14 October 2002.

39. Augustine, *Concerning the City of God Against the Pagans*, Henry Bettenson (transl), 1972, p. 862.

40. Aquinas, *Summa Theologica*, vol. 2, p. 1360.

41. Cited in Bailey, *Prohibition and Restraint in War*, p. 11.

42. Vitoria, *De Indis*, p. 303.

43. 'A just war is wont to be described as one that avenges wrongs, when a nation or a state has to be punished, for refusing to make amends for the wrongs inflicted by its subjects, or to restore what it has seized unjustly'. Augustine, *Quaestiones in Heptateuchum*, quoted in James Turner Johnson, 'Aquinas and Luther on War and

Peace', *Journal of Religious Ethics*, vol. 31, no. 1, March 2003, p. 8. See also Grotius, *De Jure Belli*, vol. 2, chapter 1, section 2, pp. 171–5.

44. Barry Paskins and Michael Dockrill, *The Ethics of War*, 1979, p. 215.
45. Bailey, *Prohibitions and Restraint in War*, p. 41.
46. According to Freedman and Karsh, for the Gulf War 'resisting aggression provided the classic basis for a just war', *The Gulf Conflict: Diplomacy and War in the New World Order*, 1994, p. 167. Also see Johnson, *Just War and the Gulf War*, 1991, for a detailed analysis.
47. David Rodin, *War and Self-Defense*, 2003, p. 104.
48. See Walzer, *Just and Unjust Wars*, pp. 51–73.
49. There exists an international society of independent states; this international society has a law establishing rights for states; the use of force constitutes aggression and is a criminal act; aggression justifies two types of violent response—a war of self-defence by the victim and a war of law enforcement by any other state; nothing but aggression can justify war; once an aggressor state has been militarily repulsed, it can also be punished. See *Just and Unjust Wars*, pp. 60–3.
50. 'President's Remarks at the United Nations General Assembly', 12 September 2002.
51. 'President Delivers Remarks on National Day of Prayer', 1 May 2003. For bin Laden's declaration of war, see his 'Declaration of *Jihad* Against the Americans Occupying the Land of the Two Holy Sanctuaries', reprinted in Bruce Lawrence, *Messages to the World: The Statements of Osama bin Laden*, 2004, pp. 24–30. Unless otherwise stated, citations of Osama bin Laden's statements in this book will refer to the Lawrence collection.
52. Cheney, 'Remarks by the Vice President to the Heritage Foundation', 10 October 2003.
53. Bush repeats this three times in an interview with Tim Russert. See transcript of *NBC*'s 'Meet the Press', 7 February 2004.
54. Wolfowitz, 'Building the Bridge to a More Peaceful Future', 6 December 2002. Unless otherwise noted, references to remarks made by the staff of the Department of Defense were accessed at http://www.defenselink.mil/speeches/archive.html.
55. Feith, 'Address to American Israeli Public Affairs Committee', 21 April 2002.
56. Aquinas, *Summa Theologica*, vol. 2, p. 1360.
57. Bush, 'State of the Union Address', 29 January 2002.
58. Bush, 'State of the Union Address', 28 January 2003.
59. 'The National Security Strategy of the United States of America', September 2002, p. 7.
60. 'President Bush Discusses Iraq Policy at Whitehall Palace in London', 19 November 2003.
61. 'President Outlines Steps to Help Iraq Achieve Democracy and Freedom', 24 May 2004.
62. 'State of the Union', 2003.

63. 'National Security Advisor Rice Remarks to Veterans of Foreign Wars', 25 August 2003.

64. Bush, 'State of the Union', 2002.

65. Rice, 'Remarks to Veterans of Foreign Wars', 25 August 2003.

66. 'President's Remarks to the Nation', 11 September 2002.

67. Feith, 'Iraq: One Year Later', 2 May 2004.

68. Bush, 'State of the Union', 2003.

69. 'President Discusses Operation Iraqi Freedom at Camp Lejeune', 3 April 2003.

70. For example, Bush: 'we will meet that threat now with our Army, Air Force, Navy, Coast Guard and Marines, so that we do not have to meet it later with armies of fire-fighters and police and doctors on the streets of our cities'. In 'President Bush Addresses the Nation', 19 March 2003.

71. 'National Strategy to Combat Weapons of Mass Destruction', December 2002.

72. 'President Says Saddam Hussein Must Leave Iraq Within 48 Hours', 17 March 2003.

73. For a detailed catalogue of the administration's accusations, see Powell, 'Remarks to the United Nations Security Council', 5 February 2003.

74. Powell, ibid.

75. Rumsfeld, 'Remarks to FORTUNE Global Forum', 11 November 2002.

76. Powell, 'Remarks to the UNSC', 5 February 2002.

77. 'Meet the Press' interview, 7 February 2004.

78. 'Dr Condoleezza Rice Interviewed by Jim Lehrer', 30 July 2003.

79. For example, in America, both CIA Director George Tenet and Director of Operations James Pavitt resigned suddenly in June 2004 amid allegations that they were pressured to leave because of intelligence concerning the failed weapons search in Iraq. In Britain, it was discovered that the source of BBC Journalist Andrew Gilligan's news report, Iraq arms expert Dr David Kelly, had committed suicide.

80. In February 2004, the US President established an independent, bipartisan commission to investigate the quality of US intelligence on WMD. Similarly, the 'Butler Report' assessed British intelligence, while the 'Hutton Inquiry' investigated the death of Dr Kelly.

81. 'The British government has learned that Saddam Hussein recently sought significant quantities of uranium from Africa.' In 'State of the Union', 28 January 2003.

82. See 'Dr Condoleezza Rice Interviewed by Jim Lehrer', 30 July 2003.

83. Bush, 'Remarks to the UNGA', 12 September 2002.

84. Dr Mohammad El Baradei, 'The Status of Nuclear Inspections in Iraq: An Update', 7 March 2003.

85. See 'Iraq's Weapons of Mass Destruction: The Assessment of the British Government', also known as the 'September Dossier', 24 September 2002, chapter 3 at http://www.number10.gov.uk/output/Page271.asp. The claim was said to be based on a questionable source and almost certainly pertained to battlefield weapons.

86. Woodward, *Plan of Attack*, p. 190.

87. On 26 September 2002. Cited in Woodward, *Plan of Attack*, p. 189.

88. El Baradei, 'The Status of Nuclear Inspections in Iraq', 7 March 2003.

89. This is the 12,200-page declaration submitted by the Iraqi government to the IAEA on 7 December 2002.

90. 'US Secretary of State Colin Powell's Statement on Iraq's Weapons Declaration', 20 December 2002.

91. 'Our greatest fear is that terrorists will find a shortcut to their mad ambitions . . .' Bush, 'Remarks to the UNGA', 12 September 2002. 'September 11 should say to the American people that we're now a battlefield, that weapons of mass destruction in the hands of terrorists could be deployed here at home.' Answering questions from journalists in 'President Bush Discusses Iraq in National Press Conference', 6 March 2003.

92. For example, Bush: 'evidence from intelligence sources, secret communications and statements by people now in custody reveal that Saddam Hussein aids and protects terrorists, including members of al-Qaeda'. 'State of the Union', 28 January 2003.

93. See Section 1.2.1.2.

94. 'He possesses weapons of terror. He provides funding and training and safe havens to terrorists—terrorists who would willingly use weapons of mass destruction against America and other peace-loving countries. Saddam Hussein and his weapons are a direct threat to this country, to our people, and to all free people.' From 'President Bush Discusses Iraq', 6 March 2003.

95. 'President's Remarks in Springfield, Missouri', 30 July 2004.

96. 'President Remarks on National Day of Prayer', 1 May 2003.

97. Powell, 'Remarks to the UNSC', 5 February 2003.

98. Cheney, 'Remarks to the Heritage Foundation', 10 October 2003.

99. Bush, 'President Discusses the Future of Iraq', 26 February 2003.

100. On 'Meet the Press', 14 September 2003.

101. As early as December 2001, a Czech newspaper was casting doubt on the meeting. See 'Czech Papers Casts Doubt on Suicide Bomber's Meeting with Iraqi Agent', *CTK*, 13 December 2001.

102. Quoted in Woodward, *Plan of Attack*, p. 4.

103. Dana Priest and Glenn Kessler, 'Iraq, 9/11, Still Linked by Cheney', *Washington Post*, 29 September 2003.

104. 'Clarke's Take on Terror', broadcast on '60 Minutes' (*CBS*), 22 March 2004. Transcript at http://www.cbsnews.com/stories/2004/03/19/60minutes/main607356.shtml.

105. Brent Scowcroft, 'Don't Attack Saddam: It Would Undermine our Antiterror Efforts', *Wall Street Journal*, 15 August 2002, p. B6.

106. Testimony made by members of a Zarqawi cell in Germany indicated that his group was founded for Jordanians who did not want to be members of al-Qaeda. Even in 2006, operating under the banner 'al-Qaeda in Mesopotamia', it was believed that Zarqawi's group was independent. See Richard Beeston and Catherine Philp, 'Bin Laden's Ruthless Rival Spreads Tentacles of Jihad Across Region', *Times*, 18 November 2005.

107. 'Remarks to the UNSC', 5 February 2003.
108. Jean-Charles Brisard, *Zarqawi: The New Face of Al-Qaeda*, 2005, pp. 85–8.
109. See, for example, Stephen F. Hayes, *The Connection: How al Qaeda's Collaboration with Saddam Hussein Has Endangered America*, 2004.
110. Quoted in Eric Schmitt, 'Rumsfeld Says US Has "Bulletproof" Evidence of Iraq's Links to Al Qaeda', *New York Times*, 28 September 2002.
111. Jane Harman, ranking Democrat on the House Permanent Select Committee on Intelligence, quoted in Peter H. Stone, 'Iraq II: Al-Qaeda Links With Baghdad Were Exaggerated', *National Journal*, 8 August 2003.
112. Jay Rockefeller, ranking Democrat on the Senate Select Committee on Intelligence, ibid.
113. 'President Addresses the Nation in Prime Time Press Conference', 13 April 2004.
114. Bush, 'Remarks to the UNGA', 12 September 2002.
115. See Rohan Gunaratna, *Inside al-Qaeda: Global Network of Terror*, 2002, p. 89. Gunaratna argues that this is al-Qaeda's mid-term strategy. While its immediate goal is the withdrawal of US troops from Saudi Arabia and the creation there of a caliphate, its long-term objective is the construction of 'a formidable array of Islamic states—including ones with nuclear capability—to wage war on the US and its allies'. However, though this book concurs with the analysis that al-Qaeda desires the end to many regimes in the Middle East and links their brutality to the abandonment of Islam, Part II will suggest that al-Qaeda describes its *jihad* against the United States as limited and defensive. Indeed, when bin Laden refers to nuclear weapons, he says he has them 'as a deterrent'. See interview with Hamid Mir, 12 November 2001, p. 142.
116. Interview with Robert Fisk, 'Why We Reject the West', *Independent*, 10 July 1996, p. 14.
117. Videotape message to the people of Iraq, 19 October 2003, p. 209.
118. Statement of 16 December 2004, p. 255.
119. Efraim Karsh and Inari Rautsi, *Saddam Hussein: A Political Biography*, 2002, p. 2.
120. 'Remarks by the President at Florida Rally', 20 March 2004.
121. Rumsfeld, 'July 4 Message to the Troops', 4 July 2003.
122. Wolfowitz, 'Building the Bridge', 6 December 2002.
123. 'Meet the Press' interview, 7 February 2004.
124. Referring to Afghanistan, Rumsfeld mused that it was 'ironic' that 'the terrorists' attacked Americans because they are a free people but the result of their attacks was the liberation of the Afghani people which 'those terrorist had so mercilessly oppressed', in 'Beyond Nation Building', 14 February 2003. But it was the Taliban regime that oppressively ruled Afghanistan, it was the Taliban regime that was deposed as the result of the invasion, and it was al-Qaeda (rather than the Taliban regime) which planned and executed the September 11 attacks.
125. Quoted in Woodward, *Plan of Attack*, p. 407.
126. 'Washington Post Poll: Saddam Hussein and the Sept. 11th Attacks', 7–11 August 2003, http://www.washingtonpost.com/wp-srv/politics/polls/vault/stories/data082303.htm.

127. 'President Bush Outlines Iraqi Threat', 7 October 2002.
128. Bush, 'President Discusses Future of Iraq', 26 February 2003.
129. Powell, 'Remarks to the UNSC', 5 February 2003.
130. *De Jure Belli*, vol. 2, p. 584.
131. See, for example, Walzer, *Just and Unjust Wars*, 1977 and *Arguing About War*, 2004, pp. 67–81.
132. See, for example, Simon Chesterman, *Just War or Just Peace?*, 2002.
133. See, for example, Nicholas Wheeler, *Saving Strangers: Humanitarian Intervention in International Society*, 2003 and R. J. Vincent, *Human Rights and International Relations*, 1986.
134. Jennifer Welsh, *Humanitarian Intervention and International Relations*, 2004, p. 3.
135. Ken Roth, 'Human Rights Watch World Report: War in Iraq—Not a Humanitarian Intervention', January 2004. Luban underlines that 'the most salient moment to launch a humanitarian war against Iraq would have been in 1988, during the Anfal campaign of crimes against humanity against the Kurds, a period when the United States was backing Iraq, not opposing it'. David Luban, 'Preventive War', *Philosophy and Public Affairs*, vol. 32, no. 3, 2004.
136. Some writers, such as the international lawyer Fernando Teson and normative theorist Nicholas Wheeler, argue that humanitarian motives need not be paramount—instead, what matters is whether the grave human rights abuses have ended as a consequence of the force employed. However, this presumes that mass slaughter was indeed taking place, which was not the case in Iraq.
137. Bush, 'Remarks to the UNGA', 12 September 2002.
138. 'National Security Strategy (2002)', foreword.
139. Bush, 'President Addresses the Nation', 13 April 2004.
140. Wolfowitz, 'Building a Better World: One Path From Crisis to Opportunity', 5 September 2002.
141. Gilles Kepel, *Jihad: The Trail of Political Islam*, 2004, p. 95.
142. Videotape address to the American people, 29 October 2004, p. 238. Beyond extremist groups, the tension between the west and Islamic states about human rights illustrates the contest over conceptions of even basic humanitarian ideas. At the UN Conference on Human Rights in 1993, for example, states like Malaysia and Indonesia upheld that Islamic principles of human rights differ from those found in the west. For an overview of the Islamic human rights debate and an analysis of the politics behind specific declarations, see Ann Elizabeth Mayer, *Islam and Human Rights: Tradition and Politics*, 1999.
143. My italics. Rice, 'Remarks to Veterans of Foreign Wars', 25 August 2003.
144. 'President Bush concluded in the light of the 9/11 attacks that it was necessary to remove the Saddam Hussein regime by force. The danger was too great that Saddam might give the fruits of his WMD programs to terrorists for use against the United States.' Feith, 'Iraq: One Year Later', 4 May 2004.
145. 'The legal position of the UK after 9/11 was that it would welcome a regime change in Iraq if that was a *consequence* of its actions, but that this would not be

the *aim* of any use of force. Whereas the US policy was regime change, it was not that of the UK; the UK's purpose was disarmament.' Christine Gray, *International Law and the Use of Force*, 2008, p. 232.

146. In his 2005 State of the Union Address, any reference to Iraq's alleged WMD capacity was markedly absent, with Bush instead devoting a significant portion of the speech to lauding the recent Iraqi elections. By his final speech as president in 2009, Bush summarized the venture in Iraq as the transformation 'from a brutal dictatorship to an Arab democracy'.

147. Aquinas, *Summa Theologica*, vol. 2, p. 1359.

148. This was also reflected in the theological debate leading up to the war: while the World Council of Churches argued for the UN as 'the custodian of lawful action against Iraq' (see Executive Committee, 'Statement Against Military Action in Iraq', 18 February 2003), the president of the Southern Baptist Convention's Ethics and Religious Liberty Commission advised the President that 'a resolution from Congress would provide the proper authority' (see Tom Strode, 'Attack on Iraq Justified, Land, Others Tell Bush', *Baptist Press News*, 3 October 2002).

149. Cheney, 'Remarks to the Heritage Foundation', 10 October 2003.

150. 'Remarks by the Vice President at the Ronald Reagan Presidential Library and Museum', 17 March 2004.

151. Bush, 'Remarks by the President', 20 March 2004.

152. He suggested, for example, that any US military action first be subject to a 'global test' of legitimacy.

153. Cheney, 'Vice President's Remarks at a Victory 2004 Rally in Ft. Myers, Florida', 14 October 2004.

154. Bush, 'Remarks to the UNGA', 12 September 2002.

155. For example, 'We will consult, but let there be no misunderstanding: if Saddam Hussein does not fully disarm for the safety of our people and the peace of the world, we will lead a coalition to disarm him'. 'State of the Union', 2003.

156. 'It's been the position of the United States all along that we didn't need a second resolution. But, as the President said, it would be welcome to have a second resolution. . . . It was also, of course, important to a number of other countries that we seek a second resolution. I think you know that for a number of our closest allies it was an important step to take.' Rice, 'Press Briefing by Dr Condoleezza Rice', 24 February 2003.

157. Lord Robin Butler, 'The Case for the Iraq War', lecture at St Antony's College, Oxford University, 17 November 2004.

158. Powell, 'Remarks to the UNSC', 5 February 2003.

159. Bush, 'Saddam Hussein Must Leave Iraq', 17 March 2003.

160. Bush, 'Remarks to the UNGA', 12 September 2002.

161. Bush, 'President Discusses Future of Iraq', 26 February 2003.

162. 'President Bush Discusses Iraq Policy at Whitehall', 19 November 2003.

163. Bush, 'President Discusses Future of Iraq', 26 February 2003.

164. Ari Fleischer, quoted in 'White House Touts International Support for Military Campaign', *CNN*, 21 March 2003. The coalition's make-up, however, was the

subject of fierce criticism, labelled as a 'coalition of the coerced and the bribed' by John Kerry and 'a cash register coalition' by Avi Shlaim.

165. Lord Goldsmith, 'Iraq: Legality of Armed Force', 17 March 2003, online at United Kingdom Parliament website, http://www.parliament.the-stationery-office.co.uk/ pa/ld199900/ldhansrd/pdvn/lds03/text/30317w01.htm. It was later alleged that Lord Goldsmith initially thought the war illegal without a UN resolution but 'changed his mind' ten days later. See Foreign Office lawyer Elizabeth Wilmshurst's resignation letter in 'Straw Facing War Advice Critics', *BBC News*, 24 March 2005.

166. 'War Would be Illegal', *Guardian*, 7 March 2003.

167. 'Iraq War Was Illegal, Chirac Tells Bush', *Irish Examiner*, 4 June 2003.

168. Anne Penketh, 'Blix: Iraq War Was Illegal', *Independent*, 5 March 2004.

169. 'Iraq War Illegal, Says Annan', *BBC News*, 16 September 2004.

170. See Professor Nicholas Grief and Professor Colin Warbrick's comments in Peter Gould, 'War with Iraq "Could Be Illegal" ', *BBC News*, 10 March 2003. A group of twenty-four Danish citizens brought a lawsuit against their Prime Minister, Anders Fogh Rasmussen, in 2005 for breaching the constitution by committing troops to the war. The crux of their ongoing case is that Rasmussen took the country to war without a valid United Nations Security Council resolution.

171. 'New Zealand Church Leaders Joint Statement on the Threat of War Against Iraq', 10 September 2002.

172. 'President Bush Addresses the Nation', 19 March 2003.

173. Aquinas, *Summa Theologica*, vol. 2, p. 1360.

174. Augustine, *Answer to Faustus: A Manichean*, Roland Teske (transl), 2007, p. 351.

175. Aquinas, *Summa Theologica*, vol. 2, p. 1360.

176. Johnson, *Morality and Contemporary Warfare*, p. 50.

177. G. Scott Davis, *Warcraft and the Fragility of Virtue: An Essay in Aristotelian Ethics*, 1992, p. 56.

178. O'Brien, *The Conduct of Just and Limited War*, p. 35.

179. Johnson, *Morality and Contemporary Warfare*, p. 33.

180. From 'Fallujah: The Real Fall', reported by Dr Ali Fadhil, *Channel 4 News*, aired 11 January 2005.

181. Douglas Lackey, *The Ethics of War and Peace*, 1989, p. 32.

182. In the second part of this book we will see that, with his *fatwas* in the 1990s, bin Laden conjured the image of a religion under attack and a people besieged by hateful plunderers, and argued that US policy amounted to 'a clear declaration of war on God, his messenger, and Muslims'. In 2003, he maintained that 'the Bush–Blair axis claims that it wants to annihilate terrorism, but it is no longer a secret—even to the masses—that it really wants to annihilate Islam' (statement of 14 February 2003, p. 188).

183. 'National Security Strategy (2002)', p. 31.

184. 'Remarks by National Security Adviser Rice at the Karamah Iftaar', 4 December 2002.

185. Leaked ICRC report cited in 'Red Cross Cites "Inhumane" Treatment at Guantanamo', *Washington Post*, 1 December 2004, p. A10.

186. From 'Is Torture a Good Idea?', an investigation by Clive Stafford Smith for *Channel 4*, aired 28 February 2005.

187. Mamdouh Habib in 'Fresh Guantanamo Torture Claims', *BBC News*, 13 February 2005.

188. See Moazzam Begg, *Enemy Combatant: A British Muslim's Journey to Guantanamo and Back*, 2006, p. 158.

189. Davis, *Warcraft and the Fragility of Virtue*, p. 103–5.

190. Ibid., p. 56.

191. Johnson, 'Was the Gulf War a Just War?', in James Turner Johnson and George Weigel (eds), *Just War and the Gulf War*, 1991, p. 24.

192. Bush, 'President Addresses the Nation', 13 April 2004.

193. 'Donald Rumsfeld's Address to the Iraqi People', 30 April 2003.

194. Bush, 'President Discusses Future of Iraq', 26 February 2003.

195. Rumsfeld, 'Beyond Nation Building', 14 February 2003.

196. Feith, 'Iraq: One Year Later', 4 May 2004.

197. This view was heard from a variety of quarters. Five years before the invasion, for example, Osama bin Laden argued that the United States planned to divide Iraq into three provinces, and Saudi Arabia into two, so as to control the region's oil supplies (see Rahimullah Yousafsai, 'Terror Suspect: An Interview with Osama bin Laden', *ABC News*, 22 December 1998). In the run up to war, the former Saudi Arabian Petroleum Minister stated that 'oil is the main objective in the US seeking to occupy Iraq' (in Andrew Walker, 'US "Playing with Fire", Warns Yamani', *BBC News*, 14 March 2003), and Hasan Nasrallah of Hizballah argued shortly after that 'the United States isn't seeking democracy in Iraq, it's after the oil in Iraq, which isn't exactly a humanitarian pursuit' (20 April 2003 in Nicholas Noe, *Voice of Hezbollah: The Statements of Sayyed Hassan Nasrallah*, 2007, p. 291). Four years later, the one-time chairman of the Federal Reserve, Alan Greenspan, pointed to the same motivation in his memoirs: 'I am saddened that it is politically inconvenient to acknowledge what everyone knows: the Iraq war is largely about oil' (Graham Paterson, 'Alan Greenspan Claims Iraq War Was Really For Oil', *The Sunday Times*, 16 September 2007).

198. See the Democrat Henry A. Waxman's accusation in Robert O'Harrow Jr, 'Waxman Raises New Questions on Cheney', *Washington Post*, 14 June 2004, p. A4.

199. At anti-war demonstrations in London, for example, placards reading 'no war for Israel' were commonplace. Al-Qaeda's deputy leader, Ayman al-Zawahiri, also argued that the US goal was to 'confirm Israel's uncontested monopoly over weapons of mass destruction in the region and to ensure the submission of Arab and Islamic states'. See Audrey Woods, 'Tape Threatens More Attacks on US', *Associated Press*, 8 October 2002.

200. On 14 November 2002, Donald Rumsfeld assured CBS news 'it has nothing to do with oil, literally nothing to do with oil'; Dick Cheney rebutted claims about illicit Halliburton profiteering on Tim Russert's 'Meet the Press', *NBC News*, 14 September 2003.

201. Cheney, 'Remarks to the Heritage Foundation', 10 October 2003.

202. Wolfowitz, 'Building the Bridge', 6 December 2002.

203. Bush, 'Remarks by the President', 20 March 2004.

204. 'Letter 189: Augustine to Boniface (417)', in E. M. Atkins and R. J. Dodaro, *Augustine: Political Writings*, 2001, p. 217.

205. Michael Howard, 'Temperamenta Belli: Can War Be Controlled?', in Elshtain (ed), *Just War Theory*, p. 34.

206. Augustine, 'Letter 189', p. 217.

207. 'President Bush Addresses the Nation', 6 June 2002.

208. 'President Bush Discusses Iraq', 6 March 2003.

209. Bush, 'President Discusses Future of Iraq', 26 February 2003.

210. Powell, 'Remarks at the American Israel Public Affairs Committee's Annual Policy Conference', 31 March 2003.

211. Aquinas, *Summa Theologica*, vol. 2, p. 1360.

212. 'State of the Union', 2003.

213. Bush, 'President Bush Discusses Iraq', 6 March 2003.

214. Bush, 'President Discusses Future of Iraq', 26 February 2003.

215. *Jomhouri Eslami* cited in 'Bush Called War Monger By Iran's Conservative Press', *Agence France Presse*, 5 February 2005. The editorial went on to consider Bush's pledge to stand by Iranians yearning for liberty and concludes that 'picturing a freedom seeker and fighter from such a savage is the most ridiculous claim of the century'.

216. Gary Younge, 'No More Mr Nice Guy', *Guardian*, 19 September 2002.

217. Greek Prime Minister Costas Simitis quoted in 'EU Says No to Iraq War without UN Approval', *Reuters*, 21 January 2003.

218. Quoted in Mark and Louise Zwick, 'Pope Jean Paul II Calls War a Defeat for Humanity: Neoconservative Iraq Just War Theories Rejected', *Houston Catholic Worker*, vol. 23, no. 4, July–August 2003.

219. A. J. Coates, *The Ethics of War*, 1997, p. 170.

220. Ramsey, *The Just War*, p. 195.

221. For example, Pope Pius XII: 'the enormous violence of modern warfare means that it can no longer be regarded as a reasonable, proportionate means for settling conflicts'.

222. Coates, *The Ethics of War*, p. 168.

223. Les Roberts, Riyadh Lafta, Richard Garfield, Jamal Khudhairi, and Gilbert Burnham, 'Mortality Before and After the 2003 Invasion of Iraq: Cluster Sample Survey', *The Lancet*, vol. 364, no. 9448, 20 November 2004. In October 2006 a second team from the Johns Hopkins Bloomberg School of Public Health updated the figure to 654,965 excess Iraqi deaths as a consequence of the war (Les Roberts, Gilbert Burnham, Riyadh Lafta, Shannon Doocy, 'Mortality After the 2003 Invasion of Iraq: A Cross-Sectional Cluster Sample Survey, *The Lancet*, vol. 386, no. 9545, 21 October 2006). President Bush dismissed the team's methodology as 'not credible' and a spokesman for Tony Blair said that the figure was 'nowhere near accurate', though it did emerge that the British government's own scientific advisers had told

him the study design was reliable and close to best practice (see Owen Bennet Jones, 'Iraqi Deaths Survey was "Robust"', *BBC News*, 26 March 2007).

224. Bill Broadway, 'Evangelicals' Voices Speak Softly About Iraq', *Washington Post*, 25 January 2003, p. B9.

225. Quoted in 'War Not Justified: Chirac, Schroeder', *The Hindu*, 19 March 2003.

226. Henry Shue, 'War', in Hugh LaFollette (ed), *Oxford Handbook of Practical Ethics*, 2003, p. 749.

227. Matthew Davis, 'Counting the Civilian Cost in Iraq', *BBC News*, 22 September 2004.

228. Pope John Paul II, 'Address of His Holiness Pope John Paul II to the Diplomatic Corps', 13 January 2003.

229. Augustine, 'Letter 189', p. 217.

230. Ramsey, *The Just War*, p. 144.

231. Vitoria, *De Indis*, p. 327.

232. 'Letter 229: Augustine to Darius (429/430)', in *Augustine: Political Writings*, p. 226.

233. O'Brien, *The Conduct of Just and Limited War*, p. 31.

234. George Weigel, 'The Development of Just War Thinking in the Post-Cold War World: An American Perspective', in Charles Reed and David Ryall (eds), *The Price of Peace: Just War in the Twenty-First Century*, 2007, p. 25.

235. See ibid and James Turner Johnson, 'Just Cause Revisited', publication of the *Ethics and Public Policy Centre*, 1 September 1998, at http://www.eppc.org/publications/pubID.1998/pub_detail.asp.

236. Weigel, 'The Development of Just War Thinking', p. 26.

237. For example, the Archbishop of Canterbury, Rowan Williams, labels this 'an odd reading of, say, Aquinas' discussion in the Summa'. See 'Just War Revisited', lecture delivered at Chatham House, 12 October 2003.

238. Rumsfeld, 'Remarks to FORTUNE', 11 November 2002.

239. Powell, 'Remarks at AIPAC', 31 March 2003.

240. Bush, 'President Addresses National Day of Prayer', 1 May 2003.

241. Cheney, 'Remarks to the Heritage Foundation', 10 October 2003 and 'Remarks at the Reagan Presidential Library', 17 March 2004.

242. 'In Cheney's Words: The Administration's Case for Removing Saddam Hussein', *New York Times*, 27 August 2002.

243. Bush, 'Saddam Hussein Must Leave Iraq', 17 March 2003.

244. Wolfowitz, 'Building the Bridge', 6 December 2002.

245. Bush, 'President Bush Discusses Iraq', 6 March 2003.

246. The text of the proposed resolution was made available by *C-Span*. See 'Draft Security Council Resolution', 7 March 2003, at http://c-span.org/resources/fyi/draftresolution2.asp.

247. Joschka Fischer in John Lichfield, 'On the Brink of War', *Independent*, 8 March 2003, p. 2.

248. Tang Jiaxuan in 'Reactions to Blix Report', *BBC News*, 7 March 2003.

249. Quoted in 'Urgent: France Not to Allow Passing of Resolution Authorising War', *Xinhua General News Service*, 7 March 2003.

250. Igor Ivanov in Richard Wallace, 'Countdown to Conflict', *Daily Mirror*, 8 March 2003.

251. Luis Ernesto Derbez in 'Mexico Calls for Peaceful Solution to Iraq Crisis', *Agence France Presse*, 7 March 2003.

252. Johnson, 'Was the Gulf War a Just War?', p. 30. It is imperative to note, however, that opponents of the Gulf War insisted that the last resort had not yet been reached. For example, Archbishop Roach testified before the Senate Foreign Relations Committee that 'the ethical restraint on war requires a nation to try all means short of war. The embargo needs time to work, it is not accurate to say it has been tried and failed. . . . Thus far, I do not believe the principle of last resort has been met'. Johnson and Weigel, *Just War and the Gulf War*, p. 126.

253. Feith, 'Iraq: One Year Later', 4 May 2004.

254. Grotius, *De Jure Belli*, vol. 2, chapter 25, section 4, p. 581.

255. Ibid., p. 576.

256. Calvin, from citation in Bailey, *Prohibitions and Restraints in War*, p. 17.

257. Rumsfeld, 'Remarks to FORTUNE', 11 November 2002.

258. Powell, 'Remarks at AIPAC', 31 March 2003.

259. 'President Signs Defense Appropriations Bill at the Pentagon', 10 January 2002.

260. Bush, 'President Addresses National Day of Prayer', 1 May 2003.

261. Powell, 'Remarks at AIPAC', 31 March 2003.

262. 'In Cheney's Words', 27 August 2002. He continues: 'moderates throughout the region would take heart'.

263. In James Graff, 'France is not a Pacifist Country', *Time Magazine*, vol. 161, no. 8, 24 February 2003.

264. Cited by Jim Lobe, 'Bush Terror War Suffers Body Blow in Spain', *Inter Press Service News Agency*, 15 March 2004.

265. Speaking with *La Stampa*, quoted in ibid.

266. Jose Luis Rodriguez Zapatero, quoted in 'Spain Victor in His Own Words', *BBC News*, 15 March 2004.

267. Quoted in 'Al Qaida Still Targeting White House, Capitol', *World Tribune*, 26 February 2004.

268. See my 'Crushed in the Shadows: Why Al-Qaeda Will Lose the War of Ideas', *Studies in Conflict and Terrorism*, vol. 33, no. 2, February 2010.

269. Lakhdar Benchiba, 'Les Mutations du Terrorisme Algérien', *Politique étrangère*, vol. 2, Eté 2009, pp. 345–52.

270. 'Excerpts of Bin Laden Speech', *BBC*, 16 December 2004.

271. Document issued by the Media Commission for the Victory of the Iraqi People and dedicated to Yusuf al-Ayiri, 2003. Quoted in Mohammad M. Hafez, *Suicide Bombers in Iraq: The Strategy and Ideology of Martyrdom*, 2007, p. 74.

272. Vali Nasr, *The Shia Revival: How Conflicts Within Islam Will Shape the Future*, 2007, p. 245.

273. The Egyptian President Hosni Mubarak argued along the same lines as Chirac, suggesting that an invasion of Iraq would produce '100 new Bin Ladens'. See 'Mubarak Warns of "100 Bin Ladens"', *CNN*, 1 April 2003.

274. The Churches for Middle East Peace cautioned the President that 'US military action at this time has great potential to destabilise the region.... Militants in Arab and Islamic majority countries would seize the opportunity to incite people against not only the United States but also against other governments that cooperate with the US'. 'Letter to President Bush on Iraq', 12 September 2002.

275. Tony Blair was, for example, allegedly warned by the Joint Intelligence Committee that 'military action would increase the risks of terrorist attacks'. See Philip Webster and Michael Evans, 'Blair on the Rack Over Iraq Terror Warning', *Times*, 12 September 2003.

276. See, for example, Avi Shlaim and others in Ian Kershaw, 'Blast From the Past', *Guardian*, 19 February 2003.

277. 'In Cheney's Words', 27 August 2002.

278. Quoted in James Brandon, 'Black Watch Soldier Killed by Roadside Bomb in Basra', *Scotsman*, 13 August 2004.

279. Karl Vick and Bassam Sebti, 'Violence Spreads in Iraq, Car Bomb Kills 17 in Baghdad', *Washington Post*, 12 November 2004, p. A21.

280. From 'Iraq Coalition Casualty Count', online at http://icasualties.org.

281. 'Iraq War: The Coming Disaster', *Los Angeles Times*, 14 April 2002, p. M3.

282. 'President Addresses the Nation', 7 September 2003.

283. 'Dr Condoleezza Rice Discusses Iraq in Chicago', 8 October 2003.

284. In terms of violence, while armed militias and Islamic extremist groups were responsible for a great number of horrific scenes, the Ministry of the Interior was accused of grave abuses after 170 detainees were found at a ministry centre allegedly suffering the effects of starvation and torture. The former interim President of Iraq, Iyad Allawi, observed that 'people are doing the same as in Saddam's time, and worse.... These were the precise reasons that we fought Saddam Hussein, and now we are seeing the same things'. Quoted in 'Iraq Abuse "As Bad As Saddam Era"', *BBC News*, 27 November 2005.

285. Text available at United Nations Development Programme website, http://www. iq.undp.org/ILCS/overview.htm. In marked contrast to the figures proffered by *The Lancet*, this report estimates Iraqi civilian casualties as somewhere between 18,000 and 29,000.

286. Barham Salih, quoted in Niko Kyriakou, 'Iraqi Living Conditions Tragic— Report', *Inter Press Service News Agency*, 13 May 2005.

287. The text of 'Likely Humanitarian Scenarios' (10 December 2002) can be accessed at http://www.casi.org.uk/info/undocs/war021210scanned.pdf.

288. 'Profile: Margaret Hassan', *BBC News*, 20 October 2004.

289. Bush, 'President Bush Discusses Freedom in Iraq and the Middle East', 6 November 2003.

290. 'While threatening the integrity of universal values, the campaign to spread democracy will not succeed.... The conditions for effective democratic

government are rare: an existing state enjoying legitimacy, consent and the ability to mediate conflicts between groups'. From Eric Hobsbawm, 'Delusions about Democracy', *Counterpunch*, 26 January 2005.

291. 'To force prosperity on people who are not free is not possible. . . . Democracy is a historical process that needs to reach maturity over time.' In an address to the John F. Kennedy School of Government at Harvard University, 11 May 2004, http://www.ksg.harvard.edu/news/news/2004/ebadi_051104.htm.

292. 'Third Arab Human Development Report Called "Courageous and Impartial"', *United Nations Development Programme News*, 5 April 2005.

293. Audiotape address broadcast on Al-Jazeera, 4 January 2004, p. 214.

294. 'President Bush Discusses Iraq Policy at Whitehall', 19 November 2003.

295. Obama, 'Remarks by the President on a New Beginning', 4 June 2009.

296. Lackey, *The Ethics of War and Peace*, p. 40.

297. He had been at the intellectual forefront of the neoconservative movement. Fukayama, 'The Neoconservative Moment', in *The National Interest*, no. 76, Summer 2004.

298. From William Rees-Mogg, 'Why Bin Laden Votes Bush', *Times*, 1 November 2004.

299. John C. Ford, 'The Morality of Obliteration Bombing', *Theological Studies*, vol. 5, no. 3, September 1944, p. 267.

300. 'Editorial: God or Country?', *America: The National Catholic Weekly*, vol. 188, no. 11, 31 March 2003.

301. 'Address of His Holiness Pope John Paul II to the Diplomatic Corps.'

302. In Graff, 'France is not a Pacifist Country'.

303. DeNeen Brown, 'Chretien Tells Canadians to Respect US Decision; Leader Tries to Curb Anti-American Sentiment', *Washington Post*, 21 March 2003, p. A29.

304. In 'Just War—or Just a War?', *New York Times*, 9 March 2003.

CHAPTER 2

1. 'New Zealand Church Leaders Joint Statement on the Threat of War Against Iraq', 10 September 2002.

2. See Christine Gray, *International Law and the Use of Force*, 2008, p. 194.

3. Indeed, the Taliban had been given an ultimatum to 'surrender the terrorists or surrender power: that is your choice'. Tony Blair, quoted in 'Blair Promises Victory Over Terror', *BBC News*, 2 October 2001. Not only did Mullah Omar refuse to hand over bin Laden, he called on the world's Muslims to join him in a *jihad* against the coalition if it invaded.

4. For example, the confessions of an alleged bin Laden associate, Djamel Begal, captured in the summer of 2001, uncovered al-Qaeda plots to attack the US Embassy in Paris and to bomb a US military site in Belgium. Also, bin Laden himself had issued warnings shortly after the September 11 attacks: 'I swear by Almighty Allah who raised the heavens without effort that neither America nor anyone who lives there will enjoy safety until safety becomes a reality for us

living in Palestine and before all the infidel armies leave the land of Mohammad'.
Videotape broadcast on *Al-Jazeera*, 7 October 2001, p. 105.

5. Cheney, 'Remarks to the Heritage Foundation', 10 October 2003.

6. 'Catholic Writers Recruited to Support Bush War on Iraq: Michael Novak Hired
   to Undermine Pope John Paul II's Position', *Houston Catholic Worker*, vol. 23, no.
   1, January–February 2003.

7. Condoleezza Rice, 'To A Free World', *New York Post*, 7 October 2002.

8. For example, James Kent, Chief Justice of the New York Supreme Court, in 1826:
   'An injury, either done or threatened, to the perfect rights of the nation, or
   of any of its members, and susceptible of no other redress, is a just cause of
   war. . . . Grotius condemns the doctrine that war may be undertaken to weaken
   the power of a neighbour, under the apprehension that its further increase
   may render him dangerous. This would be contrary to justice, unless we were
   morally certain, not only of a capacity, but of an actual intention, to injure us'.
   See James Kent, *Commentaries on American Law*, George F. Comstock (ed), 1866,
   pp. 56–79.

9. My italics. David Luban, 'Preventive War', *Philosophy and & Public Affairs*, Vol. 32,
   no. 3, 2004, p. 207.

10. See Bob Woodward, *Plan of Attack*, p. 411.

11. Cheney, 'Remarks to the Heritage Foundation', 10 October 2003.

12. 'Remarks by the President at Florida Rally', 20 March 2004; 'President's Remarks
    in Springfield, Missouri', 30 July 2004.

13. Wolfowitz, 'Building a Better World', 5 September 2002.

14. 'President Delivers State of the Union Address', 29 January 2002. These were the
    words which ended the telephone call between an operator and a passenger on
    one of the hijacked aeroplanes on 9/11. Todd Beamer and others aboard United
    Airlines Flight 93 had resolved to tackle the hijackers, and the plane, intended for
    a target in Washington DC, crashed into a field in Pennsylvania.

15. Cheney, 'Remarks to the Heritage Foundation', 10 October 2003.

16. 'Remarks by the President', 20 March 2004; 'President's Remarks in Springfield,
    Missouri', 30 July 2004; 'President's Remarks at the Republican National Conven-
    tion', 2 September 2004.

17. 'President Discusses the Future of Iraq', 26 February 2003.

18. Mary Ellen O'Connell, 'The Myth of Pre-emptive Self-Defense', *The American
    Society of International Law Task Force on Terrorism*, August 2002, p. 2.

19. See for example, Chris Brown, 'Self-Defence in An Imperfect World', part of a
    round-table discussion entitled 'Evaluating the Pre-emptive Use of Force', printed
    in *Ethics & International Affairs*, vol. 17, no. 1, Spring 2003.

20. See, for example, Michael Walzer, *Just and Unjust Wars: A Moral Argument with
    Historical Illustration*, 1977, pp. 74–85.

21. Neta C. Crawford, 'The Best Defense: The Problem with Bush's "Pre-emptive"
    War Doctrine', *Boston Review*, February–March 2003.

22. Still, it is worth bearing in mind that some scholars maintain that self-defence is
    only legal if it is in response to an attack that has already begun. See Ian Brownlie,

International Law and the Use of Force by States, 1963, and Christine Gray, *International Law and the Use of Force*, 2008.

23. Henry Shue, *Nuclear Deterrence and Moral Restraint*, 1989, p. 36. Shue recognizes that the very purity of the example makes it somewhat disanalogous to the context in which he is writing, which is the possible exchange of nuclear missiles in the Cold War.

24. Quoted in Gray, *International Law and the Use of Force*, p. 196.

25. Judge Rosalyn Higgins quoted in Christopher Greenwood, 'International Law and the Pre-emptive Use of Force: Afghanistan, Al-Qaida and Iraq', in *San Diego International Law Journal*, vol. 4, no.7, 2003, p. 15.

26. Shue, *Nuclear Deterrence and Moral Restraint*, p. 37.

27. Hew Strachan, 'Preemption and Prevention in Historical Perspective', in Henry Shue and David Rodin, eds, *Preemption: Military Action and Moral Justification*, 2007, p. 36.

28. Secretary of State Daniel Webster in a letter to British Ambassador to the United States, Henry Fox, 24 April 1841. See 'Extract from Note of April 24', online at http://www.yale.edu/lawweb/avalon/diplomacy/britain/br-1842d.htm.

29. Quoted in David E. Sanger, 'Beating Them to Prewar', *New York Times*, 27 September 2002.

30. Greenwood, 'International Law and the Pre-emptive Use of Force', p. 15.

31. Pompe, *Aggressive War: An International Crime*, 1953, p. 113.

32. Terence Taylor, 'The End of Imminence?', *The Washington Quarterly*, 27:4, Autumn 2004, p. 58.

33. Gray, *International Law and the Use of Force*, pp. 161–2.

34. For example, after Israel launched an attack against Iraq's Osirak reactor in 1981, the Israeli delegate to the United Nations 'cited several legal authorities support-ing the view that legitimate self-defence included the right to forestall a surprise attack and described the Israeli action as fully within Article 51 of the Charter' (http://www.un.org/Depts/dpa/repertoire/81-84_08.pdf). The Security Council, however, 'strongly condemn[ed] the military attack by Israel in clear violation of the Charter of the United Nations and the norms of international conduct' (resolution 487).

35. Secretary-General's High-Level Panel on Threats, Challenges and Change, *A More Secure World: Our Shared Responsibility*, 2 December 2004, paragraph 188, p. 54.

36. My italics. Ibid., paragraph 194, p. 55.

37. Ibid., paragraph 194, p. 55.

38. Ibid., paragraph 191, p. 55.

39. For the argument that 'collective action does not eliminate or even significantly reduce the dangers of preventive war', see Neta C. Crawford, 'The False Promise of Preventive War: The 'New Security Consensus' and a More Insecure World', in Henry Shue and David Rodin, eds, *Preemption: Military Action and Moral Justification*, 2007, pp. 89–125.

40. William H. Taft IV and Todd F. Buchwald, 'Pre-emption, Iraq and International Law', *American Journal of International Law*, vol. 97, no. 3, July 2003, p. 562. Their

argument turns on the language of paragraph 12 of resolution 1441, which stipulates that the Security Council will 'consider' the situation instead of 'decide' on measures in the event of a material breach by Iraq under paragraph 4, thus implicitly authorizing, they argue, the use of force without further action by the Security Council.

41. Ibid., p. 557.
42. A senior Pentagon source quoted in James Burke and Ed Vulliamy, 'War Clouds Gather as Hawks Lay Their Plans', *Observer*, 14 July 2002.
43. Sanger, 'Beating Them to Prewar'.
44. For example, 'we are fighting that enemy in Iraq and Afghanistan today so that we do not meet him again on our own streets, in our own cities'. 'President Addresses the Nation', 7 September 2003.
45. Woodward, *Plan of Attack*, p. 133.
46. Thomas More, *Utopia*, George M. Logan and Robert M. Adams (eds), book 2, 1989, p. 95.
47. 'National Security Strategy (2002)', p. 15.
48. Ibid., p. 15.
49. 'President Bush Delivers Graduation Speech at West Point', 1 June 2002.
50. 'President Addresses the Nation', 7 September 2003; 'President Signs Defense Appropriations Bill at the Pentagon', 10 January 2002.
51. 'Address to a Joint Session of Congress and the American People', 20 September 2001.
52. Wolfowitz quoted in Mohamed Sid-Ahmed, 'Bush's "Anticipatory" War', *Al-Ahram*, no. 624, 6–12 February 2003.
53. Wolfowitz, 'Building the Bridge', 6 December 2002.
54. Bush, 'Saddam Hussein Must Leave Iraq', 17 March 2003.
55. Bush, 'President Bush Discusses Iraq', 6 March 2003.
56. 'Dr Condoleezza Rice Discusses Iraq in Chicago', 8 October 2003.
57. 'Meet the Press with Tim Russert Interview with President George W. Bush', 7 February 2004.
58. Wolfowitz, 'Building the Bridge', 6 December 2002.
59. 'Remarks by the President at Florida Rally', 20 March 2004.
60. 'Where the threat is an attack by weapons of mass destruction, the risk imposed upon a state by waiting until the attack actually takes place compounded by the impossibility for that state to afford its population any effective protection once the attack has been launched, mean that such an attack can be reasonably treated as imminent in circumstances where an attack by conventional means would not be so regarded.' Greenwood, 'International Law and the Pre-emptive Use of Force', p. 16.
61. 'It is far more difficult to determine the time scale within which a threat of attack by terrorist means would materialise than it is with threats posed by, for example, regular armed forces.' Ibid., p. 16.
62. Ibid., p. 16.

63. Joschka Fischer quoted in Richard Norton-Taylor and Ian Black, 'US Fury at European Peace Plan', *Guardian*, 10 February 2003.

64. Speech before the Commonwealth Club of San Francisco, 23 September 2002.

65. Resignation speech to the House of Commons, 18 March 2003, reprinted at http://news.bbc.co.uk/1/hi/uk_politics/2859431.stm.

66. In 'Chirac and Schroeder on US Ultimatum', *BBC News*, 18 March 2003.

67. In Polly Curtis, 'Oxford Hands Anti-War Petition to No.10', *Guardian (Education)*, 6 March 2003.

68. Greenwood, 'International Law and the Pre-emptive Use of Force', p. 15.

69. Cardinal Roger M. Mahoney, 'Statement on the Possibility of a War with Iraq', 13 November 2002.

70. Swedish Mission Covenant Church, 'No to an Attack War on Iraq!', 8 February 2003.

71. Federation of Swiss Protestant Churches, 'No Preventive War Against Iraq', 23 January 2003.

72. George Hunsinger, 'Iraq: Don't Go There', *Christian Century*, 14 August 2002, no. 17, vol. 119, p. 10.

73. John Fitzgerald Kennedy, 'Special Message to the Congress on the Defense Budget', 28 March 1961.

74. O'Connell, 'The Myth of Pre-emptive Self-Defense', p. 8.

75. Luban, 'Preventive War', p. 225. This seems to be Walzer's position against P^2 in *Just and Unjust Wars*, p. 79: it's not that wars become too frequent, but they are too common in another sense, 'too ordinary', radically underestimating the importance of the shift from diplomacy to force.

76. 'Statement on the Possibility of a War with Iraq', 13 November 2002.

77. Henry Kissinger, 'Beyond Baghdad: After Regime Change the US Must Help Craft a New International Order', *New York Post*, 11 August 2002, p. 24. Kissinger cautioned that 'it is not in the American national interest to establish pre-emption as a universal principle available to every nation', fearing the 'most fateful reaction' that India would take US action as a cue to attack Pakistan.

78. According to Robert Jervis, 'the core argument of the security dilemma is that, in the absence of a supranational authority that can enforce binding agreements, many of the steps pursued by states to bolster their security have the effect—often unintended and unforeseen—of making other states less secure'. In 'Was the Cold War a Security Dilemma?', *Journal of Cold War Studies*, vol. 3, no. 1, Winter 2001, p. 36.

79. Quoted in Shue, *Nuclear Deterrence and Moral Restraint*, p. 37.

80. For example, '"we don't have to wait for them to attack", said Condoleezza Rice on television the other day. Well no, we don't, but we do have to wait for some sign that they are going to attack. The war that is being discussed is preventive war, not pre-emptive . . . Right now the administration's war is neither just nor necessary'. Michael Walzer in Event Transcript, 'Iraq and Just War: A Symposium', Pew Forum on Religion and Public Life, 30 September 2002.

81. For example, 'the overwhelming thrust of just war theory would find fault with the use of pre-emptive military action before diplomacy and other means have been exhausted'. Editor of the Religion News Service, David Earle Anderson in 'Not a Just or Moral War', *Sojourners Magazine*, vol. 32, no. 1, January–February 2003, p. 29.

82. Doris May cited by Professor Avi Shlaim, 'Israel: Wars of Choice and Wars of No Choice', lecture for the Oxford Leverhulme Programme on the Changing Character of War, Oxford University, 1 May 2007.

83. Luban, 'Preventive War', p. 236.

84. Rep. Jane Harman in Dana Priest and Mike Allen, 'Report Discounts Iraqi Arms Threat, *Washington Post*, 6 October 2004, p. A1.

85. Cheney on National Public Radio, quoted in Greg Miller, 'Cheney is Adamant on Iraq "Evidence"', *Los Angeles Times*, 23 January 2003, p. A1.

86. The Americans were said by Saddam to be 'the evil ones', 'the followers of Satan', 'the forces of evil', and 'the enemies of God, the nation, and humanity'. For his arguments against the United States on account of its alleged imperialist ambitions, see Ofra Bengio, *Saddam's Word: Political Discourse in Iraq*, 1998, pp. 127–34.

87. Quoted in Jackson Diehl, 'Israel Launches Satellite into Surveillance Orbit', *Washington Post*, 4 April 1990, p. A35.

88. Taylor, 'The End of Imminence?', p. 66.

89. Indeed, Professor William Galston suggested that 'proponents of this new expanded view of pre-emption need to make the case that the possibility of state cooperation with terrorists, especially in the deployment and use of WMD, somehow renders governments with known addresses and a great deal to lose immune to the traditional incentive structures of deterrence; that is an important factual question with theoretical and moral consequences'. Event Transcript, 'Iraq and Just War: A Symposium'.

90. Further, former National Security Advisor Brent Scowcroft argued that 'there is little evidence to indicate that the United States itself is an object of his aggression'. See 'Don't Attack Saddam', *Wall Street Journal*, 15 August 2002, p. B6.

91. 'President Bush Announces Major Combat Operations in Iraq Have Ended', 1 May 2003.

92. See Duelfer et al., 'Findings of the Special Advisor to the DCI on Iraq's WMD', 30 September 2004.

93. My italics. 'President Bush Discusses Iraq Report', 7 October 2004.

94. In Allen and Priest, 'Report Discounts Iraqi Arms Threat'.

95. David Luban, 'Preventive War and Human Rights', in Henry Shue and David Rodin, eds, *Preemption: Military Action and Moral Justification*, 2007, p. 190.

96. Ibid., p. 192.

97. Ibid., p. 192.

98. David Rodin, 'The Problem with Prevention', in Shue and Rodin, *Preemption*, pp. 166–70.

99. Ibid., p. 166.

100. Indeed, an internal document known as the 'Defence Planning Guidance', supervised by Paul Wolfowitz in 1992 and leaked to the press, stated that 'our first objective is to prevent the emergence of a new rival...our strategy must now refocus on precluding the emergence of any potential future global competitor...we have the opportunity to meet threats at lower levels and lower costs—as long as we are prepared to reconstitute additional forces should the need to counter a global threat re-emerge'. Printed in 'Excerpts from Pentagon's Plan: Prevent the Re-Emergence of a New Rival', *New York Times*, 8 March 1992, p. 14. Carrying this over, George W. Bush's Quadrennial Defence Review of September 2001 refers to maintaining 'long term military pre-eminence' as an operational goal. See Department of Defence, 'Quadrennial Defence Review Report', 30 September 2001, at http://www.defenselink.mil/pubs/qdr2001.pdf.

101. In Grotius, *De Jure Belli*, vol. 2, chapter 1, section 5, p. 174.

102. Walzer, *Just and Unjust Wars*, p. 80. This sentiment is reflected in a comment made by the director of the Office of International Justice and Peace of the US Catholic Bishops' Conference, Gerald F. Powers: 'Why now? This war was not based on actual threat but on speculation as to what that threat might be in 2004, 2005 and beyond'. Quoted in 'Ethicists Challenge Justification for Pre-Emptive War', *Worldwide Faith News*, 5 May 2003.

103. O'Brien argues that 'there must be adequate evidence that preparations for the attack have advanced to the point where it is imminent' (*The Conduct of Just and Limited War*, p. 133); Walzer's 'point of sufficient threat' requires a degree of active preparation that makes the manifest intent to injure a positive danger (*Just and Unjust Wars*, p. 81).

104. 'Vice President Speaks at VFW 103rd National Convention', 26 August 2002.

105. 'The Case Against War on Iraq', *Boston Globe*, 19 August 2002, p. A11.

106. Council of Bishops of the United Church of Christ in the Philippines, 'Pastoral Statement: Cry Out for Peace, Say No To War', 31 January 2003.

107. In Curtis, 'Oxford Hands Anti-War Petition to No. 10'.

108. My italics. In the Church of England Board for Social Responsibility, *Iraq: Would Military Action Be Justified? The Church's Contribution to the Debate*, 2002, p. 4.

109. 'We are in a conflict between good and evil, and America will call evil by its name'. 'President Delivers Graduation Speech at West Point', 1 June 2002.

110. See 'President Commemorates 60th Anniversary of V-J Day', 30 August 2005, for Bush's claim of moral equivalence between the Iraq war and the Allies' cause in the Second World War.

111. Thomas M. Nichols, 'Just War, Not Prevention', part of roundtable discussion entitled 'Evaluating the Pre-emptive Use of Force', in *Ethics & International Affairs*, vol. 17, no. 1, Spring 2003.

CHAPTER 3

1. See Carl Von Clausewitz, *On War* (1832), Michael Howard and Peter Paret (eds), 1993, p. 76. Clausewitz's view was that it was dangerous and self-deceptive to deny the full and horrible reality entailed by war. It is worth acknowledging, however, that he only postulated this 'logical absurdity' in a purely theoretical sense. He realized that, practically, 'civilized' nations did enter into compacts that made fighting less destructive but he sought to maintain that this was the result of a social process rather than any property belonging to war itself. This book, however, does not consider that any such separate entity as 'war' itself exists beyond the social frameworks in which military action takes place and the meanings attached to it at any given time.
2. 'Project of an International Declaration Concerning the Laws and Customs of War, Brussels, 27 August 1874' (article 12). Text available at http://www.icrc.org/ihl.nsf/INTRO/135?OpenDocument.
3. James Brown Scott quoted in Bailey, *Prohibitions and Restraints in War*, p. 24.
4. Grotius, *Prolegomena On the Law of War and Peace*, Francis W. Kelsey (transl), 1957, p. 21.
5. 'Hague Convention (IV) Respecting the Laws and Customs of War on Land', 18 October 1907, reprinted in Roberts and Guelff (eds), *Documents on the Laws of War*, p. 70.
6. Woodward, *Plan of Attack*, p. 405.
7. Walzer, *Just and Unjust Wars*, p. 33.
8. Dr Johnson quoted in Ramsey, *The Just War*, p. 145.
9. Ibid., p. 44.
10. Ramsey, *War and the Christian Conscience*, 1961, p. 32.
11. For his argument that 'the principal crime of the human race . . . is idolatry', and that 'the idolater is also a murderer', see Tertullian's third century work, *On Idolatry*.
12. Feith, 'Iraq: One Year Later', 4 May 2004.
13. Quoted in Richard Shelly Hartigan, 'Francesco de Vitoria and Civilian Immunity', *Political Theory*, vol. 1, no. 1, February 1973, p. 83.
14. Ramsey, *The Just War*, p. 159.
15. Francis Lieber, 'General Orders No. 100', 24 April 1863, article 15, online at http://www.au.af.mil/au/awc/awcgate/law/liebercode.htm.
16. '1977 Geneva Protocol I Additional to the Geneva Conventions', in Roberts and Guelff, *Documents on the Laws of War*, p. 450.
17. Grotius, *Prolegomena*, p. 15.
18. Best, *War and Law Since 1945*, p. 257.
19. For example, the 'Soldiers' Rules': 1. Soldiers do not harm captured enemy soldiers or civilian detainees; non-combatant civilians; medical personnel or chaplains; enemy soldiers 'out of combat'. 2. Soldiers collect and care for enemy wounded and sick. 3. Soldiers respect the medical symbol and do not attack

medical facilities. 4. Soldiers respect protected places. 5. Soldiers do not engage in treacherous acts. 6. Soldiers allow their enemy to surrender. 7. Soldiers do not steal from their enemy or from civilians. 8. Soldiers do not cause unnecessary suffering. 9. Soldiers report violations of the Law of War. 10. Soldiers obey orders and the Law of War. Reprinted in Leslie. C. Green, *The Contemporary Law of Armed Conflict*, 3rd edn., 2008, pp. 397–8.

20. 'President Bush Addresses the Nation', 19 March 2003.
21. Anne-Marie Slaughter in Robert Kuttner, 'Will Bush Wriggle Out of This One?', *Boston Globe*, 10 September 2005.
22. Quoted in Hartigan, 'Francesco de Vitoria and Civilian Immunity', p. 84.
23. Reprinted in Roberts and Guelff, *Documents on the Laws of War*, p. 448. This is also 'a norm of customary international law applicable in both international and non-international armed conflicts'—see 'Rule 1' in Jean Marie Henckaerts and Louise Doswald-Beck, *Customary International Humanitarian Law*, vol. I: *Rules* (Cambridge: Cambridge University Press, 2005), p. 3.
24. Ramsey, *The Just War*, p. 160.
25. *Just and Unjust Wars*, p. 145.
26. A. J. Coates, *The Ethics of War*, p. 235.
27. Best, *War and Law Since 1945*, p. 259.
28. O'Brien, *The Conduct of Just and Limited War*, p. 46.
29. Richard J. Regan, *Just War: Principles and Cases*, 1996, p. 93.
30. Judith Gail Gardam, 'Proportionality and Force in International Law', *American Journal of International Law*, 1993, vol. 87, no. 375, p. 391.
31. The statement noted that 'the only legitimate object which states should endeavour to accomplish during war is to weaken the military forces of the enemy' and, accordingly, banned the exploding bullet. 'Declaration Renouncing the Use, in Time of War, of Explosive Projectiles Under 400 Grammes Weight, reprinted in Roberts and Guelff, *Documents on the Laws of War*, p. 55.
32. See, for example, Best, *War and Law Since 1945*, p. 326.
33. For example, John C. Ford, 'The Morality of Obliteration Bombing', *Theological Studies*, vol. 5, 1944, pp. 289–91. See also Richard Norman, *Ethics, Killing and War*, 1995, pp. 203–6.
34. Aquinas, *Summa Theologica*, vol. 2, p. 1471.
35. In such usages, 'mistaken' refers to an action which is not intended and not foreseen whereas 'accidental' refers to an action which is not intended but indeed foreseen.
36. Vitoria, *De Indis*, p. 315.
37. George Weigel, 'The Development of Just War Thinking in the Post-Cold War World: An American Perspective', in Charles Reed and David Ryall (eds), *The Price of Peace: Just War in the Twenty-First Century*, 2007, p. 25.
38. Bush, 'President Addresses National Day of Prayer', 1 May 2003.
39. 'Baghdad Wakes Up to Explosions', *Fox News*, 22 March 2003.
40. Amnesty International, 'Iraq: Civilians Under Fire', 8 April 2003, online at http://web.amnesty.org/library/index/engmde140712003.

41. Toby Hamden, 'US Attack Kills 40 at Iraqi Wedding Party', *Telegraph*, 20 May 2004. It was reported that the guests had, according to local custom, fired AK-47s into the air in celebration.

42. Michael Smith, 'Baghdad Bomb Kills 55', *Telegraph*, 29 March 2003.

43. See 'Iraqis Push Ahead with Elections', *BBC News*, 21 November 2004.

44. Pierre Kraehenbuhl, quoted in 'Red Cross Hits Out at Iraq Abuses', *BBC News*, 19 November 2004.

45. Neil Mackay, 'US Forces' Use of Depleted Uranium Weapons is "Illegal"', *Sunday Herald*, 30 March 2003. The worry about such shells is that they contaminate land, cause cancers, and lead to birth defects.

46. Andrew Buncombe, 'US Admits It Used Napalm Bombs in Iraq', *Independent*, 10 August 2003.

47. See, for example, Jeffrey Sachs, 'Iraq's Civilian Dead Get No Hearing in the United States', *Daily Star*, 2 December 2004.

48. Much media coverage was given to the hundreds of foreigners taken hostage in Iraq (see Nicholas Blanford, 'Iraq Kidnappings Hard to Stop', *Christian Science Monitor*, 9 June 2004) but less well publicized were the thousands of Iraqis kidnapped for revenge or ransom (but see, for example, '4 Iraqis Killed, Family Kidnapped', *CNN*, 11 September 2004).

49. See Rajiv Chandrasekaran, 'Police Recruits Targeted: Bomb Kills Scores Near Headquarters', *Washington Post*, 15 September 2004, p. A1.

50. Ralph Peters, 'And Now, Fallujah', *New York Post*, 4 November 2004.

51. Karl Vick, 'Fallujah Strikes Herald Possible Attacks', *Washington Post*, 16 October 2004, p. A2.

52. See, for example, 'US strikes raze Fallujah Hospital', *BBC News*, 6 November 2004.

53. Anne Barnard, 'Returning Falluhjans Will Face Clampdown', *Boston Globe*, 5 December 2004.

54. Abdul Qader-Saadi, 'Fallujah Death Toll for Week More than 600', *Associated Press*, 11 April 2004.

55. Louise Arbour, 16 November 2004, see http://www.un.org/apps/news/story.asp?NewsID=12544&Cr=iraq&Cr1.

56. Jim McDermott and Richard Rapport, 'Investigate Alleged Violations of Law in Fallujah Attack', *Seattle Post-Intelligencer*, 11 January 2005, p. B7.

57. 'More Fallout from Mosque Shooting', *CBS News*, 17 November 2004. The cameraman who recorded the incident recalled that the marine had yelled out that the injured man was 'fucking faking he's dead' and then fired into his head as another said 'well, he's dead now'. See Elaine Monaghan, 'Man Who Filmed Shooting Speaks Out', *Times*, 23 November 2004.

58. Jim Miklaszewski, 'Marine Cleared in Mosque Shootings Probe', *NBC News*, 4 May 2005. The army's investigation concluded that the marine had 'fired his weapon in self-defence'.

59. 'US Used White Phosphorous in Iraq', *BBC News*, 16 November 2005. The US Army denies that white phosphorous is a chemical weapon, referring to it as an 'incendiary device'.

60. Reuven Paz, 'The Impact of the War in Iraq on the Global Jihad', in Hillel Fradkin, Husain Haqqani, and Eric Brown, *Current Trends in Islamist Ideology*, vol. 1, 2005, p. 44.

61. Brig. Gen. Sadoun Taleb, quoted in Rod Nordland, 'Spate of Attacks Tests Iraqi City and US Pullout', *New York Times*, 24 June 2009, p. A1.

62. General Charles Swannack, Commander 82nd Airborne Division, 'Army Maj. Gen. Swannack Jr, Live Teleconference from Baghdad', Department of Defense website, 18 November 2003, http://www.dod.mil/transcripts/2003/tr20031118-0887.html.

63. Anonymous, quoted in Sean Rayment, 'US Tactics Condemned by British Officers', *Telegraph*, 11 April 2004.

64. Bishop Wilton D. Gregory, 'Statement on Moral Responsibilities for United States in Iraq', 22 June 2004.

65. Lieutenant General John Abizaid, in Eric Schmitt, 'Pentagon Keeping Some Targets Off-Limits', *International Herald Tribune*, 24 March 2003, p. 1.

66. Peter Ford, 'Surveys Pointing to High Civilian Death Toll in Iraq', *Christian Science Monitor*, 22 May 2003.

67. 'Remarks as Delivered by Secretary Rumsfeld, Camp Al-Saliyah, Doha, Qatar', 28 April 2003.

68. Brigadier General Vince Brooks, 'Centcom Operation Iraqi Freedom Briefing', 1 April 2003.

69. Human Rights Watch, *Off Target: The Conduct of the War and Civilian Casualties in Iraq*, 2003, p. 5.

70. Tim Moynihan, 'Market Deaths Set to Dash Hopes for "Clean" War', *Press Association*, 26 March 2003.

71. Gwynne Dyer, 'Odds are Against Clean War with Iraq', *Niagara Falls Review*, 13 November 2002, p. A4.

72. 'Too Late for the US to Invoke International Law, Says PM', *Malaysia General News*, 24 March 2003.

73. 'President Bush Announces Major Combat Operations in Iraq Have Ended', 1 May 2003.

74. 'The psychological effect of this unequal killing is mitigated by the fact that there is a long-standing tradition of fighting against militarily and ethnically inferior peoples in which it is proper that the latter die in much larger numbers.' Talal Asad, *On Suicide Bombing*, 2007, p. 35.

75. For example, 'legal experts argue that the war's opening "shock and awe" campaign alone—with its thousands of civilian casualties, wholesale destruction of civilian installations, and severe traumatising and terrorising of an entire population—counted as a serious crime against humanity'. Khaled Diab, 'Justice, the American Way', *Guardian*, 14 January 2009.

76. By this, I mean the use of the detainees' Islamic faith as a means to pressure them and cause them distress, which was mentioned in Chapter 1. Indeed, according to released British detainees, the Quran was routinely thrown on the floor and stamped upon, and the word 'fuck' was inscribed into that belonging to Feroz

Abbasi. Tariq Dergoul testified that, in interrogation, the US military 'concentrated more on blasphemy and humiliation than on information' (speaking at a Reprieve conference entitled 'Guantanamo and Islam', St Anne's College, Oxford, 18 March 2007).

77. 'President Announces Major Combat Operations in Iraq Have Ended', 1 May 2003.
78. Irene Khan, 'Amnesty International Report 2005 at Foreign Press Association', 25 May 2005, available at http://web.amnesty.org/library/Index/ENGPOL100142005
79. Lord Steyn quoted in Clare Dyer, 'Law Lord Castigates US Justice', *Guardian*, 26 November 2003.
80. United Nations Economic and Social Council, 'Situation of Detainees at Guantanamo Bay', 15 February 2006, http://news.bbc.co.uk/1/shared/bsp/hi/pdfs/16_02_06_un_guantanamo.pdf, p. 37.
81. 'President Bush Honours the Brave and Fallen Defenders of Freedom', 26 May 2003.
82. 'President Discusses War on Terrorism', 8 November 2001.
83. 'Address to a Joint Session of Congress and the American People', 20 September 2001.
84. A. N. Cochrane, quoted in Bailey, *Prohibitions and Restraints in War*, p. 5. Ambrose argued that 'justice must even be preserved in all dealings with enemies ... but a deeper vengeance is taken on fiercer foes, and on those that are false as well as those who have done greater wrong'.
85. Johnson, *Just War Tradition and the Restraint of War*, p. 338.
86. By this I mean such policies as evident in medieval canon law which banned the use of crossbows in wars among Christians but permitted them in wars in which Christendom was fighting Islam.
87. Vitoria, *De Indis*, p. 315.
88. Grotius, *De Jure Belli*, vol. 1, p. 40.
89. Cited in David Luban, 'Liberalism, Torture and the Ticking Bomb', *Virginia Law Review*, vol. 91, no. 6, October 2005, p. 1447.
90. This would violate Norway's neutrality but the idea was to force German merchant ships out into the Atlantic where they could be sunk by the British.
91. Quoted in Walzer, *Just and Unjust Wars*, p. 245.
92. Ramsey's idea is that 'since it was for the sake of the innocent and the helpless of the earth that the Christian first thought himself obliged to make war against an enemy whose objective deeds had to be stopped, since only for their sakes does a Christian justify himself in resisting by any means even an enemy-neighbour, he could never proceed to kill equally innocent people as a means of getting at the enemy's forces'. *The Just War*, p. 143.
93. Vitoria, *De Indis*, p. 314.
94. Orend, 'Is There a Supreme Emergency Exemption?', in M. Evans (ed), *Just War Theory: A Reappraisal*, 2005, p. 135.
95. Walzer, *Just and Unjust Wars*, p. 251.

96. With reference to the behaviour of the British, Walzer argues that 'the supreme emergency passed long before the British bombing reached its crescendo' and that Dresden, Hamburg, and Berlin were destroyed simply for the sake of terror. The main thrust of his argument is that the end was not victory itself but the time and price of victory decreed by the British. In a similar vein, the US's actions in Japan were about the speed and scope of winning the war rather than a last resort to avert imminent destruction. In addition, Walzer maintains that Japanese militarism posed an entirely different sort of threat than did the Nazis.

97. Walzer, *Just and Unjust Wars*, p. 253.

98. Ibid, p. 259.

99. Shue, 'Liberalism: The Impossibility of Justifying WMD', in Sohail Hashmi and Steven Lee (eds), *Ethics and Weapons of Mass Destruction: Religious and Secular Perspectives*, 2004, p. 154.

100. Walzer, *Just and Unjust Wars*, p. 262.

101. See Walzer, ibid., pp. 53–5 and pp. 135–7.

102. Ibid., p. 228.

103. Ibid., p. 326.

104. 'Dr Condoleezza Rice Discusses the President's National Security Strategy', 1 October 2002.

105. Bush, 'Address to a Joint Session of Congress and the American People', 20 September 2001.

106. 'Vice President's Remarks at a Rally for the Troops', 27 July 2004.

107. 'Remarks at National Press Club', 2 February 2006.

108. 'President Bush Speaks to the United Nations', 10 November 2001.

109. Rowan Scarborough, 'Gitmo Called Death Camp', *Washington Times*, 16 June 2005.

110. Bill Frist, 'First Floor Statement on Guantanamo Bay', 17 June 2005. While in no way equivalent to execution, it is worth noting that in June 2006 two Saudi nationals and one Yemeni committed suicide. After partaking in hunger strikes, a widespread form of protest in Guantanamo that was met by the authorities with forced feeding, the three inmates were found hanging from clothing and bed sheets in their cells. Although one commander described the deaths as 'an act of asymmetrical warfare waged against us', Human Rights Watch explained that 'these people are despairing because they are being held lawlessly. There's no end in sight. They're not being brought before any independent judges. They're not being charged and convicted for any crime'. See 'Triple Suicide at Guantanamo Camp', *BBC News*, 11 June 2006. In May 2007 a third Saudi man was found hanging in his cell. In June 2009, a second Yemeni national was believed to have committed suicide after a prolonged hunger strike, bringing the total suicide count to five. One other detainee also died from cancer (in December 2007). See William Glaberson and Margot Williams, 'Officials Report Suicide of Guantanamo Detainee', *New York Times*, 2 June 2009.

111. Human rights lawyer Louise Christian in 'Guantanamo Bay: A Global Experiment in Inhumanity', *Guardian*, 10 January 2004.

112. Archbishop Desmond Tutu in 'Tutu Calls for Guantanamo Closure', *BBC News*, 17 February 2006.

113. David Luban, Testimony Presented to the Senate Judiciary Committee, 13 May 2009.

114. Joshua Dratel, 'The Legal Narrative', in *The Torture Papers: The Road to Abu Ghraib*, 2004, p. xxii.

115. All memoranda to be referred to in the following section are contained in Karen J. Greenberg and Joshua L. Dratel (eds), *The Torture Papers: The Road to Abu Ghraib*, 2004.

116. See, for example, Jay S. Bybee, 'Standards of Conduct for Interrogation Under 18 USC 2340-2340A', Memo 14, 1 August 2002, pp. 204–7.

117. See, for example, Patrick F. Philbin and John C. Yoo, 'Memorandum for William J. Haynes, II General Counsel, Department of Defense', Memo 3, 28 December 2001, pp. 29–37.

118. David Luban, 'Liberalism, Torture and the Ticking Bomb', p. 1453. See also Dratel in *The Torture Papers*, p. xxii.

119. See Jane Mayer, 'The Memo: How an Internal Effort to Ban the Abuse and Torture of Detainees was Thwarted', *The New Yorker*, 27 February 2006, pp. 32–41.

120. See Major General Antonio Taguba, 'The Taguba Report: Article 15-6 Investigation of the 800th Military Police Brigade', March 2004, printed in *The Torture Papers*, p. 416.

121. 'Translation of Statement Provided by Detainee # 151108', 18 January 2004 in *The Torture Papers*, p. 504.

122. 'Translation of Statement Provided by Detainee # 150542', 18 January 2004, in *The Torture Papers*, p. 506.

123. See 'Prisoners "Killed" at US Base', *BBC News*, 6 March 2003. See also Jameel Jaffer and Amrit Singh, eds, *Administration of Torture: A Documentary Record from Washington to Abu Ghraib and Beyond*, 2007, pp. A-185–8 and pp. A-288–9.

124. 'Remarks by the National Security Advisor at the Karamah Iftaar', 4 December 2002.

125. Alberto R. Gonzales, 'Decision Re: Application of the Geneva Convention on Prisoners of War to the Conflict with Al Qaeda and the Taliban', Memo 7, 25 January 2002, p. 119.

126. Philippe Sands, *Torture Team: Uncovering War Crimes in the Land of the Free*, 2009, p. 39.

127. Jay S. Bybee, 'Application of Treaties and Laws to al Qaeda and Taliban Detainees', Memo 6, 22 January 2002, p. 81.

128. Ibid, p. 90.

129. The White House, 'Humane Treatment of al Qaeda and Taliban Detainees', Memo 11, 7 February 2002, p. 134.

130. 'Working Group Report on Detainee Interrogations in the Global War on Terrorism', Memo 26, 4 April 2003.

131. John C. Yoo, Deputy Assistant Attorney General, in an interview for *PBS*'s 'Frontline', 19 July 2005.

132. Working Group, Memo 26, p. 287.

133. Bybee, Memo 14, p. 207.

134. Working Group, Memo 26, p. 287.

135. 'Statement of Alberto R. Gonzales before the Committee on the Judiciary United States Senate', 6 January 2005, http://judiciary.senate.gov/testimony.cfm?id=1345&wit_id=3936.

136. See 'Secretary Rumsfeld Roundtable with Radio Media', 15 January 2002.

137. 'Remarks by the President to the Travel Pool', 20 March 2002.

138. Clive Stafford Smith in 'Torture: An Idea for Our Time', *Open Democracy*, 11 August 2005, published online at http://www.opendemocracy.net/debates/article.jsp?id=2&debateId=124&articleId=2749.

139. Bradford Berenson, associate White House Counsel 2001–2003, in an interview for *PBS*'s 'Frontline', 14 July 2005.

140. Ibid.

141. Gonzales, Memo 7, p. 120.

142. The term was first used by the US Supreme Court in 1942 with reference to eight captured Germans who had landed on US soil bent on a mission of sabotage. See Richard R. Baxter, 'So-called "Unprivileged Belligerency": Spies, Guerrillas and Saboteurs', *British Yearbook of International Law*, vol. 28, 1951, p. 339.

143. Geneva III defines these as the wearing of distinctive insignia, carrying arms openly, conducting operations according to the laws of war and acting under responsible command (article 4).

144. See John Yoo and Robert J. Delahunty, 'Application of Treaties and Laws to Al Qaeda and Taliban Detainees', Memo 4, 9 January 2002, pp. 48–50.

145. See ibid., p. 55.

146. Ibid, p. 59.

147. Bybee, 'Application of Treaties and Laws to Al Qaeda and Taliban Detainees', Memo 6, 22 January 2002, p. 91.

148. See for example, the point-by-point rebuttal by the Chief Executive of Human Rights Watch, Kenneth Roth, 'US Officials Misstate Geneva Conventions Requirements', 28 January 2002, http://hrw.org/press/2002/01/us012802-ltr.htm.

149. Colin L. Powell, 'Memorandum to Counsel to the President and Assistant to the President for National Security Affairs', Memo 8, 26 January 2002, p. 123. The Geneva Conventions were less than sixty years old at Powell's time of writing, but perhaps he was referring to the first Geneva Convention of 1864 which dealt exclusively with care for wounded soldiers. The Conventions were revised and expanded in 1949. He may also have been referring to the international legal regime more generally.

150. In Sands, *Torture Team*, p. 40.

151. William Taft IV, Legal Adviser to Secretary Powell in an interview for *PBS*'s 'Frontline', 14 July 2005.

152. Thomas E. Ayres, 'Six Floors of Detainee Operations in the Post-9/11 World', p. 37.

153. Yoo, interview on *PBS*'s 'Frontline', 19 July 2005.

154. Gonzales, Memo 7, p. 119

155. Roberts and Guelff, *Documents on the Laws of War*, p. 198. Indeed, it was the Bush administration's controversial view that Common Article 3 applied only

to 'armed conflicts not of an international character'. Sands, *Torture Team*, p. 41.

156. David J. Luban, 'Selling Indulgences: The Unmistakeable Parallel Between Lynne Stewart and the President's Torture Lawyers', *Slate*, 14 February 2005. The 'torture lawyers' are White House counsel Alberto Gonzales, vice-presidential counsel David Addington, Justice Department lawyers Jay Bybee and John Yoo, and Pentagon counsel William Haynes. See also David Luban, *Legal Ethics and Human Dignity*, 2007, pp. 162–205.

157. The administration's 'new paradigm' appeared to filter down the chain of command, as one detainee was allegedly told by a CIA agent: 'After 9/11, Moazzam, the rules changed. We have new laws, and according to them, you're already convicted. The US has done with fighting wars with its hands tied behind its back'. See Begg, *Enemy Combatant*, p. 149.

158. Rumsfeld's Principal Deputy Assistant Secretary to a meeting of JAGs in Sands, *Torture Team*, p. 166.

159. This is 'United States Code: Title 18: Part I: Chapter 113C'.

160. While the Convention Against Torture prohibits acts by which 'severe pain or suffering, whether physical or mental [are] intentionally inflicted upon a person for such purposes as obtaining from him or a third person information or a confession' (article 1), the Torture Statute prohibits acts 'committed by a person under the color of law specifically intended to inflict severe physical or mental pain or suffering' (section 2340).

161. Although the United States is not a party to the two Additional Protocols, article 75 is regarded as customary international law that is binding on all states.

162. Torture here is defined as a 'crime against humanity'.

163. 'Situation of Detainees at Guantanamo Bay', p. 8.

164. Office of the High Commissioner for Human Rights, 'United Nations Convention Against Torture and Other Cruel, Inhuman or Degrading Treatment or Punishment (1984)', article 2, online at http://www.unhchr.ch/html/menu3/b/h_cat39.htm.

165. Diane E. Beaver, 'Legal Brief on Proposed Counter-Resistance Strategies', Memo 20, 11 October 2002, p. 229.

166. Bybee, Memo 14, p. 199. It is worth noting that the Bush administration subsequently distanced itself from the content of this, the 'torture memo'.

167. Ibid., p. 176.

168. Ibid., p. 183.

169. Ibid., p. 172.

170. Luban, *Legal Ethics and Human Dignity*, pp. 178–9. Philippe Sands observes that Bybee had 'no background in international law or issues of war or interrogation'—*Torture Team*, p. 88.

171. Lieutenant Colonel Thomas S. Berg, interview for *PBS*'s 'Frontline', 18 July 2005.

172. A recurring argument is that, to constitute torture, the infliction of pain must be the precise objective of an act, whereas an interrogator aims merely to extract information. While he may foresee that a particular result is certain to occur

from his actions, this does not count as specific intent. See, for example, 'Working Group Report on Detainee Interrogations in the Global War on Terrorism—Draft', Memo 25, 6 March 2003, pp. 245–7.

173. See John Yoo, 'Letter Regarding the Views of our Office Concerning the Legality, Under International Law, of Interrogation Methods to be Used On Captured Al Qaeda Operatives', Memo 15, 1 August 2002, pp. 221–2.

174. Bybee, Memo 14, p. 207.

175. Ibid., p. 208.

176. Ibid., p. 209.

177. Working Group, Memo 26, p. 308.

178. Bybee, Memo 14, p. 211.

179. Ibid., p. 212.

180. Vitoria, *De Indis*, p. 316.

181. Department of the US Army, *FM 34-52*, May 8, 1987, chapter 1, available online at http://www.globalsecurity.org/intell/library/policy/army/fm/fm34-52/chapter1.htm.

182. *Just and Unjust Wars*, p. 257. For dissenting voices from within the US military establishment with reference to torture, see, for example, Donald P. Gregg, 'Fight Fire with Compassion', *New York Times*, 10 June 2004 and Lieutenant Colonel Berg's interview for PBS.

183. Alex J. Bellamy, 'Supreme Emergencies and the Protection of Non-combatants in War', *International Affairs*, vol. 80, no. 5, 2004, p. 845.

184. Sands, *Torture Team*, p. 270.

185. FBI email to T. J. Harrington, 10 May 2004, in Jaffer and Singh, *Administration of Torture*, p. A-131.

186. FBI email to Maj. Gen. Miller, undated, in Jaffer and Singh, *Administration of Torture*, p. A-139.

187. FBI draft letter to Maj. Gen. Miller, 22 November 2002, in Jaffer and Singh, *Administration of Torture*, p. A-140.

188. FBI internal memorandum, 13 July 2004, in Jaffer and Singh, *Administration of Torture*, p. A-155.

189. FBI email subj. 'Impersonating FBI at GTMO', 5 December 2003, in Jaffer and Singh, *Administration of Torture*, p. A-159.

190. Bellamy, 'Supreme Emergencies', p. 845.

191. Orend, 'Is There a Supreme Emergency Exemption?', p. 138.

192. Walzer, *Just and Unjust Wars*, p. 253.

193. Wolfowitz argued that 'our forces today face the most recent evil mutation of totalitarianism'. See 'Wolfowitz Says Patience Key to Success in War on Terror', 10 July 2004.

194. 'President Commemorates 60th Anniversary of V-J Day', 30 August 2005.

195. Peter Baker and Josh White, 'Bush Calls Iraq War Moral Equivalent of Allies' WWII Fight Against the Axis', *Washington Post*, 31 August 2005, p. A7.

196. 'Remarks by the President Upon Arrival', 16 September 2001.

197. 'President Bush Delivers Graduation Speech at West Point', 1 June 2002. See also 'World Must Act Now to Prevent Evil', 2 February 2002.

198. Department of Defence, 'Quadrennial Defence Review Report', 30 September 2001.

199. 'The Vice President Receives the International Republican Institute's 2001 Freedom Award', 23 October 2001.

200. 'President's Remarks at the 2004 Republican National Convention', 2 September 2004.

201. For an elaboration of this view, see Ulrich Raulff, 'Interview with Georgio Agamben—Life, a Work of Art Without an Author: The State of Exception, the Administration of Disorder and Private Life', *German Law Journal*, vol. 5, no. 5, 1 May 2004, pp. 609–14. In addition, the detainees, often imprisoned in isolation and all without access to their families, can be seen as socially dead. Moazzam Begg suggested that the denial of family visits 'separates you from being a complete human being . . . you no longer have the right to be a member of any society, including a family'—From Reprieve's 'Guantanamo and Islam' conference.

202. 'Interrogation Log of Detainee 063: Day 20, 12 December 2002', reprinted in Sands, *Torture Team*, p. 61.

203. On Chris Suellentrop, 'Pentagon Official Douglas Feith and His Possible Connection to Major Tactical Errors in Iraq', *National Public Radio*, 24 May 2004, aired 4 pm. In the end, Feith maintained that he sought to *protect* the Geneva Conventions, rather than contravene them, because any protections extended to irregular fighters (and therefore terrorists) undermined the incentive system built into the Conventions. See Sands, *Torture Team*, pp. 35–45. His argument might be regarded as a *jus in bello* parallel to Bush's claim to have been protecting the UN Security Council by invading Iraq without Security Council approval: 'we believe in the Security Council—so much that we want its words to have meaning'.

204. Lord Falconer, Britain's Lord Chancellor, in 'UK Minister Condemns Guantanamo', *BBC News*, 13 September 2006. The Attorney General, Lord Goldsmith, also called for its closure.

205. At the Baptist World Alliance conference in Birmingham, quoted in Cassandra Vinograd, 'Former US President Carter Blasts Guantanamo Bay Detention Camp', *Associated Press*, 30 July 2005.

206. Captain Ian Fishback, 'A Matter of Honour', *Washington Post*, 28 September 2005, p. A21.

207. Major General Jack L. Rives quoted in Luban, *Legal Ethics and Human Dignity*, p. 173.

208. Dr John Sentamu in David Charter, Ruth Gledhill, and Greg Hurst, 'Blair Condones Amin-style Tactics Against Terrorism, says Archbishop', in the *Times*, 24 February 2006, p. 3.

209. National Council of Churches, 'A Statement on the Disavowal of Torture', 9 November 2005.

210. Robert W. Tucker, *The Just War: A Study in American Contemporary Doctrine*, 1960, p. 21. Interestingly, Tucker singles out 'freedom' as the guiding ideal, extrapolated from America's own domestic experience.
211. 'President Bush Speaks to the United Nations', 10 November 2001.
212. Ralph B. Potter, *War and Moral Discourse*, 1969, p. 51.
213. Ibid., p. 52.
214. *Just War Tradition and the Restraint of War*, p. xxxiii.
215. Rice, 'Transformational Diplomacy: Question-and-Answer Session', 18 January 2006.

CHAPTER 4

1. 'Public Report of National Commission on Terrorist Attacks Upon the United States', 22 July 2004, chapter 11, section 1.
2. Statement of 14 February 2003, reprinted in Bruce Lawrence, *Messages to the World: The Statements of Osama bin Laden*, 2004, p. 194. Unless otherwise stated, citations of Osama bin Laden's statements will refer to the Lawrence collection.
3. Interview with Hamid Mir (*Ausaf*), 12 November 2001, p. 141.
4. Two thousand West Bank Palestinians were said to have chanted slogans in honour of bin Laden, and it was reported that wedding tunes were honked out in celebration in East Jerusalem. Shots were exultantly fired into the air by Palestinian militants in the Ain Al-Helwah refugee camp in Lebanon, and some Egyptians, too, were said to be 'thrilled by the attacks'. See Ben Barber, 'Arabs Exult, but Leaders Denounce Killing', *Washington Times*, 12 September 2001 and 'Arafat Condemns, Palestinians Celebrate', *Statesman* (India), 12 September 2001.
5. Dr Mustafa Ceric in 'Head of Bosnia's Muslims Urges Bush to Exercise Caution', *BH Press (Sarajevo)*, 16 September 2001.
6. Major General Amin al-Hindi quoted in Ala al-Mashharawi, 'PA Intelligence Chief on Contacts with US Following Terrorist Attacks', *Al-Quds*, 17 September 2001.
7. 'Leaders of 46 Islamic Groups and Movements Condemn the Attacks on the US', *Al-Sharq Al-Awsat*, 14 September 2001.
8. Jiang Xiaofeng, 'Iran Shows Human Touch as Hopes of Thawing Ties With US Remain Dim', *Xinhua News Agency*, 19 September 2001.
9. Mohammad Khatami, 'Address to the United Nations General Assembly', 9 November 2001.
10. 'Xinhua Reports Taliban Condemn the Attacks in US', *Xinhua News Agency*, 11 September 2001.
11. Uthman Mirghani, 'Jihad for Who?', *Al-Sharq Al-Awsat*, 24 October 2001.
12. Quoted in Eric Rouleau, 'Terrorism and Islamism: Politics in the Name of the Prophet', *Le Monde Diplomatique*, 1 November 2001.
13. 'Ghana: Chief Imam Condemns US Attacks, Urges Global Definition of Terrorism', *Ghana Broadcasting Corporation Radio 1*, 21 September 2001.

14. In Alpha Barry's report, 'Burkina Faso: Reactions of Muslim Community to US Attacks', *Radio France Internationale*, 15 September 2001.
15. The agency staunchly supported the Taliban government of Afghanistan and it was integral to the *mujahidin's* war against the Soviets in the 1980s when it was believed to have acted as a link between the *mujahidin* and the CIA.
16. 'Pakistani Leaders Condemn Terrorism and Criticise US Policies', *Nawa-i-Waqt*, 12 September 2001, p. 8.
17. In 'Hizballah's Spiritual Leader Advocates Fatwah Against Terrorists', *Der Spiegel*, 15 October 2001.
18. 'Muslim Cleric Faults Taliban's "Backward" Mentality', *Radio Monte Carlo*, 15 November 2001.
19. Nicholas Noe, *Voice of Hezbollah: The Statements of Sayyed Hassan Nasrallah*, 2007, p. 291.
20. Ahmad Zakayev in 'Radical Chechens Deny Links With Bin Laden, Admit Contacts With Taliban', *Agence France Presse*, 27 September 2001.
21. Sheikh Abdullah bin Hussein al-Ahmar in 'Yemeni Parliament Speaker: NY, DC Operations Express Anger, Frustration', *Al-Quds Al-Arabi*, 5 October 2001.
22. Bassam Tibi, 'War and Peace in Islam', in Sohail Hashmi (ed), *Islamic Political Ethics: Civil Society, Pluralism, and Conflict*, 2002, p. 178.
23. Enormous importance was attached, by Muslims, to the teachings of Mohammad. After his death, there burgeoned a vast literature which sought to record his word and deed. Such *hadiths* formed an important part of the Islamic legal system: 'the Muhammadan community found itself at the death of Muhammad with a holy book and the living memory of a prophet; from these two sources the ecclesiastical and temporal polity of the Islamic world was for all time built up'. Alfred Guillaume, *The Traditions of Islam: An Introduction to the Study of the Hadith Literature*, 1966, p. 9.
24. Ibn Taymiyyah, *Public Policy in Islamic Jurisprudence*, Omar Farrukh (transl), 1966, p. 140.
25. Ibn Taymiyyah, *Public Duties in Islam: The Institution of the Hisba*, Muhtar Holland (transl), 1982, p. 128.
26. Ibid., p. 106.
27. Ibid., p. 109.
28. Ibid., p. 133.
29. *In the Shade of the Quran*, M. A. Salahi (ed), vol. 1, 2001, p. 270.
30. Azzam, *Defence of Muslim Lands*, 1986, chapter 1, online at http://www.islamist watch.org/texts/azzam/defense/defense.html.
31. Azzam, *Join the Caravan*, 1987, part 1, online at http://www.islamistwatch.org/texts/azzam/caravan/caravan.html.
32. For Khadduri, see *War and Peace in the Law of Islam*, 1962, p. 59; for Moinuddin see *The Charter of the Islamic Conference*, 1987, p. 28 ('[*jihad* is qualified] to be considered as the *bellum justum* of Islam because it is waged for a just cause as a consequence of some wrong or injury inflicted upon the Muslims; it includes the

inherent right of self-defence; and it must be conducted in accordance with upright intentions and not for material gains or for the sake of glory and power').

33. Mawdudi, *Towards Understanding the Quran*, Zafar Ishaq Ansari (ed), 1988, vol. 1, p. 152.

34. Madeleine Bunting, 'Friendly Fire: Madeleine Bunting Meets Sheikh Yusuf al-Qaradawi in Qatar', *Guardian*, 29 October 2005.

35. *Fatwa* entitled 'Jihad in Chechnya', 19 April 2004, at http://www.islamonline.net/servlet/Satellite?pagename=IslamOnline-English-Ask_Scholar/FatwaE/FatwaE&cid=1119503543542.

36. David Cook, *Understanding Jihad*, 2005, p. 30.

37. In 'Sayyed Hasan Nasrallah's Autobiography', *Ya Lesarat Ol-Hosayn*, 10 August 2006.

38. 'Islam and Violence in Political Reality', *Middle East Insight*, vol. 4, no. 4, 1986, p. 9.

39. George Nader, 'Interview with Sheikh Muhammed Hussein Fadl Allah', *Middle East Insight*, vol. 4, no. 2, 1985, p. 12.

40. Yusuf Qaradawi, *State in Islam*, el-Falah (transl), 1998, p. 3.

41. Quoted in Dale Eickelman and James Piscatori, *Muslim Politics*, 1996, p. 49.

42. Just as the tribes of pre-Islamic Arabia frequently fought each other, so they developed chivalric codes of combat whereby attacking non-combatants, for example, was 'considered bad form'. For the influence of pre-Islamic cultural norms upon the classical conception of *jihad* see Fred M. Donner, 'The Sources of Islamic Conceptions of War' in John Kelsay and James Turner Johnson (eds), *Just War and Jihad*, 1991, pp. 33–46.

43. Khadduri, *War and Peace in the Law of Islam*, p. 53.

44. Indeed, the notion of a single Islamic community united under one leader was short-lived. The Prophet left no sons, and two of the four caliphs from the supposed 'golden era' of Islam were assassinated by their own kin. Well before the Mongol invasions in the thirteenth century, there existed distinct Islamic dynasties, with the Fatimids in North Africa and the Seljuks in Iran, as well as other independent Muslim states. After the Mongols precipitated the fall of the Abassid caliphate, the Mughal Empire emerged in the east, the Safavids in Iran, and the Ottomans in the west.

45. Abdulaziz Abdulhussein Sachedina, *The Just Ruler in Shite Islam: The Comprehensive Authority of the Jurist in Imamite Jurisprudence*, 1988, p. 106.

46. Ibn Rushd, *Bidayat al-Mujtahid wa Nihayat al-Muqtasid* (1167), part 3, reprinted in Rudolph Peters, *Jihad in Classical and Modern Islam*, 1996, pp. 27–42. This directly parallels Francisco di Vitoria's non-combatant immunity proviso, as considered in chapter three: 'it follows that even in wars against the Turks we may not kill children, who are obviously innocent, nor women, who are to be presumed innocent at least as far as the war is concerned (unless, that is, it can be proved of a particular woman that she was implicated in guilt)'. Vitoria, *De Indis*, p. 315.

47. Khadduri argues that the sources of Islamic international law conform to the same categories defined by modern jurists and the International Court of Justice: agreement, as with rules expressed in treaties with non-Muslims; custom,

including the *sunna* and norms of the Arabian *jus gentium*; reason, as expressed in *fatwas*, opinions of rulers and the use of analogical reasoning; and authority, comprised of the Quran and the *hadith*. See Khadduri, *War and Peace in the Law of Islam*, p. 48.

48. Bruce Lawrence, 'Jihad in Islamic Religion and Nation State Ideologies', in John Kelsay and James Turner Johnson (eds), *Just War and Jihad*, 1991, p. 142.

49. John Kelsay, *Arguing the Just War in Islam*, 2007, p. 5.

50. Ibid, p. 77.

51. Address to 'our neighbours north of the Mediterranean' (the people of Europe), broadcast on *Al-Jazeera* and *Al-Arabiyya*, 15 April 2004, p. 234.

52. Interview with *Al-Jazeera*, December 1998, p. 76.

53. Ibid., p. 84.

54. Released from prison in the general amnesty granted when King Abdullah of Jordan ascended to the throne in 1999, Abu Musab al-Zarqawi went on to become involved in al-Qaeda's organizational activities in Afghanistan, and was eventually killed by an American bomb in Iraq in 2006. As the insurgency raged in post-invasion Iraq, Zarqawi was said to have become leader of 'al-Qaeda in Mesopotamia'. However, as noted on p. 30, this was seen as an attempt to challenge the conventional authority of al-Qaeda. Indeed, while in Iraq, he masterminded an independent and ruthless Sunni campaign of slaughter against the Iraqi Shia, hence Zawahiri's letter. When Zarqawi first joined al-Qaeda in Afghanistan in 1999, it was not long before his camp in Herat was regarded as a rival by the al-Qaeda leadership. Indeed, some had always been suspicious of Zarqawi, and 'for several months certain [al-Qaeda] dignitaries had suspected him of being 'turned' by the Jordanian services during his five years of incarceration'. The sign above the entryway to Zarqawi's camp in Herat read 'Tawhid wa Jihad', and it was populated mainly by fellow Jordanians, Iraqis, and Palestinians 'who were much too young to have known the years of *jihad* against the Soviets', and who were required to take an oath of allegiance to Zarqawi. It is said that Zarqawi very quickly sought ideological and operational independence from bin Laden: 'the Saudi had the reputation of constructing his own myth to the detriment of the common cause aimed at restoring the caliphate, and two "foreign factions" in Afghanistan, one of which was Zarqawi's, were said to be hostile to him'. Thus, Zarqawi extended his 'Tawhid wa Jihad' network in Europe—especially Germany and the United Kingdom—and established a firm foothold in Kurdistan. He is also said to have planned a chemical attack in downtown Amman which could have killed 80,000 were it not thwarted by the Jordanian authorities shortly before its planned execution. See Jean-Charles Brisard, *Zarqawi: The New Face of Al-Qaeda*, 2005, pp. 55–89.

55. Letter from Ayman al-Zawahiri to Abu Musab al-Zarqawi, 11 October 2005, reprinted in Laura Mansfield, *In His Own Words: A Translation of the Writings of Dr. Ayman Al-Zawahiri*, 2006, p. 259. Unless otherwise stated, citations of Zawahiri's statements will refer to this collection.

56. Rudolph Peters, *Jihad in Classical and Modern Islam*, 1996, p. 125.

57. Cheragh Ali, *A Critical Exposition of the Popular Jihad*, 1885, p. 115.
58. Reprinted in Rudolph Peters, *Islam and Colonialism: The Doctrine of Jihad in Modern History*, 1979, p. 90.
59. Quoted in Sohail Hashmi, 'Interpreting the Islamic Ethics of War and Peace', in Sohail Hashmi (ed), *Islamic Political Ethics: Civil Society, Pluralism, and Conflict*, 2002, p. 208.
60. Ayatollah Murtada Mutahhari, 'The First Lecture: Questions About Jihad', reprinted in Mehdi Abedi and Gary Legenhausen (eds), *Jihad and Shahadat: Struggle and Martyrdom in Islam*, 1986, p. 92. For Mutahhari's position that 'all the scholars are agreed that *jihad* and war must be for the sake of defence', see all three of his lectures in this compilation.
61. Qutb *In the Shade of the Quran*, M. A Salahi and A. A. Shamis (eds), 2001, vol. 1, p. 276.
62. Djamchid Momtaz, 'The Inherent Right of Self-Defence in the Iran-Iraq War', in Farhang Rajaee (ed), *The Iran-Iraq War: The Politics of Aggression*, 1993, p. 183.
63. Communiqué from the Armed Forces General Command in Robin Wright, 'The War and the Spread of Islamic Fundamentalism', in Efraim Karsh (ed), *The Iran-Iraq War: Impact and Implications*, 1989, p. 110. It is worth noting that Iran also invoked its right to self-defence under Article 51 of the UN Charter.
64. Muhtar Holland, *Public Duties in Islam*, p. 8.
65. 'Fatwa Pronounced by ibn Taymiyyah on the Mongols, 1303', reprinted in Richard Bonney, *Jihad: from Quran to Bin Laden*, 2004, p. 425.
66. Stephen Frederic Dale, 'Religious Suicides in Islamic Asia: Anticolonial Terrorism in India, Indonesia, and the Philippines', *Journal of Conflict Resolution*, vol. 32, no. 1, March 1988, p. 47.
67. Qutb *Social Justice in Islam* (1945), 1953, p. 91.
68. See Sachedina, *The Just Ruler in Shite Islam*, p. 113.
69. David C. Rapoport, 'Fear and Trembling: Terrorism in Three Religious Traditions', *The American Political Science Review*, vol. 78, no. 3, September 1984, p. 668.
70. Fadlallah *fatwa*, 'Rules of Self-Defence: Part One', no date given, posted on Fadlallah's website at http://english.bayynat.org.lb/Fatawa/s10p1.htm.
71. Interview on *Al-Arabiyah* Television, 2 September 2005.
72. Nasrallah: We Criticise and Disapprove of the Hizballah in Turkey', *Istanbul Hurriyet*, 30 May 2000, p. 4.
73. In *Channel 4* documentary 'Inside Hamas' (broadcast 10 February 2008).
74. See Alia Brahimi, 'Poisoned Chalice: The Taliban, al Qaeda and the Globalised Jihad', Lecture at the University of Cambridge, 3 June 2010, online at http://sms.cam.ac.uk/media/851919.
75. 'Lahore Conference Celebrates Jihad', *MEMRI: Special Dispatch Series*, no. 2042, 5 September 2008.
76. In 'Taliban: No Jihad Unless US Attacks', *Guardian*, 18 September 2001.
77. Nazri Adlani in 'Indonesian Islamic Chief Says Jihad Not Necessarily Call for War', *Agence France-Presse* (Hong Kong), 30 September 2001.
78. This verse is often translated as 'fight in the cause of Allah those who fight you, but do not commit *aggression*; for verily Allah loveth not *aggressors*'. All of the

author's own references to the Quran use the translation by Abdullah Yusuf Ali (*The Holy Quran*, 1946).

79. See Wael B. Hallaq, *The Origins and Evolution of Islamic Law*, 2005, p. 67.
80. Khadduri (ed), *The Islamic Law of Nations: Shaybani's Siyar*, 1966, p. 58.
81. *Public Duties in Islam*, p. 128.
82. Mawdudi, *Towards Understanding the Quran*, Zafar Ishaq Ansari (transl), vol. 1, 1988, p. 153.
83. 'The New World Order and the Middle East—An Islamic Perspective', *Middle East Insight*, vol. 8, no. 1, July/August 1991, p. 11.
84. 'Interview with George Nader', p. 13.
85. *Defence of Muslim Lands*, chapter 4, question 3.
86. William Cleveland, *A History of the Modern Middle East*, 1994, p. 15.
87. Qutb, *In the Shade of the Quran*, p. 272.
88. See Sachedina, *The Just Ruler in Shite Islam*, p. 111.
89. Mohammad Shahrour, 'The Divine Text and Pluralism in Muslim Societies', online at https://www.quran.org/shahrour.htm.
90. Hamas Charter, article 6, available online at http://www.mideastweb.org/hamas.htm.
91. Patricia Crone, *Medieval Islamic Political Thought*, 2005, p. 372.
92. M. Cherif Bassiouni, 'Evolving Approaches to Jihad: From Self-Defence to Revolutionary and Regime-Change Political Violence', *Journal of Islamic Law and Culture*, vol. 10, no. 1, April 2008, p. 70.
93. Interview with Taysir Alluni (*Al-Jazeera*), 21 October 2001, p. 129.
94. Declaration of *Jihad* Against the Americans Occupying the Land of the Two Holy Sanctuaries, 23 August 1996, p. 30.
95. Statement broadcast on *Al-Jazeera*, 26 December 2001, p. 146.
96. Letter delivered to *Al-Jazeera*, 3 November 2001, p. 135.
97. See translation of Mohammad Abd al-Salam Faraj's 'Al Farida al-Ghaiba' in Jansen, *The Neglected Duty*, pp. 159–230.
98. Interview with *Al-Jazeera*, December 1998, p. 87.
99. In *Knights Under the Prophet's Banner* (autobiography, 2001), reprinted in Mansfield, *In His Own Words*, p. 25.
100. My italics. Ibid., p. 75.
101. My italics. World Islamic Front *fatwa*, 23 February 1998, p. 60.
102. My emphasis. Interview with *Al-Jazeera*, December 1998, p. 73.
103. My emphasis. In an interview with *Al-Muhajiroun*, 24 June 2002, online at http://www.why-war.com/news/2002/06/24/intervie.html.
104. My italics. Letter from Zawahiri to Zarqawi, 11 October 2005, p. 273.
105. Audiotape address to the People of Iraq, 11 February 2003, p. 181.
106. Interview with Hamid Mir, 12 November 2001, p. 141.
107. Letter to the Americans, 6 October 2002, p. 162.
108. Audiotape address entitled '*Hurriya*', 5 February 2005, p. 242.
109. Ibid, p. 240.
110. Videotape message, 29 November 2004, p. 236.

111. Zawahiri, *Knights Under the Prophet's Banner* (Autobiography, 2001), p. 128.
112. Interview with *Nida'ul Islam*, November 1996, p. 42.
113. World Islamic Front *fatwa*, 23 February 1998, p. 61.
114. Letter to the Americans, 6 October 2002, p. 161.
115. Ibid, p. 164.
116. In the full text of the interview bin Laden gave to *Al-Jazeera* in December 1998, available at http://www.robert-fisk.com/usama_interview_aljazeera.htm.
117. Sulaiman Abu Ghaith, 'Under the Shadow of Spears', June 2002, posted on the Centre for Islamic Studies and Research website, reposted at http://www.out-therenews.com/modules.php?op=modload&name=News&file=article&sid=55. Partial reprint also in *MEMRI: Special Dispatch Series*, no. 388, 12 June 2002, http://www.memri.org/bin/articles.cgi?ID=SP38802.
118. Letter to the Chief Mufti of Saudi Arabia, 29 December 1994, p. 9.
119. Interview with *Nida'ul Islam*, November 1996, p. 42.
120. In a speech posted on a number of Islamic websites, reprinted as 'A New Bin Laden Speech', *MEMRI: Special Dispatch Series*, no. 539, 18 July 2003, http://www.memri.org/bin/articles.cgi?Area=sd&ID=SP53903.
121. World Islamic Front *fatwa*, 23 February 1998, p. 61.
122. Audiotape address (broadcast on *Al-Jazeera*), 12 November 2002, p. 174.
123. Interview with Robert Fisk, 'Why We Reject the West', *Independent*, 10 July 1996, p. 14.
124. Audiotape address, 12 November 2002, p. 173.
125. Interview with Peter Arnett (*CNN*), March 1997, p. 52.
126. In Christopher Blanchard, 'Al-Qaeda: Statements and Evolving Ideology', *Congressional Research Service Report for Congress*, 9 July 2007, code RL32759.
127. Address to the people of Europe, 15 April 2004, p. 234. On the morning of 11 March 2004, ten bombs on four commuter trains in Madrid were detonated in a coordinated attack by a group of Islamic extremists connected with al-Qaeda. A videotaped message from the group calling itself 'the Brigades of Al-Mufti and Ansar Al-Qaeda' was found in the rubble of the flat where seven of the bombing suspects blew themselves up as police closed in on them. See 'Threat Video in Spain Flat Rubble', *BBC News*, 9 April 2004.
128. Videotape broadcast on *Al-Jazeera* Television, 7 October 2001, p. 104.
129. Zawahiri's message to the British, 4 August 2005, p. 280.
130. Interview with Taysir Alluni, 21 October 2001, p. 114.
131. Audiotape address, 12 November 2002, p. 175.
132. Videotape address to the American people, 29 October 2004, p. 238.
133. Rahimullah Yousafsai, 'Terror Suspect: An Interview with Osama bin Laden', *ABC News*, 22 December 1998, transcript at http://www.jihadunspun.com/BinLadensNetwork/interviews/abc01-1998.html.
134. Address to the people of Europe, 15 April 2004, p. 234.
135. Ibid., p. 234.
136. Videotape address of 29 October 2004, p. 244.
137. Ibid, p. 240.

138. Interview with Hamid Mir, 12 November 2001, p. 141.
139. Bin Laden was born and raised in Saudi Arabia but he went to Afghanistan in the 1980s in order to fight the Soviets. In 1991, he moved to Sudan where a number of attacks on Western targets were organized. He surfaced again in Afghanistan in May 1996 after it was alleged that the Sudanese had succumbed to international pressure and finally expelled him. Al-Qaeda was known to have entrenched itself in Afghanistan, with permission by the Taliban government, until the attacks of 11 September 2001. It is worth noting that limited operations were mounted by the US against alleged al-Qaeda targets in Afghanistan and Sudan in response to the al-Qaeda bombings of the US embassies in Tanzania and Kenya in 1998, which killed 220 people.
140. *Defence of Muslim Lands*, ch. 4.
141. Ibid., ch. 2.
142. *Join the Caravan*, part 2.
143. Audiotape address to the International Conference of Deobandis, 9 April 2001, p. 96.
144. Statement of 26 December 2001, p. 148.
145. Bin Laden made this statement in December of 2001, before the US invasion of Iraq in 2003. His complaint was with the rigorous sanctions regime levied by the United Nations against Iraq, which UNICEF estimated led to the preventable deaths of 500,000 Iraqi children denied access to food and basic medicines. See 'Iraqis Blame Sanctions for Child Deaths', *BBC News*, 12 August 1999.
146. Statement of 26 December 2001, p. 153.
147. Audiotape address, 9 April 2001, p. 96.
148. Letter to the Americans, 6 October 2002, p. 171.
149. Address to the scholars of Arabia, c.1995/1996, p. 16.
150. Interview with Peter Arnett, March 1997, p. 52. The *qibla* is the direction of prayer for Muslims: the Ka'ba in Mecca.
151. Interview with *Al-Jazeera*, December 1998, p. 68.
152. Ibid, p. 68.
153. Interview with John Miller (*ABC Television*), May 1998, text available online at http://www.pbs.org/wgbh/pages/frontline/shows/binladen/who/interview.html.
154. Bin Laden, 'To the Islamic Umma, on the First Anniversary of the New American Crusader War', 11 September 2002, http://www.jihadunspun.com/articles/ 10152002-To.The.Islamic.Ummah/.
155. Declaration of *Jihad*, 23 August 1996, p. 25.
156. World Islamic Front *fatwa*, 23 February 1998, p. 60.
157. Interview with Rahimullah Yousafsai (*ABC*), 22 December 1998.
158. Letter delivered to *Al-Jazeera*, 3 November 2001, p. 135.
159. World Islamic Front *fatwa*, 23 February 1998, p. 59.
160. Videotape Message to the people of Iraq, 19 October 2003, p. 210.
161. Bruce Reidel, 'The Return of the Knights: Al-Qaeda and the Fruits of Middle East Disorder', *Survival*, vol. 49, no. 3, September 2007, p. 117.
162. World Islamic Front *fatwa*, p. 61.

163. Interview with John Miller, May 1998.
164. Statement of 14 February 2003, p. 191.
165. Statement faxed to *Al-Jazeera*, 24 September 2001, p. 101.
166. Statement of 14 February 2003, p. 193.
167. Letter of 3 November 2001, p. 138.
168. *Knights Under the Prophet's Banner*, p. 192.
169. From a document entitled 'The Mujahidin's Roadmap', 1 July 2004, quoted in Reuven Paz, 'The Impact of the War in Iraq on the Global Jihad', in Hillel Fradkin, Husain Haqqani, and Eric Brown, *Current Trends in Islamist Ideology*, vol. 1, 2005, p. 42.
170. Interview with Taysir Alluni, 21 October 2001, p. 121. Talking to reporters on the White House lawn on 16 September 2001, Bush veered off script and stated that 'this Crusade, this war on terrorism is going to take a while'.
171. Quoted in Cook, *Understanding Jihad*, p. 98.
172. *In the Shade of the Quran*, vol. 1, p. 273.
173. 'Tantawi Says Jihad Meant for Self-Defence', *Arabic News*, 23 August 2005.
174. Cited in Ann Elizabeth Mayer, 'War and Peace in the Islamic Tradition and International Law', in John Kelsay and James Turner Johnson (eds), *Just War and Jihad*, 1991, p. 204.
175. *Towards Understanding Islam*, Khurshid Ahmad (transl), 1980, p. 150.
176. Alistair Horne argues that it was the Islamic 'Association des Ulema', founded in 1931, 'which provided the nationalists with their first momentum'. See *A Savage War of Peace: Algeria 1954–1962*, 1977, p. 38. It is worth remembering, however, the role of Les Jeunes Algeriens, French-educated intellectuals who emerged thirty years earlier advocating assimilation into the French community on terms of equality. And the Marxist-inspired Etoile Nord-Africaine, which was founded to protect the rights of North African workers in France, is especially important in this respect. Established in 1926, it was the first organized movement to totally reject Algeria's association with France, and its leader, Massali Hadj, 'became the head of an important mass nationalist movement'. See Jamil Abu Nasr, *A History of the Maghrib in the Islamic Period*, 1987, pp. 328–37. Yet, as T. O. Ranger argued, African decolonization movements embodied a complex interplay between the early traditional 'primary resistance' to occupation and the later 'secondary resistance', which mobilized modernist nationalism. Abdulqader's *jihad* against the French invasion in 1830 is thus an inextricable part of the process which gave rise to populist nationalism and eventually to Algerian independence in 1962. See T. O. Ranger, 'Connexions between "Primary Resistance" Movements and Modern Mass Nationalism in East and Central Africa', *The Journal of African History*, vol. 9, no. 3, 1968.
177. Khomeini was influenced by, and appropriated the ideas of, Ali Shariati who incorporated Marxist ideas about 'the disinherited' into his Islamic theories of liberation. See Gilles Kepel, *Jihad: The Trail of Political Islam*, 2004, p. 39.
178. Shahrour, 'The Divine Text'.

179. Usually translated as either 'internal dissension' or 'civil strife'. Yahya Michot points out that, contrary to much misrepresentation, the true heirs of ibn Taymiyyah would not advocate violence against a domestic tyrant: 'the hero of a *jihad* against foreign invaders, he urged only honest speech against domestic abuse of power and forbade violence or revolt'. See his *Muslims Under Non-Muslim Rule*, 2006.

180. World Islamic Front *fatwa*, 23 February 1998, p. 61.

181. 'Sheikh Yusuf Al-Qaradawi Condemns Attacks Against Civilians: Forbidden in Islam', 13 September 2001, online at http://www.islamonline.net/English/News/2001-09/12/article25.shtml.

182. In Bunting, 'Friendly Fire'.

183. Quoted in 'Islam for International Anti-terror Campaign', *Al-Akhbar*, 8 November 2001.

184. 'Arab NGOs Condemn Attacks on US, Palestinians, Iraq', *Middle East News Agency*, 13 September 2001.

185. 'Divisions Evident in Islamic Mideast, N. Africa', *CNN*, 24 September 2001. Nasrallah similarly condemned the Madrid bombings as 'a horrendous crime and a flagrant aggression on innocent people' on *Al-Manar* Television, 14 March 2004.

186. 'Egyptian Mufti Does Not Approve 11 September Attacks Against US', *Middle East News Agency*, 26 October 2001.

187. 'Islam for International Anti-terror Campaign', *Al-Akhbar*, 8 November 2001.

188. Roula Khalaf, 'Saudi Rulers Seek to Counter Calls for Jihad', *Financial Times*, 26 October 2001, p. 2.

189. Ismail Haniyeh in 'Palestinians React to US attacks with Condemnation', *Agence France Presse*, 11 September 2001.

190. 'Muslims Disagree on When Jihad OK', *Seattle Times*, 17 September 2001, p. A8.

191. Videotape of 7 October 2001, p. 105.

192. Interview with Taysir Alluni, 21 October 2001, p. 128.

193. Letter of 3 November 2001, p. 134.

194. Interview with Taysir Alluni, p. 124.

195. Audiotape address broadcast on *Al-Jazeera*, 4 January 2004, p. 217.

196. Interview with Hamid Mir, 12 November 2001, p. 142.

197. Address to the people of Europe, 15 April 2004, p. 235.

198. Audiotape address to the people of Iraq, 11 February 2003, p. 185.

199. *Knights Under the Prophet's Banner*, p. 202.

200. Letter to Zarqawi, 21 February 2005, p. 252.

201. Videotape message, 29 October 2004, p. 237.

202. In *Al-Muhajiroun* interview.

203. Interview with Taysir Alluni, 21 October 2001, p. 121.

204. 'Under the Shadow of Spears', June 2002.

205. Statement of 26 December 2001, p. 146.

206. 'Osama bin Laden to the Iraqi People', *MEMRI: Special Dispatch Series*, no. 837, 27 December 2004.

207. Peters, *Jihad in Classical and Modern Islam*, p. 123.
208. Interview with Taysir Alluni, 21 October 2001, p. 121.
209. Asad Abu Khalil, in 'Muslims Disagree on When Jihad OK'.
210. Tibi, 'War and Peace in Islam', p. 180.
211. Sheikh Qaradawi in Volkhard Windfuhr and Bernhard Zand, 'God Has Disappeared', *Der Spiegel*, 26 September 2005. For Ayatollah Fadlallah's argument that 'anyone committing this kind of thing must be . . . punished for it by an Islamic court' see Adel S. Elias, 'Bin Laden Is a Legend', *Der Spiegel*, October 2001.

CHAPTER 5

1. Statement of 14 February 2003, p. 194.
2. Videotape address to the American people, 29 October 2004, p. 238.
3. Interview with John Miller, May 1998.
4. Interview with Peter Arnett, March 1997, p. 45.
5. Sachedina, *The Just Ruler in Shite Islam*, p. 110.
6. Yusuf Qaradawi, *Priorities of the Islamic Movement in the Coming Phase*, 2001, p. 177.
7. Gilles Kepel, *Jihad: The Trail of Political Islam*, 2004, p. 27. It is worth noting that scholars such as George Joffe would stress that Hasan al-Banna, the Muslim Brotherhood's founder, intended the recreation of *society* as opposed to the formation of a political movement which would invite state attack. Certainly, the *Ikhwan* cut their teeth through philanthropy and the provision of welfare services, but the organization was quickly, perhaps inevitably, politicized, and within a decade it was the most prominent nationalist force against British colonialism and Zionism in Palestine. Indeed, the Muslim Brotherhood allied with the Free Officers in their coup against the monarchy in 1952, but it went on to oppose Nasserist rule. It also inspired a slew of Islamist organizations across the Islamic world.
8. Eickelman and Piscatori argue that three factors have combined to 'objectify' Islam in the consciousness of many Muslims. Firstly, mass education, which is relatively recent in the Middle East, has democratized access to sacred texts and made religious belief a conscious system that broadens the scope of authority as well as the community. Secondly, increasing numbers of Muslims have taken it upon themselves to interpret the textual sources of Islam such that activist discourse is not limited to the traditional establishment. Finally, objectification reconfigures the symbolic production of Muslim politics, leading to a competition between the state, the *ulema*, and new religious intellectuals over the arbitration of Islamic practice. See Dale F. Eickelman and James Piscatori, *Muslims Politics*, 1996, pp. 37–45.
9. Tilman Seidensticker, 'The Religious and Historical Background of Suicide Attacks in the Name of Islam', *The 9/11 Handbook: Annotated Translation and Interpretation of the Attackers' Spiritual Manual*, 2006, p. 35.

10. Patricia Crone, *Medieval Islamic Political Thought*, 2005, p. 297.
11. B. Lewis, C. H. Pellat, and J. Schacht, *The Encyclopaedia of Islam: New Edition*, vol. 2, 1965, p. 539.
12. Mawdudi, *Towards Understanding Islam*, vol. 1, p. 150.
13. Cited in Ann Elizabeth Mayer, 'War and Peace in the Islamic Tradition and International Law', in John Kelsay and James Turner Johnson (eds), *Just War and Jihad*, 1991, p. 207.
14. *Ibn Taymiyyah Expounds on Islam: Selected Writings of Shaykh al-Islam Taqi ad-Din Ibn Taymiyyah on Islamic Faith, Life, and Society*, Muhammad Abdul-Haqq Ansari (ed), 2000, p. 547.
15. Azzam, *Join the Caravan*, conclusion.
16. Azzam, *Defence of Muslim Lands*, ch. 1.
17. *Join the Caravan*, part 2.
18. *Defence of Muslim Lands*, ch. 4.
19. Interview with Peter Arnett (*CNN*), March 1997, p. 48.
20. 'Jihad for the Sovereignty of Allah Alone: The Latest Interview with Al-Qaeda's Abu Ghaith', no date given, online at www.jihadunspun.com/BinLadensNetwork/interviews/iwag01.html.
21. Interview with Taysir Alluni (*Al-Jazeera*), 21 October 2001, p. 110.
22. Kelsay, *Arguing the Just War in Islam*, p. 135.
23. Ibid., p. 115.
24. These were Abdel-Salam Mohammad, leader of the Jihad Movement in Bangladesh; Maulana Fazlur Rahman, the head of the Jamiat Ulema i-Islam party in Pakistan, who has been elected to the Pakistani National Assembly three times; Sheikh Mir Hamza, Secretary General of Jamiat Ulema i-Pakistan, the biggest Barelvi party in Pakistan which gained 11 per cent of the popular vote in the 2002 legislative elections; Sheikh Rifai Ahmad Taha, who signed on behalf of Gama'at Islamiya, Egypt's largest militant group. The Gama'at Islamiya later revoked its signature of the *fatwa*, claiming Taha had thought it was a statement supporting the Iraqi people against the Anglo-American bombing of Iraq rather than the announcement of a 'World Islamic Front' against Israel and America. Indeed, as early as 1988 the Gama'at had refused to join al-Qaeda and thereby relinquish its leadership—in December 1998 bin Laden described the World Islamic Front's dispute as 'some confusion over an administrative issue ... [the Gama'at] did sign the juridicial ruling, but it is not part of the World Islamic Front'. Nonetheless, in August 2006 Ayman al-Zawahiri claimed that the group had unified completely with al-Qaeda.
25. Abdel Bari Atwan, *The Secret History of Al-Qaeda*, 2006, p. 31.
26. Burke contends that by 1998 there were tensions between bin Laden and Mullah Omar due to the latter's annoyance at the former's impudent issuing of *fatwas* and reckless agenda of international terrorism. Apparently, Omar had even arranged to hand over bin Laden to the Saudis, but pulled out at the last minute due to 'Operation Infinite Reach': the US missile strikes on al-Qaeda targets in Sudan and Afghanistan in response to the East Africa bombings in the summer of 1998.

Burke argues, however, that relations warmed up again when, after failing to get formal recognition from the international community, the Taliban 'turned to an alternative international community, the Islamic international radical fringe'. See Jason Burke, *Al-Qaeda: Casting The Shadow of Terror*, 2002, pp. 164–77.

27. Interview with Taysir Alluni, 21 October 2001, p. 110.

28. Ibid., p. 117.

29. Interestingly, bin Laden is systematically hostile to Saudi Arabia's Chief Mufti Sheikh Abdul Aziz bin Baz (see e.g. statement of 29 December 1994), whereas Abdullah Azzam could draw upon bin Baz's authority in direct support of his *jihad*: 'the major scholars, the foremost among them, the Honourable Sheikh Abdul Aziz Bin Baz, have passed a *fatwa* which declares that directing the *zakat* to the Afghani *mujahidin* is of the finest deeds and the best charity'. See *Defence of Muslims Lands*, ch. 3.

30. For example, in the February 1998 *fatwa* he quotes the belligerent verse, 'when the forbidden months are over, wherever you find the polytheists, kill them, seize them, besiege them, ambush them', leaving out the crucial remainder of the verse which reads, 'but if they repent, and establish regular prayers and practise regular charity, then open the way for them, for Allah is oft-forgiving, most Merciful' (Quran 9:5).

31. World Islamic Front *fatwa*, 23 February 1998, p. 61.

32. Bin Laden has great disdain for 'infidel parties, like the Arab Baath Socialist Party' and later argues, in October 2003, that whoever cooperates with them can be killed.

33. Audiotape address to the people of Iraq, 11 February 2003, p. 184.

34. Videotape message to the people of Iraq, 19 October 2003, p. 209.

35. Bernard Lewis, 'License to Kill: Usama bin Laden's Declaration of Jihad', *Foreign Affairs*, November/December 1998, p. 14.

36. Professor Flagg Miller in John Harlow, 'Pray Silence for bin Laden the Wedding Poet', *Sunday Times*, 21 September 2008.

37. Jansen, *The Neglected Duty*, p. 17.

38. Azzam, *Join the Caravan*, part 1.

39. Azzam, 'Martyrs: the Building Blocks of Nations', online at http://www.religio-scope.com/info/doc/jihad/azzam_martyrs.htm.

40. Mohammad Abdul-Haqq Ansari in *Ibn Taymiyyah Expounds on Islam*, p. lxviii.

41. Quoted in Rohan Gunaratna, *Inside al-Qaeda: Global Network of Terror*, 2002, p. 16.

42. My emphasis. Interview with *Al-Jazeera*, December 1998, p. 80.

43. Videotape message to the people of Iraq, 19 October 2003, p. 209. In a 'Dispatches' documentary for *Channel 4* entitled 'Iraq: the Lost Generation' (broadcast 6 November 2006), a 19 year-old insurgent from Fallujah, who also attends school at night, portrayed himself in a similar way, making reference to the fact he wages *jihad* with the gun in one hand and pen in the other.

44. Cook, *Understanding Jihad*, p. 6.

45. Interview with Rahimullah Yousafsai (*ABC*), 22 December 1998.

46. For an exploration of the legitimating concept of *hijra*, and its different interpretations at various historical junctures, see Mohammad Khalid Masud, 'The Obligation to Migrate: The Doctrine of Hijra in Islamic Law', Dale F. Eickelman and James Piscatori (eds), *Muslims Travellers*, 1990, pp. 29–49.
47. Statement of 16 December 2004, p. 265.
48. Interview with *Al-Jazeera*, December 1998, p. 73.
49. Statement of 26 December 2001, p. 146.
50. World Islamic Front *fatwa*, 23 February 1998, p. 61.
51. Declaration of *Jihad*, 23 August 1996, p. 26. Khurasan was the Sassanian name given to a region which encompassed parts of present-day Iran, Afghanistan, Tajikistan, Turkmenistan, and Uzbekistan. One messianic trend in Islam expects that the Mahdi (redeemer) will appear with Jesus in Khurasan before the end of time to fill the world with peace and justice.
52. Interview with *Al-Jazeera*, December 1998, p. 88.
53. Ibid., p. 74.
54. Statement of 16 December 2004, p. 269.
55. Interview with *Al-Jazeera*, December 1998, p. 83.
56. Interview with *Al-Jazeera*, December 1998, full version online at http://www.robert-fisk.com/usama_interview_aljazeera.htm. The Lawrence reproduction omits the first question—'what is your history?'—and bin Laden's answer.
57. Interview with Rahimullah Yousafsai, 22 December 1998.
58. Fisk, 'Anti-Soviet Warrior Puts His Army on the Road to Peace', *Independent*, 6 December 1993, p. 10.
59. Statement of 16 December 2004, p. 259.
60. Declaration of *Jihad*, 23 August 1996, p. 26.
61. Audiotape address, 4 January 2004, p. 216.
62. This idea that the authorities have sold the Muslims down the river for a paltry sum appears to be widespread among al-Qaeda linked militants. Sentenced to death for his role in the 'millennium plot' to blow up civilian targets in Jordan, Ra'id Hijazi told the judge: 'you are fighting your own fellow citizens for a few dinar'. Quoted in Brissard, *Zarqawi*, p. 83.
63. 'A New Bin Laden Speech', *MEMRI: Special Dispatch Series*, no.539, 18 July 2003, online at http://www.memri.org/bin/articles.cgi?Area=sd&ID=SP53903.
64. Statement of 16 December 2004, p. 252.
65. 'A New Bin Laden Speech', 18 July 2003.
66. Interview with *Al-Jazeera*, December 1998, p. 80.
67. Declaration of *Jihad*, 23 August 1996, p. 28.
68. Interview with *Al-Jazeera*, December 1998, p. 68.
69. Ibid., p. 90.
70. Audiotape address (broadcast on *Al-Jazeera*), 4 January 2004, p. 219.
71. Statement of 16 December 2004, p. 251.
72. Interview with *Al-Jazeera*, December 1998, p. 75.
73. Statement of 14 February 2003, p. 198.
74. Interview with *Nida'ul Islam*, November 1996, p. 34.

75. Audiotape address of 4 January 2004, p. 228.

76. Statement of 16 December 2004, p. 260.

77. The verbal declaration is the *shahada*, one of the five pillars of Islam. It is the testimony that 'there is no god but God and Mohammad is his messenger'.

78. Richard Bonney, *Jihad: From Quran to Bin Laden*, 2004, p. 120.

79. Kepel, *Jihad*, p. 32.

80. This was the name given to the group by the Egyptian media, keen to depict its members as a gang of fanatics. In fact, never in its entire coverage of the group did the media ever mention its real name. See Gilles Kepel, *Muslim Extremism in Egypt*, 1984, pp. 70–102.

81. Barry Rubin, *Islamic Fundamentalism in Egyptian Politics*, 2002, p. 18.

82. Emmanuel Sivan, *Radical Islam: Medieval Theology and Modern Politics*, 1985, p. 16.

83. See translation in Jansen, *The Neglected Duty*, especially pp. 166–75.

84. Peters, *Jihad in Classical and Modern Islam*, p. 166.

85. Mawdudi, 'Mischief of Takfir', 1935.

86. See Mohammad Zafrullah Khan, *Punishment of Apostasy in Islam*, 1984.

87. 'Friday Sermons Condemn Iraqi Prisoner Abuse, Israeli Actions Against Palestinians', *FBIS Report*, 14 May 2004. Grand Mufti Abdul Aziz al-Sheikh likewise insists that the matter should be left to competent religious scholars—see 'Saudi Arabia's Grand Mufti Says Suicide Bombing UnIslamic', *Jedda Arab News*, 21 April 2002.

88. Declaration of *Jihad*, 23 August 1996, p. 28.

89. Television message to the People of Iraq, 19 October 2003, p. 208. While bin Laden is antipathetic to democracy, he urges that politics in the region be conducted in accordance with the Islamic principle of *shura*. For example, in 1996 he stated that he would be willing to reconcile with the Saudi regime if it brought back Islamic law and practised 'real consultative government'.

90. Audiotape address of 4 January 2004, p. 229.

91. Interview with Peter Arnett, March 1997, p. 45.

92. Statement of 14 February 2003, p. 196.

93. Interview with Rahimullah Yousafsai, 22 December 1998.

94. Statement of 16 December 2004, p. 255.

95. Interview with Taysir Alluni, 21 October 2001, p. 128.

96. Zawahiri, televised statement (broadcast on *Al-Jazeera*), 1 October 2004, transcript online at http://edition.cnn.com/2004/WORLD/meast/10/01/zawahiri. transcript/.

97. Audiotape address, 4 January 2004, p. 218. The Banu Ghasan was an Arab tribe in Syria which was sponsored by the Byzantines against the Persians. After the rise of Islam, the Ghassanid ruler accepted the new religion but then baulked at the fact it was too democratic—he discovered he was made the equal of a Bedouin—and returned to Christianity.

98. Statement of 16 December 2004, p. 248.

99. Audiotape address, 4 January 2004, p. 216.

100. Statement of 16 December 2004, p. 272.
101. Ibid., p. 249.
102. Ibid., p. 260.
103. Ibid., p. 262. For an overview of the use of the term by various groups in order to denounce each other, see Jeffrey Kenney, *Muslim Rebels: Kharijites and the Politics of Extremism in Egypt*, 2006. Kenney demonstrates how the example of the early Kahrijis was constructed into a mythical system of rebellion 'by medieval thinkers more concerned with establishing and preserving a system of authority than with accurately telling history'. This myth, as invoked in the modern era, communicates a moral lesson on the limits of protest against authority, for 'a symbolic name such as Kharijite holds special communicative power because it carries with it an authority to act. . . . The presence of Kharijites in the Muslim community, according to the Islamic historical record, authorizes Muslims to act to eliminate them, to remove this threat to the well-being of the community'. Indeed, this idiom of the religious past plays a formative role in thinking about the present, as Kenney shows how the historical symbol of the Kharijis has been used since the mid-twentieth century, by Egyptian regimes and Islamists alike, to delegitimize their opponents.
104. Audiotape address, 4 January 2004, p. 227.
105. Ibid., p. 229.
106. Indeed, bin Laden refers to himself as 'this poor slave bin Laden' (Statement of 26 December 2001, p. 152).
107. The other two objectives were to retaliate against the United States for its aggression in the Muslim world and to provoke the United States 'out of its hole'. See Christopher M. Blanchard, 'Al-Qaeda: Statements and Evolving Ideology', *CRS Report for Congress* (code RL32759), 9 July 2007, p. 5.
108. 'Letter to the *Umma*', 9 April 2002, online at http://www.jihadunspun.com/articles/04152002-al-Qaeda.Letter/index.html.
109. Audiotape address, 4 January 2004, p. 226.
110. '*Jihad* for the Sovereignty of Allah Alone: the Latest Interview with Al-Qaeda's Abu Ghaith'.
111. 'Hizballah Chief: US Makes "Big Mistake" If It Chooses Mideast for Its War', *Al-Safir*, 27 November 2001.
112. Anwar Ibrahim, 'Who Hijacked Islam? Repressive Muslim Regimes Are Partly to Blame for Bin Laden's Rise', *Time* (Asia Edition), 15 October 2001.
113. Arnaud de Borchgrave, 'Osama bin Laden— "Null and Void"', *United Press International*, 14 June 2001. Interestingly, the very same authority card is sometimes used against the Taliban, as when Egypt's Mufti Dr Nasr Wasil criticized the Afghan *ulema's* unwillingness to hand over bin Laden by observing that 'they are a group of students who did not complete their studies and who know nothing about jurisprudence and hence they tend to stick to the text'. See Mohammad Khalil, 'Egypt's Mufti Urges Taliban to Opt for Lesser of Two Evils and Hand Over UBL', *Al-Sharq Al-Awsat*, 9 October 2001.
114. 'Interpreting Islam', *Indian Currents*, 6 June 2004.

115. Sheikh Ali Gum'a in an interview with *Al-Haqiqa*, reprinted in 'The New Egyptian Mufti- Dr Sheikh Ali Gum'a: Opinions About Jihad, Supporting Suicide Bombings, and Forbidding Muslims in the US Military From Fighting Other Muslims', *MEMRI: Special Dispatch Series*, no. 580, 1 October 2003.

116. Interview in Al Watan, 18 June 2006, reprinted in 'Saudi Imam Al-Hawashi Opposes Women's Driving; Criticises Jihadis', *BBC Monitoring International Reports*, 4 July 2006.

117. 'Egypt: Al-Azhar Grand Sheikh Condemns Terrorism', *Middle East News Agency*, 20 October 2001.

118. In Lawrence Wright, 'The Rebellion Within', *New Yorker*, 2 June 2008.

119. Peter Bergen and Paul Cruickshank, 'The Unravelling: The Jihadist Revolt Against bin Laden', *The New Republic*, 11 June 2008.

120. BBC Radio 4, *Analysis: Al-Qaeda's Enemy Within*, broadcast 7 August 2008 at 8.30pm.

121. See 'Islamist Osama Rushdie Responds to Al-Zawahiri's Memoirs', *Al-Sharq Al-Awsat*, 13 December 2001.

122. For more on al-Qaeda's more reckless franchises jeopardizing bin Laden's 'hearts and minds' campaign, see my 'Crushed in the Shadows: Why Al-Qaeda Will Lose the War of Ideas', *Studies in Conflict and Terrorism*, vol. 33, no. 2, forthcoming February 2010.

123. Faisal Devji, *Landscapes of the Jihad: Militancy, Morality, Modernity*, 2005, p. 162.

124. Sayyid Qutb, *In the Shade of the Quran*, M. A Salahi and A. A. Shamis (eds), 2001, vol. 1, p. 326.

125. Mawdudi, *Towards Understanding the Quran*, Zafar Ishaq Ansari (ed), 1988, vol. 1, p. 152.

126. Fadlallah, '*Fatwa*: Rules of Self-Defence'.

127. Ayatollah Mohammad Hussein Fadlallah, 'Islam and Violence in Political Reality', *Middle East Insight*, vol. 4, no. 4, 1986.

128. Alwani, 'Live Dialogue: Islam and Prisoner Abuse', 13 May 2004, posted at http://www.islamonline.net/livedialogue/english/Browse.asp?hGuestID=nZfwfq.

129. Qaradawi, '*Fatwa*: Abode of Peace and Abode of War', 14 August 2004, posted at http://www.islamonline.net/servlet/Satellite?pagename=IslamOnline-English-Ask_Scholar/FatwaE/FatwaE&cid=1123585750474.

130. 'Nasrallah: Israeli Withdrawal From Gaza Another Victory for the Logic of the Weapon Of the Resistance', *Al-Safir*, 16 August 2005.

131. Khadduri, *War and Peace in the Law of Islam*, p. 96. Though the general principle of sending an invitation was agreed upon by all the schools of law, there were idiosyncratic differences in details. The Hanafi and Malaki jurists held that an invitation should be sent before fighting begins, while the Shafiis maintained that the leader was not under a strict obligation to send an invitation a second time if the adversary had received an invitation once before. Hanbalis claimed that those who had already received an invitation should never be reinvited.

132. Kelsay, *Arguing the Just War in Islam*, p. 37.
133. Letter to the Americans, 6 October 2002, p. 166.
134. Interview with Peter Arnett, March 1997, p. 53.
135. Letter to the Americans, 6 October 2002, p. 171.
136. Videotape address of 29 October 2004, p. 240.
137. In Christoph Reuter, *My Life is a Weapon: A Modern History of Suicide Bombing*, 2004, p. 144.
138. Interview with Rahimullah Yousafsai, 22 December 1998.
139. Audiotape address, 12 November 2002, p. 175.
140. Zawahiri's message to the British, 4 August 2005, p. 280.
141. Address to the people of Europe, 15 April 2004, p. 235.
142. Audiotape address, 4 January 2004, p. 231.
143. Interview with Hamid Mir, 12 November 2001, p. 141.
144. Zawahiri, *Knights Under the Prophet's Banner*, p. 205.
145. Bin Laden, 'To the Islamic *Umma*, On the First Anniversary of the New American Crusader War', 11 September 2002, online at http://www.jihadunspun.com/articles/10152002-To.The.Islamic.Ummah/faotnacw01.html.
146. Interview with Rahimullah Yousafsai, 22 December 1998.
147. Letter to the Americans, 6 October 2002, p. 165.
148. Interview with Taysir Alluni, 21 October 2001, p. 114.
149. *Knights Under the Prophet's Banner*, p. 223.
150. In 'Under the Shadow of Spears', June, 2002.
151. Incidentally, bin Laden extends this courtesy because 'when disasters happen, intelligent people look for the reasons behind them so that they can avoid them in the future. But I am amazed by you. Although we are now into the fourth year since the events of September 11, Bush is still practicing his deception, misleading you about the real reason behind it. As a result, there are still motives for a repeat'. Videotape address of 29 October 2004, p. 238.
152. Ibid., p. 239.
153. Statement of 14 February 2003, p. 199.
154. Interview with Hamid Mir, 12 November 2001, p. 144.
155. Letter to the Afghanis, 25 August 2002, p. 159.
156. 'Nigeria; Terror Attacks: The World Needs to Exercise Restraint— Sheikh Orire', *Africa News*, 23 September 2001. Sheikh Orire is the Secretary General of Jamaatu Nasril Islam, which is headed by the Sultan of Sokoto (considered to be the leader of Nigeria's 70 million Muslims until his death in 2006).
157. See, for example, Qutb, *In the Shade of the Quran*, vol. 1, p. 267.
158. *Siyar* as reprinted in Khadduri, *The Islamic Law of Nations: Shaybani's Siyar*, 1966, p. 154.
159. Yasir S. Ibrahim, *Al-Tabari's Book of Jihad*, 2007, p. 86.
160. Khadduri, *War and Peace in the Law of Islam*, p. 67.
161. Ibn Rushd, *Bidayat al-Mujtahid wa Nihayat al-Muqtasid* (1167), part 5, reprinted in Peters, *Jihad in Classical and Modern Islam*, 1996, pp. 27–42.

162. Sayyid Qutb, *Fi Dhilal al-Quran*, vol. 30, M. A Salahi and A. A. Shamis (eds), 1979, p. 184.
163. Peters, *Jihad in Classical and Modern Islam*, p. 164.
164. In Wright, 'The Rebellion Within', p. 4 and p. 10.
165. Fadlallah, '*Fatwa*: Rules of Self-defence'.
166. Zawahiri, *Knights Under the Prophet's Banner*, p. 55.
167. Ibid., p. 60.
168. In Fisk, 'Anti-Soviet Warrior Puts His Army on the Road to Peace'.
169. Interview with *Al-Jazeera*, December 1998, p. 80.
170. Audiotape of 8 April 2003, transcript online at http://www.guardian.co.uk/alqaida/story/0,,932283,00.html.
171. Videotape message to the people of Iraq, 19 October 2003, p. 210.
172. Audiotape address to the people of Iraq, 11 February 2003, p. 181.
173. *Knights Under the Prophet's Banner*, p. 212.
174. Audiotape address to the people of Iraq, 11 February 2003, p. 181.
175. 'The Arabic Text of the Spiritual Manual', *The 9/11 Handbook*, p. 81. The text is also known as 'The Doomsday Document'.
176. Ibid., p. 88.
177. Interview with Peter Arnett, March 1997, p. 48.
178. Interview with Rahimullah Yousafsai, 22 December 1998.
179. *Knights Under the Prophet's Banner*, p. 38.
180. Videotape address of 29 October 2004, p. 241.
181. Interview with John Miller, May 1998.
182. Interview with Peter Arnett, March 1997, p. 50.
183. Interview with *Al-Jazeera*, December 1998, p. 82.
184. Interview with Taysir Alluni, 21 October 2001, p. 109.
185. Interview with John Miller, May 1998, op cit.
186. Interview with *Al-Jazeera*, December 1998, p. 82.
187. Interview with Taysir Alluni, 21 October 2001, p. 109.
188. For an authoritative, in-depth account of the Battle of Mogadishu see Mark Bowden, *Black Hawk Down: The Extraordinary Story of the Most Dramatic US Military Operation Since Vietnam*, 1999.
189. Interview with John Miller, May 1998.
190. Jason Burke points out that, when asked in 1999, Aidid's aides 'laughed at the claim that bin Laden helped them and said unanimously that they had never heard of bin Laden until he began boasting about Somalia some years later'. Further, he notes that bin Laden's involvement in Somalia was suggested by the prosecutor during the African embassy bombing trial in New York, but it was struck from the record due to a lack of evidence. The tribes named by witnesses as having had ties with al-Qaeda were in fact fighting against Aidid. Though a number of 'Afghan Arabs' went to east Africa after the Soviet withdrawal from Afghanistan, Burke contends that there is no evidence that those dealing with various Somali tribes had anything to do with al-Qaeda specifically. See Burke, *Al-Qaeda*, pp. 134–6.

191. Statement of 14 February 2003, p. 192.
192. Interview with *Al-Jazeera*, 1998, full transcript.
193. Interview with John Miller, May 1998.
194. Interview with *Al-Jazeera*, 1998, full transcript.
195. Interview with Peter Arnett, March 1997, p. 54.
196. Ibid., p. 56.
197. During the civil war in Lebanon, 241 servicemen were killed by a suicide bomber who detonated a truckload of explosives at US Marine barracks in Beirut.
198. 'Letter to the *Umma*', 9 April 2002.
199. Statement of 14 February 2003, p. 191.
200. In response to 9/11 and the Taliban's refusal to hand over Osama bin Laden, the United States invaded Afghanistan in October 2001 with the aim of taking bin Laden 'dead or alive'. In November, bin Laden and some 1500 al-Qaeda fighters took refuge at Tora Bora, a fortified cave system comprised of a labyrinth of interconnected tunnels in the White Mountains of eastern Afghanistan. The United States mounted a ten-day B-52 bombing campaign against the facility and enlisted local warlords to launch a ground assault, but bin Laden eluded the manhunt as he and many of his fighters escaped over the border into Pakistan. Indeed, by the time the Afghans had advanced into the last of the caves, only twenty-one fighters remained sheltering there. See, for example, Philip Smucker, 'How Bin Laden Got Away', *Christian Science Monitor*, 4 March 2002.
201. Audiotape address to the people of Iraq, 11 February 2003, p. 182.
202. 'Bin Laden Lieutenant Admits to September 11 and Explains Al-Qaida's Combat Doctrine', *MEMRI: Special Dispatch Series*, no.344, 10 February 2002.
203. Bin Laden, 'To the Islamic *Umma*, On the First Anniversary of the New American Crusader War', 11 September 2002. During a Senate hearing on the success of Operation Enduring Freedom (the US-led war in Afghanistan which commenced in October 2001), Georgia Democrat Max Cleland remarked that 'to me, Operation Enduring Freedom has become Operation Enduring Frustration... because we still have not killed or captured Osama bin Laden'. See 'Rumsfeld Questioned in US Senate About bin Laden', *Agence France Presse*, 1 August 2002.
204. John Lewis Gaddis, *The United States and the End of the Cold War*, 1992, p. 166.
205. In Afghanistan, the proxy funded by the CIA was the *mujahidin* in which bin Laden fought. This is a sensitive issue for bin Laden, who dismisses the notion as a distortion and a conspiracy and points out that 'unintended confluence of interests does not mean there is any kind of link or tacit agreement'. As with allowing the Muslims in Iraq to fight alongside Baathists, he employs the Islamic precedent of the Muslims warring with Byzantium, mentioned in Chapter 4 (arguing that, just because both the Muslims and the Persians were fighting the Byzantines, this did not make the Muslims agents of the Persians). Interview with *Al-Jazeera*, December 1998, p. 87.
206. Garthoff, for example, customarily argues that 'it was Gorbachev who brought the Cold War to an end'. See, Raymond L. Garthoff, 'Why Did the Cold

War Arise and Why Did It End?' in Michael J. Hogan (ed), *The End of the Cold War: Its Meanings and Implications*, 1992, and Garthoff, *The Great Transition: American-Soviet Relations and the End of the Cold War*, 1994.

207. For the argument that ideological shift is the key explanatory variable see John Mueller, 'What Was the Cold War About? Evidence from Its Ending', *Political Science Quarterly*, vol. 119, no. 4, 2004–05.

208. William C. Wohlforth, 'The Stability of a Unipolar World', *International Security*, vol. 24, no. 1, 1999. Christopher Layne, on the other hand, warned in 1993 of a 'unipolar illusion' and suggested that states will be compelled by the logic of the international system to balance against the predominant power: history has shown that 'unipolar moments cause geopolitical backlashes that lead to multipolarity'. See 'The Unipolar Illusion', *International Security*, vol. 17, no. 4, 1993.

209. The term 'hyperpower' was first used in 1991 by Peregrine Worsthorne, the editor of the *Sunday Telegraph*. But French Foreign Minister Hubert Vedrine popularized it later with his lamentations on US unilateralism and America's 'abusive' tendencies. He held that 'superpower' was a Cold War term which did not adequately take into account American material strength as well as its 'domination of attitudes, concepts, language and modes of life'. See 'To Paris, US Looks Like a "Hyperpower"', *International Herald Tribune*, 5 February 1999.

210. Ethan B. Kapstein, 'Does Unipolarity Have a Future?, in Ethan Kapstein and Michael Mastanduno (eds), *Unipolar Politics: Realism and State Strategies After the Cold War*, 1999, p. 486.

211. For example, 'so watch as the amount reaches no less than $1 trillion by the lowest estimate, due to these successful and blessed attacks'. Interview with Taysir Alluni, 21 October 2001, p. 112.

212. I say ironically because bin Laden would, presumably, like to take credit for this heavy toll upon the US economy and its military personnel and Bush would, presumably, seek to justify this expenditure with reference to bin Laden. However, as considered in Chapter 1, it transpired that there was no connection between Saddam Hussein and al-Qaeda and the Iraq war did little to curb the threat from Islamic extremists.

213. According to the Congressional Budget Office, the Iraq war could total $600 billion by 2010 (see Peter Grier, 'The Rising Economic Cost of the Iraq War', *Christian Science Monitor*, 19 May 2005). Joseph Stiglitz included interest accrued on the national debt, the negative impact from high oil prices and future health-care costs for wounded troops in his estimate of an overall cost of 1–2 trillion dollars (see Martin Wolk, 'Cost of Iraq War Could Surpass $1 Trillion', *MSNBC*, 17 March 2006). The Pentagon admitted in 2005 that the invasion and occupation of Iraq costs an average of $4.8 billion per month (see 'Iraq War Cost $102 Billion Through September, Pentagon Says', *Bloomberg News*, 13 January 2005).

214. Nicholas Wheeler, *Saving Strangers: Humanitarian Intervention in International Society*, 2000, pp. 180–2.

215. American motives did seem to shift after the murders of UN peacekeepers in the summer of 1993. The United States spearheaded a manhunt for General Aidid (even offering a reward for his capture) and started using gunships to destroy his weapons sites, radio stations, and command and control facilities. However, these developments, while concerned with retaliation and the credibility of UN peacekeeping missions, did not constitute dealing with strategic threats to the United States itself.
216. Audiotape address to the people of Iraq, 11 February 2003, p. 183.
217. See 'Bin Laden on Tape: "Attacks Benefited Islam Greatly"', *CNN*, 14 December 2001.
218. 'Mekkah Imam Calls for Wisdom in Fight Against Terrorism', *Middle East Newsfile*, 29 September 2001.
219. In the first week alone, two Muslim Americans were murdered in hate crimes. CNN reported that much of the anger following the attacks 'is directed at Arab-Americans, Muslims and South Asians, some of whom look like those believed to have carried out the attacks'. A Sikh man, Balbir Singh Sodhi, was shot dead in his Arizona petrol station which, according to the county prosecutor, was 'for no other apparent reason than that he was dark-skinned and wore a turban'. Waqar Hasan, a Dallas grocer originally from Pakistan, was also shot and killed. See 'Immigrants Fear Backlash to Terror Attacks', *CNN*, 19 September 2001. Mosques were also petrol bombed and, on university campuses, Muslim students were spat at and had their turbans and *hijabs* pulled off as walls were defaced with racist, anti-Muslim graffiti.
220. Chaiwat Satha-Anand, 'Understanding Terrorism Is Vital', *Bangkok Post*, 18 September 2001.
221. Sana Al-Said, 'Interview with Pope Shinudah III', *Al-Musawwar*, 5 October 2001.
222. 'Muslim Clerics Repeat: US Attacks are UnIslamic', *Agence France Press*, 14 September 2001.
223. A report by Human Rights Watch noted that 'in the days following September 11, various governments tried to take advantage of the tragedy by touting their own internal struggles as battles against terrorism'. For example, Ariel Sharon began to speak of Yasir Arafat as 'our bin Laden' and the Zimbabwean authorities justified a crackdown on journalists critical of the regime by labelling them 'supporters of terrorism'. The report singles out the governments of Uzbekistan, Egypt, and Russia as the main offenders in using the 'war on terror' to wage war against political opponents they claim to be 'terrorists'. It also states that the United States and its Western allies were turning a blind eye to such abuses in exchange for support in the 'war on terror'. See 'Human Rights Watch World Report 2002', online at http://hrw.org/wr2k2/. The Russian leader, Vladimir Putin, also switched from referring to Chechnya as a 'stronghold of separatism' to an 'international terror enclave'. Ahmed Taya of Mauritania took to branding his political opponents as al-Qaeda-type extremists, and claimed that international terrorists were responsible for a coup attempt in 2003 (Raffi Katchadourian, 'Pursuing Terrorists in the Desert', *Village Voice*, 31 January 2006). Zaki Chehab

suggests that a document was sent out to all Israeli embassies advising diplomats to use every media opportunity to make a connection between al-Qaeda and the Palestinian leadership. Chehab, *Inside Hamas*, 2007, p. 186.

224. 'The War That Started: Why and Whereto?', *Al-Ray*, 8 October 2001.

225. In Zaki Chehab, *Inside Hamas*, 2007, p. 182.

226. This initiative, sponsored by the 'quartet' comprised of America, Russia, the United Nations and the European Union, was said to have been one of the conditions upon which Blair agreed to support Bush in the invasion of Iraq. It aimed at a two-state solution by 2005 based on concessions from both sides. Broadly, the Palestinian Authority was to appoint a Prime Minister and desist from aiding terrorist activities, and Israel was to support the establishment of a viable Palestinian government and halt its settlement activity in the territories. Then, an independent Palestinian state was to be created with provisional borders after which the hard questions of water, refugees' right of return, the status of Jerusalem, and final borders were to be tackled. Though violence flared up by mid-2003 and the peace talks stalled, the Israeli government made the unilateral decision to withdraw from Gaza in the summer of 2005. This did not, however, stop the violence as IDF forces engaged in a prolonged Gaza battle with Hamas in 2006. Indeed, Hamas won an historic victory in the Palestinian elections of January 2006 and neither the United States nor the Israelis would deign to deal with an armed 'terrorist organization' which sought the destruction of Israel. Meanwhile, Israeli settlement activity continued apace (see Amos Harel, 'Settlements Grow on Arab Land Despite Promises Made to US', *Haaretz*, 24 October 2006). At the time of writing little progress has been made towards the goal of a two-state solution.

227. Even if all of the victims of the al-Qaeda related attacks in Djerba, Bali, Mombasa, Riyadh, Casablanca, Jakarta, Istanbul, Madrid, Khobar, London, Amman, Algiers, Mumbai, and Islamabad are assumed to be non-Muslims, the total death toll is 1003. In Iraq that death toll can be matched by al-Qaeda related killings in Sadr City on 23 November 2006, in Najaf on 10 August 2006, in Kufa on 18 July 2006, and in the Ashura bombings on 2 April 2004, in the spate of reprisals for the Asqariya mosque attack in February 2006, and in the assault on the Yazidi community of Sinjar in August 2007. In the first three months of 2006 alone at least 3800 Iraqi civilians were killed in Baghdad as a result of Sunni–Shia violence. See Louis Roug, 'Targeted Killings Surge in Baghdad', *Los Angeles Times*, 7 May 2006, p. A1. These al-Qaeda related attacks were selected at random; there are dozens more.

228. Zawahiri, *Knights Under the Prophet's Banner*, p. 117.

229. Al-Odah, 'A Ramadan Letter'.

230. Wright, 'The Rebellion Within', p. 11.

231. 'Major Jihadi Cleric and Author of Al-Qaeda's Sharia Guide to Jihad Sayyed Imam vs. Al-Qaeda (2), MEMRI, 25 January 2008.

232. Bergen and Cruickshank, 'The Unravelling'.

233. See Gunaratna, *Inside al-Qaeda*, pp. 92–4.

234. Neofundamentalism emerged in the wake of the failure of the political Islamist project. With its puritanical emphasis on morality in daily life and the application of the *sharia*, neofundamentalism 'replaces a discourse on the state with a discourse on society' (see Olivier Roy, *The Failure of Political Islam*, 1994, pp. 75–88). It is both a product and an agent of globalization. See Roy, *Globalised Islam: The Search for a New Umma*, 2004, pp. 232–89.

235. Roy argues that 'there is a strange mix of deep personal pessimism and collective millenarianist optimism among this type of terrorists: they do not trust the people they are fighting for (they are also indifferent to killing Muslims), they are sure to die, and as political scientist Farhad Khosrokhavar pointed out in the case of the Iranian martyrs of the Iran–Iraq War, they know that even if they succeed, the future society will not match the ideals for which they are fighting'. See *Globalised Islam*, p. 43 and p. 246.

236. Fisk, 'Anti-Soviet Warrior Puts His Army on the Road to Peace'.

237. Address to the scholars of Arabia, *c*.1995/1996, p. 17.

CHAPTER 6

1. Interview with *Nida'ul Islam*, November 1996, p. 40.

2. Mawdudi, *Towards Understanding the Quran*, vol. 1, p. 151.

3. Ayatollah Mohammad Hussein Fadlallah, 'Islam and Violence in Political Reality', in *Middle East Insight*, vol. 4, no. 4, 1986, p. 12.

4. Statement of 26 December 2001, p. 153.

5. Khadduri, *The Islamic Law of Nations*, p. 13.

6. See for example Shaybani, *Siyar*, pp. 106–29.

7. See, for example, Ibn Rushd's *Bidayat al-Mujtahid wa-Nihayat al-Muqtasid* (1167), part 3, reprinted in Peters, *Jihad in Classical and Modern Islam*, pp. 31–7.

8. See e.g. Muhammad Hamidullah, *Muslim Conduct of State*, 1941, pp. 204–14.

9. Ibid., p. 66.

10. Qutb, *In the Shade of the Quran*, vol. 1, p. 272.

11. Mowdudi, *Towards Understanding the Quran*, vol. 3, p. 276.

12. Mowdudi, *Towards Understanding the Quran*, vol. 1, p. 153.

13. Ibn Taymiyyah, *Public Duties in Islam*, p. 133.

14. Ibid., p. 106.

15. Ibid., p. 133.

16. Fadlallah, '*Fatwa*: Rules of Self-Defence'.

17. My italics. Fadlallah, ibid.

18. Qaradawi, '*Fatwa*: Bali Attacks, Juristic Approach', 15 October 2002.

19. Khadduri, *War and Peace in the Law of Islam*, p. 102.

20. Ibid., p. 103.

21. 'If then any one transgresses the prohibition against you, Transgress ye likewise against him. But fear Allah, and know that Allah is with those who restrain themselves'.

22. *In the Shade of the Quran*, vol. 1, p. 275.

23. Fadlallah, '*Fatwa*: Rules of Self-Defence'.

24. Interview with Rahimullah Yousafsai, 22 December 1998.

25. Statement of 26 December 2001, p. 151.

26. Azyumardi Azra, rector of Jakarta's Syarif Hidayatullah State Institute of Islamic Studies, in Mohammad Nafik, 'Mainstream Islamic Groups to Cooperate in Countering Radicals', *Jakarta Post*, 9 November 2001.

27. Shaybani, *Siyar*, p. 102.

28. In Thomas Patrick Hughes, *A Dictionary of Islam*, 1885, p. 246.

29. Khadduri, *War and Peace in the Law of Islam*, p. 107.

30. *Defence of Muslim Lands*, ch. 1.

31. Interview with Hamid Mir, 12 November 2001, p. 140. Yusuf al-Ayyiri makes exactly the same argument. Because the Muslims are living among legitimate targets, they are effectively acting as human shields for the enemy.

32. Statement of 16 December 2004, p. 262.

33. Shaybani, *Siyar*, p. 91.

34. In *Al-Siyasa Al-Shariyya fi Islah Al-Rai wa Al-Ra'iyya*, reprinted in Peters, *Jihad in Classical and Modern Islam*, p. 50.

35. Yusuf al-Ayyiri, 'A Guide for the Perplexed on the Permissibility of Killing Prisoners', published at www.qoqaz.com, reprinted in 'Pro-Chechen Islamist Website: Islamic Religious Interpretation Permits Killing of Prisoners', *MEMRI*, 27 October 2001, at http://www.memri.org/bin/articles.cgi?Page=subjects&Area=jihad&ID=SP43402 [accessed 9 May 2005].

36. Sayyid Qutb, *Fi Dhilal al-Quran (In the Shade of the Quran)*, vol. 30, M. A Salahi and A. A. Shamis (eds) (London: MWH, 1979), p. 301.

37. Sayyid Abu Ala Mawdudi, *Tafhim al-Quran (Towards Understanding the Quran)*, Zafar Ishaque Ansari and Abdul Aziz Kamal (eds), online at www.tafheem.net, discussion at 47:4.

38. '*Ahkam al-Bughat*: Irregular Warfare and the Law of Rebellion in Islam', in Johson and Kelsay (eds), *Cross, Crescent and Sword*, p. 165. See also Khaled Abou El Fadl, *Rebellion and Violence in Islamic Law*, 2001.

39. Hashmi, 'Interpreting the Islamic Ethics of War and Peace', p. 212.

40. Al-Tawhidi in Franz Rosenthal, 'Suicide in Islam', *Journal of the American Oriental Society*, vol. 66, no. 3, 1946, p. 249.

41. Ibid., p. 240.

42. 'Arab News Provides Profiles of "Well Educated" Hijackers', *Arab News*, 1 October 2001.

43. Hans G. Kippenberg, 'Background to the Spiritual Manual: Its Discovery, Interrogation and Disregard', in *The 9/11 Handbook*, p. 6.

44. Statement of 26 December 2001, p. 155.

45. In Elias, 'Bin Laden Is a Legend'.

46. Verse 3:140 speaks of being wounded or killed in battle and notes that Allah 'may take *shuhada* from among you'. Though this could still mean 'witness', the martial context makes it conceivable that the meaning is 'martyr'.

47. Brian Wicker (ed), *Witnesses to Faith? Martyrdom in Christianity and Islam*, 2006, p. 2.

48. Asma Afsaruddin, 'Competing Perspectives on Jihad and Martyrdom in Early Islamic Sources', in Brian Wicker (ed), ibid., p. 22.

49. Ariel Merari, 'The Readiness to Kill and Die: Suicidal Terrorism in the Middle East', in Walter Reich (ed), *Origins of Terrorism: Psychologies, Ideologies, Theologies, States of Mind*, 1990, p. 197.

50. Mohammad in *Death in Gaza* (2004), directed by James Miller, distributed by Channel Four Television Corporation.

51. J. M. Davis quoted in Stephen Holmes, 'Al Qaeda September 11, 2001', in Diego Gambetta (ed), *Making Sense of Suicide Missions*, 2006, p. 147.

52. At the Battle of Karbala, Husayn and less than 100 men loyal to him faced a 40,000 strong Umayyad army. Knowing that certain death was imminent, it is said the Husayn permitted his men to defect the night before the battle, but all refused.

53. Observances include processions and plays, pilgrimages to Husayn's shrine in Karbala, and ritualistic self-flagellation to connect the believer with Husayn's suffering.

54. Cited in Mehdi Abedi and Gary Legenhausen (eds), *Jihad and Shahadat: Struggle and Martyrdom in Islam*, 1986, p. 27.

55. Cook, *Understanding Jihad*, p. 142.

56. That is not to say, however, that the 'martyrdom' discourse in Palestine was always Islamic. The 'first martyrs', a group of unarmed demonstrators shot by Israeli forces in 1976, were mainly Marxist-Leninists, and George Habash's communist organization, the PFLP, took the lead in the use of terror missions in the 1970s. Additionally, suicide bombings today are sometimes carried out by secular groups, such as the Fatah-linked Al-Aqsa Martyrs' Brigades. That said, since the early 1990s, the self-consciously Muslim group, Hamas, has appropriated the tactic of 'martyrdom operations' with an explicitly Islamic dimension.

57. This battle, in which the Prophet was injured, took place between the Muslims and Meccan forces in AD 625.

58. The Muslims prevailed in the Battle of Badr in AD 624 despite being vastly outnumbered by their polytheistic, Meccan foes.

59. Brian Wicker, Maha Azzam, and Peter Bishop, 'Martyrdom and Murder: Aspects of Suicidal Terrorism', in Wicker (ed), *Witnesses to Faith?*, p. 133.

60. In Razzuq al-Ghawi, 'Khaled Mish'al: Israel Has Cornered the Palestinians, Halting Martyrdom Operations Depends on Field Conditions', *Al-Sharq Al-Awsat*, 22 September 2002.

61. 'What did Jesus do for the people? He sacrificed himself. The Palestinians are doing the same thing. They are sacrificing themselves to defend their people'. In

Susanne Knaul, 'If a Civil War Should Break Out Here, Every Home Will Burn', *Die Presse*, 16 November 2001.

62. Ayman al-Zawahiri, 'Jihad and the Superiority of Martyrdom', reprinted in Raymond Ibrahim (ed), *The Al-Qaeda Reader*, 2007, p. 157. This tract, written for the Islamic Jihad group in Egypt, begins by stating that it was prepared under the supervision of Dr Ayman al-Zawahiri—thus it is commonly attributed to him.

63. Abu Ruqiyah, 'The Islamic Legitimacy of the "Martyrdom Operations"', *Nida'ul Islam*, December 1996–January 1997.

64. Ayyiri, 'The Islamic Ruling on the Permissibility of Martyrdom Operations: Did Hawa Barayev Commit Suicide or Achieve Martyrdom?', online at http://journal. maine.com/pdf/martyrdom.pdf, p. 2.

65. Durkheim, *Suicide: A Study in Sociology*, 1952, p. 219.

66. Ibid., p. 14.

67. 'Jihad and the Superiority of Martyrdom', p. 150.

68. Ayyiri insists that 'yes, he did not take his life by his own hand, but his opinion was the sole factor leading to it'.

69. Ibrahim, *The Al-Qaeda Reader*, p. 138.

70. Abu Ruqiyah, 'The Islamic Legitimacy of the "Martyrdom Operations"'.

71. 'The Islamic Ruling on the Permissibility of Martyrdom Operations', p. 9.

72. Ibid., p. 6.

73. Ibid., p. 14.

74. 'Jihad and the Superiority of Martyrdom Operations', p. 143.

75. Kermani, 'A Dynamite of the Spirit'.

76. Cook, *Martyrdom in Islam*, 2007, p. 159.

77. 'The Islamic Ruling on the Permissibility of Martyrdom Operations', p. 2.

78. Taken from Al-Albani, *Al Masjid Al-Aqsa: The Path to Its Freedom*, extract online at http://www.allaahuakbar.net/scholars/albaani/suicide_bombing.htm.

79. 'Muslim Clerics Disagree About the Judgement of Islamic Law Concerning Suicide Operations', *Al-Sharq Al-Awsat*, 8 May 2001.

80. In Imam Mohammad Imam, 'Interview with Muslim Scholar Sheikh Dr Yusuf Al-Qaradawi', *Al-Sharq Al-Awsat*, 12 December 2001.

81. See Nadia Abou El-Magd, 'The Politics of Fatwa', *Al-Ahram*, no. 532, 3–9 May 2001.

82. See Magdi Abdelhadi, 'Controversial Preacher with "Star Status"', *BBC News*, 7 July 2004.

83. In 'Mecca's Imam Sides with Al-Azhar Despite Al-Qaradawi's Objections', *Al-Musawwar*, 7 December 2001.

84. From Emile Henri's Defence Speech, 1894, available at http://www.marxists.org/ reference/archive/henry/1894/defence-speech.htm.

85. 'Egyptian Mufti Says Martyrdom Operations Legitimate', *Middle East News Agency*, 2 August 2002.

86. 'Amal, Hizballah Leadership Discuss Local, Regional Issues', *Al-Safir*, 20 June 2002.

87. Interview with *Al-Haqiqa* reprinted in 'The New Egyptian Mufti'. This argument about Israeli society is shunned by Tantawi who describes it as 'ridiculous, ugly talk that is totally rejected. And it totally contradicts the recommendations of the Prophet. Aggression against honest people is completely prohibited in Islamic law' (quoted in Frank Gardner, 'Restoring Faith in Islam', *BBC News*, 26 December 2001).

88. In Imam, 'Interview with Muslim Scholar Sheikh Dr Yusuf Al-Qaradawi'.

89. In Bunting, 'Friendly Fire'.

90. Interview with Egyptian Islamic website www.lailatalqadr.com, reprinted in 'Egypt's Mufti: We Condemned the September 11 Attacks, But Since Then Our Feelings Have Changed', *MEMRI: Special Dispatch Series*, no. 402, 23 July 2002.

91. For example, 'the Mufti's answer . . . is a message to the new American adminis-tration. Al-Sheikh was addressing, and trying to prevent, the recurrence of the suicide bombings against American military targets in Saudi Arabia and the hijackings of the Saudi planes'. Nabil Abdel Fattah, in Abou El-Magd, 'The Politics of Fatwa'.

92. Maha Azzam, 'Al-Qaeda: The Misunderstood Wahabi Connection and the Ideology of Violence', p. 4.

93. After a spate of suicide bombings attributed to Islamic militants, Mawlana Obaidul Haq told a demonstration of hundreds of Muslims that 'Islam prohibits suicide bombings. These bombers are enemies of Islam'. See 'Protest Against Bangladesh Bombs', *BBC News*, 9 December 2005.

94. Khatami stated that 'suicide bombers did Islam an injustice and would not go to heaven'. See 'Khatami: Suicide Bombings are an Injustice and Hurt Islam', *Haaretz*, 9 September 2006.

95. Sheikh Mohammad bin Abdullah al-Sabil, in Abdelbari Atwan, 'Imam Bush's Fatwas', *Al-Quds Al-Arabi*, 5 December 2001.

96. Interview with Peter Arnett, March 1997, p. 47.

97. World Islamic Front *fatwa*, 23 February 1998, p. 61.

98. Sheikh Abdul Aziz al-Sheikh quoted in Hasan Adawi, 'Terrorism Is Alien to Islam: Mufti', *Jedda Arab News*, 22 February 2002.

99. Khadduri, *War and Peace in the Law of Islam*, p. 104.

100. Shaybani, *Siyar*, p. 87.

101. In the time of the Prophet and the first Muslim community, women visibly participated in battle. For famous examples of this see Leila Ahmed, *Women and Gender in Islam*, 1992, pp. 69–72. Such was the norm that the Kharijis instituted *jihad* as a religious duty for all women. But, as the orthodox opposed *jihad* for women, they killed and exposed naked the women captured in battles with the Kharijis, which eventually led them to withdraw women from the theatre of war.

102. In *Bidayat al-Mujtahid wa-Nihayat al-Muqtasid*, p. 33.

103. Quoted in Kelsay, 'Islam and the Distinction Between Combatants and Noncombatants', in Johnson and Kelsay (eds), *Cross, Crescent and Sword*, p. 214.
104. 'Those Who Die Fighting US Occupation Forces are Martyrs, But Distinguish Between American Civilians and the Government and Military, Says Scholar, Qaradawi', 19 June 2003, online at http://www.islamfortoday.com/qaradawi04.htm.
105. *In the Shade of the Quran*, vol. 1, p. 270.
106. Ibn Taymiyyah, *Public Policy and Islamic Jurisprudence*, Omar Farrukh (transl), 1966, p. 141.
107. Aytollah Murtada Mutahhari, 'Jihad in the Quran: The Second Lecture', reprinted in Abedi and Legenhausen (eds), *Jihad and Shahadat*, p. 95.
108. International Association of Muslim Scholars' statement, 'Bombing Innocents', 25 2005, online at http://www.islamonline.net/English/In_Depth/ViolenceCausesAlternatives/Articles/topic08/2005/07/01.shtml.
109. Ramsey, *The Just War*, p. 144.
110. In 'Mecca's Imam Sides with Al-Azhar Despite Al-Qaradawi's Objections'.
111. In Leon Usigbe, 'Terror Attacks: The World Needs to Exercise Restraint-Sheikh Orire', *Africa News*, 23 September 2001.
112. 'Leaders of 46 Islamic Groups and Movements Condemn the Attacks on the US', *Al-Sharq Al-Awsat*, 14 September 2001.
113. Imad Shihab, leader of the Islamic Cultural Society, quoted in Suha Ma'ayeh, 'Jordanian Muslim, Christian Clerics Mourn Victims of US Terrorist Attacks', *Jordan Times*, 18 September 2001.
114. In 'Iran Expresses Rare Sympathy for US Over Attacks', *Gulf News*, 13 September 2001. The article notes that 'no president since the 1979 Islamic revolution has ever before openly expressed sympathy for the United States, regarded by Iran as its arch-enemy'.
115. 'Megawati Heads to US Amid Controversy', *BBC News*, 17 September 2001.
116. R. Xhuvani, 'Assembly of Albania Passes Resolution', *ATA (Tirana)*, 27 September 2001.
117. In 'National Assembly and Liberal Group Condemn Attacks', *Le Soleil (Dakar)*, 13 September 2001.
118. Ali Karimli in 'Azeri Politicians Blast "Monstrous Terrorist Attacks in US"', *Turan (Baku)*, 11 September 2001.
119. Report in 'Turkey: Religious Affairs Director Rejects Link Between Islam, Terrorism', *Ankara Anatolia*, 30 November 2001.
120. Statement reprinted in 'Palestinian Intellectuals Condemn Terror Attack on US Targets', *Al-Quds*, 17 September 2001.
121. Hatim Abu-Sha'ban in 'Why Were Arabs and Muslims Accused of Terrorism?', *Al-Quds*, 18 September 2001.
122. Imam Mohammad Imam, 'Islamic Jurisprudence Assembly Says Terrorist Acts Are Impermissible Crimes', *Al-Sharq Al-Awsat*, 17 December 2003.

123. Abdulkarim Ould Adda on 'Algeria: FIS Says Attack on WTC, Pentagon "Ignoble Act of Violence"', *Radio France Internationale*, 17 September 2001.

124. Nafez Azzam in 'Palestinians React to US Attacks with Condemnation—and Celebrations', *Agence France Presse*, 11 September 2001.

125. Rif'at Sayyid Ahmad, 'Is Usama Bin Laden the Culprit? Has World War III Started?', *Al-Safir*, 14 September 2001.

126. Quoted in report by Boris Bachorz, 'AFP Examines Support for Islamic Fundamentalism, Bin Laden in Britain', *Agence France Presse*, 17 September 2001.

127. Quoted in Charles Kurzman, 'Pro-US Fatwas', *Middle East Policy*, vol. 10, no. 3, September, 2003, p. 155.

128. In interview by Juan Cierco,, *ABC News* (Spain), 18 September 2001.

129. 'Sheikh Yusuf Al-Qaradawi Condemns Attacks Against Civilians: Forbidden in Islam', on Qaradawi's website, 13 September 2001, at http://www.islamonline.net/English/News/2001-09/13/article25.shtml.

130. Ann Coulter, for example, famously stated on 12 September 2001 that 'we know who the homicidal maniacs are. They are the ones cheering and dancing right now. We should invade their countries, kill their leaders, and convert them to Christianity'. See 'This Is War', weblog entry on 12 September 2001, at http://www.anncoulter.org/columns/2001/091301.htm.

131. Interview with John Miller, May 1998.

132. Interview with *Al-Jazeera*, December 1998, full version.

133. Interview with Hamid Mir, 12 November 2001, p. 141.

134. Letter to the Americans, 6 October 2002, p. 165.

135. Interview with *Nida'ul Islam*, November 1996, p. 41.

136. Interview with Taysir Alluni, 21 October 2001, p. 118.

137. Interview with John Miller, May 1998.

138. Interview with Peter Arnett, March 1997, p. 56.

139. *Knights Under the Prophet's Banner*, p. 222.

140. Ibid, p. 51.

141. Interview with *Nida'ul Islam*, November 1996, p. 40.

142. Interview with John Miller, May 1998.

143. Videotape of 7 October 2001, p. 105.

144. Interview with Peter Arnett, March 1997, p. 47.

145. Videotape of 7 October 2001, p. 104.

146. Letter of 3 November 2001, p. 137.

147. During the 1996 invasion of southern Lebanon, the Israeli Defence Forces shelled a UN compound in Qana where hundreds of civilians had taken refuge, killing 106 people. Another 100 were injured by the lethal showers of shrapnel released by the anti-personnel shells. A UN report concluded that it was unlikely that the compound had been hit by accident. Qana shot to worldwide renown again in the 2006 Israel–Lebanon conflict. It was estimated that twenty-eight people died when Israeli forces dropped a massive bomb on a three-storey building, causing it to collapse on civilians, many of them children, who had been sheltering there.

148. Interview with Peter Arnett, March 1997, p. 47.
149. Bin Laden, 'To the Islamic *Umma*', 11 September 2002.
150. Letter to the Americans, 6 October 2002, p. 170.
151. As a delegitimizing device, bin Laden frequently employs the charge of moral hypocrisy. Indeed, the Quran explicitly condemns hypocrites, both morally and for the danger they pose to the Muslims (*Surat Al-Munafiqun*). Bin Laden's accusations began with his diatribes against the Saudi regime for crying in public over pan-Islamic issues, yet doing nothing, in practice, to stop the injustices. He also refers to 'the immoral United Nations', lambasting it for 'being an organisation that is overseeing with all its capabilities the annihilation blockade of a million Muslims under the sanctions, and yet is still not ashamed to talk about human rights!' Likewise, at almost every turn, America is labelled a hypocrite. Some examples include condemning Saddam Hussein for using chemical weapons against Iran and the Kurds, when the United States was actually supporting Iraq at that time; the US failure to ratify the treaty establishing the International Criminal Court; America's unerring support for Israel while Palestinian children who throw stones are labelled 'terrorists'; the fact that Gerry Adams is received in the White House but 'woe, all woe if the Muslims cry out for their rights'; the fact that the Twin Towers were supposed to represent America's commitment to freedom, human rights, and equality, but after they were destroyed the US government acted quickly to interfere in the media and prevent bin Laden's speeches from being aired; the denial of Geneva Conventions protections at Guantanamo Bay, which 'is a historical embarrassment to America and its values, and it screams in your hypocritical faces: what is the value of your signature on any agreement or treaty?' Thus, hypocrisy is one of America's major characteristics, as 'all manners, principles, and values have two scales: one for you and one for everybody else'. The 'terrorism' discourse itself constitutes a double standard that is employed to weaken Muslims and keep them subservient, for, in the end, Americans believe that 'freedom only has meaning for the white race'.
152. Interview with Taysir Alluni, 21 October 2001, p. 117.
153. Address to the people of Europe, 15 April 2004, p. 234.
154. Interview with Rahimullah Yousafsai, 22 December 1998.
155. Interview with John Miller, May 1998.
156. Audiotape address, 9 April 2001, p. 96.
157. Interview with John Miller, May 1998.
158. Interview with Taysir Alluni, 21 October 2001, p. 119.
159. This personal form of responsibility was articulated by the Prophet in opposition to the pre-Islamic practice of blood feuding, in which it was permissible to take revenge upon any member of the perpetrator's clan.
160. M. Th. Houtsma, A. J. Wensinck, T. W. Arnold, W. Heffening, and E. Levi-Provencal, *The Encyclopaedia of Islam*, vol. 2, 1927, p. 1038.
161. Qutb, *In the Shade of the Quran*, vol. 1, p. 272.
162. Ibid., p. 329.

163. 'Islam and International Law', *International Review of the Red Cross*, vol. 87, no. 858, June 2005, p. 275.

164. Ahmad Kutty in *fatwa* entitled 'Even in Retaliation . . . Ethics Must Be Honoured', 12 May 2004.

165. Ibrahim, *Al-Tabari's Book of Jihad*, p. 29.

166. My translation. See Mohammad Rawaas Qalahji, *Mu'jam Lughat Al-Fuqahaa*, 1988, p. 438.

167. Interview with Hamid Mir, p. 140.

168. 'Jihad and the Superiority of Martyrdom', pp. 161–71.

169. Interview with Hamid Mir, p. 140.

170. Rahimullah Yousafsai interview with Osama bin Laden, 22 December 1998.

171. p. 163.

172. See my 'Crushed in the Shadows: Why Al-Qaeda Will Lose the War of Ideas', Studies in conflict and terrorism, 33: 2, February 2010.

173. See 'Audio Message from Abu Musab Al-Zarqawi—Commander of Al-Qaeda's Jihad Committee in Mesopotamia', 18 November 2005.

174. 'An Interview with Abdulmalek Droukdal', *New York Times*, 1 July 2008.

175. For a summary of the issues and answers, see 'Open Meeting with Sheikh Ayman Al-Zawahiri', *MEMRI: Special Dispatch Series No. 1887*, 4 April 2008.

176. 'Expatriate Syrian Sheikh Al-Tartusi Comes Out Against Suicide Attacks', *MEMRI: Special Dispatch Series No.40*, 10 February 2006.

177. Interview with Rahimullah Yousafsai, 22 December 1998.

178. Statement of 26 December 2001, p. 147.

179. Videotape address to the American people, 29 October 2004, p. 240.

180. Interview with John Miller, May 1998.

181. Interview with *Al-Jazeera*, December 1998, p. 70.

182. Interview with Hamid Mir, 12 November 2001, p. 140.

183. Interview with Taysir Alluni, 21 October 2001, p. 118.

184. See Ibn Taymiyya, *Le Statut Des Moines*, Nasreddin Lebatelier (ed), 1997, pp. 27–30.

185. Aisha Bewley (ed), *Tafsir Al-Qurtubi: Classical Commentary of the Holy Quran*, 2003, p. 492.

186. Ibid., p. 498.

187. Interview with Taysir Alluni, 21 October 2001, p. 119.

188. Ibid., p. 119.

189. Interview with John Miller, May 1998.

190. Quoted in Zawahiri, *Knights Under the Prophet's Banner*, p. 160. On 17 November 1997, fifty-eight foreign tourists were massacred at the Temple of Queen Hatshepsut in Luxor, Egypt. During the ensuing firefight with Egyptian security services, each of the six gunmen either was killed or committed suicide. The assault was attributed to a splinter group of the Gama'at Islamiya, but the Egyptian government went on to claim that Osama bin Laden financed the attack (see 'Bin Laden "Behind Luxor Massacre"', *BBC News*, 13 May 1999). Burke notes that the event 'caused a huge swathe of the Egyptian middle and

lower classes to withdraw their support for radical Islam and forced the more moderate elements among the militants to declare a truce'. See Burke, *Al-Qaeda*, p. 216.
191. In a statement delivered to the *El Youm* newspaper, reprinted in 'Algerian Islamist Guerrillas Threaten to Attack US Interests', *Agence France Presse*, 17 September 2001.
192. In Izhar Bhatti and Irshad Bhatti, 'After Afghanistan It Will Be Pakistan's Turn', *Al-Akhbar* (*Islamabad*), 5 October 2001.

CONCLUSION

1. 'Giuliani Rejects $10 Million from Saudi Prince', *CNN*, 12 October 2001.
2. Department of Defence, 'Quadrennial Defence Review Report', 30 September 2001.
3. Interview with Taysir Alluni, 21 October 2001, p. 120.
4. Wolfowitz, 'Building a Better World: One Path From Crisis to Opportunity', 5 September 2001.
5. Letter from Ayman al-Zawahiri to Abu Musab al-Zarqawi, 11 October 2005, p. 273.
6. Finnemore and Sikkink observe that norms do not appear out of thin air but are actively built by norm entrepreneurs who call attention to issues by using language that names, interprets, and dramatizes them. In doing so, however, norm entrepreneurs face firmly embedded alternative norms and frames that create alternative perceptions of both appropriateness and interest. Again, competition is fundamental to this process: 'new norms never enter a normative vacuum but instead emerge in a highly contested normative space where they must compete with other norms and perceptions of interest'. See Martha Finnemore and Kathryn Sikkink, 'International Norm Dynamics and Political Change', *International Organization*, vol. 52, no. 4, Autumn 1998, pp. 894–905.
7. James Tully, 'The Pen Is a Mighty Sword: Quentin Skinner's Analysis of Politics', in Tully (ed), *Meaning and Context*, p. 14.
8. Abedi and Legenhausen, *Jihad and Shahadat*, p. 5.
9. Kelsay, *Arguing the Just War in Islam*, p. 97.
10. In the tape released on 7 October 2001, bin Laden praised the 9/11 attacks but did not claim them as his own. When he finally took personal responsibility for the attacks in a television address on 29 October 2004, his speech was devoted almost in its entirety to the argument that the Muslims were acting in self-defence, and must continue to do so until America desists from its aggressive wars.
11. See, for example, Danielle Archibugi, David Held and Martin Kohler (eds), *Re-imagining Political Community: Studies in Cosmopolitan Democracy*, 1998. See also Charles Jones, *Global Justice: Defending Cosmopolitanism*, 1999 and Jeremy Waldron, 'Minority Cultures and the Cosmopolitan Alternative', in Will Kymlicka (ed), *The Rights of Minority Cultures*, 1995.

12. Kamal Kharazi quoted in 'Mideast News Summary', *Xinhua News Agency*, 19 September 2001.
13. Quoted in 'Sudan: Anti-US Supporters Express Support for Bin Laden, Afghanistan, Intifada', *Agence France Presse*, 4 October 2001.
14. In 'Divisions Evident in Islamic Mideast, N. Africa', *CNN*, 24 September 2001.
15. 'Egyptian Shura Council Supports Mubarak's International Efforts', *Middle East News Agency*, 25 September 2001.
16. Holmes, *On War and Morality*, p. 3.
17. Letter to the Americans, 6 October 2002, p. 165.
18. Hashmi, 'Interpreting the Islamic Ethics of War and Peace', p. 212.
19. For an example, see Tariq Ali's *The Clash of Fundamentalisms: Crusades, Jihad and Modernity*, 2002, in which he argues that 'to combat a single-minded and ruthless fanaticism by becoming equally fanatical and ruthless will not further the cause of justice or bring about a meaningful democracy' (p. 3).
20. Suleiman Abu Ghaith, statement released on 10 October 2001, online at http://news.bbc.co.uk/1/hi/world/middle_east/1590350.stm.
21. For example, Bush: 'the terrorist threat to America and the world will be diminished the moment Saddam Hussein is disarmed'. In 'President Says Saddam Hussein Must Leave Iraq Within 48 Hours', 17 March 2003.
22. 'Give Blix the Chance to Finish His Job', *Daily Mirror*, 8 March 2003, p. 6.
23. This theory was explicitly rejected by a series of influential Muslim leaders after 9/11. For example, Sheikh Ahmad Yasin of Hamas observed that 'we are not facing a war between the west and the Arab countries, between Christians and Muslims. Islam speaks of forgiveness, of coexistence, of tolerance, not of hatred or revenge' (interview by Juan Cierco, *ABC News*, 18 September 2001). Sheikh Tantawi similarly stated that 'Islam rejects so-called clashes of civilisations and wars of faith, because they are untruths that humanity has suffered from in past centuries' (in 'Islam for International Anti-terror Campaign', *Al-Akhbar*, 8 November 2001). Ayatollah Fadlallah, too, explained that 'Islam tries to open channels of dialogue between various religions, trends, and civilisations without trying to cancel others and without considering violence as a basis for resolving problems' ('Muslim Cleric Faults Taliban's "Backward" Mentality', *Radio Monte Carlo*, 15 November 2001). Moreover, Hamad bin al-Rafae, chief of the International Islamic Forum, argued that 'the dialogue among cultures and civilisations is a religious duty, a cultural inevitability and a security necessary for co-existence' ('Participants in Islamic-Christian Forum Reject Clash of Civilisations', *Middle East News Agency*, 20 December 2001).
24. Just as the United States cited 9/11 in each of its actions taken in the 'war on terror', including the war with Iraq, terrorist attacks after 9/11 have been justified in terms of the Iraq war and self-defence. For example, a video message left by one of the '7/7' London bombers explained that 'I am directly responsible for protecting and avenging my Muslim brothers and sisters. . . . Until you stop the bombing, gassing, imprisonment and torture of my people, we will not stop this fight. We are at war and I am a soldier' (Mohammad Sidique Khan tape aired on *Al-Jazeera*

television on 1 September 2005, transcript available at http://news.bbc.co.uk/1/hi/uk/4206800.stm). Similarly, the perpetrators of the Madrid train bombings of March 2004 described it as 'a response to your collaboration with the criminal Bush and his allies. This is a response to the crimes that you have caused in the world, and specifically in Iraq and Afghanistan, and there will be more, if God wills it' (Abu Dukan al-Afghani, a Moroccan who claimed to be the military spokesman for al-Qaeda in Europe, transcript at http://news.bbc.co.uk/1/hi/world/europe/3509556.stm).

25. David Luban, *Legal Ethics and Human Dignity*, 2007, p. 166.
26. Bush, 'President to Send Secretary Powell to the Middle East', 4 April 2002.
27. Bush, 'President Discusses War on Terrorism', 8 November 2001.
28. Interview with Taysir Alluni, 21 October 2001, p. 127.
29. Quoted in Christina Lamb, 'The Invisible Man', *Sunday Times Magazine*, 18 March 2007, p. 54.
30. Talal Asad, *On Suicide Bombing*, 2007, p. 21.
31. Interview with Taysir Alluni, 21 October 2001, p. 110.
32. Ibid., p. 117.
33. Videotape address, 29 October 2004, p. 242.
34. Zawahiri, *Knights Under the Prophet's Banner*, p. 183.
35. Letter from Zawahiri to Zarqawi, 11 October 2005, p. 270.
36. Letter to the Americans, 6 October 2002, p. 168.
37. Interview with John Miller, May 1998.
38. Letter to the Americans, 6 October 2002, p. 164.
39. Stephen Holmes, 'Al Qaeda September 11, 2001', in Diego Gambetta (ed), *Making Sense of Suicide Missions*, 2006, p. 139.
40. Azzam, 'Al-Qaeda: The Misunderstood Wahabi Connection and the Ideology of Violence', p. 4.
41. John L. Esposito, *Political Islam: Revolution, Radicalism, or Reform?*, 1997, p. 5.
42. Shelley Widhalm, 'Understand Jihad: Author Seeks to Arm West with Information', *Washington Times*, 6 February 2008, p. A2.
43. Lewis, 'License to Kill', 1998, p. 19.
44. Statement on Iraq, 7 May 2004, online at http://news.bbc.co.uk/1/hi/world/middle_east/3693969.stm.

Bibliography

This bibliography is arranged into seven sections:

1. Books
2. Articles
   A. Journal/Online/Book Chapters
   B. Newspaper/Newswire/Magazine/Television/Online News
3. Statements
   A. Bush Administration Statements
   B. Al-Qaeda Statements
   C. Other Statements/Fatawa
4. Policy Documents/Reports
5. Lectures/Conferences
6. Films/Television and Radio Documentaries
7. Additional Internet Sources

1. Books

Abedi, Mehdi and Gary Legenhausen, *Jihad and Shahadat: Struggle and Martyrdom in Islam* (Houston, TX: Institute for Research and Islamic Studies), 1986.

Abou El Fadl, Khaled, *Rebellion and Violence in Islamic Law* (Cambridge; New York: Cambridge University Press), 2001.

Abu Nasr, Jamil, *A History of the Maghrib in the Islamic Period* (Cambridge: Cambridge University Press), 1987.

Ahmed, Leila, *Women and Gender in Islam: Historical Roots of a Modern Debate* (New Haven, CT; London: Yale University Press), 1992.

Alderson, Kai and Andrew Hurrell, *Hedley Bull on International Society* (Basingstoke, UK: Macmillan), 2000.

Ali, Abdullah Yusuf, *The Holy Qur'an: Translation & Commentary By Abdullah Yusuf Ali* (Birmingham, UK: Islamic Propagation Centre International), 1946.

Ali, Cheragh, *A Critical Exposition of the Popular Jihad* (Calcutta, India: Thacker, Spink and Co.), 1885.

Ali, Tariq, *The Clash Of Fundamentalisms: Crusades, Jihads And Modernity* (London: Verso), 2002.

Aquinas, Thomas, *Summa Theologica*, Fathers of the English Dominican Province, transl., 5 vols (Westminster, MD: Christian Classics), 1981.

Archibugi, Daniele, David Held, and Martin Köhler, *Re-Imagining Political Community: Studies in Cosmopolitan Democracy* (Cambridge: Polity Press), 1998.

Atkins, E. M. and R. J. Dodaro, *Augustine: Political Writings* (Cambridge: Cambridge University Press), 2001.

Atwan, Abdel Bari, *The Secret History of Al-Qaeda* (Berkeley, CA: University of California Press), 2006.

Augustine, Saint, *Answer to Faustus, A Manichean*, Roland Teske, transl. (Hyde Park, NY: New City Press), 2007.

——, *Concerning the City of God Against the Pagans*, Henry Bettenson, transl. (Harmondsworth: Penguin Books; Pelican Classics), 1972.

Azzam, Abdullah, *Defence of Muslim Lands* (London: Azzam Publications), 1986 [consulted online edition at http://www.islamistwatch.org/texts/azzam/defense/defense.html].

——, *Join the Caravan* (London: Azzam Publications), 1987 [consulted online edition at http://www.islamistwatch.org/texts/azzam/caravan/caravan.html].

Bailey, Sydney Dawson, *Prohibitions and Restraints in War* (London: Oxford University Press for The Royal Institute of International Affairs), 1972.

Begg, Moazzam, *Enemy Combatant: A British Muslim's Journey to Guantánamo and Back* (London: Free Press), 2006.

Bengio, Ofra, *Saddam's Word: Political Discourse in Iraq* (New York; Oxford: Oxford University Press), 1998.

Best, Geoffrey F., *War And Law Since 1945* (Oxford: Clarendon Press), 1994.

Bonney, Richard, *Jihad: From Quran to Bin Laden* (Basingstoke, UK: Palgrave Macmillan), 2004.

Bowden, Mark, *Black Hawk Down: The Extraordinary Story of the Most Dramatic US Military Operation Since Vietnam* (London: Bantam), 1999.

Brisard, Jean-Charles, *Zarqawi: The New Face of Al-Qaeda* (Cambridge: Polity), 2005.

Brownlie, Ian, *International Law and the Use of Force by States* (Oxford: Clarendon Press), 1963.

Burchill, Scott and Andrew Linklater, *Theories of International Relations* (Basingstoke, UK: Macmillan), 2005.

Burke, Jason, *Al-Qaeda: Casting the Shadow of Terror* (London: I. B. Tauris), 2003.

Chehab, Zaki, *Inside Hamas: The Untold Story of Militants, Martyrs and Spies* (London: I. B. Tauris), 2007.

Chesterman, Simon, *Just War Or Just Peace? Humanitarian Intervention and International Law* (Oxford: Oxford University Press), 2002.

Church of England Board for Social Responsibility, *Iraq: Would Military Action Be Justified? The Church's Contribution to the Debate* (London: General Synod of The Church of England), 2002.

Clarke, Richard A., *Against All Enemies: Inside America's War On Terror* (New York: Free Press), 2004.

Clausewitz, Carl Von, *On War*, Michael Howard and Peter Paret, eds. (London: David Campbell), 1993.

Cleveland, William L., *A History of the Modern Middle East* (Boulder, CO; Oxford: Westview), 1994.

Coates, A. J., *The Ethics Of War* (Manchester, UK: Manchester University Press), 1997.

Cook, David, *Understanding Jihad* (Berkeley, CA; London: University Of California Press), 2005.

Cook, David, *Martyrdom in Islam* (Cambridge: Cambridge University Press), 2007.

Coulson, Noel J., *A History of Islamic Law* (Edinburgh, UK: Edinburgh University Press), 1964.

Crawford, Neta, *Argument and Change in World Politics: Ethics, Decolonization, and Humanitarian Intervention* (Cambridge: Cambridge University Press), 2002.

Crone, Patricia, *Medieval Islamic Political Thought* (Edinburgh, UK: Edinburgh University Press), 2005.

Dark, K. R., *Religion and International Relations* (Basingstoke, UK: Macmillan), 2000.

Davis, G. Scott, *Warcraft and the Fragility of Virtue: An Essay in Aristotelian Ethics* (Moscow, ID: University of Idaho Press), 1992.

de Vaus, Daniel. A., *Research Design in Social Research* (London: Sage), 2001.

Devji, Faisal, *Landscapes of The Jihad: Militancy, Morality, Modernity* (London: Hurst), 2005.

Durkheim, Emile, *Suicide: A Study in Sociology* (London: Routledge & Kegan Paul), 1952.

Eickelman, Dale F. and James P. Piscatori, *Muslim Travellers: Pilgrimage, Migration and the Religious Imagination* (London: Routledge), 1990.

——, *Muslim Politics* (Princeton, NJ: Princeton University Press), 1996.

Elshtain, Jean Bethke, *Just War Theory* (New York: New York University Press), 1992.

——, *Just War Against Terror: The Burden of American Power in a Violent World* (New York: Basic Books), 2003.

Esposito, John L., *Political Islam: Revolution, Radicalism, or Reform?* (London: Lynne Rienner), 1997.

Farouk-Sluglett, Marion and Peter Sluglett, *Iraq Since 1958: From Revolution to Dictatorship* (London: Tauris), 2001.

Freedman, Lawrence, *War* (Oxford: Oxford University Press), 1994.

——and Efraim Karsh, *The Gulf Conflict, 1990–1991: Diplomacy and War in the New World Order* (London: Faber), 1994.

Gaddis, John Lewis, *The United States and the End of the Cold War: Implications, Reconsiderations, Provocations* (New York; Oxford: Oxford University Press), 1992.

Gambetta, Diego, *Making Sense of Suicide Missions* (Oxford: Oxford University Press), 2006.

Garthoff, Raymond L., *The Great Transition: American-Soviet Relations and the End of the Cold War* (Washington, DC Brookings Institution), 1994.

Goldstein, Judith and Robert O. Keohane, *Ideas and Foreign Policy: Beliefs, Institutions, and Political Change* (Ithaca, NY; London: Cornell University Press), 1993.

Gray, Christine D., *International Law and the Use of Force* (3rd edn., Oxford: Oxford University Press), 2008.

Green, Leslie. C., *The Contemporary Law of Armed Conflict* (3rd edn., Manchester, UK: Manchester University Press), 2008.

Greenberg, Karen J. and Joshua L. Dratel, *The Torture Papers: The Road to Abu Ghraib* (New York: Cambridge University Press), 2005.

Grotius, Hugo, *De Jure Belli Ac Pacis Libri Tres*, vols.1–3, Francis W. Kelsey, transl. (Oxford: Clarendon Press), 1925.

Guillaume, Alfred, *The Traditions of Islam: An Introduction to the Study of the Hadith Literature* (Oxford: The Clarendon Press), 1924.

Gunaratna, Rohan, *Inside Al Qaeda: Global Network Of Terror* (London: Hurst), 2002.

Hafez, Mohammad M., *Suicide Bombers in Iraq: The Strategy and Ideology of Martyrdom* (Washington, DC: US Institute of Peace Press), 2007.

Hallaq, Wael B., *The Origins and Evolution of Islamic Law* (Cambridge: Cambridge University Press), 2005.

Hamidullah, Muhammad, *Muslim Conduct of State* (Lahore, Pakistan: M. Ashraf), 1945.

Hashmi, Sohail H., *Islamic Political Ethics: Civil Society, Pluralism, and Conflict* (Princeton, NJ; Oxford: Princeton University Press), 2002.

——and Steven Lee, *Ethics and Weapons of Mass Destruction: Religious and Secular Perspectives* (Cambridge: Cambridge University Press), 2004.

Hatzopoulos, Pavlos and Fabio Petito, *Religion in International Relations: The Return From Exile* (New York; Basingstoke, UK: Palgrave Macmillan), 2003.

Hayes, Stephen F., *The Connection: How Al Qaeda's Collaboration with Saddam Hussein Has Endangered America* (New York: Harper Collins), 2004.

Helgeland, John, Robert J. Daly, and J. Patout Burns, *Christians and the Military: The Early Experience* (London: SCM), 1985.

Henckaerts, Jean Marie and Louise Doswald-Beck, *Customary International Humanitarian Law*, vol. I: *Rules* (Cambridge: Cambridge University Press), 2005.

Hogan, Michael J., *The End of the Cold War: Its Meaning and Implications* (Cambridge: Cambridge University Press), 1992.

Hollis, Martin and Steve Smith, *Explaining and Understanding International Relations* (Oxford: Clarendon Press), 1990.

Holmes, Robert L., *On War and Morality* (Princeton, NJ: Princeton University Press), 1989.

Horne, Alistair, *A Savage War of Peace: Algeria 1954–1962* (London: Macmillan), 1977.

Houtsma, M. Th., A. J. Wensinck, T. W. Arnold, W. Heffening, and E. Levi-Provencal, *The Encyclopaedia of Islam: A Dictionary of the Geography, Ethnology and Biography of the Muhammadan Peoples*, 5 vols. (Leiden, The Netherlands: E. J. Brill), 1927.

Hroub, Khalid, *Hamas: Political Thought and Practice* (Washington, DC: Institute for Palestine Studies), 2000.

Hughes, John. A. and Wes Sharrock, *The Philosophy Of Social Research* (3rd edn., Harlow: Longman), 1997.

Hughes, Thomas Patrick, *A Dictionary of Islam: Being a Cyclopaedia of the Doctrines, Rites, Ceremonies, and Customs, Together with the Technical and Theological Terms, of the Muhammedan Religion* (London: W.H. Allen,), 1885.

Ibrahim, Yasir S., *Al-Tabari's Book of Jihad* (Lewiston, NY: Edwin Mellen Press), 2007.

Ibn Taymiyyah, Taqi al-Din, *On Public And Private Law in Islam: Or, Public Policy in Islamic Jurisprudence*, Omar Farrukh, transl. (Beirut, Lebanon: Khayats), 1966.

——, *Ibn Taymiyyah Expounds on Islam: Selected Writings of Shaykh Al-Islam Taqi Ad-Din Ibn Taymiyyah on Islamic Faith, Life, and Society*, Muhammad Abdul Haq Ansari, transl. (Riyadh: General Administration of Culture and Publication), 2000.

Ibn Taymiyyah, Taqi al-Din, *Public Duties In Islam: The Institution of the Hisba*, Muhtar Holland, transl. (Leicester, UK: Islamic Foundation), 1982.

——, *Le Statut Des Moines*, Nasreddin Lebatelier, ed. (Beirut: El-Safina Editions), 1997.

Jaffer, Jameel and Amrit Singh, eds, *Administration of Torture: A Documentary Record from Washington to Abu Ghraib and Beyond* (New York: Columbia University Press), 2007.

Jansen, Johannes J. G., *The Neglected Duty: The Creed of Sadat's Assassins and Islamic Resurgence in the Middle East* (New York: Macmillan), 1986.

Johnson, James Turner, *Just War Tradition and the Restraint of War: A Moral and Historical Inquiry* (Princeton, NJ: Princeton University Press), 1981.

——, *Can Modern War Be Just?* (New Haven, CT: Yale University Press), 1984.

——, *Morality & Contemporary Warfare* (New Haven, CT: Yale University Press), 1999.

——and John Kelsay, *Cross, Crescent, and Sword: The Justification and Limitation of War in Western and Islamic Tradition* (New York; London: Greenwood), 1990.

——, *Just War and Jihad: Historical and Theoretical Perspectives on War and Peace in Western and Islamic Traditions* (New York; London: Greenwood), 1991.

—— and George Weigel, *Just War and the Gulf War* (Washington, DC: Ethics and Public Policy Center), 1991.

Johnston, Douglas M. and Cynthia Sampson, *Religion: The Missing Dimension of Statecraft* (New York; Oxford: Oxford University Press), 1994.

Jones, Charles, *Global Justice: Defending Cosmopolitanism* (Oxford: Oxford University Press), 1999.

Kapstein, Ethan B. and Michael Mastanduno, *Unipolar Politics: Realism and State Strategies After The Cold War* (New York; Chichester, UK: Columbia University Press), 1999.

Karsh, Efraim, *The Iran-Iraq War: Impact and Implications* (London: Macmillan), 1989.

——and Inari Rautsi, *Saddam Hussein: A Political Biography* (New York: Free Press), 1991.

Kelsay, John, *Arguing the Just War in Islam* (Cambridge, MA; London: Harvard University Press), 2007.

Kenney, Jeffrey T., *Muslim Rebels: Kharijites and the Politics of Extremism in Egypt* (Oxford: Oxford University Press), 2006.

Kent, James, *Commentaries on American Law*, George F. Comstock, ed. (11th edn.; Boston, MA: Little, Brown and Company), 1866.

Kepel, Gilles, *Jihad: The Trail of Political Islam* (London: I. B. Tauris), 2004.

——, *Muslim Extremism in Egypt: The Prophet and the Pharaoh* (Berkeley, CA: University of California Press), 1984.

Khadduri, Majid, *War and Peace in the Law of Islam* (Baltimore, MD: Johns Hopkins Press), 1962.

Khan, Muhammed Zafrullah, *Punishment of Apostasy in Islam* (London: London Mosque), 1984.

King, Gary, Robert O. Keohane, and Sidney Verba, *Designing Social Inquiry: Scientific Inference in Qualitative Research* (Princeton, NJ; Chichester, UK: Princeton University Press), 1994.

Kippenberg, Hans G., and Tilman Seidensticker, *The 9/11 Handbook: Annotated Translation and Interpretation of the Attackers' Spiritual Manual* (London: Equinox), 2006.

Kymlicka, Will, *The Rights of Minority Cultures* (Oxford: Oxford University Press), 1995.

Lackey, Douglas, *The Ethics of War and Peace* (Englewood Cliffs, NJ: Prentice-Hall), 1989.

Lafollette, Hugh, ed., *The Oxford Handbook of Practical Ethics* (Oxford; New York: Oxford University Press), 2003.

Lawrence, Bruce, *Messages to The World: The Statements of Osama Bin Laden* (London; New York: Verso), 2005.

Lewis, Bernard, C. H. Pellat and J. Schacht, *The Encyclopaedia of Islam: New Edition*, 5 vols. (Leiden, The Netherlands: E. J. Brill), 1965.

Luban, David, *Legal Ethics and Human Dignity* (Cambridge: Cambridge University Press), 2007.

McElroy, Robert W., *Morality and American Foreign Policy: The Role of Ethics in International Affairs* (Princeton, NJ: Princeton University Press), 1992.

Macintyre, Alasdair C., *The Macintyre Reader*, Kelvin M. Knight, ed. (Oxford: Polity Press), 1998.

Makiya, Kanan, *Republic of Fear: The Politics of Modern Iraq* (London: Hutchinson Radius), 1989.

Mansfield, Laura, *In His Own Words: A Translation of the Writings of Dr. Ayman Al-Zawahiri* (Old Tappan, NJ: TLG Publications), 2006.

Mawdudi, Sayyid Abu Ala, *Towards Understanding Islam*, Ahmad Kurshid, transl. (Leicester, UK: Islamic Foundation), 1980.

——, *Towards Understanding the Quran*, Zafar Ishaq Ansari, transl., vols. 1–7 (Leicester, UK: Islamic Foundation), 1988.

Mayer, Ann Elizabeth, *Islam And Human Rights: Tradition and Politics* (Boulder, CO; Oxford: Westview), 1999.

Michot, Yahya, *Ibn Taymiyyah: Muslims Under Non-Muslim Rule* (Oxford; London: Interface), 2006.

Moinuddin, Hasan, *The Charter of The Islamic Conference* (Oxford; New York: Clarendon Press), 1987.

More, Thomas, *Utopia*, George M. Logan and Robert M. Adams, eds. (Cambridge: Cambridge University Press), 1989.

Nardin, Terry and David Mapel, *Traditions of International Ethics* (Cambridge: Cambridge University Press), 1992.

Nasr, Vali, *The Shia Revival: How Conflicts Within Islam Will Shape the Future* (New York: Norton), 2007.

Noe, Nicholas, *Voice of Hezbollah: The Statements of Sayyed Hassan Nasrallah* (London: Verso), 2007.

Nys, Ernest, *Les Origines Du Droit International* (Bruxelle: A. Castaigne), 1894.

O'Brien, William Vincent, *The Conduct of Just and Limited War* (New York: Praeger), 1981.

Pagden, Anthony and Jeremy Lawrance, *Vitoria: Political Writings* (Cambridge: Cambridge University Press), 1991.

Pape, Robert Anthony, *Dying to Win: The Strategic Logic of Suicide Terrorism* (1st edn.; New York: Random House), 2005.

Paskins, Barrie and Michael L. Dockrill, *The Ethics of War* (London: Duckworth), 1979.

Peters, Rudolph, *Islam and Colonialism: The Doctrine of Jihad in Modern History* (The Hague; New York: Mouton), 1979.

——, *Jihad in Classical and Modern Islam: A Reader* (Princeton, NJ: Markus Wiener), 1996.

Piscatori, James P., *Islam in a World of Nation-States* (Cambridge: Cambridge University Press in Association with The Royal Institute of International Affairs), 1986.

Pogge, Thomas, *World Poverty and Human Rights: Cosmopolitan Responsibilities and Reforms* (Cambridge: Polity Press), 2002.

Pompe, Cornelis Arnold, *Aggressive War: An International Crime* (The Hague: M. Nijhoff), 1953.

Potter, Ralph B., *War And Moral Discourse* (Richmond, VA: John Knox Press), 1969.

Qalahji, Mohammad Rawaas, *Mu'jam Lughat Al-Fuqahaa* (Beirut: Dar Al-Nafais), 1988.

Qaradawi, Yusuf, *State in Islam* (Cairo: El-Falah), 1998.

——, *Priorities of the Islamic Movement in the Coming Phase* (Swansea, UK: Awakening Publications), 2000.

Qutb, Sayyid, *Social Justice in Islam* (Washington, DC: American Council Of Learned Societies), 1953.

——, *In the Shade of the Quran (Fi Dhilal Al-Quran)*, M. A Salahi and A. A. Shamis, eds., vols. 1, 2, and 30 (Leicester, UK: Islamic Foundation), 2001.

Qurtubi, Mohammad ibn Ahmad, *Tafsir Al-Qurtubi: Classical Commentary of the Holy Quran*, Aisha Bewley, ed. (London: Dar Al-Taqwa), 2003.

Rajaee, Farhang, *The Iran-Iraq War: The Politics of Aggression* (Gainesville, FL: University Press Of Florida), 1993.

Ramsey, Paul, *War and the Christian Conscience: How Shall Modern War Be Conducted Justly?* (Durham, NC: Duke University Press), 1961.

——, *The Just War: Force and Political Responsibility* (Oxford: Rowman & Littlefield), 2002.

Reed, Charles and David Ryall (eds), *The Price of Peace: Just War in the Twenty-First Century* (Cambridge: Cambridge University Press), 2007.

Regan, Richard J., *Just War: Principles and Cases* (Washington, DC: Catholic University Of America Press), 1996.

Reich, Walter, *Origins of Terrorism: Psychologies, Ideologies, Theologies, States Of Mind* (Cambridge: Cambridge University Press), 1990.

Reus-Smit, Christian, *The Moral Purpose of the State: Culture, Social Identity, and Institutional Rationality in International Relations* (Princeton, NJ: Princeton University Press), 1999.

Reuter, Christoph, *My Life Is a Weapon: A Modern History of Suicide Bombing* (Princeton, NJ: Princeton University Press), 2004.

Roberts, Adam and Richard Guelff, *Documents on the Laws of War* (3rd edn.; Oxford: Oxford University Press), 2000.

Rodin, David, *War and Self-Defense* (Oxford: Clarendon Press), 2002.

Roy, Olivier, *Globalised Islam: The Search For a New Ummah* (London: Hurst), 2004.

——, *The Failure of Political Islam* (London: Tauris), 1994.

Rubin, Barry M., *Islamic Fundamentalism in Egyptian Politics* (Basingstoke, UK: Palgrave Macmillan), 2002.

Sachedina, Abdulaziz, *The Just Ruler (Al-Sultan Al-Adil) in Shite Islam: The Comprehensive Authority of the Jurist in Imamite Jurisprudence* (New York; Oxford: Oxford University Press), 1988.

Sands, Philippe, *Torture Team: Uncovering War Crimes in the Land of the Free* (London: Penguin), 2009.

Shaybani, Mohammad ibn Al-Hasan, *The Islamic Law of Nations: Shaybani's Siyar*, Majid Khadduri, ed. (Baltimore, MD: Johns Hopkins Press), 1966.

Shils, Edward, *Tradition* (London: Faber & Faber), 1981.

Shue, Henry, *Nuclear Deterrence and Moral Restraint: Critical Choices for American Strategy* (Cambridge: Cambridge University Press), 1989.

——and David Rodin, eds, *Preemption: Military Action and Moral Justification* (Oxford: Oxford University Press), 2007.

Silverman, David, *Interpreting Qualitative Data: Methods for Analysing Talk, Text and Interaction* (London: Sage), 1993.

Sivan, Emmanuel, *Radical Islam: Medieval Theology and Modern Politics* (New Haven, CT: Yale University Press), 1985.

Tan, Kok-Chor, *Toleration, Diversity and Global Justice* (University Park, PA.: Pennsylvania State University Press), 2000.

Thomas, Scott, *The Global Resurgence of Religion and the Transformation of International Relations: The Struggle for the Soul of the Twenty-First Century* (New York; Basingstoke, UK: Palgrave Macmillan), 2005.

Thomas, Ward, *The Ethics of Destruction: Norms and Force in International Relations* (Ithaca, NY; London: Cornell University Press), 2001.

Tucker, Robert W., *The Just War: A Study in Contemporary American Doctrine* (Baltimore, MD: Johns Hopkins Press), 1960.

Tully, James, *Meaning and Context: Quentin Skinner and His Critics* (Princeton, NJ: Princeton University Press), 1988.

United States Conference of Catholic Bishops, *The Challenge of Peace: God's Promise and Our Response* (Washington, DC: Office of Publicity and Promotion Services, United States Catholic Conference), 1983.

Vincent, R. J., *Human Rights and International Relations* (Cambridge: Cambridge University Press), 1986.

Walzer, Michael, *Just and Unjust Wars: A Moral Argument With Historical Illustrations* (3rd edn.; New York: Basic Books), 2000.

———, *Arguing About War* (New Haven, CT: Yale University Press), 2004.

Weber, Max, *Max Weber on the Methodology of the Social Sciences*, Edward Shils and Henry Finch, eds. (Glencoe, IL: Free Press), 1949.

Welsh, Jennifer M., *Humanitarian Intervention and International Relations* (Oxford: Oxford University Press), 2004.

Wheeler, Nicholas J., *Saving Strangers: Humanitarian Intervention in International Society* (Oxford: Oxford University Press), 2000.

Wicker, Brian, *Witnesses to Faith? Martyrdom in Christianity and Islam* (Aldershot: Ashgate), 2006.

Woodward, Bob, *Plan of Attack* (New York; London: Simon & Schuster), 2004.

2. Articles

A. Articles: Journal/Online/Book Chapters

Abou El-Fadl, Khaled, 'Ahkam al-Bughat: Irregular Warfare and the Law of Rebellion in Islam', in James Turner Johson and John Kelsay, *Cross, Crescent, and Sword: The Justification and Limitation of War in Western and Islamic Tradition* (New York; London: Greenwood), 1990, pp. 149–76.

Afsaruddin, Asma, 'Competing Perspectives on Jihad and Martyrdom in Early Islamic Sources', in Brian Wicker, *Witnesses to Faith? Martyrdom in Christianity and Islam* (Aldershot: Ashgate), 2006, pp. 15–32.

Al-Albani, Mohammad Nasr Al Din, 'Extract from *Al Masjid Al-Aqsa: The Path to Its Freedom*', at http://www.allaahuakbar.net/scholars/albaani/suicide_bombing.htm [accessed 3 February 2007].

Ali, Imtiaz, 'Preparing the Mujahidin: The Taliban's Military Field Manual', *CTC Sentinel*, September 2008, vol. 1, no. 10, pp. 5–7.

Ayers, Thomas E., 'Six Floors of Detainee Operations in the Post-9/11 World', *Parameters*, vol. 35, Autumn 2005, pp. 33–53.

Azzam, Abdullah, 'Martyrs: the Building Blocks of Nations', date unknown, at http://www.religioscope.com/info/doc/jihad/azzam_martyrs.htm [accessed 12 May 2006].

Azzam, Maha, 'Al-Qaeda: The Misunderstood Wahabi Connection and the Ideology of Violence', Royal Institute of International Affairs Briefing Paper No. 1, February 2003, at http://www.chathamhouse.org.uk/pdf/briefing_papers/Azzaml.pdf [accessed 16 January 2006].

Bassiouni, M. Cherif, 'Evolving Approaches to Jihad: From Self-Defence to Revolutionary and Regime-Change Political Violence', *Journal of Islamic Law and Culture*, vol. 10, no. 1, April 2008, pp. 61–83.

Baxter, Richard R., 'So-called "Unprivileged Belligerency": Spies, Guerrillas and Saboteurs', *British Yearbook of International Law*, vol. 28, 1951, pp. 324–45.

Bellamy, Alex J., 'Supreme Emergencies and the Protection of Non-combatants in War', *International Affairs*, vol. 80, no. 5, 2004, pp. 829–50.

Benchiba, Lakhdar, 'Les Mutations du Terrorisme Algérien', *Politique étrangère*, vol. 2, Eté 2009, pp. 345–52.

Brahimi, Alia, 'Crushed in the Shadows: Why Al-Qaeda Will Lose the War of Ideas', *Studies in Conflict and Terrorism*, vol. 33, no. 2, February 2010, pp. 93–110.

Bull, Hedley, 'Recapturing the Just War for Political Theory', *World Politics*, vol. 31, no. 4, July 1979, pp. 588–99.

Crawford, Neta C., 'The Best Defense: The Problem with Bush's "Pre-emptive" War Doctrine', *Boston Review*, February/March 2003, at http://www.bostonreview.net/BR28.1/crawford.html [accessed 12 November 2004].

——, 'Just War Theory and the US Counterterror War', *Perspectives on Politics*, vol. 1, no. 1, March 2003, pp. 5–25.

Dale, Stephen Frederic, 'Religious Suicides in Islamic Asia: Anticolonial Terrorism in India, Indonesia, and the Philippines', *Journal of Conflict Resolution*, vol. 32, no. 1, March 1988, pp. 37–59.

Donner, Fred M., 'The Sources of Islamic Conceptions of War' in John Kelsay and James Turner Johnson, *Just War and Jihad: Historical and Theoretical Perspectives on War and Peace in Western and Islamic Traditions* (New York; London: Greenwood), 1991, pp. 31–70.

Fadlallah, Mohammad Hussein, 'Islam and Violence in Political Reality', *Middle East Insight*, vol. 4, no. 4, 1986, pp. 5–13.

——, 'The New World Order and the Middle East—An Islamic Perspective', *Middle East Insight*, vol. 8, no. 1, 1991, pp. 9–13.

Faraj, Mohammad Abd al-Salam Faraj, 'Al Farida al-Ghaiba' in Johannes J. G. Jansen, *The Neglected Duty: The Creed of Sadat's Assassins and Islamic Resurgence in the Middle East* (New York: Macmillan), 1986, pp. 159–230.

Finnemore, Martha, and Kathryn Sikkink, 'International Norm Dynamics and Political Change', *International Organization*, vol. 52, no. 4, Autumn 1998, pp. 887–917.

Ford, John C., 'The Morality of Obliteration Bombing', *Theological Studies*, vol. 5, no. 3, September 1944, pp. 261–309.

Fukuyama, Francis, 'The Neoconservative Moment', *The National Interest*, no. 76, Summer 2004, pp. 57–68.

Gardam, Judith G., 'Proportionality and Force in International Law', *American Journal of International Law*, 1993, vol. 87, no. 375, pp. 391–413.

Garthoff, Raymond L., 'Why Did the Cold War Arise and Why Did It End?' in Michael J. Hogan, *The End of the Cold War: Its Meaning and Implications* (Cambridge: Cambridge University Press), 1992, pp. 127–36.

Greenwood, Christopher, 'International Law and the Pre-emptive Use of Force: Afghanistan, Al-Qaida and Iraq', in *San Diego International Law Journal*, vol. 4, no. 7, 2003, pp. 7–38.

Hartigan, Richard S., 'Francesco de Vitoria and Civilian Immunity', *Political Theory*, vol. 1, no. 1, February 1973, pp. 79–91.

Hashmi, Sohail, 'Interpreting the Islamic Ethics of War and Peace', in Sohail Hashmi, *Islamic Political Ethics: Civil Society, Pluralism, and Conflict* (Princeton, NJ; Oxford: Princeton University Press), 2002, pp. 194–216.

Hobsbawm, Eric, 'Delusions about Democracy', *Counterpunch*, 26 January 2005, at http://www.counterpunch.org/hobsbawm01252005.html [accessed 12 December 2005].

Holmes, Stephen, 'Al Qaeda September 11, 2001', in Diego Gambetta, ed., *Making Sense of Suicide Missions* (Oxford: Oxford University Press), 2006, pp. 131–72.

Howard, Michael, 'Temperamenta Belli: Can War Be Controlled?', in Jean Bethke Elshtain, *Just War Theory* (New York: New York University Press), 1992, pp. 23–35.

Hurka, Thomas, 'Proportionality in the Morality of War', *Philosophy and Public Affairs*, vol. 33, no. 1, 2005, pp. 34–66.

Jackson, Robert, 'Dialectical Justice in the Gulf War', *Review of International Studies*, vol. 18, 1992, pp. 335–54.

Jervis, Robert, 'Was the Cold War a Security Dilemma?', *Journal of Cold War Studies*, vol. 3, no. 1, Winter 2001, pp. 36–60.

Joffe, George, 'Democracy, Islam and the Culture of Modernism', *Democratization*, vol. 4, no. 3, 1997, pp. 133–51.

Johnson, James Turner, 'Just Cause Revisited', publication of the Ethics and Public Policy Centre, 1 September 1998, at http://www.eppc.org/publications/pubID.1998/pub_detail.asp [accessed 8 March 2005].

——, 'Aquinas and Luther on War and Peace', *Journal of Religious Ethics*, vol. 31, no. 1, March 2003, pp. 3–20.

Kapstein, Ethan, B., 'Does Unipolarity Have a Future?', in Ethan Kapstein and Michael Mastanduno, *Unipolar Politics: Realism and State Strategies After the Cold War* (New York; Chichester, UK: Columbia University Press), 1999, pp. 464–90.

Kelsay, John, 'Islam and the Distinction Between Combatants and Noncombatants', in James Turner Johson and John Kelsay, *Cross, Crescent, and Sword: The Justification and Limitation of War in Western and Islamic Tradition* (New York; London: Greenwood), 1990, pp. 197–220.

Kurzman, Charles, 'Pro-US Fatwas', *Middle East Policy*, vol. 10, no. 3, September, 2003, pp. 155–66.

Lawrence, Bruce, 'Jihad in Islamic Religion and Nation State Ideologies', in John Kelsay and James Turner Johnson, *Just War and Jihad: Historical and Theoretical Perspectives on War and Peace in Western and Islamic Traditions* (New York; London: Greenwood), 1991, pp. 141–59.

Layne, Christopher, 'The Unipolar Illusion', *International Security*, vol. 17, no. 4, 1993, pp. 5–51.

Lewis, Bernard, 'License to Kill: Usama bin Laden's Declaration of Jihad', *Foreign Affairs*, vol. 77, no. 6, November/December 1998, pp. 14–19.

Luban, David J., 'Liberalism, Torture and the Ticking Bomb', *Virginia Law Review*, vol. 91, no. 6, October 2005, pp. 1425–61.

——, 'Preventive War', *Philosophy and Public Affairs*, vol. 32, no. 3, July 2004, pp. 207–48.

Lynch, Cecilia, 'Dogma, Praxis and Religious Perspectives on Multiculturalism', in Pavlos Hatzopoulos and Fabio Petito, *Religion in International Relations: The*

Return From Exile (New York; Basingstoke, UK: Palgrave Macmillan), 2003, pp. 55–78.

Masud, Mohammad Khalid, 'The Obligation to Migrate: The Doctrine of Hijra in Islamic Law', in Dale F. Eickelman and James Piscatori, *Muslim Travellers: Pilgrimage, Migration and the Religious Imagination* (London: Routledge), 1990, pp. 29–49.

Mawdudi, Sayyid Abu Ala, 'Mischief of Takfir', 1935, at http://www.muslim.org/movement/maudoodi/art-takfir.htm [accessed 2 June 2006].

Mayer, Ann Elizabeth, 'War and Peace in the Islamic Tradition and International Law', in John Kelsay and James Turner Johnson, *Just War and Jihad: Historical and Theoretical Perspectives on War and Peace in Western and Islamic Traditions* (New York; London: Greenwood), 1991, pp. 195–226.

Merari, Ariel, 'The Readiness to Kill and Die: Suicidal Terrorism in the Middle East', in Walter Reich, *Origins of Terrorism: Psychologies, Ideologies, Theologies, States Of Mind* (Cambridge: Cambridge University Press), 1990, pp. 192–210.

Momtaz, Djamchid, 'The Inherent Right of Self-Defence in the Iran-Iraq War', in Farhang Rajaee, *The Iran-Iraq War: The Politics of Aggression* (Gainesville, FL: University Press Of Florida), 1993, pp. 183–90.

Mueller, John, 'What Was the Cold War About? Evidence from Its Ending', *Political Science Quarterly*, vol. 119, no. 4, 2004–05, pp. 609–31.

Mutahhari, Murtada, 'The First Lecture: Questions About Jihad', reprinted in Mehdi Abedi and Gary Legenhausen, *Jihad and Shahadat: Struggle and Martyrdom in Islam* (Houston, TX: Institute for Research and Islamic Studies), 1986, pp. 81–92.

——, 'The Second Lecture: Questions About Jihad', reprinted in Mehdi Abedi and Gary Legenhausen, *Jihad and Shahadat: Struggle and Martyrdom in Islam* (Houston, TX: Institute for Research and Islamic Studies), 1986, pp. 93–102.

Nader, George, 'Interview with Sheikh Muhammed Hussein Fadl Allah', *Middle East Insight*, vol. 4, no. 2, 1985, pp. 12–20.

Navid, Kermani, 'A Dynamite of the Spirit: Why Nietzsche, Not the Koran, Is the Key to Understanding the Suicide Bombers', *Times Literary Supplement*, 29 March 2002, pp. 13–15.

O'Connell, Mary Ellen, 'The Myth of Pre-emptive Self-Defense', *The American Society of International Law Task Force on Terrorism*, August 2002, at http://www.asil.org/taskforce/oconnell.pdf [accessed 12 June 2005].

Orend, Brian, 'Is There a Supreme Emergency Exemption?', in M. Evans, ed., *Just War Theory: A Reappraisal* (Edinburgh, UK: Edinburgh University Press), 2005, pp. 134–53.

Paz, Reuven, 'The Impact of the War in Iraq on the Global Jihad', in Hillel Fradkin, Husain Haqqani and Eric Brown, *Current Trends in Islamist Ideology*, vol. 1, 2005, pp. 39–49.

Ranger, T. O., 'Connexions between "Primary Resistance" Movements and Modern Mass Nationalism in East and Central Africa', *The Journal of African History*, vol. 9, no. 3, 1968, pp. 437–53.

Rapoport, David C., 'Fear and Trembling: Terrorism in Three Religious Traditions', *The American Political Science Review*, vol. 78, no. 3, September 1984, pp. 658–77.

Raulff, Ulrich, 'Interview with Georgio Agamben— Life, a Work of Art Without an Author: The State of Exception, the Administration of Disorder and Private Life', *German Law Journal*, vol. 5, no. 5, 1 May 2004, pp. 609–14.

Reidel, Bruce, 'The Return of the Knights: Al-Qaeda and the Fruits of Middle East Disorder', *Survival*, vol. 49, no. 3, September 2007, pp. 107–20.

Rengger, Nicholas, 'On the Just War Tradition in the Twenty-First Century', *International Affairs*, vol. 78, no. 2, April 2002, pp. 353–63.

Reus-Smit, Christian, 'Constructivism', Scott Burchill and Andrew Linklater, *Theories of International Relations* (Basingstoke, UK: Macmillan), 2005, pp. 188–212.

Roberts, Les, Riyadh Lafta, and Richard Garfield, Jamal Khudhairi and Gilbert Burnham, 'Mortality Before and After the 2003 Invasion of Iraq: Cluster Sample Survey', *The Lancet*, vol. 364, no. 9448, 20 November 2004, pp. 1857–64.

——, Gilbert Burnham, Riyadh Lafta, and Shannon Doocy, 'Mortality After the 2003 Invasion of Iraq: A Cross-Sectional Cluster Sample Survey', *The Lancet*, vol. 368, no. 9545, 21 October 2006, pp. 1421–8.

Rosen, Lawrence, 'Orientalism Revisited: Edward Said's Unfinished Critique', *Boston Review*, January/February 2007, at http://bostonreview.net/BR32.1/rosen.html [accessed 2 March 2007].

Shahrour, Mohammad, 'The Divine Text and Pluralism in Muslim Societies', no date given, online at https://www.quran.org/shahrour.htm [accessed 12 November 2006].

Shue, Henry, 'Liberalism: The Impossibility of Justifying Weapons of Mass Destruction', in Sohail Hashmi and Steven Lee, *Ethics and Weapons of Mass Destruction: Religious and Secular Perspectives* (Cambridge: Cambridge University Press), 2004, pp. 139–62.

——, 'War', in Hugh LaFollette, *The Oxford Handbook of Practical Ethics* (Oxford; New York: Oxford University Press), 2003, pp. 734–62.

Skinner, Quentin, 'Some Problems in the Analysis of Political Thought and Action', in James Tully, *Meaning and Context: Quentin Skinner and His Critics* (Princeton, NJ: Princeton University Press), 1988, pp. 97–118.

——, 'Language and Social Change', in James Tully, *Meaning and Context: Quentin Skinner and His Critics* (Princeton, NJ: Princeton University Press), 1988, pp. 119–34.

Stafford Smith, Clive, 'Torture: An Idea for Our Time', *Open Democracy*, 11 August 2005, at http://www.opendemocracy.net/debates/article.jsp?id=2&debateId=124&articleId=2749 [accessed 12 August 2005].

Taft, William H. and Todd F. Buchwald, 'Pre-emption, Iraq and International Law', *American Journal of International Law*, vol. 97, no. 3, July 2003, pp. 557–63.

Taylor, Terence, 'The End of Imminence?', *The Washington Quarterly*, vol. 27, no. 4, Autumn 2004, pp. 57–72.

Thomas, Scott, 'The Global Resurgence of Religion and the Study of World Politics', *Millennium*, vol. 24, no. 2, June 1995, pp. 289–300.

——, 'Religion and International Conflict', K. R. Dark, *Religion and International Relations* (Basingstoke, UK: Macmillan), 2000, pp. 1–23.

Tully, James, 'The Pen Is a Mighty Sword: Quentin Skinner's Analysis of Politics', in James Tully, *Meaning and Context: Quentin Skinner and His Critics* (Princeton, NJ: Princeton University Press), 1988, pp. 7–28.

Tibi, Bassam, 'War and Peace in Islam', in Sohail Hashmi, *Islamic Political Ethics: Civil Society, Pluralism, and Conflict* (Princeton, NJ; Oxford: Princeton University Press), 2002, pp. 175–93.

van Tongeren, Paul, 'Ethics, Tradition and Hermeneutics', *Ethical Perspectives*, vol. 3, no. 3, 1996, pp. 175–83.

Waldron, Jeremy, 'Minority Cultures and the Cosmopolitan Alternative', in Will Kymlicka, *The Rights of Minority Cultures* (Oxford: Oxford University Press), 1995, pp. 93–122.

Walzer, Michael, 'So, Is This a Just War?', *Dissent Magazine*, web exclusive, posted 20 March 2003, reprinted in Michael Walzer, *Arguing About War* (New Haven, CT: Yale University Press), 2004, pp. 160–2.

Wheeler, Nicholas J., 'The Humanitarian Responsibilities of Sovereignty: Explaining the Development of a New Norm of Military Intervention for Humanitarian Purposes in International Society' in Jennifer M. Welsh, *Humanitarian Intervention and International Relations* (Oxford: Oxford University Press), 2004, pp. 29–51.

Wicker, Brian, Maha Azzam, and Peter Bishop, 'Martyrdom and Murder: Aspects of Suicidal Terrorism', in Brian Wicker, ed., *Witnesses to Faith? Martyrdom in Christianity and Islam* (Aldershot: Ashgate), 2006, pp. 123–38.

Wohlforth, William C., 'The Stability of a Unipolar World', *International Security*, vol. 24, no. 1, 1999, pp. 5–41.

Wright, Robin, 'The War and the Spread of Islamic Fundamentalism', in Efraim Karsh, *The Iran-Iraq War: Impact and Implications* (London: Macmillan), 1989, pp. 110–20.

Zuhili, Wahbeh al-, 'Islam and International Law', *International Review of the Red Cross*, vol. 87, no. 858, June 2005, pp. 269–83.

B. News Articles: Newspaper/Newswire/Magazine/Television/Online News

'4 Iraqis Killed, Family Kidnapped', *CNN*, 11 September 2004, at http://edition.cnn.com/2004/WORLD/meast/09/11/iraq.main/ [accessed 12 January 2005].

'A New Bin Laden Speech', *MEMRI: Special Dispatch Series*, no. 539, 18 July 2003, http://www.memri.org/bin/articles.cgi?Area=sd&ID=SP53903 [accessed 6 March 2006].

'Al Qaida Still Targeting White House, Capitol', *World Tribune*, 26 February 2004.

'Algeria: FIS Says Attack on WTC, Pentagon "Ignoble Act of Violence"', *Radio France Internationale*, 17 September 2001 [title by *Foreign Broadcast Information Service*].

'Algerian Islamist Guerrillas Threaten to Attack US Interests', *Agence France Presse*, 17 September 2001 [original title of publication not supplied by *Foreign Broadcast Information Service*].

'Amal, Hizballah Leadership Discuss Local, Regional Issues', *Al-Safir*, 20 June 2002.

'An Interview with Abdulmalek Droukdal', *New York Times*, 1 July 2008.

'Arab News Provides Profiles of "Well Educated" Hijackers', *Arab News*, 1 October 2001 [original title of publication not supplied by *Foreign Broadcast Information Service*].

'Arab NGOs Condemn Attacks on US, Palestinians, Iraq', *Middle East News Agency*, 13 September 2001.

'Arafat Condemns, Palestinians Celebrate', *Statesman* (India), 12 September 2001.

'As Bad as the Nazis? What the Red Cross Thinks About the US Military', *Wall Street Journal: Opinion Journal*, 23 May 2005, at http://www.opinionjournal.com/editorial/feature.html?id=110006725 [accessed 2 June 2005].

'Azeri Politicians Blast "Monstrous Terrorist Attacks in US"', *Turan (Baku)*, 11 September 2001 [original title of publication not supplied by *Foreign Broadcast Information Service*].

'Baghdad Wakes Up to Explosions', *Fox News*, 22 March 2003, http://www.foxnews.com/story/0,2933,81791,00.html [accessed 2 February 2006].

'Bin Laden "Behind Luxor Massacre"', *BBC News*, 13 May 1999, at http://news.bbc.co.uk/1/hi/world/middle_east/343207.stm [accessed 12 November 2006].

'Bin Laden On Tape: "Attacks Benefited Islam Greatly"', *CNN*, 14 December 2001, at http://archives.cnn.com/2001/US/12/13/ret.bin.laden.videotape/[accessed 15 December 2001].

'Blair Promises Victory Over Terror', *BBC News*, 2 October 2001, at http://news.bbc.co.uk/1/hi/uk_politics/1575293.stm [accessed 2 October 2001].

'Bush Called War Monger By Iran's Conservative Press', *Agence France Presse*, 5 February 2005.

'Condemning Aggression', *Al Ahram*, no. 551, 13–19 September 2001, at http://weekly.ahram.org.eg/2001/551/fo2.htm [accessed 5 March 2005].

'Catholic Writers Recruited to Support Bush War on Iraq: Michael Novak Hired to Undermine Pope John Paul II's Position', *Houston Catholic Worker*, vol. 23, no. 1, January–February 2003.

'Chirac and Schroeder on US Ultimatum', *BBC News*, 18 March 2003, at http://news.bbc.co.uk/1/hi/world/europe/2860715.stm [accessed 12 January 2006].

'Czech Papers Casts Doubt on Suicide Bomber's Meeting with Iraqi Agent', *CTK*, 13 December 2001 [original title of publication not supplied by *Foreign Broadcast Information Service*].

'Divisions Evident in Islamic Mideast, N. Africa', *CNN*, 24 September 2001.

'Editorial: God or Country?', *America: The National Catholic Weekly*, vol. 188, no. 11, 31 March 2003.

'Egypt: Al-Azhar Grand Sheikh Condemns Terrorism', *Middle East News Agency*, 20 October 2001.

'Egypt's Mufti: We Condemned the September 11 Attacks, But Since Then Our Feelings Have Changed', *MEMRI: Special Dispatch Series*, no. 402, 23 July 2002, at http://memri.org/bin/articles.cgi?Page=archives&Area=sd&ID=SP40202 [accessed 3 July 2006].

'Egyptian Mufti Does Not Approve 11 September Attacks Against US', *Middle East News Agency*, 26 October 2001.

'Egyptian Mufti Says Martyrdom Operations Legitimate', *Middle East News Agency*, 2 August 2002.

'Egyptian Shura Council Supports Mubarak's International Efforts', *Middle East News Agency*, 25 September 2001.

'Ethicists Challenge Justification for Pre-Emptive War', *Worldwide Faith News*, 5 May 2003.

'EU Says No to Iraq War Without UN Approval', *Reuters*, 21 January 2003.

'Excerpts from Pentagon's Plan: Prevent the Re-Emergence of a New Rival', *New York Times*, 8 March 1992, p. 14.

'Expatriate Syrian Sheikh Al-Tartusi Comes Out Against Suicide Attacks', *MEMRI: Special Dispatch Series No. 40*, 10 February 2006 at http://www.memri.org/bin/articles.cgi?Page=archives&Area=sr&ID=SR4006 [accessed 10 February 2006].

'Fresh Guantanamo Torture Claims', *BBC News*, 13 February 2005, at http://news.bbc.co.uk/1/hi/world/asia-pacific/4262095.stm [accessed 14 February 2005].

'Friday Sermons Condemn Iraqi Prisoner Abuse, Israeli Actions Against Palestinians', *Foreign Broadcast Information Service Report*, 14 May 2004.

'Ghana: Chief Imam Condemns US Attacks, Urges Global Definition of Terrorism', *Ghana Broadcasting Corporation Radio 1*, 21 September 2001.

'Giuliani Rejects $10 Million from Saudi Prince', *CNN*, 12 October 2001, at http://archives.cnn.com/2001/US/10/11/rec.giuliani.prince/index.html [accessed 12 November 2004].

'Give Blix the Chance to Finish His Job', *Daily Mirror*, 8 March 2003, p. 6.

'GU Professor William O'Brien Dies', *Washington Post*, 19 July 2003, p. B6.

'Head of Bosnia's Muslims Urges Bush to Exercise Caution', *BH Press (Sarajevo)*, 16 September 2001.

'Hizballah Chief: US Makes "Big Mistake" If It Chooses Mideast for Its War', *Al-Safir*, 27 November 2001.

'Hizballah's Spirtual Leader Advocates Fatwah Against Terrorists', *Der Spiegel*, 15 October 2001.

'Immigrants Fear Backlash to Terror Attacks', *CNN*, 19 September 2001, at http://archives.cnn.com/2001/US/09/19/gen.hate.crimes/index.html [accessed 3 December 2005].

'Indonesian Islamic Chief Says Jihad Not Necessarily Call for War', *Agence France-Presse* (Hong Kong), 30 September 2001.

'Interpreting Islam', *Indian Currents*, 6 June 2004.

'Iran Expresses Rare Sympathy for US Over Attacks', *Gulf News*, 13 September 2001.

'Iraq Abuse "As Bad as Saddam Era"', *BBC News*, 27 November 2005, at http://news.bbc.co.uk/1/hi/world/middle_east/4475030.stm [accessed 27 November 2005].

'Iraq War Cost $102 Billion Through September, Pentagon Says', *Bloomberg News*, 13 January 2005.

'Iraq War Illegal, Says Annan', *BBC News*, 16 September 2004, at http://news.bbc.co.uk/1/hi/world/middle_east/3661134.stm [accessed 16 September 2004].

'Iraq War: The Coming Disaster', *Los Angeles Times*, 14 April 2002, p. M3.

'Iraq War Was Illegal, Chirac Tells Bush', *Irish Examiner*, 4 June 2003.

'Iraqis Blame Sanctions for Child Deaths', *BBC News*, 12 August 1999, at http://news.bbc.co.uk/1/hi/world/middle_east/418625.stm [accessed 7 March 2006].

'Iraqis Push Ahead with Elections', *BBC News*, 21 November 2004, at http://news.bbc.co.uk/1/hi/world/middle_east/4030323.stm [accessed 22 November 2004].

'Islam for International Anti-terror Campaign', *Al-Akhbar*, 8 November 2001.

'Islamist Osama Rushdie Responds to Al-Zawahiri's Memoirs', *Al-Sharq Al-Awsat*, 13 December 2001.

'Khatami: Suicide Bombings Are an Injustice and Hurt Islam', *Haaretz*, 9 September 2006.

'Lahore Conference Celebrates Jihad', *MEMRI: Special Dispatch Series*, no. 2042, 5 September 2008, at http://www.memri.org/bin/latestnews.cgi?ID=SD204208 [accessed 5 September 2008].

'Leaders of 46 Islamic Groups and Movements Condemn the Attacks on the US', *Al-Sharq Al-Awsat*, 14 September 2001.

'Major Jihadi Cleric and Author of Al-Qaeda's Sharia Guide to Jihad Sayyed Imam vs. Al-Qaeda (2), MEMRI, 25 January 2008, http://www.memri.org/bin/articles.cgi?Page=archives&Area=sd&ID=SP182608 [accessed 25 January 2008].

'Mecca's Imam Sides with Al-Azhar Despite Al-Qaradawi's Objections', *Al-Musawwar*, 7 December 2001.

'Megawati Heads to US Amid Controversy', *BBC News*, 17 September 2001, at http://news.bbc.co.uk/1/hi/world/asia-pacific/1548607.stm [accessed 6 August 2006].

'Mekkah Imam Calls for Wisdom in Fight Against Terrorism', *Middle East Newsfile*, 29 September 2001.

'Mexico Calls for Peacful Solution to Iraq Crisis', *Agence France Presse*, 7 March 2003.

'Mideast News Summary', *Xinhua News Agency*, 19 September 2001.

'More Fallout from Mosque Shooting', *CBS News*, 17 November 2004, at http://www.cbsnews.com/stories/2004/11/15/iraq/main655898.shtml [accessed 2 December 2005].

'Mubarak Warns of "100 Bin Ladens"', *CNN*, 1 April 2003.

'Muslim Cleric Faults Taliban's "Backward" Mentality', *Radio Monte Carlo*, 15 November 2001 [title by *Foreign Broadcast Information Service*].

'Muslim Clerics Disagree About the Judgement of Islamic law Concerning Suicide Operations', *Al-Sharq Al-Awsat*, 8 May 2001.

'Muslim Clerics Repeat: US Attacks Are UnIslamic', *Agence France Press*, 14 September 2001.

'Muslims Disagree on When Jihad OK', *Seattle Times*, 17 September 2001, p. A8.

'Nasrallah: Israeli Withdrawal From Gaza Another Victory for the Logic of the Weapon Of the Resistance', *Al-Safir*, 16 August 2005.

'Nasrallah: We Criticise and Disapprove of the Hizballah in Turkey', *Istanbul Hurriyet*, 30 May 2000, p. 4.

'National Assembly and Liberal Group Condemn Attacks', *Le Soleil (Dakar)*, 13 September 2001.

'Newshour with Jim Lehrer: War or Diplomacy', *PBS Television*, 5 March 2003, transcript at http://www.pbs.org/newshour/bb/middle_east/jan-june03/diplomacy_3–5.html [accessed 7 September 2005].

'Nigeria; Terror Attacks: The World Needs to Exercise Restraint— Sheikh Orire', *Africa News*, 23 September 2001.

'Osama bin Laden to the Iraqi People', *MEMRI: Special Dispatch Series*, no. 837, 27 December 2004, at http://www.memri.org/bin/articles.cgi?Page=archives&Area=sd&ID=SP83704 [accessed 6 March 2006].

'Pakistani Leaders Condemn Terrorism and Criticise US Policies', *Nawa-i-Waqt*, 12 September 2001, p. 8.

'Palestinian Intellectuals Condemn Terror Attack on US Targets', *Al-Quds*, 17 September 2001 [original title of publication not supplied by *Foreign Broadcast Information Service*].

'Palestinians React to US attacks with Condemnation—and Celebrations', *Agence France Presse*, 11 September 2001.

'Participants in Islamic-Christian Forum Reject Clash of Civilisations', *Middle East News Agency*, 20 December 2001.

'Prisoners "Killed" at US Base', *BBC News*, 6 March 2003, at http://news.bbc.co.uk/1/hi/world/south_asia/2825575.stm [accessed 11 February 2006].

'Profile: Margaret Hassan', *BBC News*, 20 October 2004.

'Protest Against Bangladesh Bombs', *BBC News*, 9 December 2005, at http://news.bbc.co.uk/1/hi/world/south_asia/4512406.stm [accessed 9 December 2005].

'Radical Chechens Deny Links With Bin Laden, Admit Contacts With Taliban', *Agence France Presse*, 27 September 2001.

'Reactions to Blix Report', *BBC News*, 7 March 2003, at http://news.bbc.co.uk/1/hi/world/middle_east/2830447.stm [accessed 2 July 2005].

'Reactions to Terrorist Outrages in America', *Saudi Arabia Information Source*, 15 September 2001, at http://www.saudinf.com/main/x008.htm [accessed 5 March 2005].

'Red Cross Cites "Inhumane" Treatment at Guantanamo', *Washington Post*, 1 December 2004, p. A10.

'Red Cross Hits Out at Iraq Abuses', *BBC News*, 19 November 2004, at http://news.bbc.co.uk/1/hi/world/middle_east/4027163.stm [accessed 19 November 2004].

'Rumsfeld Questioned in US Senate About bin Laden', *Agence France Presse*, 1 August 2002.

'Saudi Arabia's Grand Mufti Says Suicide Bombing UnIslamic', *Jedda Arab News*, 21 April 2002.

'Saudi Imam Al-Hawashi Opposes Women's Driving; Criticises Jihadis', *BBC Monitoring International Reports*, 4 July 2006.

'Sayyed Hasan Nasrallah's Autobiography', *Ya Lesarat Ol-Hosayn*, 10 August 2006.

'Spain Victor in His Own Words', *BBC News*, 15 March 2004, at http://news.bbc.co.uk/1/hi/world/europe/3514168.stm [accessed 6 June 2005].

'Straw Facing War Advice Critics', *BBC News*, 24 March 2005, at http://news.bbc.co.uk/1/hi/uk_politics/4377469.stm [accessed 25 March 2005].

'Sudan: Anti-US Supporters Express Support for Bin Laden, Afghanistan, Intifada', *Agence France Presse*, 4 October 2001 [original title of publication not supplied by *Foreign Broadcast Information Service*].

'Taliban: No Jihad Unless US Attacks', *Guardian*, 18 September 2001.

'Tantawi Says Jihad Meant for Self-Defence', *Arabic News*, 23 August 2005, at http://www.arabicnews.com/ansub/Daily/Day/050823/2005082324.html [accessed 12 June 2006].

'The Case Against War on Iraq', *Boston Globe*, 19 August 2002, p. A11.

'The New Egyptian Mufti— Dr. Sheikh Ali Gum'a: Opinions About Jihad, Supporting Suicide Bombings, and Forbidding Muslims in the US Military From Fighting Other Muslims', *MEMRI: Special Dispatch Series*, no. 580, 1 October 2003, at http://memri.org/bin/articles.cgi?Page=archives&Area=sd&ID=SP58003 [accessed 10 October 2003].

'The War That Started: Why and Whereto?', *Al-Ray*, 8 October 2001.

'Third Arab Human Development Report Called "Courageous and Impartial"', *United Nations Development Programme News*, 5 April 2005, at http://www.undp. org/dpa/pressrelease/releases/2005/april/pr5apr05.html [accessed 7 June 2005].

'Threat Video in Spain Flat Rubble', *BBC News*, 9 April 2004, at http://news.bbc.co.uk/ 1/hi/world/europe/3613775.stm [accessed 10 April 2004].

'To Paris, US Looks Like a "Hyperpower"', *International Herald Tribune*, 5 February 1999.

'Too Late for the US to Invoke International Law, Says PM', *Malaysia General News*, 24 March 2003.

'Triple Suicide at Guantanamo Camp', *BBC News*, 11 June 2006, http://news.bbc.co. uk/1/hi/world/americas/5068228.stm [accessed 11 June 2006].

'Turkey: Religious Affairs Director Rejects Link Between Islam, Terrorism', *Ankara Anatolia*, 30 November 2001 [original title of publication not supplied by *Foreign Broadcast Information Service*].

'Tutu Calls for Guantanamo Closure', *BBC News*, 17 February 2006, at http://news. bbc.co.uk/1/hi/world/americas/4723512.stm [accessed 17 February 2006].

'UK Minister Condemns Guantanamo', *BBC News*, 13 September 2006, at http://news. bbc.co.uk/1/hi/uk_politics/5340104.stm [accessed 13 September 2006].

Untitled, *Islamic Republic News Agency*, 16 September 2001, at http://www.irna.com/ en/hphoto/010916000000.ehp.shtml [accessed 5 March 2005].

'Urgent: France Not to Allow Passing of Resolution Authorising War', *Xinhua General News Service*, 7 March 2003.

'US strikes raze Fallujah Hospital', *BBC News*, 6 November 2004, at http://news.bbc. co.uk/1/hi/world/middle_east/3988433.stm [accessed 3 September 2005].

'US Used White Phosphorous in Iraq', *BBC News*, 16 November 2005, at http://news. bbc.co.uk/1/hi/world/middle_east/4440664.stm [accessed 16 November 2005].

'War Not Justified: Chirac, Schroeder', *The Hindu*, 19 March 2003.

'War Would Be Illegal', *Guardian*, 7 March 2003.

'Washington Post Poll: Saddam Hussein and the Sept. 11th Attacks', 7–11 August 2003, at http://www.washingtonpost.com/wp-srv/politics/polls/vault/stories/ data082303.htm [accessed 12 December 2004].

'White House Touts International Support for Military Campaign', *CNN*, 21 March 2003, http://edition.cnn.com/2003/ALLPOLITICS/03/20/sprj.irq.bush [accessed 16 February 2005].

'Xinhua Reports Taliban Condemn the Attacks in US', *Xinhua News Agency*, 11 September 2001 [original title of publication not supplied by *Foreign Broadcast Information Service*].

'Yemeni Parliament Speaker: NY, DC Operations Express Anger, Frustration', *Al-Quds Al-Arabi*, 5 October 2001.

Abou El-Magd, Nadia, 'The Politics of Fatwa', *Al-Ahram*, no. 532, 3–9 May 2001.

Abdelhadi, Magdi, 'Controversial Preacher with "Star Status"', *BBC News*, 7 July 2004, at http://news.bbc.co.uk/1/hi/uk/3874893.stm [accessed 12 May 2006].

Abu-Sha'ban, Hatim, 'Why Were Arabs and Muslims Accused of Terrorism?', *Al-Quds*, 18 September 2001.

Ackerman, Spencer, 'Is Al-Jazeera the Next PBS?', *The New Republic*, 1 May 2006.

Adawi, Hasan, 'Terrorism is Alien to Islam: Mufti', *Jedda Arab News*, 22 February 2002.

Anderson, David Earle, 'Not a Just or Moral War: The Churches' Pre-Emptive Response to Bush's Iraq Plans', *Sojourners Magazine*, January–February 2003.

Atwan, Abdelbari, 'Imam Bush's Fatwas', *Al-Quds Al-Arabi*, 5 December 2001.

Baker, Peter, and Josh White, 'Bush Calls Iraq War Moral Equivalent of Allies' WWII Fight Against the Axis', *Washington Post*, 31 August 2005, p. A7.

Bachorz, Boris, 'AFP Examines Support for Islamic Fundamentalism, Bin Laden in Britain', *Agence France Presse*, 17 September 2001 [original title of publication not supplied by *Foreign Broadcast Information Service*].

Barber, Ben, 'Arabs Exult, but Leaders Denounce Killing', *Washington Times*, 12 September 2001.

Barnard, Anne, 'Returning Falluhjans Will Face Clampdown', *Boston Globe*, 5 December 2004.

Barry, Alpha, 'Burkina Faso: Reactions of Muslim Community to US Attacks', *Radio France Internationale*, 15 September 2001.

Beeston, Richard and Catherine Philp, 'Bin Laden's Ruthless Rival Spreads Tentacles of Jihad Across Region', *Times*, 18 November 2005.

Bennet Jones, Owen, 'Iraqi Deaths Survey Was "Robust"', *BBC News*, 26 March 2007, at http://news.bbc.co.uk/1/hi/uk_politics/6495753.stm [accessed 26 March 2007].

Bergen, Pater and Paul Cruickshank, 'The Unravelling: The Jihadist Revolt Against bin Laden', *The New Republic*, 11 June 2008.

Bhatti, Izhar and Irshad Bhatti, 'After Afghanistan It Will Be Pakistan's Turn', *Al-Akhbar (Islamabad)*, 5 October 2001.

Blanford, Nicholas, 'Iraq Kidnappings Hard to Stop', *Christian Science Monitor*, 9 June 2004.

de Borchgrave, Arnaud, 'Osama bin Laden- "Null and Void"', *United Press International*, 14 June 2001.

Borger, Julian, 'Bush Aiming at Wrong Target, US Critics Fear', *Guardian*, 14 October 2002.

Brandon, James, 'Black Watch Soldier Killed by Roadside Bomb in Basra', *Scotsman*, 13 August 2004.

Broadway, Bill, 'Evangelicals' Voices Speak Softly About Iraq', *Washington Post*, 25 January 2003, p. B9.

Brown, DeNeen, 'Chretien Tells Canadians to Respect US Decision; Leader Tries to Curb Anti-American Sentiment', *Washington Post*, 21 March 2003, p. A29.

Buncombe, Andrew, 'US Admits It Used Napalm Bombs in Iraq', *Independent*, 10 August 2003.

Bunting, Madeleine, 'Friendly Fire: Madeleine Bunting Meets Sheikh Yusuf al-Qaradawi in Qatar', *Guardian*, 29 October 2005.

Burke, James and Ed Vulliamy, 'War Clouds Gather as Hawks Lay Their Plans', *Observer*, 14 July 2002.

Carter, Jimmy, 'Just War – or Just a War?', *New York Times*, 9 March 2003.

Chandrasekaran, Rajiv, 'Police Recruits Targeted: Bomb Kills Scores Near Headquarters', *Washington Post*, 15 September 2004, p. A1.

Charter, David, Ruth Gledhill and Greg Hurst, 'Blair Condones Amin-style Tactics Against Terrorism, Says Archbishop', *Times*, 24 February 2006, p. 3.

Christian, Louise, 'Guantanamo Bay: A Global Experiment in Inhumanity', *Guardian*, 10 January 2004.

Cierco, Juan, Interview with Sheikh Ahmad Yasin, *ABC News* (Spain), 18 September 2001.

Curtis, Polly, 'Oxford Hands Anti-War Petition to No. 10', *Guardian (Education)*, 6 March 2003.

Davis, Matthew, 'Counting the Civilian Cost in Iraq', *BBC News*, 22 September 2004, at http://news.bbc.co.uk/1/hi/world/middle_east/3672298.stm [accessed 9 October 2004].

Diehl, Jackson, 'Israel Launches Satellite into Surveillance Orbit', *Washington Post*, 4 April 1990, p. A35.

Dyer, Clare, 'Law Lord Castigates US Justice', *Guardian*, 26 November 2003.

Dyer, Gwynne, 'Odds Are Against Clean War with Iraq', *Niagara Falls Review*, 13 November 2002, p. A4.

Elias, Adel S., 'Bin Laden Is a Legend', *Der Spiegel*, 15 October 2001.

Fishback, Ian, 'A Matter of Honour', *Washington Post*, 28 September 2005, p. A21.

Ford, Peter, 'Surveys Pointing to High Civilian Death Toll in Iraq', *Christian Science Monitor*, 22 May 2003.

Gardner, Frank, 'Restoring Faith in Islam', *BBC News*, 26 December 2001, at http://news.bbc.co.uk/1/hi/world/middle_east/1721907.stm [accessed 6 June 2006].

Ghawi, Razzuq al-, 'Khaled Mish'al: Israel Has Cornered the Palestinians, Halting Martyrdom Operations Depends on Field Conditions', *Al-Sharq Al-Awsat*, 22 September 2002.

Glaberson, William and Margot Williams, 'Officials Report Suicide of Guantanamo Detainee', *New York Times*, 2 June 2009.

Gould, Peter, 'War With Iraq "Could Be Illegal"', *BBC News*, 10 March 2003, at http://news.bbc.co.uk/1/hi/uk/2826331.stm [accessed 11 March 2003].

Graff, James, 'France Is not a Pacifist Country', *Time Magazine*, vol. 161, no. 8, 24 February 2003.

Gregg, Donald P., 'Fight Fire with Compassion', *New York Times*, 10 June 2004.

Grier, Peter, 'The Rising Economic Cost of the Iraq War', *Christian Science Monitor*, 19 May 2005.

Hamden, Toby, 'US Attack Kills 40 at Iraqi Wedding Party', *Telegraph*, 20 May 2004.

Harel, Amos, 'Settlements Grow on Arab Land Despite Promises Made to US', *Haaretz*, 24 October 2006.

Harlow, John, 'Pray Silence for bin Laden the Wedding Poet', *Sunday Times*, 21 September 2008.

Hunsinger, George, 'Iraq: Don't Go There', *Christian Century*, 14 August 2002, no. 17, vol. 119.

Ibrahim, Anwar, 'Who Hijacked Islam? Repressive Muslim Regimes Are Partly to Blame for Bin Laden's Rise', *Time* (Asia Edition), 15 October 2001.

Imam, Imam Mohammad, 'Interview with Muslim Scholar Sheikh Dr. Yusuf Al-Qaradawi', *Al-Sharq Al-Awsat*, 12 December 2001.

——, 'Islamic Jurisprudence Assembly Says Terrorist Acts Are Impermissible crimes', *Al-Sharq Al-Awsat*, 17 December 2003.

Jain, Sandhya, 'Post 9/11: Clash of Civilisations', *The Pioneer (Delhi)*, 10 September 2002.

Katchadourian, Raffi, 'Pursuing Terrorists in the Desert: The US Military's $500 Million Gamble to Prevent the Next Afghanistan', *Village Voice*, 31 January 2006.

Kershaw, Ian, 'Blast From the Past', *Guardian*, 19 February 2003.

Khalaf, Roula, 'Saudi Rulers Seek to Counter Calls for Jihad', *Financial Times*, 26 October 2001, p. 2.

Khalil, Mohammad, 'Egypt's Mufti Urges Taliban to Opt for Lesser of Two Evils and Hand Over UBL', *Al-Sharq Al-Awsat*, 9 October 2001.

Kissinger, Henry, 'Beyond Baghdad: After Regime Change the US Must Help Craft a New International Order', *New York Post*, 11 August 2002.

Knaul, Susanne, 'If a Civil War Should Break Out Here, Every Home Will Burn', *Die Presse*, 16 November 2001.

Kuttner, Robert, 'Will Bush Wriggle Out of This One?', *Boston Globe*, 10 September 2005.

Kyriakou, Niko, 'Iraqi Living Conditions Tragic—Report', *Inter Press Service News Agency*, 13 May 2005.

Lamb, Christina, 'The Invisible Man', *Sunday Times Magazine*, 18 March 2007, p. 54.

Lichfield, John, 'On the Brink of War', *Independent*, 8 March 2003, p. 2.

Lobe, Jim, 'Bush Terror War Suffers Body Blow in Spain', *Inter Press Service News Agency*, 15 March 2004.

Luban, David J., 'Selling Indulgences: The Unmistakeable Parallel Between Lynne Stewart and the President's Torture Lawyers', *Slate*, 14 February 2005, www.slate.com/id/2113447 [accessed 14 February 2005].

McCarthy, Rory, 'Clerics Called to Council of Holy War', *Guardian*, 19 September 2001.

McDermott, Jim and Richard Rapport, 'Investigate Alleged Violations of Law in Fallujah Attack', *Seattle Post-Intelligencer*, 11 January 2005, p. B7.

Ma'ayeh, Suha, 'Jordanian Muslim, Christian Clerics Mourn Victims of US Terrorist Attacks', *Jordan Times*, 18 September 2001.

Mackay, Neil, 'US Forces' Use of Depleted Uranium Weapons Is "Illegal"', *Sunday Herald*, 30 March 2003.

Makiya, Kanan and Hassan Mneimneh, 'Manual for a "Raid"', *The New York Review of Books*, 49:1, 17 January 2002.

Mashharawi, Ala al-, 'PA Intelligence Chief on Contacts With US Following Terrorist Attacks', *Al-Quds*, 17 September 2001.

Matthews, Athalie, 'US Begins Battle for Baghdad', *Guardian*, 2 April 2003.

Mayer, Jane, 'The Memo: How an Internal Effort to Ban the Abuse and Torture of Detainees Was Thwarted', *The New Yorker*, 27 February 2006, pp. 32–41.

Miklaszewski, Jim, 'Marine Cleared in Mosque Shootings Probe', *NBC News*, 4 May 2005, http://www.msnbc.msn.com/id/7738733/Marine [accessed 11 September 2005].

Miller, Greg, 'Cheney Is Adamant on Iraq "Evidence"', *Los Angeles Times*, 23 January 2003, p. A1.

Mirghani, Uthman, 'Jihad for Who?', *Al-Sharq Al-Awsat*, 24 October 2001.

Monaghan, Elaine, 'Man Who Filmed Shooting Speaks Out', *Times*, 23 November 2004.

Moynihan, Tim, 'Market Deaths Set to Dash Hopes for "Clean" War', *Press Association*, 26 March 2003.

Nafik, Mohammad, 'Mainstream Islamic Groups to Cooperate in Countering Radicals', *Jakarta Post*, 9 November 2001.

Nasrawi, Salah, 'Al Qaeda Recruiting Made Web of Militants', *Associated Press*, 15 March 2004.

Nordland, Rod, 'Spate of Attacks Tests Iraqi City and US Pullout', *New York Times*, 24 June 2009, p. A1.

Norton-Taylor, Richard, 'Law Unto Themselves', *Guardian*, 14 March 2003.

——and Ian Black, 'US Fury at European Peace Plan', *Guardian*, 10 February 2003.

O'Harrow Jr., Robert, 'Waxman Raises New Questions on Cheney', *Washington Post*, 14 June 2004, p. A4.

Paterson, Graham, 'Alan Greenspan Claims Iraq War Was Really For Oil', *The Sunday Times*, 16 September 2007.

Penketh, Anne, 'Blix: Iraq War Was Illegal', *Independent*, 5 March 2004.

Peters, Ralph, 'And Now, Fallujah', *New York Post*, 4 November 2004.

Petre, Zoe, 'Whom Are We Fighting Against?', *Ziua*, 21 September 2001.

Pipes, Daniel, 'What Is *Jihad*?', *New York Post*, 31 December 2002.

Priest, Dana and Glenn Kessler, 'Iraq, 9/11, Still Linked by Cheney', *Washington Post*, 29 September 2003.

Priest, Dana and Mike Allen, 'Report Discounts Iraqi Arms Threat, *Washington Post*, 6 October 2004, p. A1.

Qader-Saadi, Abdul, 'Fallujah Death Toll for Week More than 600', *Associated Press*, 11 April 2004, at http://www.usatoday.com/news/world/iraq/2004-04-11-fallujah-casualties_x.htm [accessed 1 February 2006].

Rayment, Sean, 'US Tactics Condemned by British Officers', *Telegraph*, 11 April 2004.

Rees-Mogg, William, 'Why Bin Laden Votes Bush', *Times*, 1 November 2004.

Roug, Louis, 'Targeted Killings Surge in Baghdad', *Los Angeles Times*, 7 May 2006, p. A1.

Rouleau, Eric, 'Terrorism and Islamism: Politics in the Name of the Prophet', *Le Monde Diplomatique*, 1 November 2001.

Sachs, Jeffrey, 'Iraq's Civilian Dead Get No Hearing in the United States', *Daily Star*, 2 December 2004, at http://www.dailystar.com.lb/article.asp?edition_id=10&categ_id=5&article_id=10594 [accessed 7 January 2005].

Said, Sana al-, 'Interview with Pope Shinudah III', *Al-Musawwar*, 5 October 2001.

Sanger, David E., 'Beating Them to Prewar', *New York Times*, 27 September 2002.

Satha-Anand, Chaiwat, 'Understanding Terrorism Is Vital', *Bangkok Post*, 18 September 2001.

Sayyid Ahmad, Rif'at, 'Is Usama Bin Laden the Culprit? Has World War III Started?', *Al-Safir*, 14 September 2001.

Scarborough, Rowan, 'Gitmo Called Death Camp', *Washington Times*, 16 June 2005.

Schmitt, Eric, 'Rumsfeld Says US Has "Bulletproof" Evidence of Iraq's Links to Al Qaeda', *New York Times*, 28 September 2002.

——, 'Pentagon Keeping Some Targets Off-Limits', *International Herald Tribune*, 24 March 2003, p. 1.

Scowcroft, Brent, 'Don't Attack Saddam: It Would Undermine Our Antiterror Efforts', *Wall Street Journal*, 15 August 2002, p. B6.

Shadid, Anthony, 'Maverick Cleric Is a Hit on Arab TV', *Washington Post*, 14 February 2003.

Sid-Ahmed, Mohamed, 'Bush's "Anticipatory" War', *Al-Ahram*, no. 624, 6–12 February 2003.

Smith, Michael, 'Baghdad Bomb Kills 55', *Telegraph*, 29 March 2003.

Smucker, Philip, 'How Bin Laden Got Away', *Christian Science Monitor*, 4 March 2002.

Solomou, George, 'Why I'll Refuse to Fight in this Immoral War', *Independent*, 21 January 2005.

Stone, Peter H., 'Iraq II: Al-Qaeda Links With Baghdad Were Exaggerated', *National Journal*, 8 August 2003.

Strode, Tom, 'Attack on Iraq Justified, Land, Others Tell Bush', *Baptist Press News*, 3 October 2002.

Suellentrop, Chris, 'Pentagon Official Douglas Feith and His Possible Connection to Major Tactical Errors in Iraq', *National Public Radio*, 24 May 2004, aired 4pm.

Usigbe, Leon, 'Terror Attacks: The World Needs to Exercise Restraint-Sheikh Orire', *Africa News*, 23 September 2001.

Uwaydah, Bakr, 'We Want to Know', *Al-Sharq al-Awsat*, 4 October 2001.

Vick, Karl, 'Fallujah Strikes Herald Possible Attacks', *Washington Post*, 16 October 2004, p. A2.

Vick, Karl and Bassam Sebti, 'Violence Spreads in Iraq, Car Bomb Kills 17 in Baghdad', *Washington Post*, 12 November 2004, p. A21.

Vinograd, Cassandra, 'Former US President Carter Blasts Guantanamo Bay Detention Camp', *Associated Press*, 30 July 2005.

Walker, Andrew, 'US "Playing with Fire", Warns Yamani', *BBC News*, 14 March 2003, at http://news.bbc.co.uk/1/hi/business/2851723.stm [accessed 12 May 2006].

Wallace, Richard, 'Countdown to Conflict', *Daily Mirror*, 8 March 2003.

Webster, Philip and Michael Evans, 'Blair on the Rack Over Iraq Terror Warning', *Times*, 12 September 2003.

Widhalm, Shelley, 'Understand Jihad: Author Seeks to Arm West with Information', *Washington Times*, 6 February 2008, p. A2.

Windfuhr, Volkhard and Bernhard Zand, 'God Has Disappeared', *Der Spiegel*, 26 September 2005.

Wright, Lawrence, 'The Rebellion Within', *New Yorker*, 2 June 2008, at http://www.newyorker.com/reporting/2008/06/02/080602fa_fact_wright?currentPage=all [accessed 8 June 2008].

Wolk, Martin, 'Cost of Iraq War Could Surpass $1 Trillion', *MSNBC*, 17 March 2006, at http://www.msnbc.msn.com/id/11880954/[accessed 17 March 2006].

Woods, Audrey, 'Tape Threatens More Attacks on US', *Associated Press*, 8 October 2002.

Xhuvani, R., 'Assembly of Albania Passes Resolution', *ATA (Tirana)*, 27 September 2001 [original title of publication not supplied by *Foreign Broadcast Information Service*].

Xiaofeng, Jiang, 'Iran Shows Human Touch as Hopes of Thawing Ties With US Remain Dim', *Xinhua News Agency*, 19 September 2001.

Younge, Gary, 'No More Mr. Nice Guy', *Guardian*, 19 September 2002.

Yousafsai, Rahimullah, 'Terror Suspect: An Interview with Osama bin Laden', *ABC News*, 22 December 1998, at http://www.jihadunspun.com/BinLadensNetwork/interviews/abc01-1998.html [accessed 6 March 2006].

Zwick, Mark and Louise Zwick, 'Pope Jean Paul II Calls War a Defeat for Humanity: Neoconservative Iraq Just War Theories Rejected', *Houston Catholic Worker*, vol. 23, no. 4, July–August 2003.

3. Statements

A. Bush Administration Statements

Berenson, Bradford, Interview on 'Frontline' (PBS), 14 July 2005, at http://www.pbs.org/wgbh/pages/frontline/torture/interviews/berenson.html [accessed 30 March 2006].

Brooks, Vince, 'Centcom Operation Iraqi Freedom Briefing', 1 April 2003, at http://www.whitehouse.gov/news/releases/2003/04/20030401-6.html [accessed 1 February 2006].

Bush, George W., 'Remarks by the President Upon Arrival', 16 September 2001, at http://www.whitehouse.gov/news/releases/2001/09/20010916-2.html [accessed 12 October 2004].

——, 'Address to a Joint Session of Congress and the American People', 20 September 2001, at http://www.whitehouse.gov/news/releases/2001/09/20010920-8.html [accessed 12 October 2004].

Bush, George W., 'President Discusses War on Terrorism', 8 November 2001, at http://www.whitehouse.gov/news/releases/2001/11/20011108-13.html [accessed 12 October 2004].

——, 'President Bush Speaks to the United Nations', 10 November 2001, at http://www.whitehouse.gov/news/releases/2001/11/20011110-3.html [accessed 12 October 2004].

——, 'President Signs Defense Appropriations Bill at the Pentagon', 10 January 2002, http://www.defenselink.mil/speeches/2002/s20020111-secdef.html [accessed 12 October 2004].

——, 'State of the Union Address', 29 January 2002, at http://www.whitehouse.gov/news/releases/2002/01/20020129-11.html [accessed 12 October 2004].

——, 'Remarks by the President to the Travel Pool', 20 March 2002, at http://www.whitehouse.gov/news/releases/2002/03/20020320-17.html [accessed 13 October 2004].

——, 'President to Send Secretary Powell to the Middle East', 4 April 2002, at http://www.whitehouse.gov/news/releases/2002/04/20020404-1.html [accessed 12 October 2004].

——, 'President Delivers Graduation Speech at West Point', 1 June 2002, at http://www.whitehouse.gov/news/releases/2002/06/20020601-3.html [accessed 12 October 2004].

——, 'President Bush Addresses the Nation', 6 June 2002, at http://www.whitehouse.gov/news/releases/2002/06/20020606-8.html [accessed 12 October 2004].

——, 'The President's Agenda for Long-term Growth and Prosperity', 15 July 2002, at http://www.whitehouse.gov/news/releases/2002/07/20020715.html [accessed 12 October 2004].

——, 'President's Remarks to the Nation', 11 September 2002, at http://www.whitehouse.gov/news/releases/2002/09/20020911-3.html [accessed 12 October 2004].

——, 'President's Remarks at the United Nations General Assembly', 12 September 2002, at http://www.whitehouse.gov/news/releases/2002/09/20020912-1.html [accessed 12 October 2004].

——, 'President Bush Outlines Iraqi Threat', 7 October 2002, at http://www.whitehouse.gov/news/releases/2002/10/20021007-8.html [accessed 12 October 2004].

——, 'President Delivers State of the Union Address', 28 January 2003, at http://www.whitehouse.gov/news/releases/2003/01/20030128-19.html [accessed 12 October 2004].

——, 'President Discusses the Future of Iraq', 26 February 2003, at http://www.whitehouse.gov/news/releases/2003/02/20030226-11.html [accessed 12 October 2004].

——, 'President Bush Discusses Iraq in National Press Conference', 6 March 2003, at http://www.whitehouse.gov/news/releases/2003/03/20030306-8.html [accessed 12 October 2004].

——, 'President Says Saddam Hussein Must Leave Iraq Within 48 Hours', 17 March 2003, at http://www.whitehouse.gov/news/releases/2003/03/20030317-7.html [accessed 12 October 2004].

——, 'President Bush Addresses the Nation', 19 March 2003, at http://www.whitehouse.gov/news/releases/2003/03/20030319-17.html [accessed 12 October 2004].

——, 'President Discusses Operation Iraqi Freedom at Camp Lejeune', 3 April 2003, at http://www.whitehouse.gov/news/releases/2003/04/20030403-3.html [accessed 12 October 2004].

——, 'Operation Iraqi Freedom: President's Radio Address', 5 April 2003, at http://www.whitehouse.gov/news/releases/2003/04/20030405.html [accessed 12 October 2004].

——, 'President Bush Announces Major Combat Operations in Iraq Have Ended', 1 May 2003, at http://www.whitehouse.gov/news/releases/2003/05/20030501–15.html [accessed 12 October 2004].

——, 'President Delivers Remarks on the National Day of Prayer', May 2003, at http://www.whitehouse.gov/news/releases/2003/05/20030501-4.html [accessed 12 October 2004].

——, 'President Bush Honours the Brave and Fallen Defenders of Freedom', 26 May 2003, at http://www.whitehouse.gov/news/releases/2003/05/20030526-1.html [accessed 12 October 2004].

——, 'President Addresses the Nation', 7 September 2003, at http://www.whitehouse.gov/news/releases/2003/09/20030907-1.html [accessed 12 October 2004].

——, 'President Bush Discusses Freedom in Iraq and the Middle East', 6 November 2003, at http://www.whitehouse.gov/news/releases/2003/11/20031106-2.html [accessed 12 October 2004].

——, 'President Bush Discusses Iraq Policy at Whitehall Palace in London', 19 November 2003, at http://www.whitehouse.gov/news/releases/2003/11/20031119-1.html [accessed 12 October 2004].

——, Interview on Meet the Press with Tim Russert (NBC), 7 February 2004, at http://www.msnbc.msn.com/id/4179618/ [accessed 16 May 2005].

——, 'Remarks by the President at Florida Rally', 20 March 2004, at http://www.whitehouse.gov/news/releases/2004/03/20040320-4.html [accessed 12 October 2004].

——, 'President Addresses the Nation in Prime Time Press Conference', 13 April 2004, at http://www.whitehouse.gov/news/releases/2004/04/20040413-20.html [accessed 12 October 2004].

——, 'President Outlines Steps to Help Iraq Achieve Democracy and Freedom', 24 May 2004, at http://www.whitehouse.gov/news/releases/2004/05/20040524-10.html [accessed 12 October 2004].

——, 'President's Remarks in Springfield, Missouri', 30 July 2004, at http://www.whitehouse.gov/news/releases/2004/07/20040730-3.html [accessed 12 October 2004].

——, 'President's Remarks at the Republican National Convention', 2 September 2004, at http://www.whitehouse.gov/news/releases/2004/09/20040902-2.html [accessed 12 October 2004].

——, 'President Bush Discusses Iraq Report', 7 October 2004, at http://www.whitehouse.gov/news/releases/2004/10/20041007-6.html [accessed 6 January 2006].

Bush, George W., 'President Commemorates 60th Anniversary of V-J Day', 30 August 2005, at http://www.whitehouse.gov/news/releases/2005/08/20050830-1. html [accessed 6 January 2006].

Cheney, Richard B., 'The Vice President Receives the International Republican Institute's 2001 Freedom Award', 23 October 2001, at http://www.whitehouse.gov/vice-president/news-speeches/speeches/vp20011023.html [accessed 12 October 2004].

——, 'Vice President Speaks at VFW 103rd National Convention', 26 August 2002, at http://www.whitehouse.gov/news/releases/2002/08/20020826.html [accessed 12 October 2004].

——, 'In Cheney's Words: The Administration's Case for Removing Saddam Hussein', *New York Times*, 27 August 2002.

——, 'Vice President's Remarks at 30th Political Action Conference', 30 January 2003, at http://www.whitehouse.gov/news/releases/2003/01/20030130-16.html [accessed 12 October 2004].

——, Interview on Meet the Press with Tim Russert (NBC), 14 September 2003, at http://msnbc.msn.com/id/3080244/default.htm [accessed 2 December 2004].

——, 'Remarks by the Vice President to the Heritage Foundation', 10 October 2003, at http://www.whitehouse.gov/news/releases/2003/10/20031010-1.html [accessed 12 October 2004].

——, 'Remarks by the Vice President at the Ronald Reagan Presidential Library and Museum', 17 March 2004, at http://www.whitehouse.gov/news/releases/2004/03/20040317-3.html [accessed 12 October 2004].

——, 'Vice President's Remarks at a Rally for the Troops', 27 July 2004, at http://63.161.169.137/news/releases/2004/07/20040727-3.html [accessed 12 October 2004].

——, 'Vice President's Remarks at a Victory 2004 Rally in Ft. Myers, Florida', 14 October 2004, at http://www.whitehouse.gov/news/releases/2004/10/20041014-11.html [accessed 29 January 2005].

Feith, Douglas, 'Address to American Israeli Public Affairs Committee', 21 April 2002, at http://www.defenselink.mil/policy/sections/public_statements/speeches/archive/former_usdp/feith/2002/april_21_02.html [accessed 12 October 2004].

——, 'Iraq: One Year Later', 2 May 2004, at http://www.defenselink.mil/transcripts/transcript.aspx?transcriptid=2958 [accessed 12 October 2004].

Gonzales, Alberto R., 'Statement of Alberto R. Gonzales before the Committee on the Judiciary United States Senate', 6 January 2005, at http://judiciary.senate.gov/testimony.cfm?id=1345&wit_id=3936 [accessed 12 May 2006].

Powell, Colin L., 'US Secretary of State Colin Powell's Statement on Iraq's Weapons Declaration', 20 December 2002, reprinted in *The Guardian*, at http://www.guardian.co.uk/Iraq/Story/0,,863575,00.html [accessed 21 October 2004].

——, 'Remarks to the United Nations Security Council', 5 February 2003, at http://www.state.gov/secretary/rm/2003/17300.htm [accessed 12 October 2004].

——, 'Remarks at the American Israel Public Affairs Committee's Annual Policy Conference', 31 March 2003, at http://www.state.gov/secretary/former/powell/remarks/2003/19174.htm [accessed 12 October 2004].

Rice, Condoleezza, 'Dr. Condoleezza Rice Discusses the President's National Security Strategy', 1 October 2002, at http://www.whitehouse.gov/news/releases/2002/10/20021001-6.html [accessed 12 October 2004].

——, 'To A Free World', *New York Post*, 7 October 2002.

——, 'Remarks by National Security Adviser Rice at the Karamah Iftaar', 4 December 2002, at http://www.whitehouse.gov/news/releases/2002/12/20021204-17.html [accessed 12 October 2004].

——, 'Press Briefing by Dr. Condoleezza Rice', 24 February 2003, at http://www.whitehouse.gov/news/releases/2003/02/20030224-14.html [accessed 12 October 2004].

——, 'Dr. Condoleezza Rice Interviewed by Jim Lehrer', 30 July 2003, at http://www.whitehouse.gov/news/releases/2003/07/20030731-10.html [accessed 12 October 2004].

——, 'National Security Advisor Condoleezza Rice Remarks to Veterans of Foreign Wars', 25 August 2003, at http://www.whitehouse.gov/news/releases/2003/08/20030825-1.html [accessed 12 October 2004].

——, 'Dr. Condoleezza Rice Discusses Iraq in Chicago', 8 October 2003, at http://www.whitehouse.gov/news/releases/2003/10/20031008-4.html [accessed 12 October 2004].

——, 'Transformational Diplomacy: Question-and-Answer Session', 18 January 2006, at http://www.state.gov/secretary/rm/2006/59375.htm [accessed 20 January 2006].

Rumsfeld, Donald H., 'Secretary Rumsfeld Roundtable with Radio Media', 15 January 2002, at http://www.defenselink.mil/transcripts/2002/t01152002_t0115sdr.html [accessed 13 October 2004].

——, 'Remarks to FORTUNE Global Forum', 11 November 2002, at http://www.defenselink.mil/releases/release.aspx?releaseid=3543 [accessed 12 October 2004].

——, 'Beyond Nation Building', 14 February 2003, at http://www.defenselink.mil/speeches/speech.aspx?speechid=337 [accessed 12 October 2004].

——, 'Remarks as Delivered by Secretary Rumsfeld, Camp Al-Saliyah, Doha, Qatar', 28 April 2003, at http://www.defenselink.mil/speeches/speech.aspx?speechid=375 [accessed 1 February 2006].

——, 'July 4 Message to the Troops', 4 July 2003, at http://www.defenselink.mil/releases/release.aspx?releaseid=5505 [accessed 12 October 2004].

——, 'Donald Rumsfeld's Address to the Iraqi People', 30 April 2003, reprinted in the *Guardian* at http://www.guardian.co.uk/Iraq/Story/0,,946567,00.html [accessed 30 November 2004].

——, 'Remarks at National Press Club', 2 February 2006, at http://www.defenselink.mil/transcripts/transcript.aspx?transcriptid=908 [accessed 5 February 2006].

Swannack, Charles, 'Army Maj. Gen. Swannack Jr., Live Teleconference from Baghdad', 18 November 2003, at http://www.dod.mil/transcripts/2003/tr20031118-0887.html [accessed 1 February 2006].

Taft, William H., Interview on 'Frontline' (PBS), 14 July 2005, at http://www.pbs.org/wgbh/pages/frontline/torture/themes/geneva.html [accessed 30 March 2006].

Wolfowitz, Paul, 'World Must Act Now to Prevent Evil', 2 February 2002, at http://www.
    defenselink.mil/news/Feb2002/n02022002_200202021.html [accessed 12 October
    2004].
——, 'Building a Better World: One Path From Crisis to Opportunity', 5 September
    2002, at http://www.defenselink.mil/speeches/speech.aspx?speechid=277 [accessed
    12 October 2004].
——, 'Building the Bridge to a More Peaceful Future', 6 December 2002, available
    at http://www.defenselink.mil/speeches/2002/s20021206-depsecdef.html [accessed
    12 October 2004].
——, 'Wolfowitz Says Patience Key to Success in War on Terror', 10 July 2004, at
    http://www.defenselink.mil/news/Jul2004/n07102004_2004071002.html [accessed
    13 October 2004].
Yoo, John C., Interview on 'Frontline' (PBS), 19 July 2005, at http://www.pbs.org/
    wgbh/pages/frontline/torture/interviews/yoo.html [accessed 30 March 2006].

B. Al-Qaeda Statements

Abu Ghaith, Suleiman, Statement released on 10 October 2001, at http://news.bbc.co.
    uk/1/hi/world/middle_east/1590350.stm [accessed 3 July 2006].
——, 'Under the Shadow of Spears' (Centre for Islamic Studies and Research web-
    site), June 2002, at http://www.outtherenews.com/modules.php?op=modload&na-
    me=News&file=article&sid=55 [accessed 3 July 2006].
——, Interview with *Al-Muhajiroun*, 24 June 2002, at http://www.why-war.com/
    news/2002/06/24/intervie.html [accessed 3 July 2006].
——, 'Jihad for the Sovereignty of Allah Alone: The Latest Interview with Al-Qaeda's
    Abu Ghaith', no date given, at www.jihadunspun.com/BinLadensNetwork/inter-
    views/iwag01.html [accessed 3 July 2006].
Bin Laden, Osama, Interview with Robert Fisk, 'Anti-Soviet Warrior Puts His Army
    on the Road to Peace', *Independent*, 6 December 1993, p. 10.
——, Letter to the Chief Mufti of Saudi Arabia, 29 December 1994, in Bruce
    Lawrence, *Messages to the World: The Statements of Osama bin Laden* (London;
    New York: Verso), 2005, pp. 4–14.
——, Address to the Scholars of Arabia, c.1995/1996, in *Messages to the World*, pp. 15–19.
——, Interview with Robert Fisk, 'Why We Reject the West', *Independent*, 10 July
    1996, p. 14.
——, Interview with *Nida'ul Islam*, November 1996, in *Messages to the World*, pp. 31–43.
——, 'Declaration of Jihad against the Americans Occupying the Land of the Two
    Holy Sanctuaries', 23 August 1996, in *Messages to the World*, pp. 24–30.
——, Interview with Peter Arnett (*CNN*), March 1997, in *Messages to the World*,
    pp. 45–57.
——, World Islamic Front Fatwa, 23 February 1998, in *Messages to the World*, pp. 59–62.
——, Interview with John Miller (ABC), May 1998, at http://www.pbs.org/wgbh/
    pages/frontline/shows/binladen/who/interview.html [accessed 6 March 2006].
——, Interview with *Al-Jazeera*, December 1998, in *Messages to the World*, pp. 66–94.

——, Interview with *Al-Jazeera*, December 1998 (full text), at http://www.robert-fisk.com/usama_interview_aljazeera.htm [accessed 6 March 2006].

——, Interview with Rahimullah Yousafsai, December 1998, at http://www.jihadunspun.com/BinLadensNetwork/interviews/abc01-1998.html [accessed 6 March 2006].

——, Audiotape address to the International Conference of Deobandis, 9 April 2001, in *Messages to the World*, pp. 95–9.

——, Statement faxed to *Al-Jazeera*, 24 September 2001, in *Messages to the World*, pp. 100–102.

——, Videotape broadcast on *Al-Jazeera* Television, 7 October 2001, in *Messages to the World*, pp. 103–105.

——, Interview with Taysir Alluni (*Al-Jazeera*), 21 October 2001, in *Messages to the World*, pp. 107–29.

——, Letter delivered to *Al-Jazeera*, 3 November 2001, in *Messages to the World*, pp. 134–8.

——, Interview with Hamid Mir (*Ausaf*), 12 November 2001, in *Messages to the World*, pp. 140–4.

——, 'Bin Laden On Tape: "Attacks Benefited Islam Greatly"', 14 December 2001, at http://archives.cnn.com/2001/US/12/13/ret.bin.laden.videotape/ [accessed 15 December 2001].

——, Statement broadcast on *Al-Jazeera*, 26 December 2001, in *Messages to the World*, pp. 146–57.

——, 'Letter to the Umma', 9 April 2002, at http://www.jihadunspun.com/articles/04152002-al-Qaeda.Letter/index.html [accessed 6 March 2006].

——, 'To the Islamic Umma, on the First Anniversary of the New American Crusader War', 11 September 2002, at http://www.jihadunspun.com/articles/10152002-To.The.Islamic.Ummah/ [accessed 6 March 2006].

——, Letter to the Afghanis, 25 August 2002, in *Messages to the World*, pp. 158–9.

——, Letter to the Americans, 6 October 2002, in *Messages to the World*, pp. 161–72.

——, Audiotape address (broadcast on *Al-Jazeera*), 12 November 2002, in *Messages to the World*, pp. 173–5.

——, Audiotape address, 12 November 2002, in *Messages to the World*, pp. 173–5.

——, Audiotape address to the People of Iraq, 11 February 2003, in *Messages to the World*, pp. 180–5.

——, Statement of 14 February 2003, in *Messages to the World*, pp. 187–206.

——, Audiotape of 8 April 2003, at http://www.guardian.co.uk/alqaida/story/0,,932283,00.html [accessed 6 March 2006].

——, Speech during July 2003, at http://www.memri.org/bin/articles.cgi?Area=sd&ID=SP53903 [accessed 6 March 2006].

——, Videotape message to the people of Iraq, 19 October 2003, in *Messages to the World*, pp. 207–11.

——, Audiotape address broadcast on *Al-Jazeera*, 4 January 2004, in *Messages to the World*, pp. 213–32.

Bin Laden, Osama., Address to the people of Europe, broadcast on *Al-Jazeera* and *Al-Arabiyya*, 15 April 2004, in *Messages to the World*, pp. 234–6.

——, Statement on Iraq, 7 May 2004, at http://news.bbc.co.uk/1/hi/world/ middle_east/3693969.stm [accessed 7 May 2004].

——, Videotape address to the American people, 29 October 2004, in *Messages to the World*, pp. 238–44.

——, 'Osama bin Laden to the Iraqi People', December 2004, at http://www.memri. org/bin/articles.cgi?Page=archives&Area=sd&ID=SP83704 [accessed 6 March 2006].

——, Statement of 16 December 2004, in *Messages to the World*, pp. 246–75.

Zawahiri, Ayman al-, *Knights Under the Prophet's Banner* (Autobiography), 2001, in Laura Mansfield, *In His Own Words: A Translation of the Writings of Dr. Ayman Al-Zawahiri* (United States: TLG Publications), 2006, pp. 18–225.

——, Statement (broadcast on *Al-Jazeera*), 1 October 2004, at http://edition.cnn. com/2004/WORLD/meast/10/01/zawahiri.transcript/ [accessed 6 March 2006].

——, Videotape message, 29 November 2004, in *In His Own Words*, pp. 236–8.

——, Audiotape address entitled 'Hurriya', 5 February 2005, in *In His Own Words*, pp. 239–44.

——, Message to the British, 4 August 2005, in *In His Own Words*, pp. 280–2.

——, Letter from Ayman al-Zawahiri to Abu Musab al-Zarqawi, 11 October 2005, in *In His Own Words*, pp. 250–79.

——, 'Jihad and the Superiority of Martyrdom', reprinted in Raymond Ibrahim (ed), *The Al-Qaeda Reader* (New York: Broadway Books), 2007, pp. 141–71.

——, 'Open Meeting with Sheikh Ayman Al-Zawahiri', *MEMRI: Special Dispatch Series No. 1887*, 4 April 2008, at http://www.memri.org/bin/articles.cgi?Page=archives&Area=sd&ID=SP188708 [accessed 10 April 2008].

Zarqawi, Abu Mus'ab al-, 'Audio Message from Abu Musab Al-Zarqawi—Commander of Al-Qaeda's Jihad Committee in Mesopotamia', 18 November 2005, at http://www.globalterroralert.com/pdf/1105/zarqawi1105-7.pdf [accessed June 2006].

C. Other Statements/Fatawa

Abu Ruqiyah, 'The Islamic Legitimacy of the "Martyrdom Operations"', *Nida'ul Islam*, December 1996–January 1997, at http://contenderministries.org/islam/jihadlegitimate.php [accessed 2 August 2006].

Afghani, Abu Dukan al-, Statement on Madrid bombings, 14 March 2004, at http://news.bbc.co.uk/1/hi/world/europe/3509556.stm [accessed 14 March 2004].

Berg, Thomas S., Interview on Frontline' (PBS), 18 July 2005, at http://www.pbs.org/ wgbh/pages/frontline/torture/interviews/berg.html [accessed 30 March 2006].

Clarke, Richard A., 'Clarke's Take on Terror', broadcast on CBS's '60 Minutes', 22 March 2004, at http://www.cbsnews.com/stories/2004/03/19/60minutes/ main607356.shtml [accessed 6 February 2005].

Churches for Middle East Peace, 'Letter to President Bush on Iraq', 12 September 2002, at http://www.cmep.org/letters/2002Sep12_BushReIraq.htm [accessed 18 June 2005].

Cook, Robin, 'Resignation Speech to the House of Commons', 18 March 2003, at http://news.bbc.co.uk/1/hi/uk_politics/2859431.stm [accessed 12 October2004].

Coulter, Ann, 'This Is War', weblog entry on 12 September 2001, at http://www.anncoulter.org/columns/2001/091301.htm [accessed 14 September 2001].

Council of Bishops of the United Church of Christ in the Philippines, 'Pastoral Statement: Cry Out for Peace, Say No to War', 31 January 2003, at http://www.warc.ch/dcw/iraq/01.html [accessed 9 January 2005].

Blanchard, Christopher, 'Al-Qaeda: Statements and Evolving Ideology', *Congressional Research Service Report for Congress*, 9 July 2007, code RL32759.

Ebadi, Shirin, Address to the John F. Kennedy School of Government at Harvard University, 11 May 2004, at http://www.ksg.harvard.edu/news/news/2004/ebadi_051104.htm [accessed 6 February 2005].

El-Baradei, Mohammad, 'The Status of Nuclear Inspections in Iraq: An Update', 7 March 2003, at http://www.iaea.org/NewsCenter/Statements/2003/ebsp2003n006.shtml [accessed 8 June 2005].

Fadlallah, Mohammed Hussein, 'Rules of Self-Defence: Part One', no date given, at http://english.bayynat.org.lb/Fatawa/s10p1.htm [accessed 16 May 2006].

Federation of Swiss Protestant Churches, 'No Preventive War Against Iraq', 23 January 2003, at http://www.warc.ch/dcw/iraq/08.html [accessed 9 October 2005].

Frist, Bill, 'First Floor Statement on Guantanamo Bay', 17 June 2005, at http://frist.senate.gov/index.cfm?FuseAction=Speeches.Detail&Speech_id=231&Month=6&Year=2005 [accessed 1 July 2005].

Gore, Albert A., Speech before the Commonwealth Club of San Francisco, 23 September 2002, at http://www.commonwealthclub.org/archive/02/02-09gore-speech.html [accessed 3 October 2005].

Gregory, Wilton D., 'Statement on Moral Responsibilities for United States in Iraq', 22 June 2004, at http://www.usccb.org/sdwp/international/iraqstatem.htm [accessed 11 June 2005].

Gum'a, Ali, 'The New Egyptian Mufti— Dr. Sheikh Ali Gum'a: Opinions About Jihad, Supporting Suicide Bombings, and Forbidding Muslims in the US Military From Fighting Other Muslims', *MEMRI: Special Dispatch Series*, no. 580, 1 October 2003, at http://memri.org/bin/articles.cgi?Page=archives&Area=sd&ID=SP58003 [accessed 10 October 2003].

Henri, Emile, 'Defence Speech', 1894, at http://www.marxists.org/reference/archive/henry/1894/defence-speech.htm [accessed 12 March 2009].

Ibn Taymiyyah, 'Fatwa Pronounced by ibn Taymiyyah on the Mongols, 1303', in Richard Bonney, *Jihad: from Quran to Bin Laden* (Basingstoke, UK: Palgrave Macmillan), 2004, pp. 423–6.

International Association of Muslim Scholars, 'Bombing Innocents', 25 July 2005, at http://www.islamonline.net/English/In_Depth/ViolenceCausesAlternatives/Articles/topic08/2005/07/01.shtml [accessed 3 August 2006].

Khatami, Mohammad, 'Address to the United Nations General Assembly', 9 November 2001, at http://former.president.ir/khatami/eng/cronicnews/1380/8008/800818/800818.htm [accessed 12 October 2008].

Kennedy, Edward M., 'Eliminating the Threat: The Right Course of Action for Disarming Iraq, Combating Terrorism, Protecting the Homeland, and Stabilising the Middle East', 27 September 2002, at http://kennedy.senate.gov/~kennedy/statements/02/09/2002927718.html [accessed 17 January 2005].

Kennedy, John F., 'Special Message to the Congress on the Defense Budget', 28 March 1961, at http://www.jfklink.com/speeches/jfk/publicpapers/1961/jfk99_61.html [accessed November 17, 2005].

Khan, Mohammad Sidique, Video message before London Bombings, aired on *Al-Jazeera* television on 1 September 2005, at http://news.bbc.co.uk/1/hi/uk/4206800.stm [accessed 1 September 2005].

Kutty, Ahmad, 'Fatwa: Even in Retaliation . . . Ethics Must Be Honoured', 12 May 2004, at http://www.islamonline.net/servlet/Satellite?cid=1119503548456&pagename=IslamOnline-English-Ask_Scholar/FatwaE/FatwaEAskTheScholar [accessed 7 June 2008].

Luban, David, Testimony Presented to the Senate Judiciary Committee, Subcommittee on Administrative Oversight and the Courts, Hearing: 'What Went Wrong: Torture and the Office of Legal Counsel in the Bush Administration', 13 May 2009, at http://judiciary.senate.gov/hearings/testimony.cfm?id=3842&wit_id=7905 [accessed 27 June 2009].

Mahoney, Roger M., 'Statement on the Possibility of a War with Iraq', 13 November 2002, at http://www.usccb.org/sdwp/peace/mahony.htm [accessed 8 October 2005].

Mujahidin in Chechnya, 'The Islamic Ruling on the Permissibility of Martyrdom Operations: Did Hawa Barayev Commit Suicide or Achieve Martyrdom?', at http://journal.maine.com/pdf/martyrdom.pdf [accessed 2 August 2006].

National Council of Churches (USA), 'A Statement on the Disavowal of Torture', 9 November 2005, at http://www.ncccusa.org/news/051130GAResolutions.html [accessed 17 January 2006].

Nasrallah, Hasan, Interview on *Al-Arabiyah* Television, 2 September 2005.

——, Interview on *Al-Manar* Television, 14 March 2004.

New Zealand Churches, 'New Zealand Church Leaders Joint Statement on the Threat of War against Iraq', 10 September 2002, at http://www.dunedinmethodist.org.nz/just/ldrs.html [accessed 21 February 2005].

Obama, Barack, 'Remarks by the President on a New Beginning', 4 June 2009, http://www.whitehouse.gov/the_press_office/Remarks-by-the-President-at-Cairo-University-6-04-09/ [accessed 5 June 2009].

Odah, Salman ibn Fahd al-, 'A Ramadan Letter to Osama bin Laden', aired on MBC Television, 14 November 2007, at http://www.islamtoday.com/showme2.cfm?cat_id=29&sub_cat_id=1521 [accessed 10 December 2007].

Pope Benedict XVI, 'Faith, Reason and the University: Memories and Reflections', 12 September 2006, at http://www.vatican.va/holy_father/benedict_xvi/speeches/2006/september/documents/hf_ben-xvi_spe_20060912_university-regensburg_en.html [accessed 14 September 2006].

Pope John Paul II, 'Address of His Holiness Pope John Paul II to the Diplomatic Corps', 13 January 2003, at http://www.vatican.va/holy_father/john_paul_ii/speeches/2003/january [accessed 16 June 2005].

Qaradawi, Yusuf al-, 'Sheikh Yusuf Al-Qaradawi Condemns Attacks Against Civilians: Forbidden in Islam', 13 September 2001, at http://www.islam-online.net/English/News/2001-09/13/article25.shtml [accessed 16 October 2005].

——, 'Fatwa: Bali Attacks, Juristic Approach', 15 October 2002, at http://www.islamon-line.net/servlet/Satellite?pagename=IslamOnline-English-Ask_Scholar/FatwaE/Fat-waE&cid=1119503546090 [accessed 6 June 2006].

——, 'Those Who Die Fighting US Occupation Forces Are Martyrs, But Distinguish Between American Civilians and the Government and Military, Says Scholar, Qaradawi', 19 June 2003, at http://www.islamfortoday.com/qaradawi04.htm [accessed 6 June 2006].

——, 'Fatwa: Jihad in Chechnya', 19 April 2004, at http://www.islamonline.net/servlet/Satellite?pagename=IslamOnline-English-Ask_Scholar/FatwaE/FatwaE&-cid=1119503543542 [accessed 6 June 2006].

——, 'Fatwa: Abode of Peace and Abode of War', 14 August 2004, at http://www.islamonline.net/servlet/Satellite?pagename=IslamOnline-English-Ask_Scholar/FatwaE/FatwaE&cid=1123585750474 [accessed 6 June 2006].

Swedish Mission Covenant Church, 'No to an Attack War on Iraq!', 8 February 2003, at http://www.warc.ch/dcw/iraq/13.html [accessed 8 October 2005].

Tayeb, Ahmad al-, Interview with Lailat Al-Qadr, 23 July 2002, at http://memri.org/bin/articles.cgi?Page=archives&Area=sd&ID=SP40202 [accessed 3 July 2006].

Williams, Rowan, 'Just War Revisited', lecture delivered at the Royal Institute for International Affairs, 12 October 2003, at http://www.archbishopofcanterbury.org/1214?q=just+war+revisited [accessed 31 October 2003].

World Council of Churches, 'Executive Committee Statement Against Military Action in Iraq', 18 February 2003, at http://www.wcc-coe.org/wcc/what/international/exco03-iraq.html [accessed 13 March 2005].

4. Policy Documents/Reports

Amnesty International, 'Iraq: Civilians Under Fire', 8 April 2003, at http://web.amnesty.org/library/index/engmde140712003 [accessed 26 November 2004].

Amnesty International (Irene Khan), 'Amnesty International Report 2005 at Foreign Press Association', 25 May 2005, at http://web.amnesty.org/library/Index/ENGPOL100142005 [accessed 6 June 2006].

Beaver, Diane E., 'Legal Brief on Proposed Counter-Resistance Strategies', 11 October 2002, in Karen J. Greenberg and Joshua L. Dratel, *The Torture Papers: The Road to Abu Ghraib* (New York: Cambridge University Press), 2005, pp. 229–36.

Brussels Declaration, 'Project of an International Declaration Concerning the Laws and Customs of War, Brussels, 27 August 1874', at http://www.icrc.org/ihl.nsf/INTRO/135?OpenDocument [accessed 21 January 2006].

Bybee, Jay S., 'Application of Treaties and Laws to al Qaeda and Taliban Detainees', 22 January 2002, in Karen J. Greenberg and Joshua L. Dratel, *The Torture Papers: The Road to Abu Ghraib* (New York: Cambridge University Press), 2005, pp. 81–117.

Bybee, Jay S., 'Standards of Conduct for Interrogation Under 18 USC 2340–2340A', 1 August 2002, in Karen J. Greenberg and Joshua L. Dratel, *The Torture Papers: The Road to Abu Ghraib* (New York: Cambridge University Press), 2005, pp. 172–217.

Detainee No. 151108 (Abu Ghraib prison), 'Translation of Statement Provided by Detainee # 151108', 18 January 2004, in Karen J. Greenberg and Joshua L. Dratel, *The Torture Papers: The Road to Abu Ghraib* (New York: Cambridge University Press), 2005, p. 504.

Detainee No. 150542 (Abu Ghraib prison), 'Translation of Statement Provided by Detainee # 150542', 18 January 2004, in Karen J. Greenberg and Joshua L. Dratel, *The Torture Papers: The Road to Abu Ghraib* (New York: Cambridge University Press), 2005, p. 506.

Department of the US Army, *FM 34-52*, 8 May 1987, at http://www.globalsecurity.org/intell/library/policy/army/fm/fm34-52/chapter1.htm [accessed 2 April 2005].

Duelfer, Charles, 'Findings of the Special Advisor to the DCI on Iraq's WMD', 30 September 2004, at https://www.cia.gov/cia/reports/iraq_wmd_2004/index.html [accessed 6 January 2006].

Goldsmith, Peter H., 'Iraq: Legality of Armed Force', 17 March 2003, online at United Kingdom Parliament website, http://www.parliament.the-stationery-office.co.uk/pa/ld199900/ldhansrd/pdvn/lds03/text/30317w01.htm [accessed 17 March 2005].

Gonzales, Alberto R., 'Decision Re: Application of the Geneva Convention on Prisoners of War to the Conflict with Al Qaeda and the Taliban', 25 January 2002, in Karen J. Greenberg and Joshua L. Dratel, *The Torture Papers: The Road to Abu Ghraib* (New York: Cambridge University Press), 2005, pp. 118–21.

Harakat Al-Muqawamah Al-Islamiyya (Hamas), 'The Covenant of the Islamic Resistance Movement', at http://www.mideastweb.org/hamas.htm [accessed 12 June 2006].

Human Rights Watch, 'Human Rights Watch World Report 2002', at http://hrw.org/wr2k2/ [accessed 3 May 2005].

——, 'Human Rights Watch World Report 2004', at http://hrw.org/wr2k4/ [accessed 3 May 2005].

——, *Off Target: The Conduct of the War and Civilian Casualties in Iraq* (New York; London: Human Rights Watch), 2003.

Lieber, Francis, 'General Orders No. 100', 24 April 1863, at http://www.au.af.mil/au/awc/awcgate/law/liebercode.htm [accessed 11 January 2005].

National Commission on Terrorist Attacks Upon the United States ('9/11 Commission'), 'Public Report of National Commission on Terrorist Attacks Upon the United States', 22 July 2004, at http://www.9-11commission.gov [accessed 1 August 2004].

Number 10 Downing Street, 'Iraq's Weapons of Mass Destruction: The Assessment of the British Government', 24 September 2002, at http://www.number10.gov.uk/output/Page271.asp [accessed 8 June 2005].

Powell, Colin L., 'Memorandum to Counsel to the President and Assistant to the President for National Security Affairs', 26 January 2002, in Karen J. Greenberg and Joshua L. Dratel, *The Torture Papers: The Road to Abu Ghraib* (New York: Cambridge University Press), 2005, pp. 122–5.

Roth, Kenneth, 'US Officials Misstate Geneva Conventions Requirements', 28 January 2002, at http://hrw.org/press/2002/01/us012802-ltr.htm [accessed 3 May 2005].

——, 'Human Rights Watch World Report: War in Iraq—Not a Humanitarian Intervention', January 2004, www.hrw.org/wr2k4/3.htm [accessed May 3, 2005].

Taguba, Antonio, 'The Taguba Report: Article 15–6 Investigation of the 800th Military Police Brigade', March 2004, in Karen J. Greenberg and Joshua L. Dratel, *The Torture Papers: The Road to Abu Ghraib* (New York: Cambridge University Press), 2005, pp. 405–556.

United Nations Commissioner for Human Rights (Louise Arbour), Statement on Civilians in Iraq, 16 November 2004, at http://www.un.org/apps/news/story.asp? NewsID=12544&Cr=iraq&Cr1 [accessed 17 January 2006].

United Nations Economic and Social Council, 'Situation of Detainees at Guantanamo Bay', 15 February 2006, at http://news.bbc.co.uk/1/shared/bsp/hi/pdfs/ 16_02_06_un_guantanamo.pdf [accessed 18 February 2006].

United Nations Development Programme, 'Iraq Living Conditions Survey 2004', released May 2005, at http://www.iq.undp.org/ILCS/overview.htm [accessed 2 August 2005].

United Nations Office of the High Commissioner for Human Rights, 'United Nations Convention Against Torture and Other Cruel, Inhuman or Degrading Treatment or Punishment (1984)', at http://www.unhchr.ch/html/menu3/b/h_cat39.htm [accessed 6 June 2006].

United Nations Office of the Secretary-General, High-Level Panel on Threats, Challenges and Change, *A More Secure World: Our Shared responsibility*, 2 December 2004, at http://www.un.org/secureworld/report.pdf [accessed 12 June 2009].

United Nations officials (anonymous), 'Likely Humanitarian Scenarios' (internal memorandum), 10 December 2002, at http://www.casi.org.uk/info/undocs/ war021210scanned.pdf [accessed 8 April 2005].

——, 'Initial Proceedings: Complaint by Iraq', 19 June 1981, at http://www.un.org/ Depts/dpa/repertoire/81-84_08.pdf [accessed 10 February 2005].

——, 'Resolution 487', 19 June 1981, at http://daccessdds.un.org/doc/RESOLUTION/ GEN/NR0/418/74/IMG/NR041874.pdf?OpenElement [accessed 1 October 2005].

——, 'Draft Resolution on Iraq', 7 March 2003, at http://c-span.org/resources/fyi/ draftresolution2.asp [accessed 26 April 2005].

United States Department of Defence, 'Quadrennial Defence Review Report', 30 September 2001, at http://www.defenselink.mil/pubs/qdr2001.pdf [accessed 3 October 2004].

Department of Defence, 'Working Group Report on Detainee Interrogations in the Global War on Terrorism— Draft', 6 March 2003, in Karen J. Greenberg and Joshua L. Dratel, *The Torture Papers: The Road to Abu Ghraib* (New York: Cambridge University Press), 2005, pp. 241–85.

——, 'Working Group Report on Detainee Interrogations in the Global War on Terrorism', 4 April 2003, in Karen J. Greenberg and Joshua L. Dratel, *The Torture Papers: The Road to Abu Ghraib* (New York: Cambridge University Press), 2005, pp. 286–359.

United States White House, 'The National Security Strategy of the United States of America', September 2002, at http://www.whitehouse.gov/nsc/nss.pdf [accessed 3 October 2004].

——, 'National Strategy to Combat Weapons of Mass Destruction', December 2002, at http://www.whitehouse.gov/news/releases/2002/12/WMDStrategy.pdf [accessed 3 October 2004].

——, 'Humane Treatment of al Qaeda and Taliban Detainees', 7 February 2002, in Karen J. Greenberg and Joshua L. Dratel, *The Torture Papers: The Road to Abu Ghraib* (New York: Cambridge University Press), 2005, pp. 134–5.

Webster, Daniel, 'Letter to the British Ambassador to the United States, Henry Fox', 24 April 1841, at http://www.yale.edu/lawweb/avalon/diplomacy/britain/br-1842d.htm [accessed 3 September 2005].

Yoo, John C., 'Letter Regarding the Views of our Office Concerning the Legality, Under International Law, of Interrogation Methods to Be Used On Captured Al Qaeda Operatives', 1 August 2002, in Karen J. Greenberg and Joshua L. Dratel, *The Torture Papers: The Road to Abu Ghraib* (New York: Cambridge University Press), 2005, pp. 218–22.

——and Patrick F. Philbin, 'Memorandum for William J. Haynes, II General Counsel, Department of Defense', 28 December 2001, in Karen J. Greenberg and Joshua L. Dratel, *The Torture Papers: The Road to Abu Ghraib* (New York: Cambridge University Press), 2005, pp. 29–37.

——and Robert J. Delabunty, 'Application of Treaties and Laws to al Qaeda and Taliban Detainees', 9 January 2002, in Karen J. Greenberg and Joshua L. Dratel, *The Torture Papers: The Road to Abu Ghraib* (New York: Cambridge University Press), 2005, pp. 38–79.

5. Lectures/Conferences

Betts, Richard K., Chris Brown, Michael Byers, Neta C. Crawford, Anthony F. Lang Jr. and Thomas M. Nichols, 'Evaluating the Pre-Emptive Use of Force', round-table discussion, printed in *Ethics and International Affairs*, vol. 17, no. 1, Spring 2003.

Bradley, Gerard, William A. Galston, John Kelsay and Michael Walzer, 'Iraq and Just War: A Symposium', discussion at the Pew Forum on Religion and Public Life, 30 September 2002, posted online at http://pewforum.org/events/index.php?EventID=36 [accessed 2 December 2005], pp. 1–36.

Butler, Robin, 'The Case for the Iraq War', lecture at St Antony's College, Oxford University, 17 November 2004.

Guthrie, Charles, 'The Just War: Ethics in Modern Warfare', lecture at Las Casas Institute, Oxford, 21 January 2009.

Reprieve, 'Guantanamo and Islam', law conference at St Anne's College, Oxford, 18 March 2007.

Shlaim, Avi, 'Israel: Wars of Choice and Wars of No Choice', lecture for the Oxford Leverhulme Programme on the Changing Character of War, Department of Politics and International Relations, Oxford University, 1 May 2007.

6. Films/Television and Radio Documentaries

'Al-Qaeda's Enemy Within', an Analysis programme for *BBC Radio 4*, broadcast 7 August 2008, 8.30pm.

Death in Gaza (2004), directed by James Miller, distributed by Channel Four Television Corporation.

'Inside Hamas', a Faith and Belief documentary for *Channel 4*, aired 10 February 2008, 7pm.

'Iraq: the Lost Generation', a Dispatches documentary for *Channel 4*, aired 10 November 2006, 8pm.

'Is Torture a Good Idea?', an investigation by Clive Stafford Smith for *Channel 4*, aired 28 February 2005, 9pm.

The Fog of War: Eleven Lessons From the Life of Robert S. McNamara (2003), directed by Errol Morris, distributed by Sony Pictures Classics.

7. Additional Internet Sources

'Iraq Coalition Casualty Count', updated daily at http://icasualties.org [last accessed 21 June 2010].

Index

Abduh, Mohammad 104, 107, 206 n. 51
Abrogation (*naskh*) 109–110, 186
Abu Ghraib 38, 86
Abu Qatada 1, 105
Abu Ruqaiyah 167, 169
Afghanistan 9, 10, 13, 26, 39, 49, 55, 62, 86,
    88, 100, 107, 108, 114, 115, 128, 132, 139,
    141, 145, 146, 148, 149–50, 152, 153,
    154, 160, 161, 164, 181–2, 188, 189, 200,
    212 n. 124, 224 n. 44, 240 n. 15, 242 n.
    54, 246 n. 139, 250 n. 26, 257 n. 190, 258
    n. 274, 258 n. 203, 258 n. 205, 273 n. 24
Agamben, Giorgio 93
Ajami, Fouad 50
al-Albani, Mohammad Nasr al-Din 171
al-Ayyiri, Yusuf 162, 167–8, 169, 171,
    263 n. 31
al-Odah, Salman ibn Fahd 139, 153
al-Qaeda; related attacks 1, 49, 50, 138, 141,
    148, 157, 194, 261 n. 227
  leadership 13, 139
  nature of 4, 106, 199–201, 201–2
al-Qaradawi, Yusuf 13, 99, 102, 120, 126,
    140, 172–3, 175, 178
al-Qurtubi, Mohammad ibn Ahmad 184–7
al-Sheikh Abd-al Aziz 2, 120, 171
al-Shaybani, Mohammad ibn al-Hasan 12,
    144, 160, 162, 175
al-Tabari, Mohammad ibn Jarir 144, 183
al-Tartousi, Abu Basir 185
al-Zarqawi, Abu Mus'ab 30, 106, 211 n. 106,
    242 n. 54
al-Zawahiri, Ayman 13, 100, 106, 112, 114,
    118, 122, 123, 136, 139, 141, 142, 145,
    168, 169, 181, 183, 184, 199–200
Ali, Cheragh 11, 107
Annan, Kofi 37
Aquinas, Thomas 11, 12, 21, 24, 35, 38, 41,
    77, 160
Ata, Mohammad 30, 146, 164, 201
St Augustine 24, 35, 38, 40, 44, 82, 109, 198
Azzam, Abdullah 102, 110, 115, 127, 128,
    130, 161, 170–1

Baathism 30–1, 130, 251 n. 32, 258 n. 205
bin Laden, Osama 2, 34, 38, 49, 95, 100, 108,
    111–2, 145, 151–3

allegations of slaughter of Muslims 116
argument that US responds only to
    violence 142–3
arguments for murder of
    non-combatants 179–185
as aggressor 120
biographical information 246 n. 139
claim of defensive *jihad* 112–4
conception of 'attack' 116–7
contradictory statements 185–8
defending own concept of American
    aggression 115–6
evidence against Manichaean
    worldview 121–3
invocation of David and Goliath 149
justification of accidental killing of
    innocents 161
justification of resort to violence 140–2
misconceptions about 4, 106
Muslim opposition to 2, 120, 176–8, 99–100
myth of superpower 146–8
on 'war of ideas' 191
on 9/11 attacks 99
on Baath party and Saddam 31
on modern war 3
Islamic credentials 128–32
view of Iraq war as opportunity 48
views against modern Muslim
    regimes 133–7
views against religious establishment 133
bin Othman, Nu'man 139, 154
Black, Cofer 3
Blix, Hans 37, 48
Burke, Jason 250–1 n. 26, 257 n. 190, 271 n. 190
Bush, George W. 1, 2, 3, 8, 13, 17, 25, 27–28,
    31, 40, 46, 48, 51, 57, 61–2, 68, 71, 77, 80,
    87, 93, 118, 122, 191–2
  'crusade language' 118, 122
Bush, George H. W. 151, 181. *See also* Gulf war
Bybee, Jay 86, 87, 90–1

Caroline incident 59
Carter, Jimmy 53, 93
Central Intelligence Agency 3, 28, 30, 49,
    68, 87, 111, 119, 236 n. 157, 240 n. 15,
    258 n. 205